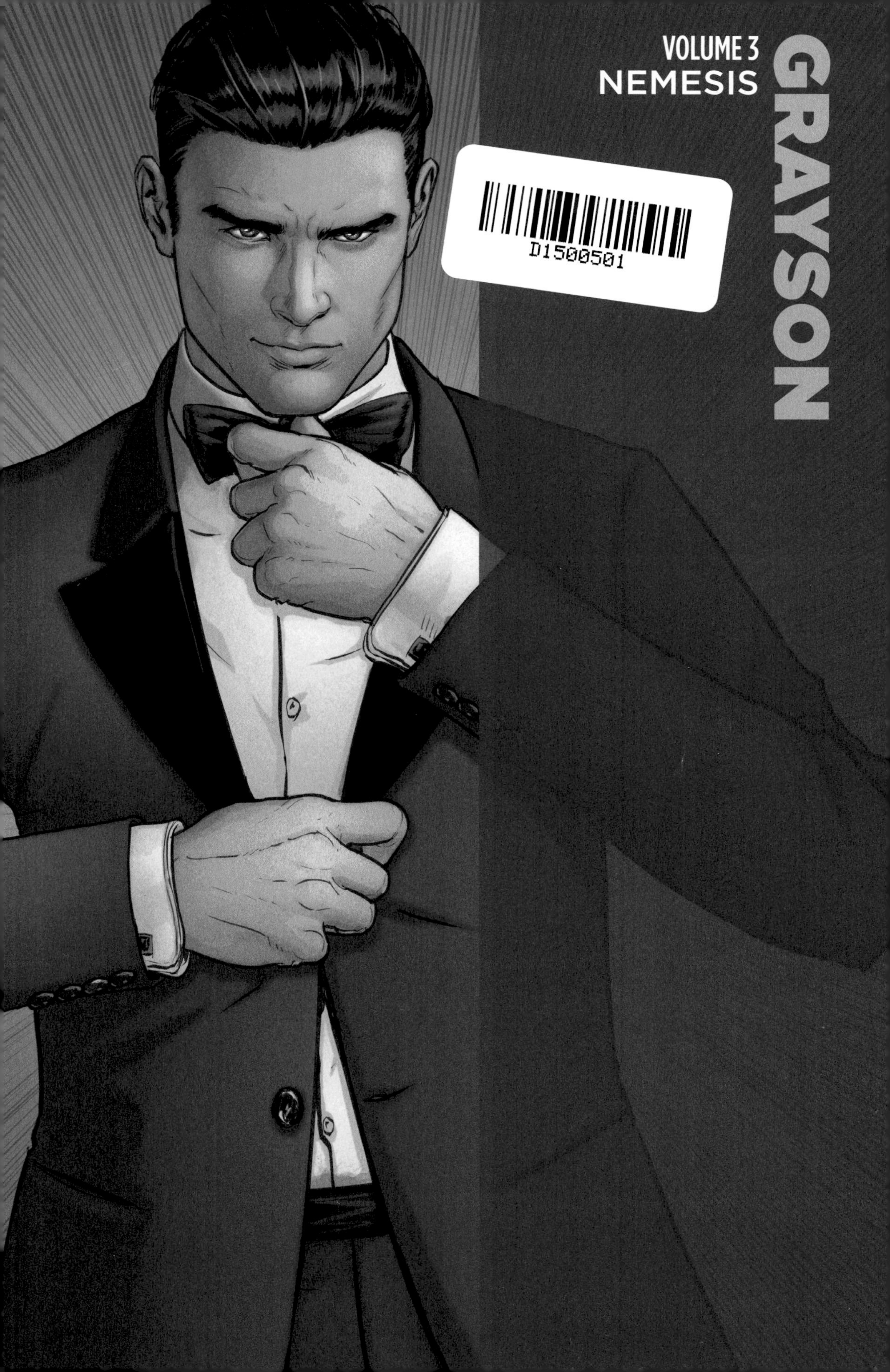
VOLUME 3
NEMESIS
GRAYSON

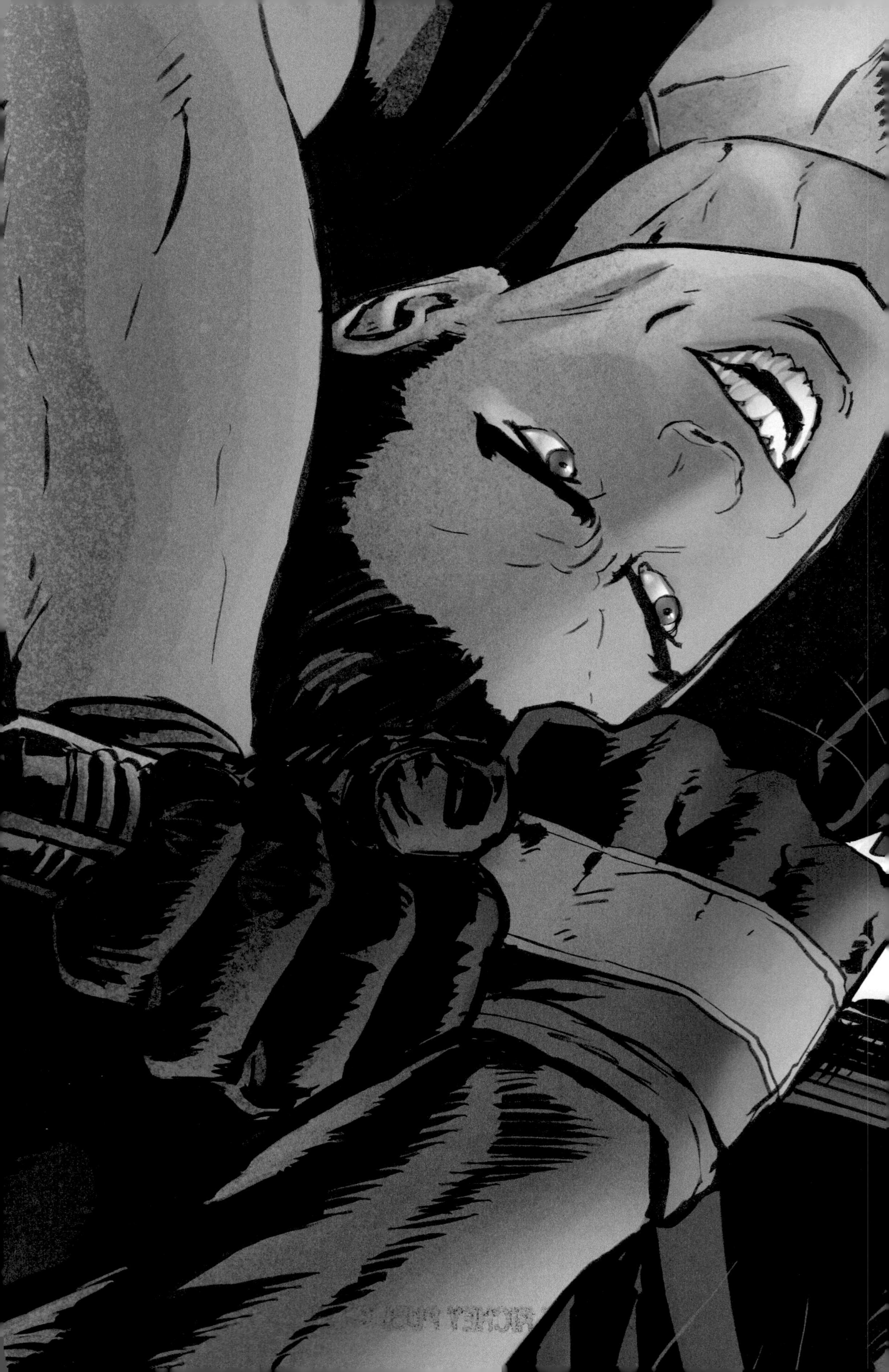

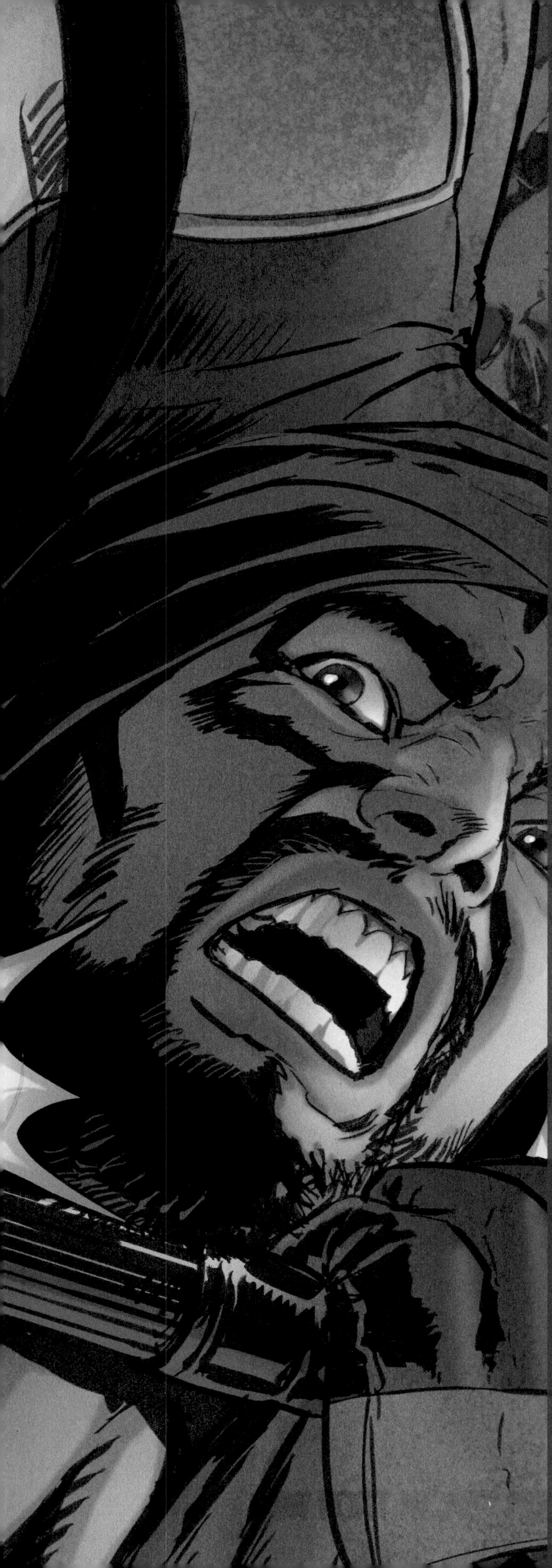

GRAYSON

VOLUME 3
NEMESIS

WRITTEN BY
TIM SEELEY
TOM KING

ART BY
MIKEL JANÍN
HUGO PETRUS
JUAN CASTRO
ALVARO MARTINEZ
RAUL FERNANDEZ

COLOR BY
JEROMY COX

LETTERS BY
CARLOS M. MANGUAL

COLLECTION COVER ARTIST
MIKEL JANÍN

SUPERMAN CREATED BY
JERRY SIEGEL &
JOE SHUSTER
BY SPECIAL ARRANGEMENT WITH
THE JERRY SIEGEL FAMILY.

REBECCA TAYLOR Editor – Original Series
JEB WOODARD Group Editor – Collected Editions
STEVE COOK Design Director – Books
DAMIAN RYLAND Publication Design

BOB HARRAS Senior VP – Editor-in-Chief, DC Comics

DIANE NELSON President
DAN DiDIO and JIM LEE Co-Publishers
GEOFF JOHNS Chief Creative Officer
AMIT DESAI Senior VP – Marketing & Global Franchise Management
NAIRI GARDINER Senior VP – Finance
SAM ADES VP – Digital Marketing
BOBBIE CHASE VP – Talent Development
MARK CHIARELLO Senior VP – Art, Design & Collected Editions
JOHN CUNNINGHAM VP – Content Strategy
ANNE DePIES VP – Strategy Planning & Reporting
DON FALLETTI VP – Manufacturing Operations
LAWRENCE GANEM VP – Editorial Administration & Talent Relations
ALISON GILL Senior VP – Manufacturing & Operations
HANK KANALZ Senior VP – Editorial Strategy & Administration
JAY KOGAN VP – Legal Affairs
DEREK MADDALENA Senior VP – Sales & Business Development
JACK MAHAN VP – Business Affairs
DAN MIRON VP – Sales Planning & Trade Development
NICK NAPOLITANO VP – Manufacturing Administration
CAROL ROEDER VP – Marketing
EDDIE SCANNELL VP – Mass Account & Digital Sales
COURTNEY SIMMONS Senior VP – Publicity & Communications
JIM (SKI) SOKOLOWSKI VP – Comic Book Specialty & Newsstand Sales
SANDY YI Senior VP – Global Franchise Management

GRAYSON VOLUME 3: NEMESIS

Published by DC Comics. Compilation and all new material Copyright © 2016 DC Comics. All Rights Reserved.
Originally published online as GRAYSON SNEAK PEEK and in single magazine form as GRAYSON 9-12, GRAYSON ANNUAL 2.
Copyright © 2015 DC Comics. All Rights Reserved. All characters, their distinctive likenesses and related elements featured in this publication are trademarks of DC Comics. The stories, characters and incidents featured in this publication are entirely fictional. DC Comics does not read or accept unsolicited ideas, stories or artwork.

DC Comics, 2900 West Alameda Ave., Burbank, CA 91505
Printed by RR Donnelley, Salem, VA. 4/8/16. First Printing.
ISBN: 978-1-4012-6276-1

LIBRARY OF CONGRESS CATALOGING-IN-PUBLICATION DATA

NAMES: SEELEY, TIM, AUTHOR. | KING, TOM, 1978- AUTHOR. | JANÍN, MIKEL,
ILLUSTRATOR.
TITLE: GRAYSON. VOLUME 3, NEMESIS / TIM SEELEY, TOM KING, WRITERS, MIKEL
JANÍN, ARTIST.
OTHER TITLES: NEMESIS
DESCRIPTION: BURBANK, CA : DC COMICS, [2016] | "ORIGINALLY PUBLISHED ONLINE
AS GRAYSON SNEAK PEEK AND IN SINGLE MAGAZINE FORM AS GRAYSON 9-12, GRAYSON
ANNUAL 2."
IDENTIFIERS: LCCN 2016006079 | ISBN 9781401262761
CLASSIFICATION: LCC PN6728.G723 S45 2016 | DDC 741.5/973–DC23
LC RECORD AVAILABLE AT HTTP://LCCN.LOC.GOV/2016006079

PEFC Certified

Printed on paper from
sustainably managed
forests and controlled
sources

PEFC/29-31-75   www.pefc.org

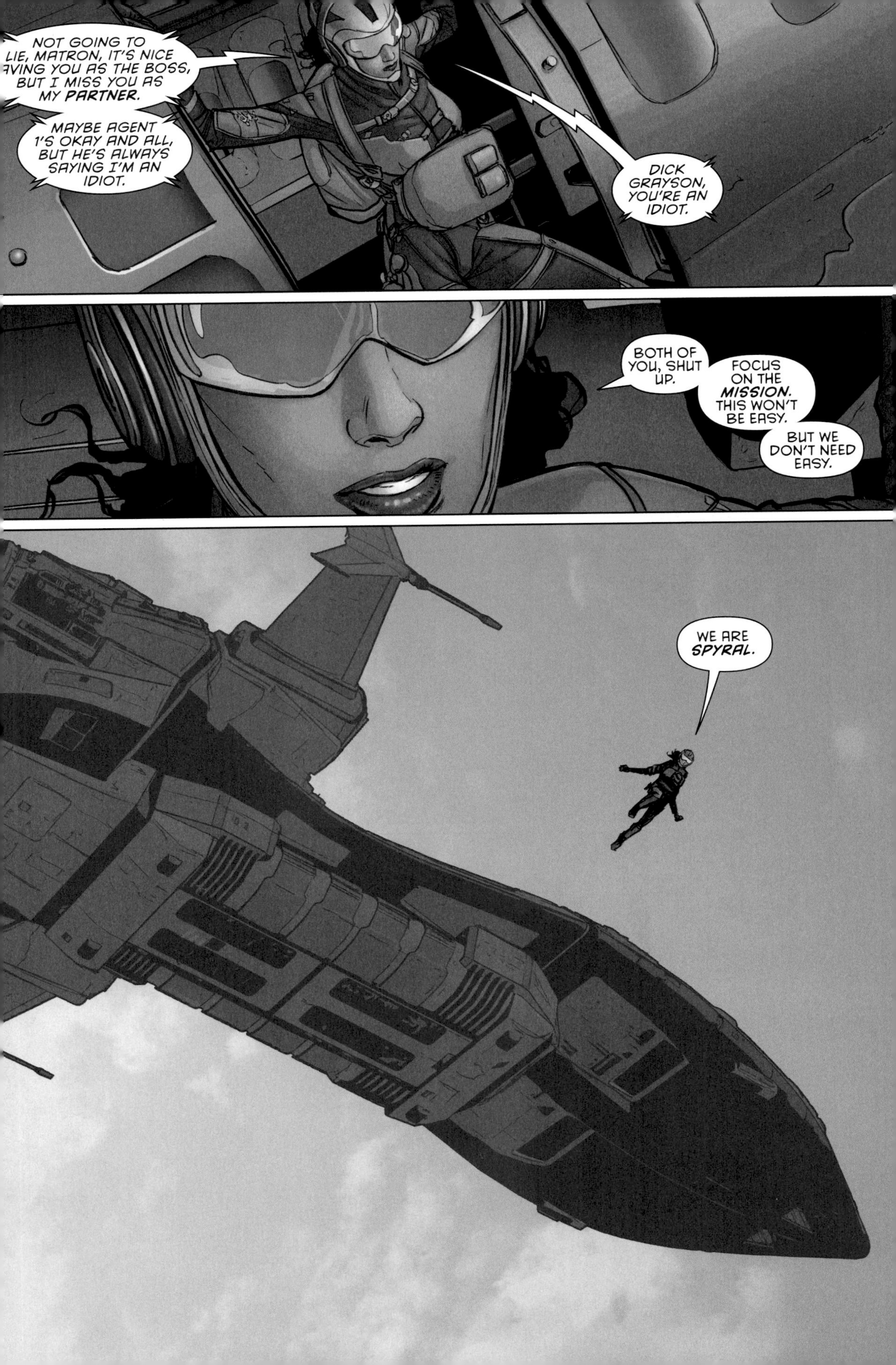
NOT GOING TO LIE, MATRON, IT'S NICE HAVING YOU AS THE BOSS, BUT I MISS YOU AS MY PARTNER.
MAYBE AGENT 1'S OKAY AND ALL, BUT HE'S ALWAYS SAYING I'M AN IDIOT.
DICK GRAYSON, YOU'RE AN IDIOT.
BOTH OF YOU, SHUT UP.
FOCUS ON THE MISSION. THIS WON'T BE EASY.
BUT WE DON'T NEED EASY.
WE ARE SPYRAL.

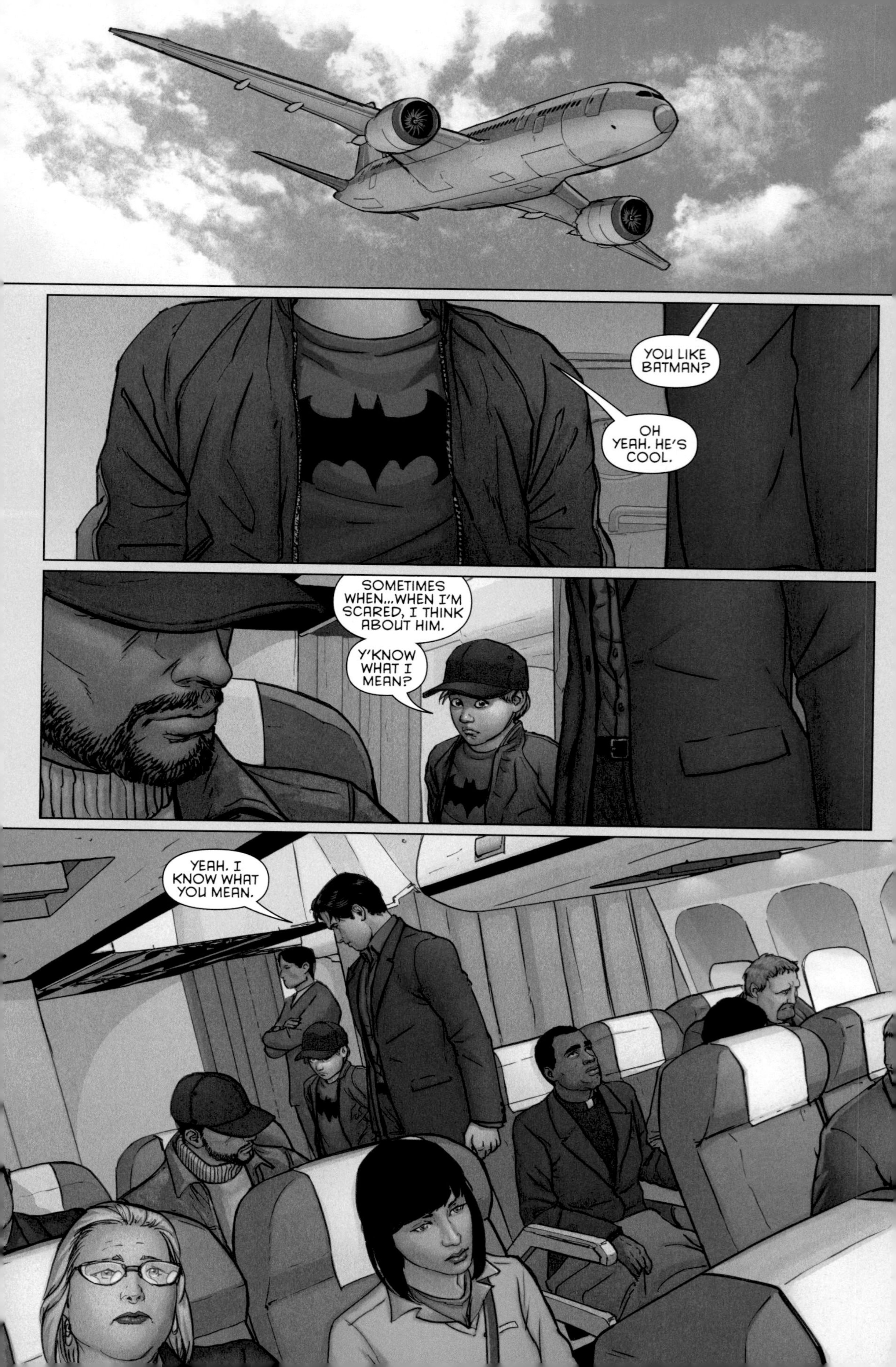
YOU LIKE BATMAN?
OH YEAH. HE'S COOL.
SOMETIMES WHEN...WHEN I'M SCARED, I THINK ABOUT HIM.
Y'KNOW WHAT I MEAN?
YEAH. I KNOW WHAT YOU MEAN.

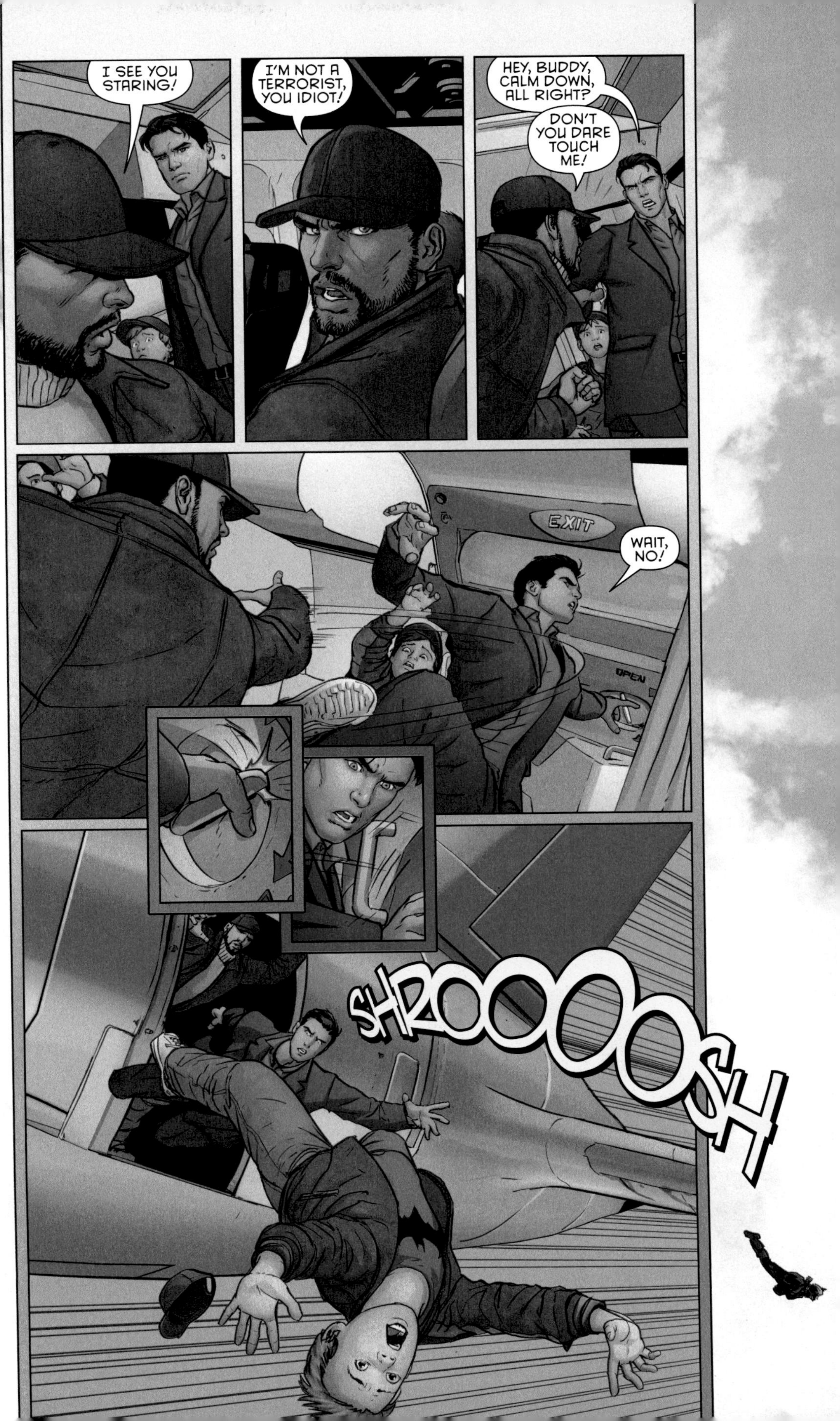
I SEE YOU STARING!
I'M NOT A TERRORIST, YOU IDIOT!
HEY, BUDDY, CALM DOWN, ALL RIGHT?
DON'T YOU DARE TOUCH ME!
EXIT
WAIT, NO!
OPEN
SHROOOOOSH

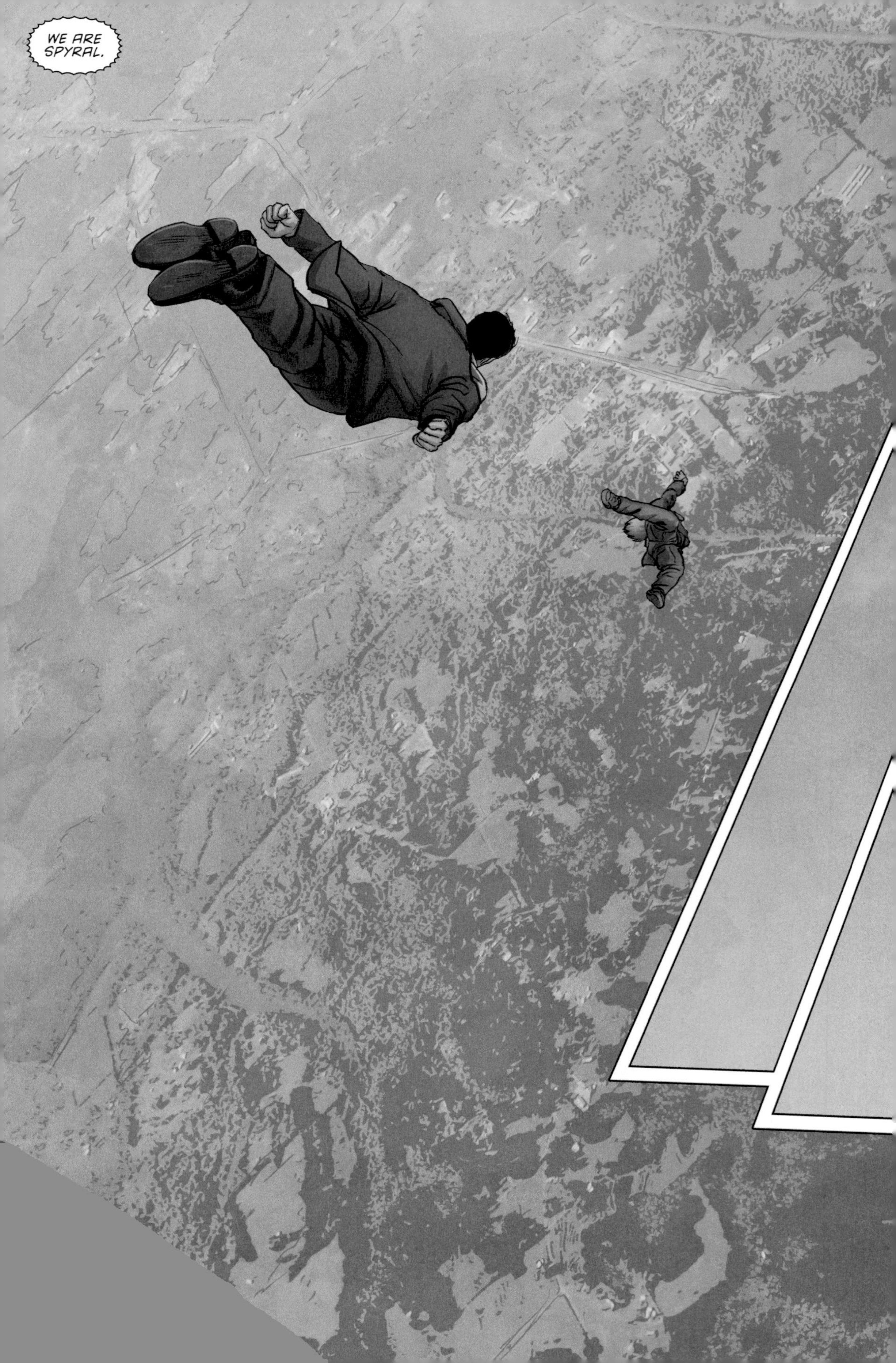
WE ARE SPYRAL.

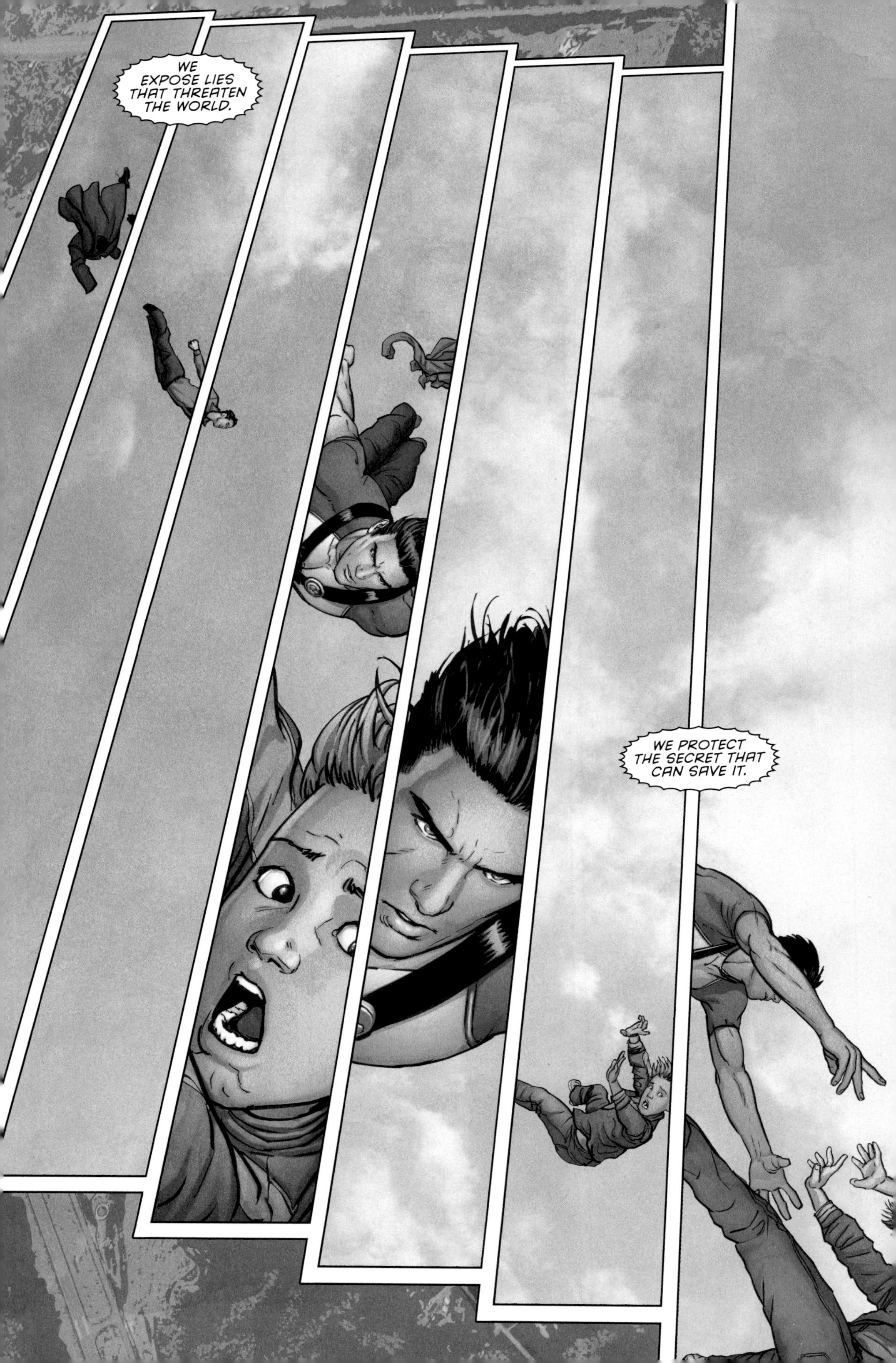
WE EXPOSE LIES THAT THREATEN THE WORLD.
WE PROTECT THE SECRET THAT CAN SAVE IT.

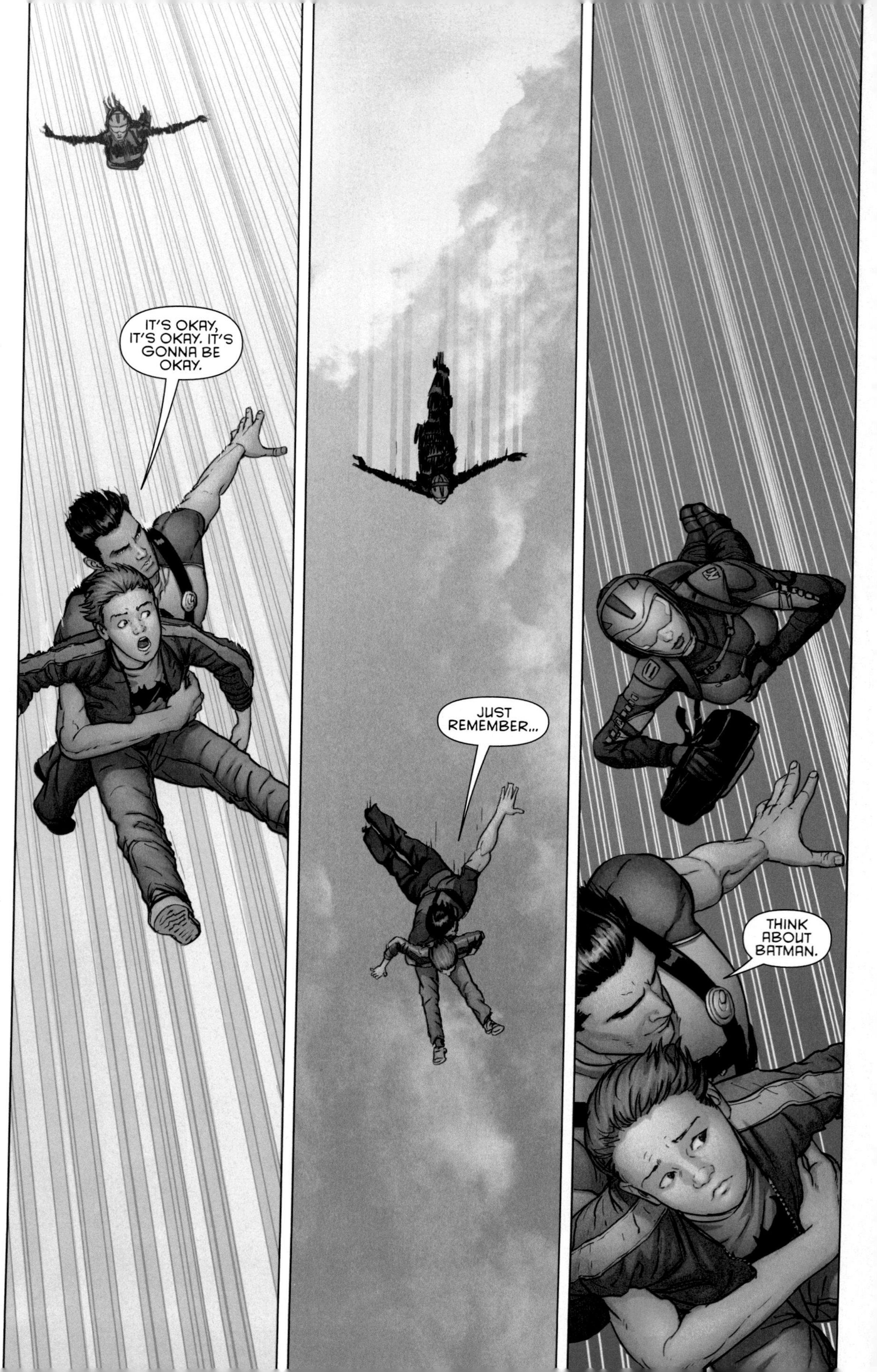
IT'S OKAY, IT'S OKAY. IT'S GONNA BE OKAY.
JUST REMEMBER...
THINK ABOUT BATMAN.

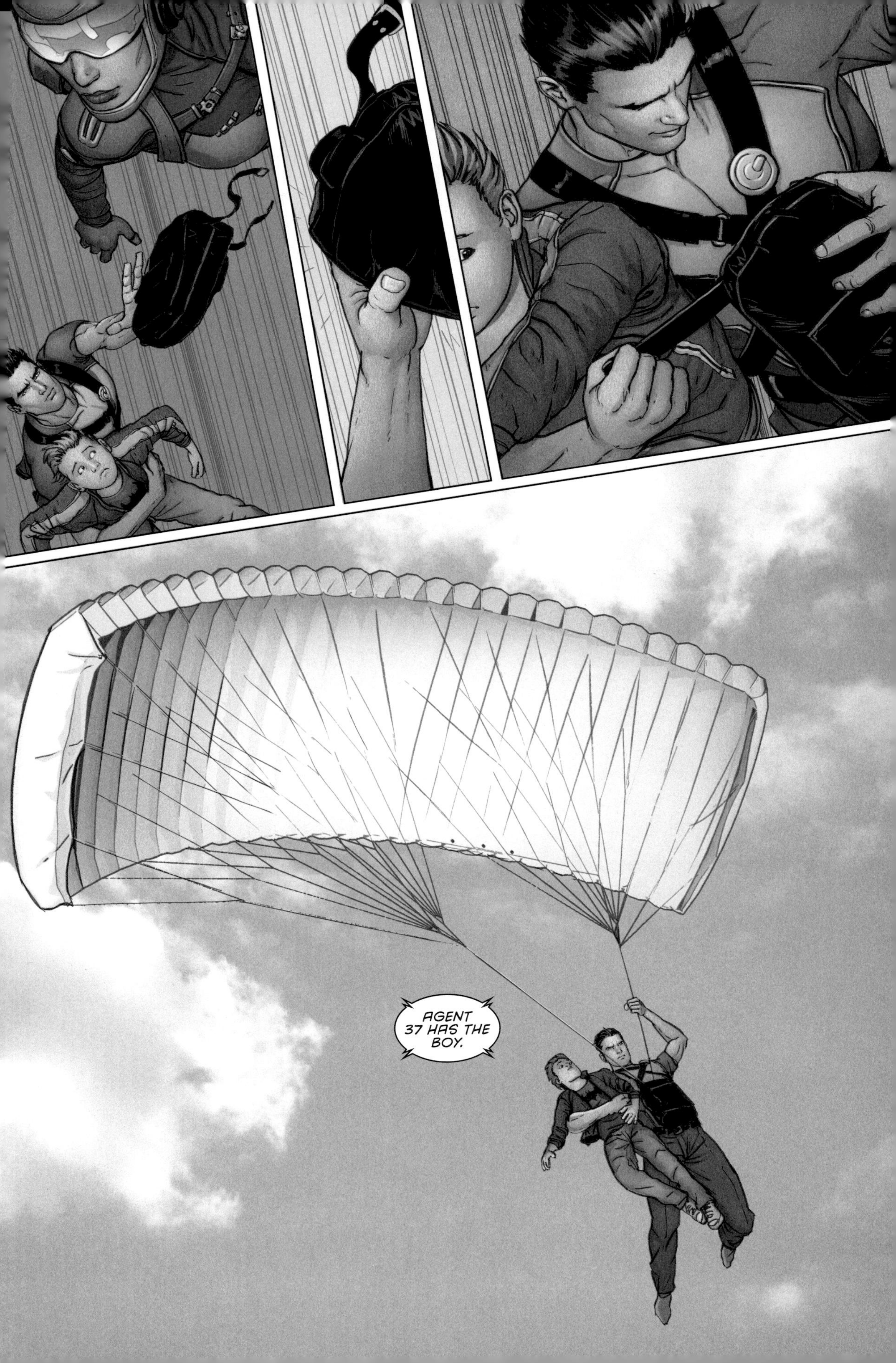
AGENT 37 HAS THE BOY.

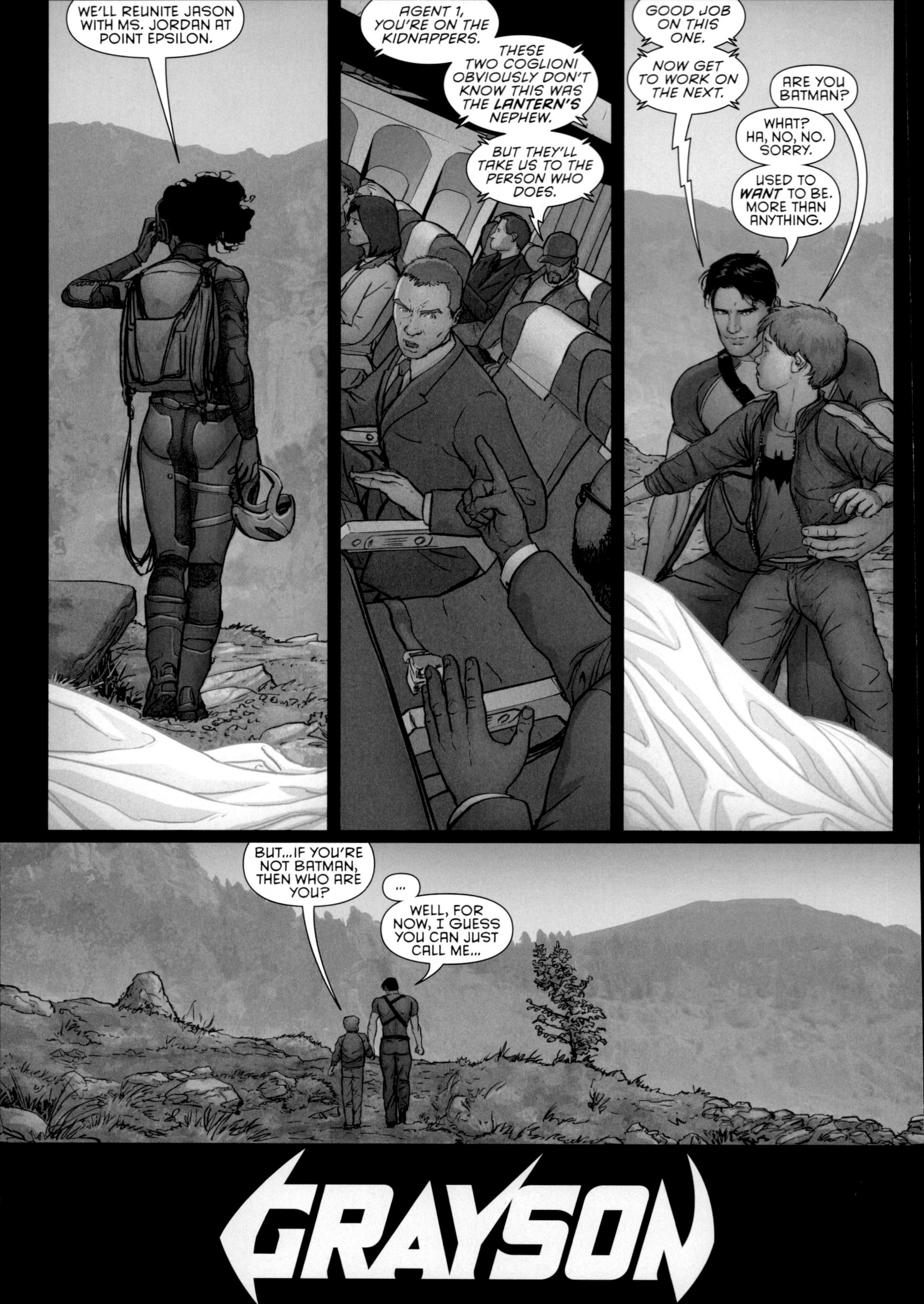
WE'LL REUNITE JASON WITH MS. JORDAN AT POINT EPSILON.
AGENT 1, YOU'RE ON THE KIDNAPPERS.
THESE TWO COGLIONI OBVIOUSLY DON'T KNOW THIS WAS THE LANTERN'S NEPHEW.
BUT THEY'LL TAKE US TO THE PERSON WHO DOES.
GOOD JOB ON THIS ONE.
NOW GET TO WORK ON THE NEXT.
ARE YOU BATMAN?
WHAT? HA, NO, NO. SORRY.
USED TO WANT TO BE. MORE THAN ANYTHING.
BUT...IF YOU'RE NOT BATMAN, THEN WHO ARE YOU?
...
WELL, FOR NOW, I GUESS YOU CAN JUST CALL ME...
GRAYSON

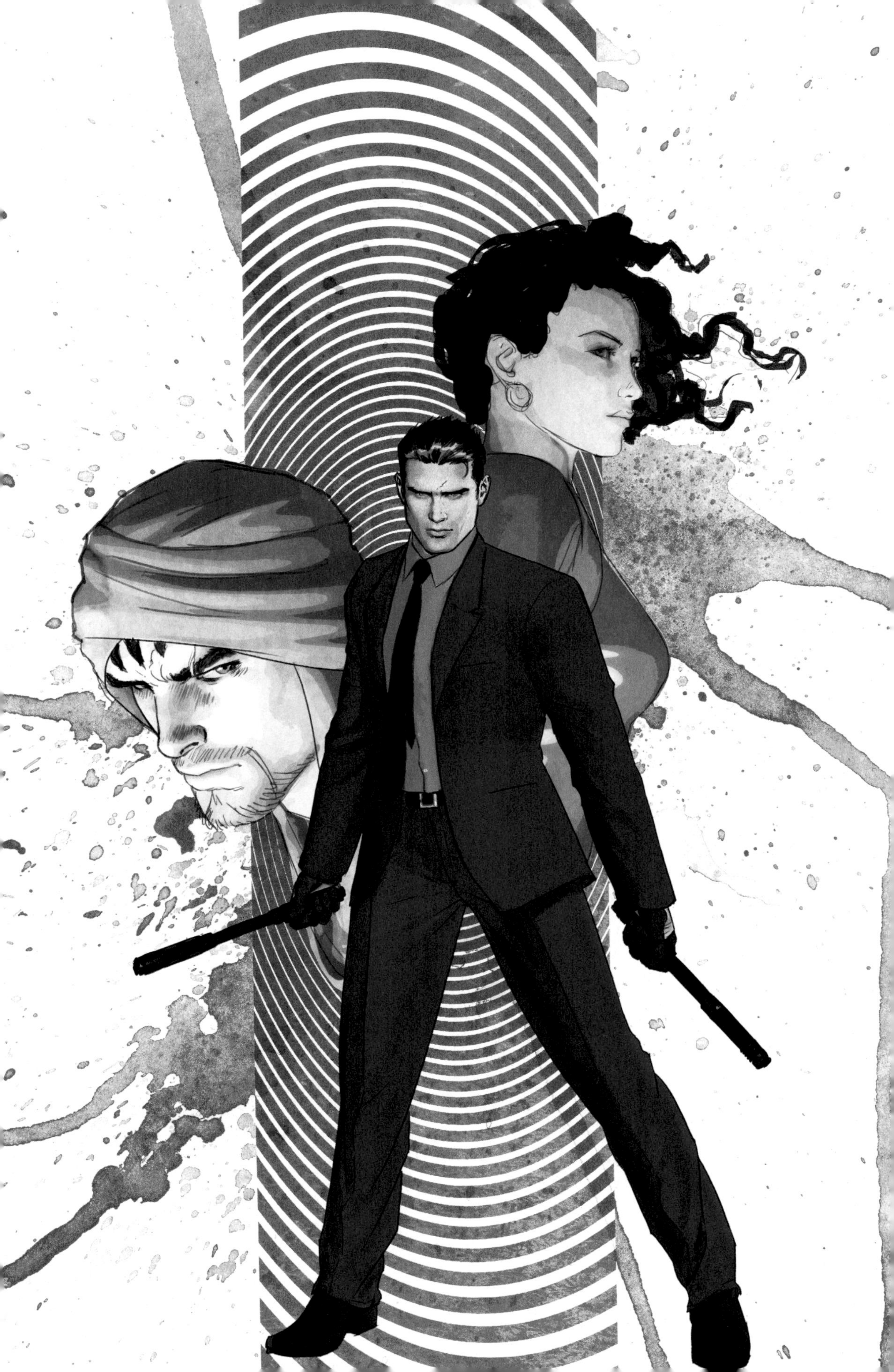

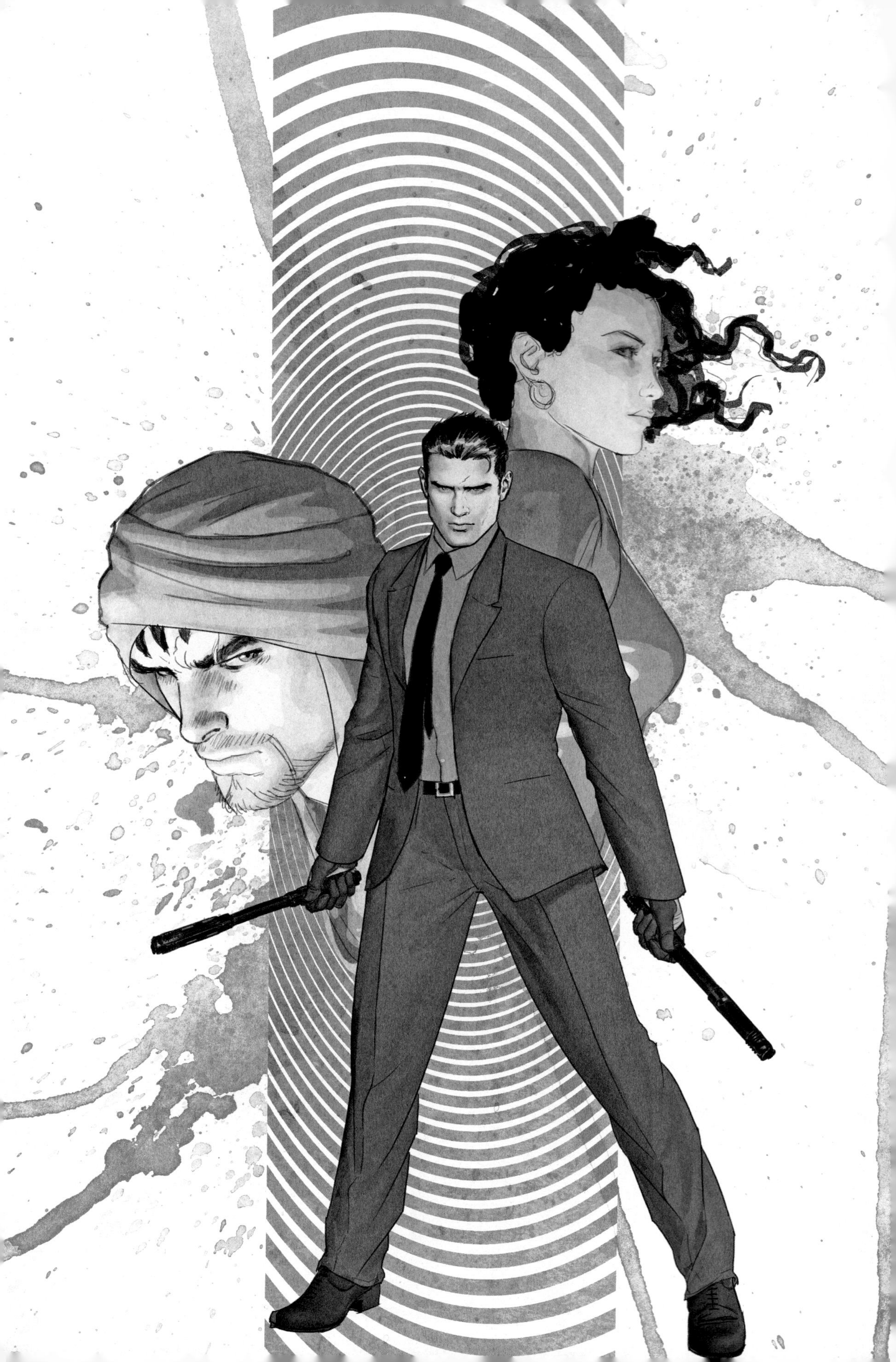

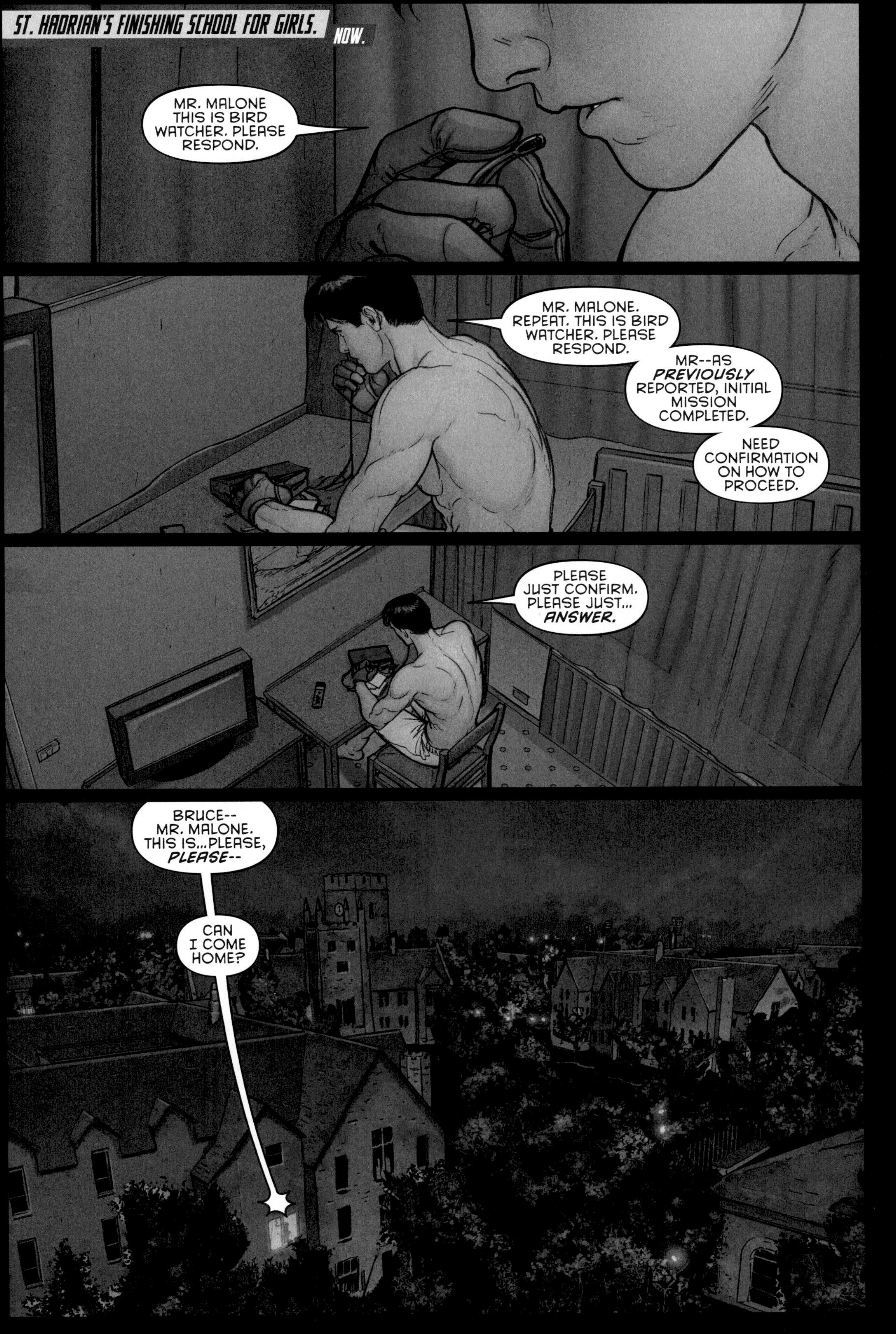
ST. HADRIAN'S FINISHING SCHOOL FOR GIRLS.
NOW.
MR. MALONE THIS IS BIRD WATCHER. PLEASE RESPOND.
MR. MALONE. REPEAT. THIS IS BIRD WATCHER. PLEASE RESPOND.
MR--AS *PREVIOUSLY* REPORTED, INITIAL MISSION COMPLETED.
NEED CONFIRMATION ON HOW TO PROCEED.
PLEASE JUST CONFIRM. PLEASE JUST... ***ANSWER.***
BRUCE-- MR. MALONE. THIS IS...PLEASE, *PLEASE*--
CAN I COME HOME?

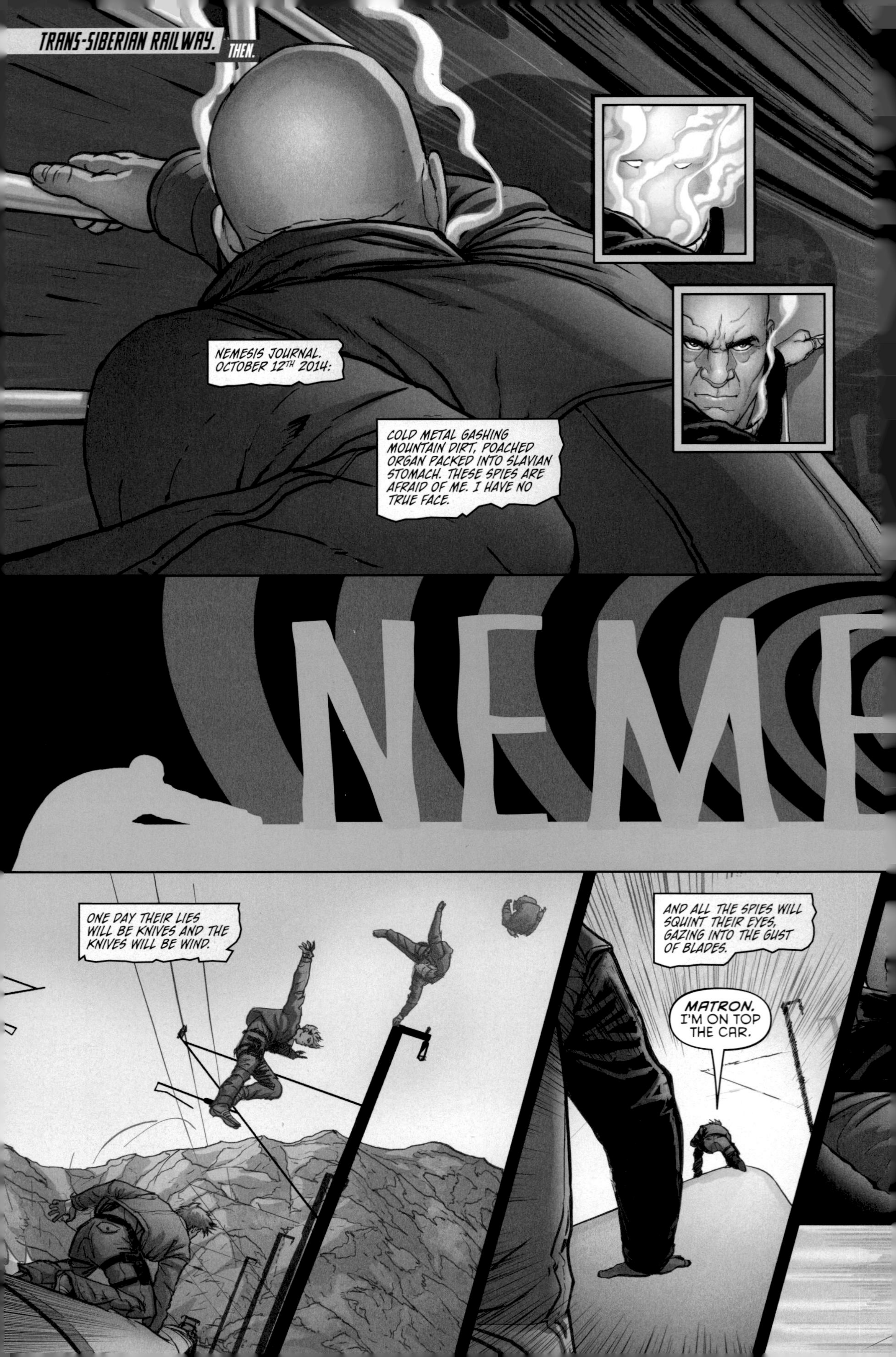
TRANS-SIBERIAN RAILWAY.
THEN.
NEMESIS JOURNAL. OCTOBER 12TH 2014:
COLD METAL GASHING MOUNTAIN DIRT, POACHED ORGAN PACKED INTO SLAVIAN STOMACH. THESE SPIES ARE AFRAID OF ME. I HAVE NO TRUE FACE.
NEME
ONE DAY THEIR LIES WILL BE KNIVES AND THE KNIVES WILL BE WIND.
AND ALL THE SPIES WILL SQUINT THEIR EYES, GAZING INTO THE GUST OF BLADES.
MATRON. I'M ON TOP THE CAR.

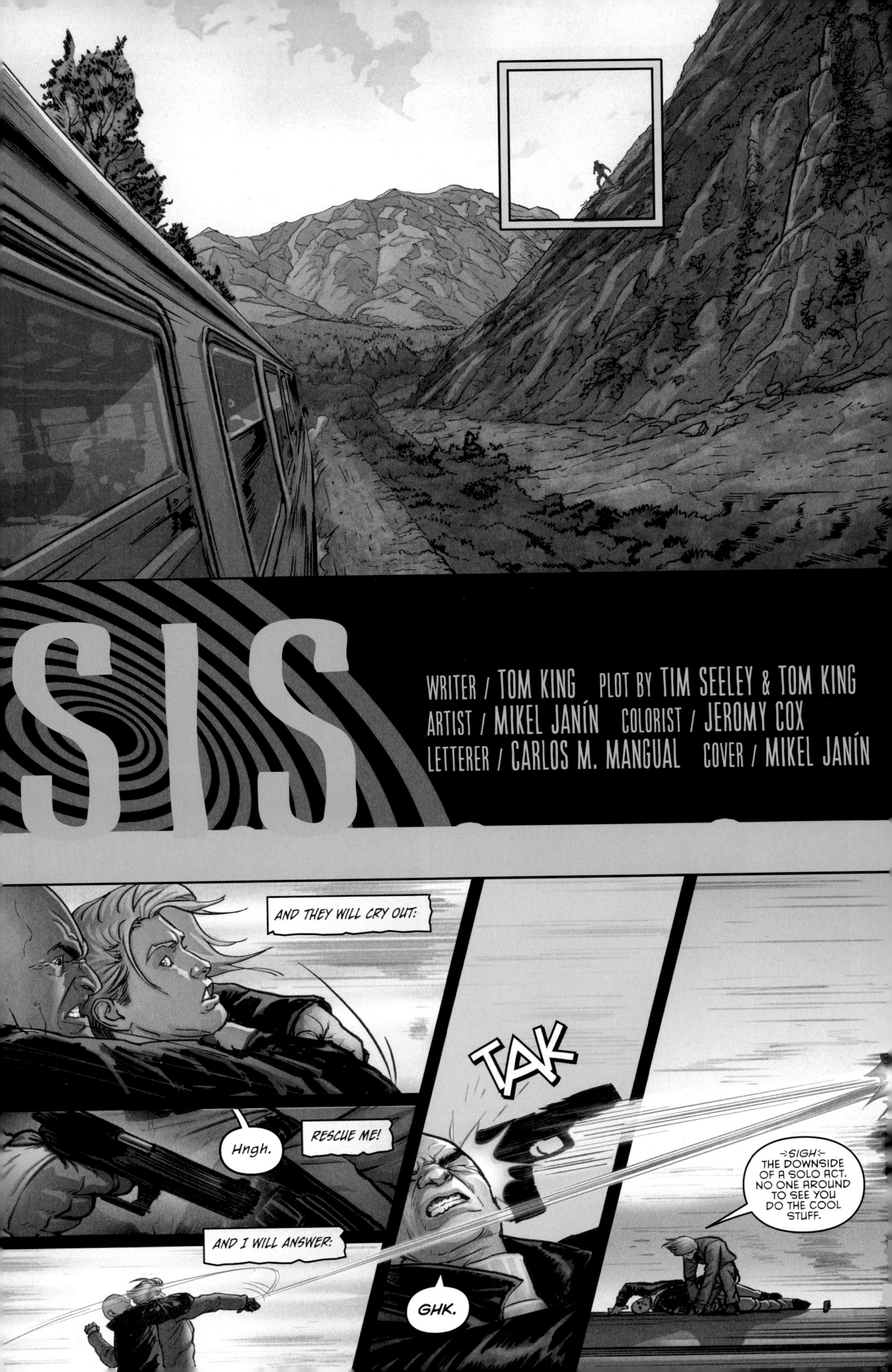
S.I.S
WRITER / TOM KING PLOT BY TIM SEELEY & TOM KING
ARTIST / MIKEL JANÍN COLORIST / JEROMY COX
LETTERER / CARLOS M. MANGUAL COVER / MIKEL JANÍN
AND THEY WILL CRY OUT:
Hngh.
RESCUE ME!
TAK
AND I WILL ANSWER:
GHK.
-SIGH- THE DOWNSIDE OF A SOLO ACT. NO ONE AROUND TO SEE YOU DO THE COOL STUFF.

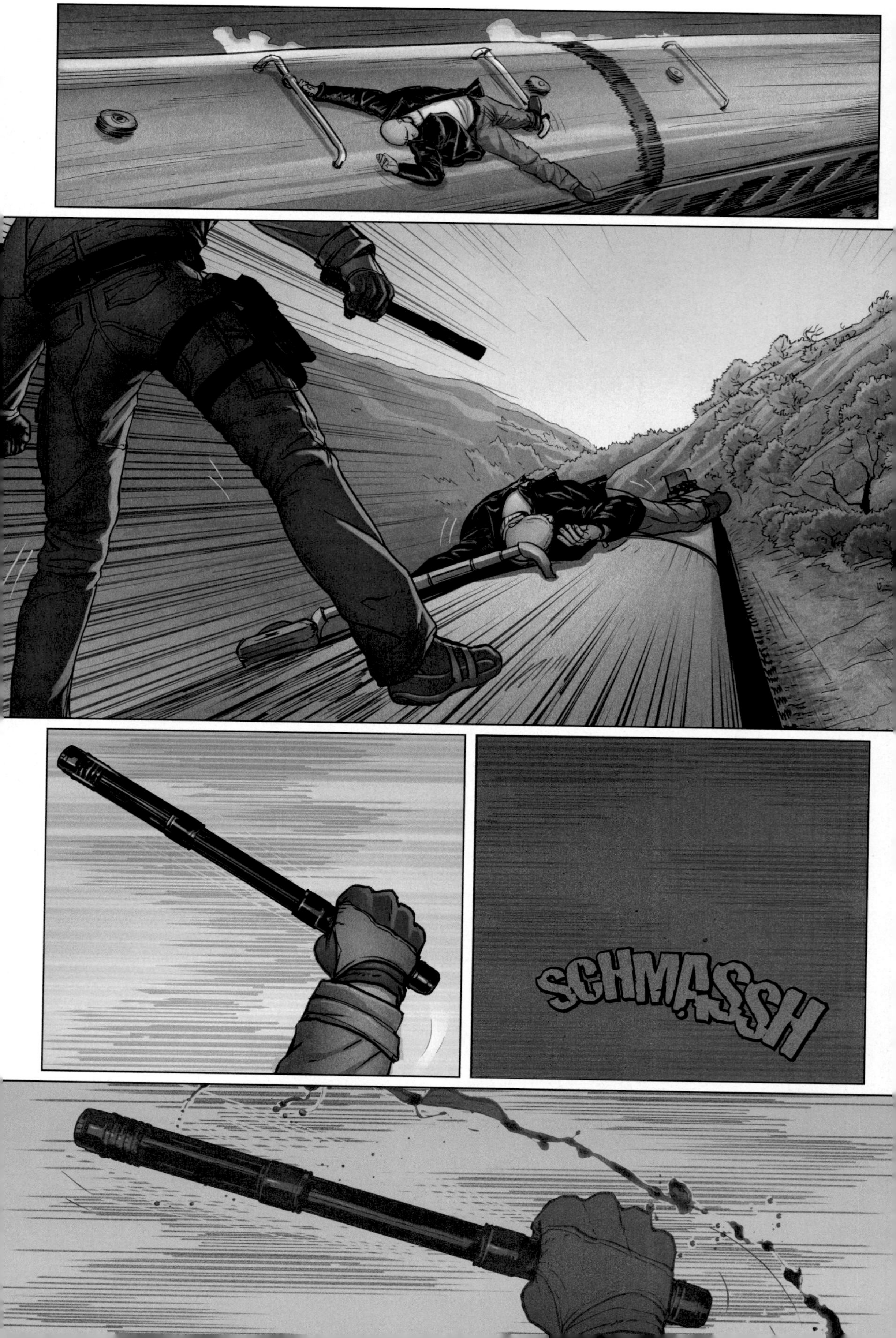
SCHMASSH

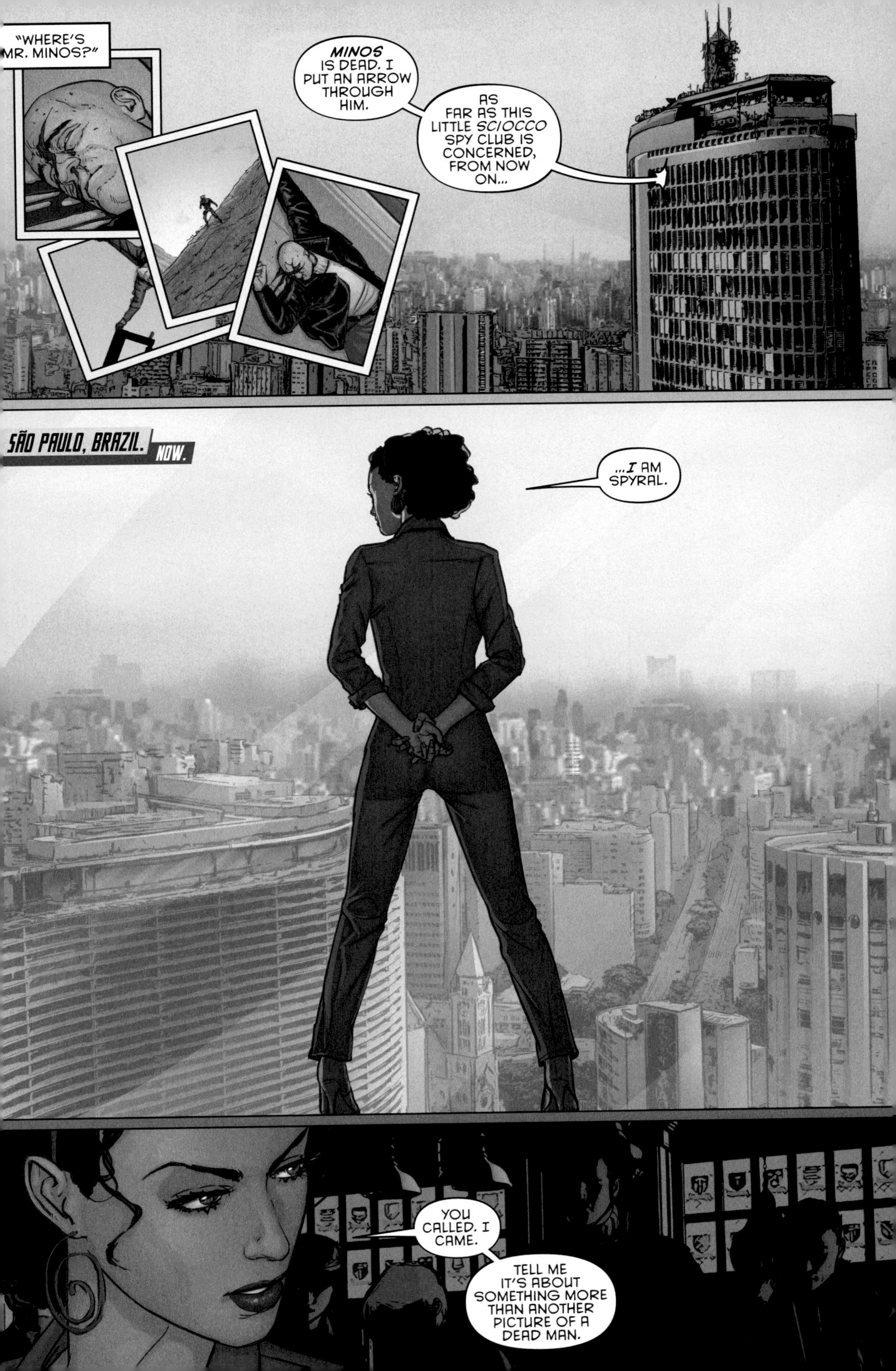
"WHERE'S MR. MINOS?"
MINOS IS DEAD. I PUT AN ARROW THROUGH HIM.
AS FAR AS THIS LITTLE SCIOCCO SPY CLUB IS CONCERNED, FROM NOW ON...
SÃO PAULO, BRAZIL. NOW.
...I AM SPYRAL.
YOU CALLED. I CAME.
TELL ME IT'S ABOUT SOMETHING MORE THAN ANOTHER PICTURE OF A DEAD MAN.

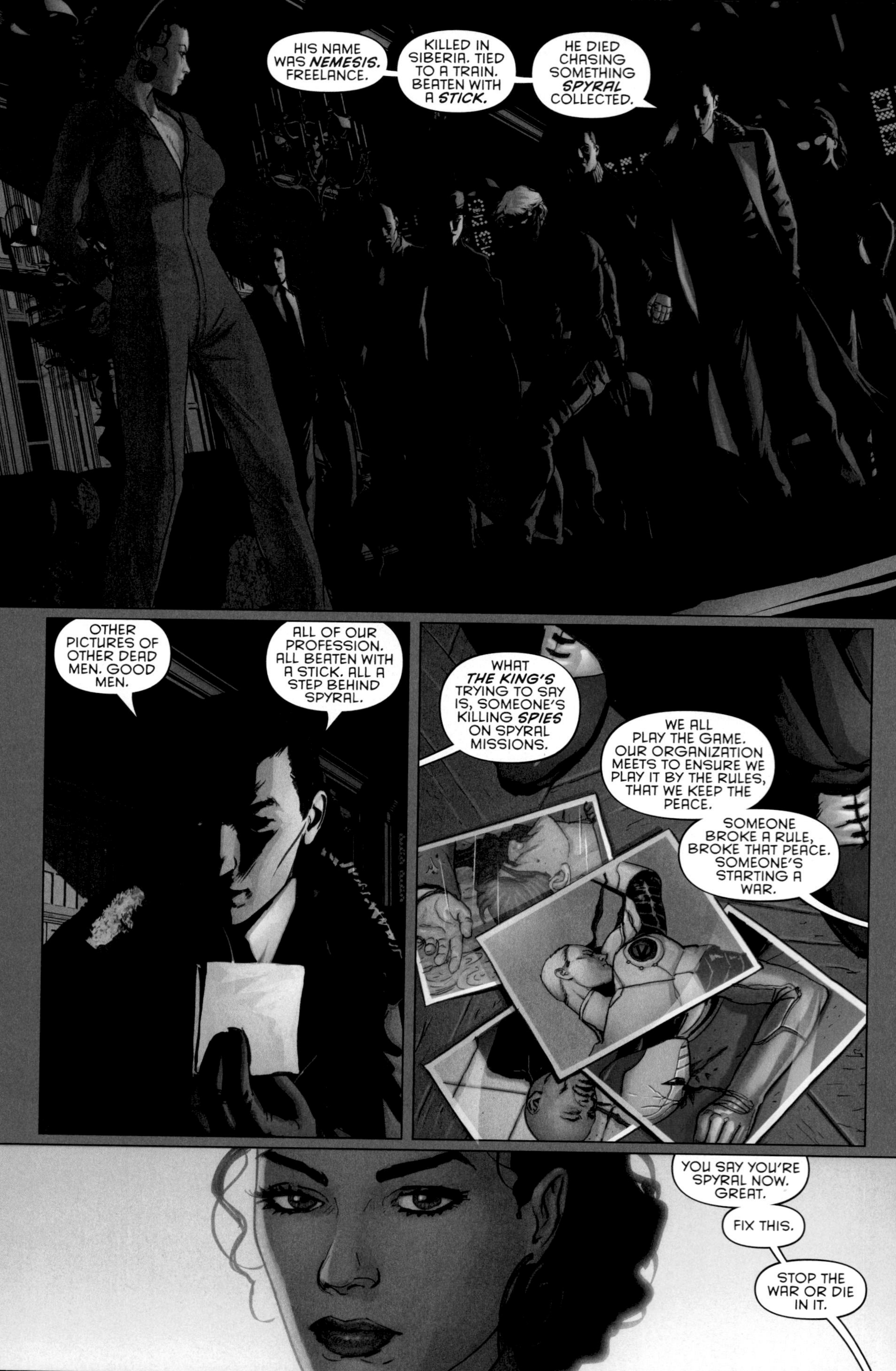
HIS NAME WAS *NEMESIS.* FREELANCE.
KILLED IN SIBERIA. TIED TO A TRAIN. BEATEN WITH A *STICK.*
HE DIED CHASING SOMETHING *SPYRAL* COLLECTED.
OTHER PICTURES OF OTHER DEAD MEN. GOOD MEN.
ALL OF OUR PROFESSION. ALL BEATEN WITH A STICK. ALL A STEP BEHIND SPYRAL.
WHAT *THE KING'S* TRYING TO SAY IS, SOMEONE'S KILLING *SPIES* ON SPYRAL MISSIONS.
WE ALL PLAY THE GAME. OUR ORGANIZATION MEETS TO ENSURE WE PLAY IT BY THE RULES, THAT WE KEEP THE PEACE.
SOMEONE BROKE A RULE, BROKE THAT PEACE. SOMEONE'S STARTING A WAR.
YOU SAY YOU'RE SPYRAL NOW. GREAT.
FIX THIS.
STOP THE WAR OR DIE IN IT.

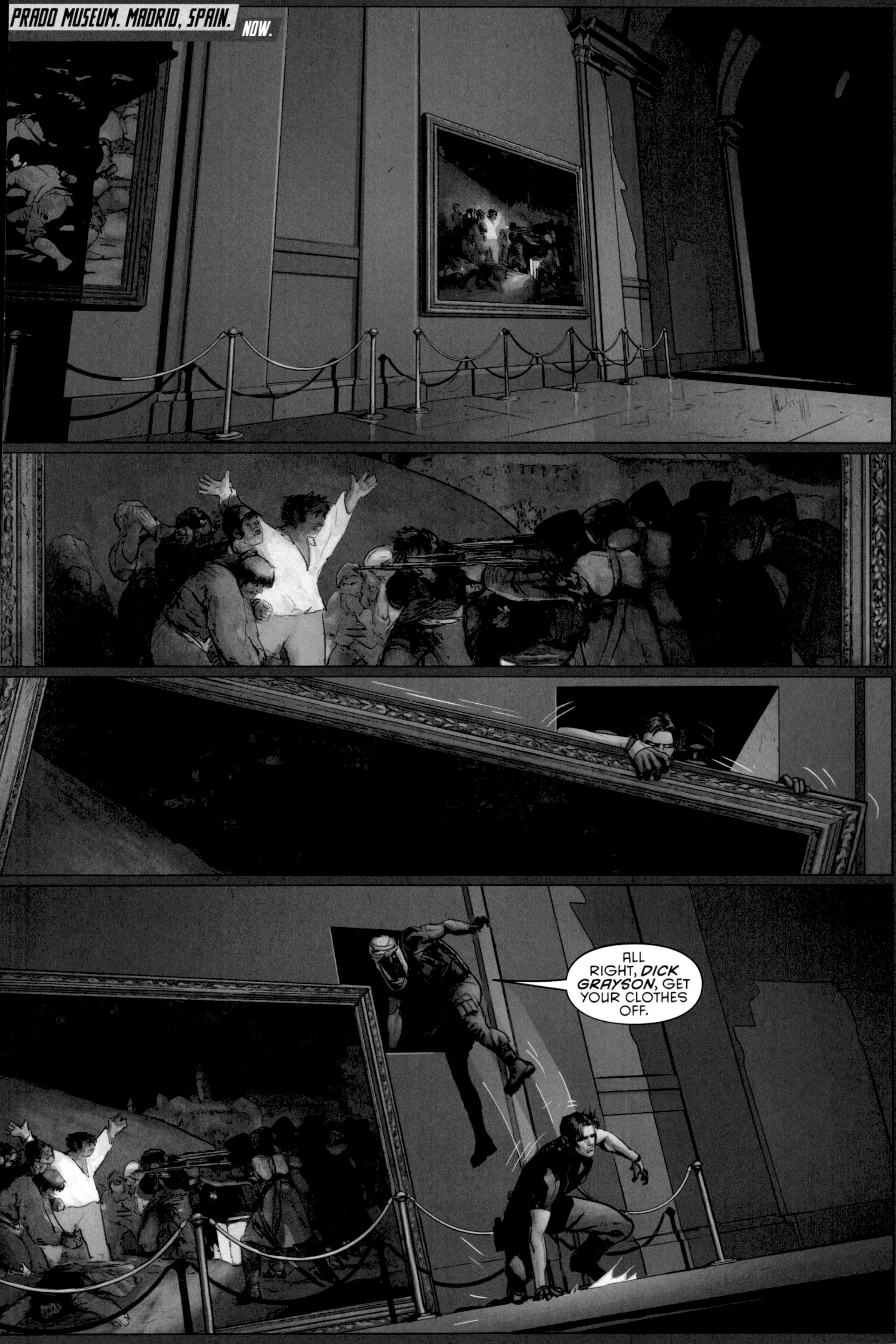
PRADO MUSEUM. MADRID, SPAIN.
NOW.
ALL RIGHT, DICK GRAYSON, GET YOUR CLOTHES OFF.

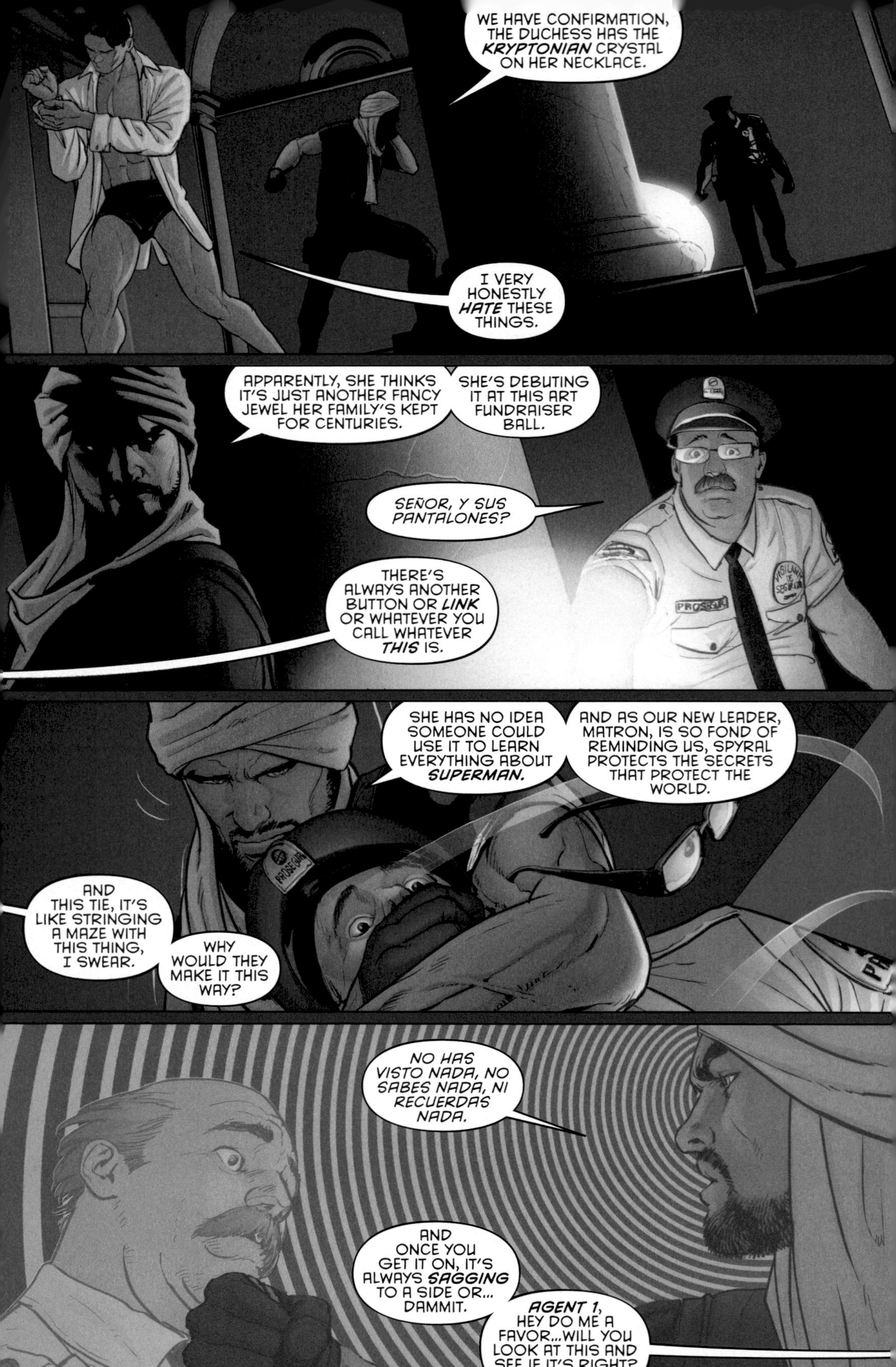
WE HAVE CONFIRMATION, THE DUCHESS HAS THE KRYPTONIAN CRYSTAL ON HER NECKLACE.
I VERY HONESTLY HATE THESE THINGS.
APPARENTLY, SHE THINKS IT'S JUST ANOTHER FANCY JEWEL HER FAMILY'S KEPT FOR CENTURIES.
SHE'S DEBUTING IT AT THIS ART FUNDRAISER BALL.
SEÑOR, Y SUS PANTALONES?
THERE'S ALWAYS ANOTHER BUTTON OR LINK OR WHATEVER YOU CALL WHATEVER THIS IS.
SHE HAS NO IDEA SOMEONE COULD USE IT TO LEARN EVERYTHING ABOUT SUPERMAN.
AND AS OUR NEW LEADER, MATRON, IS SO FOND OF REMINDING US, SPYRAL PROTECTS THE SECRETS THAT PROTECT THE WORLD.
AND THIS TIE, IT'S LIKE STRINGING A MAZE WITH THIS THING, I SWEAR.
WHY WOULD THEY MAKE IT THIS WAY?
NO HAS VISTO NADA, NO SABES NADA, NI RECUERDAS NADA.
AND ONCE YOU GET IT ON, IT'S ALWAYS SAGGING TO A SIDE OR... DAMMIT.
AGENT 1, HEY DO ME A FAVOR...WILL YOU LOOK AT THIS AND SEE IF IT'S RIGHT?

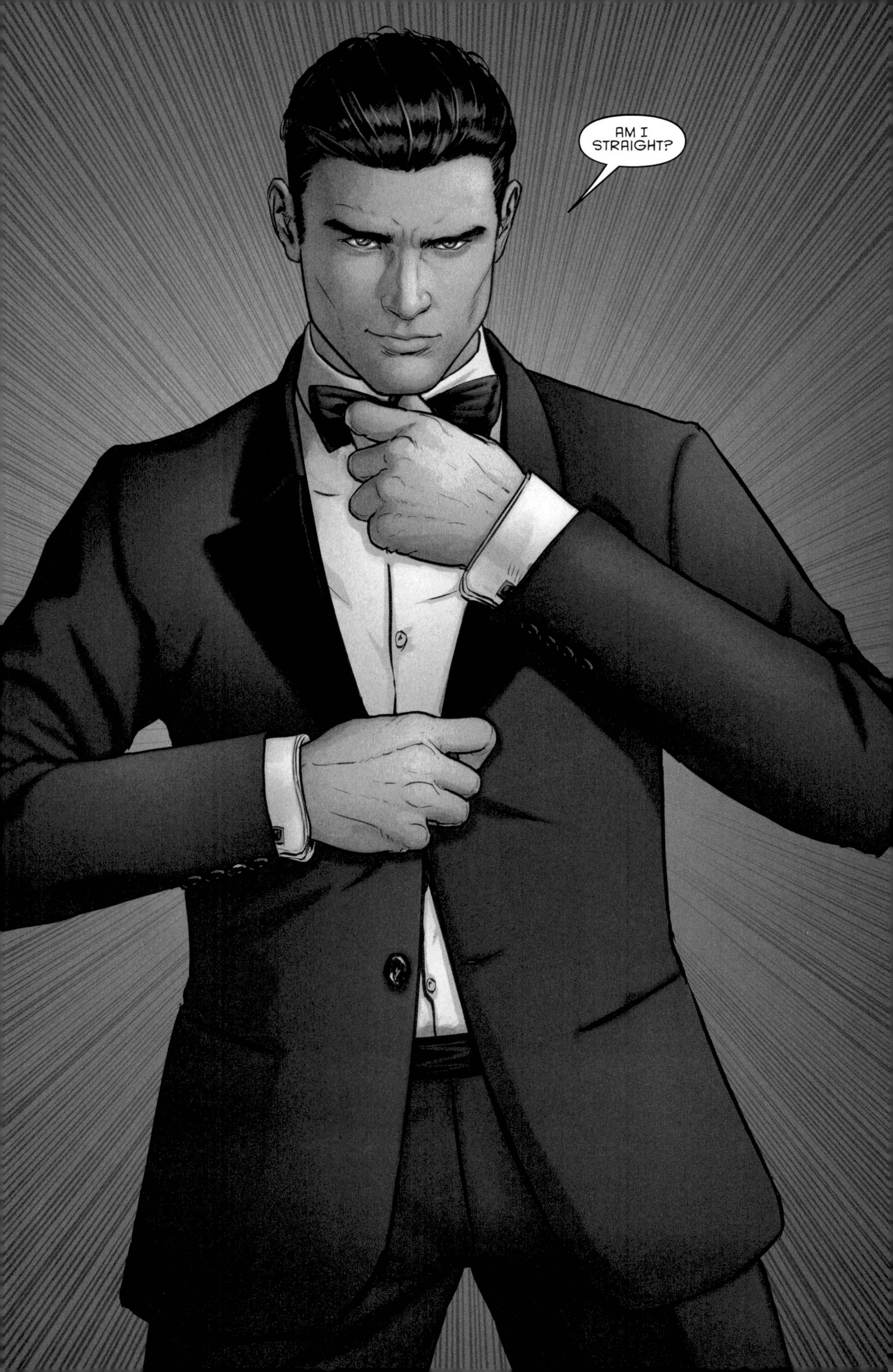
AM I STRAIGHT?

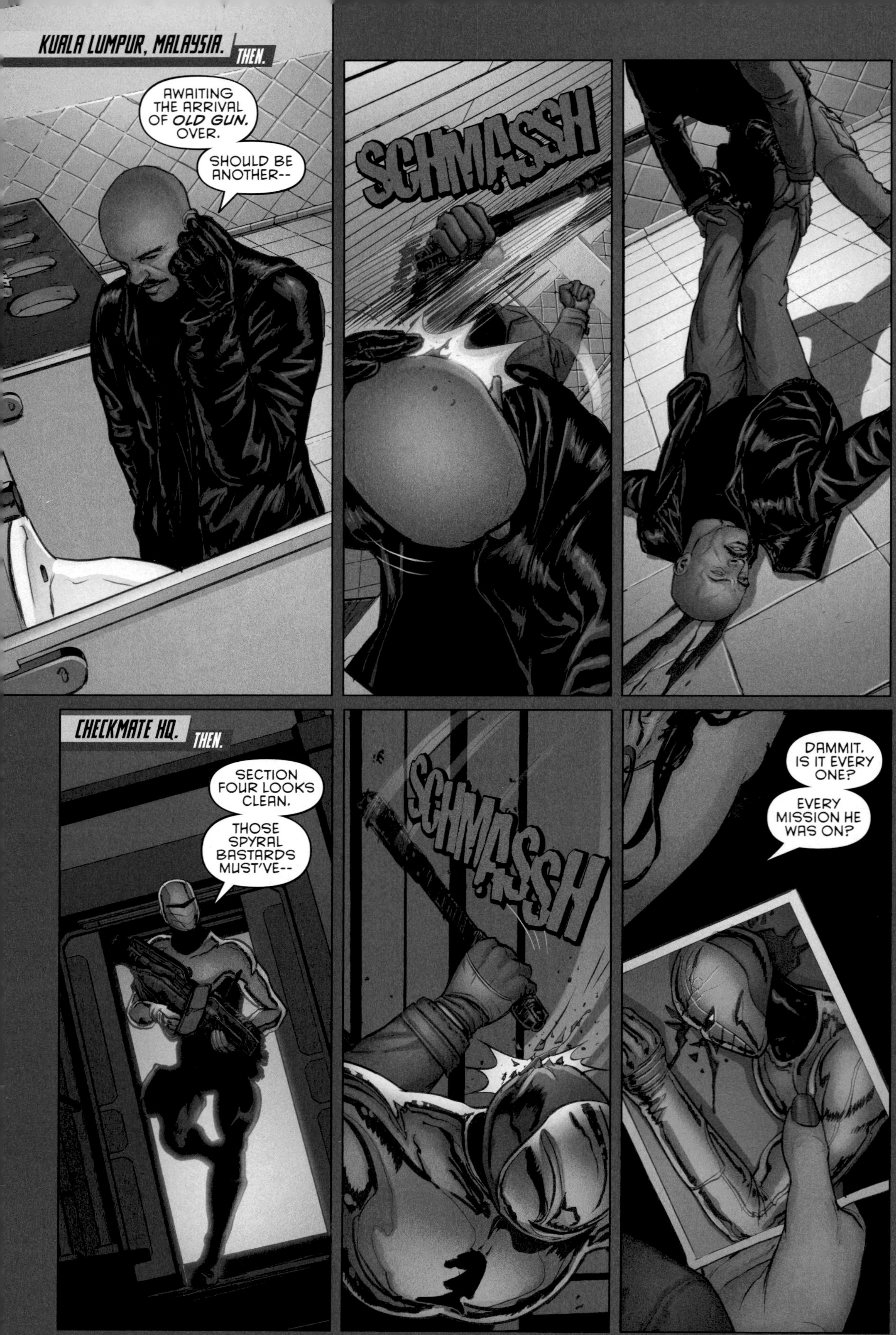
KUALA LUMPUR, MALAYSIA.
THEN.
AWAITING THE ARRIVAL OF OLD GUN. OVER.
SHOULD BE ANOTHER--
SCHMASSH
CHECKMATE HQ.
THEN.
SECTION FOUR LOOKS CLEAN.
THOSE SPYRAL BASTARDS MUST'VE--
SCHMASSH
DAMMIT. IS IT EVERY ONE?
EVERY MISSION HE WAS ON?

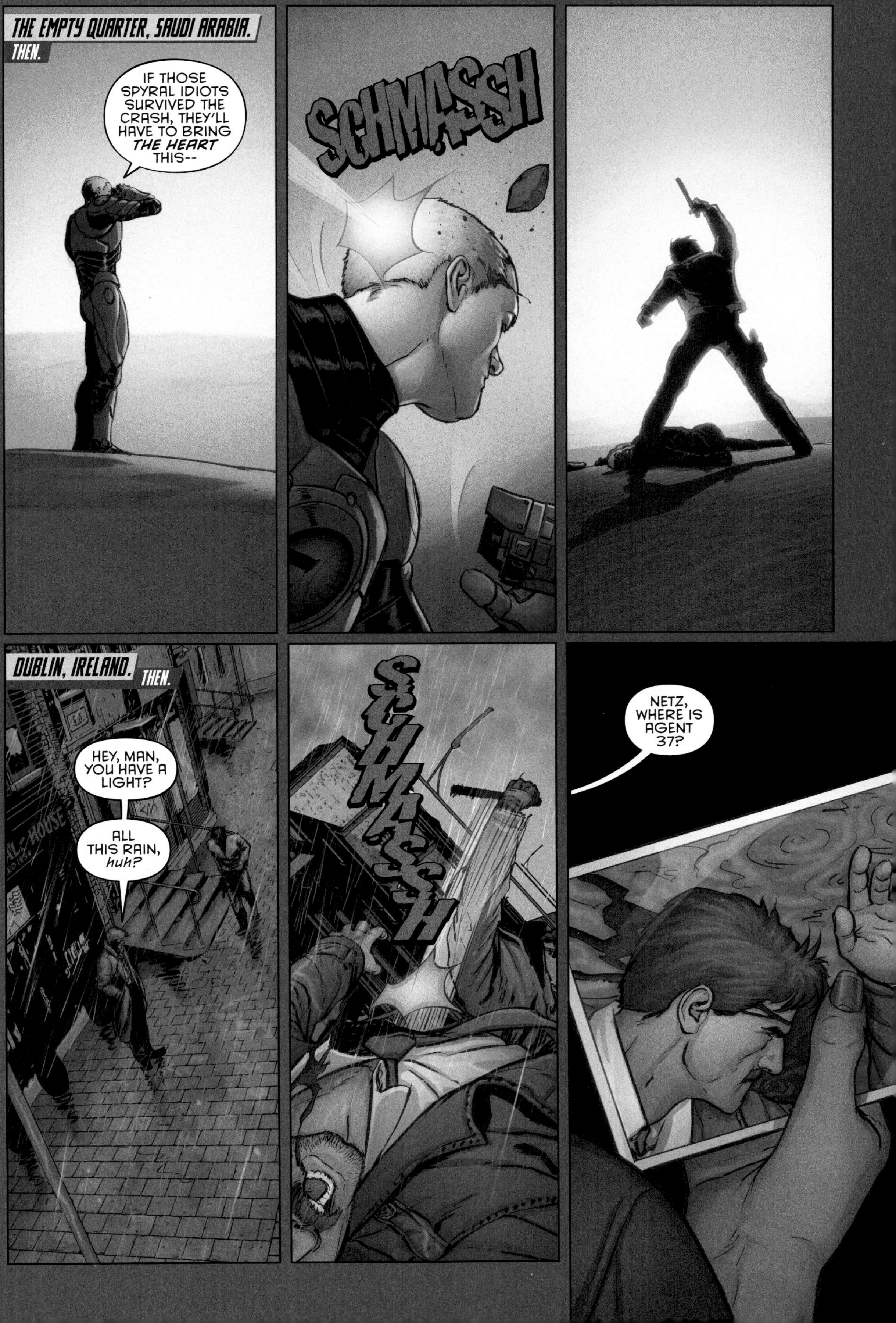
THE EMPTY QUARTER, SAUDI ARABIA.
THEN.
IF THOSE SPYRAL IDIOTS SURVIVED THE CRASH, THEY'LL HAVE TO BRING THE HEART THIS--
SCHMASSH
DUBLIN, IRELAND.
THEN.
HEY, MAN, YOU HAVE A LIGHT?
ALL THIS RAIN, huh?
SCHMASSH
NETZ, WHERE IS AGENT 37?

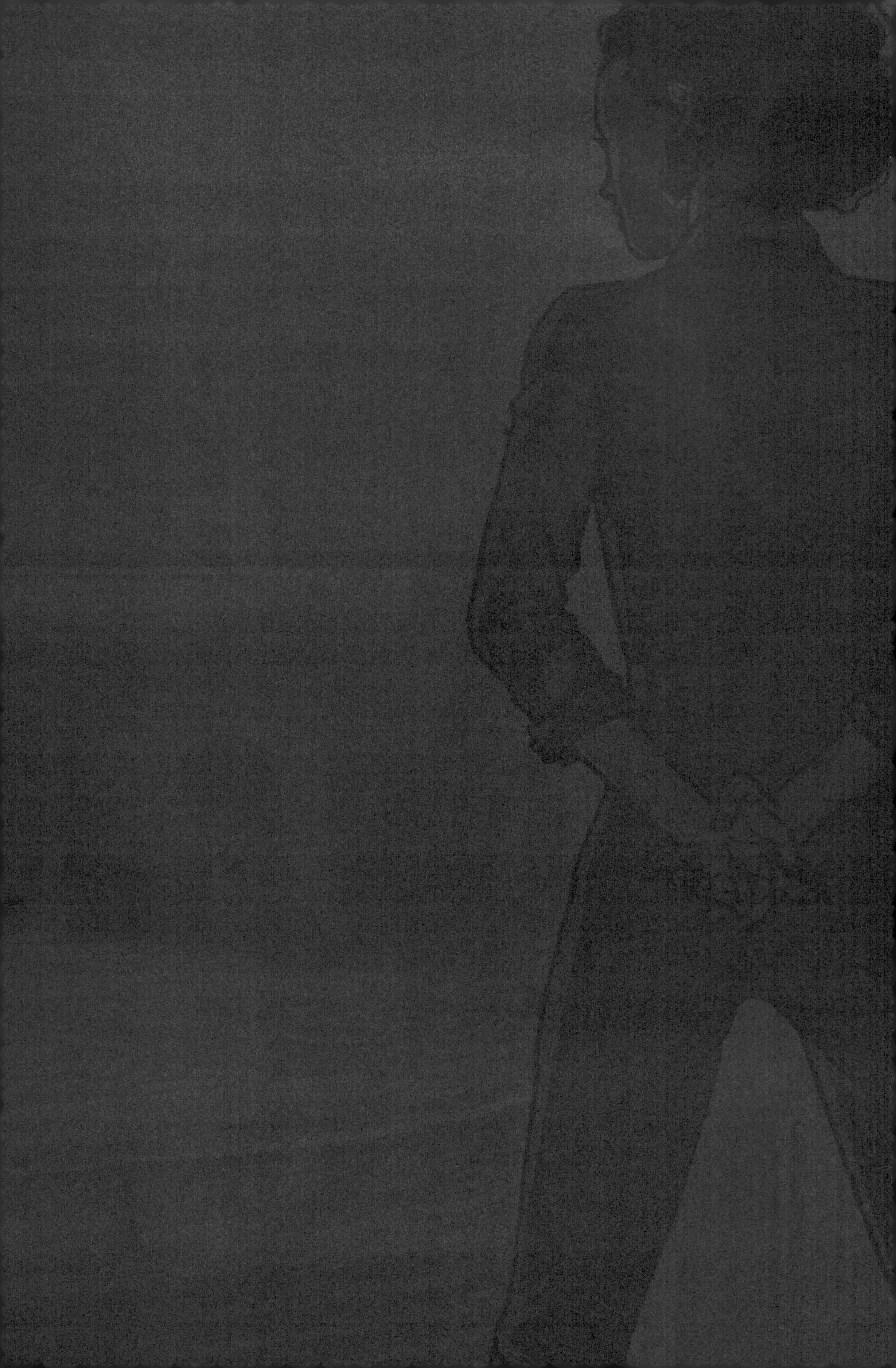

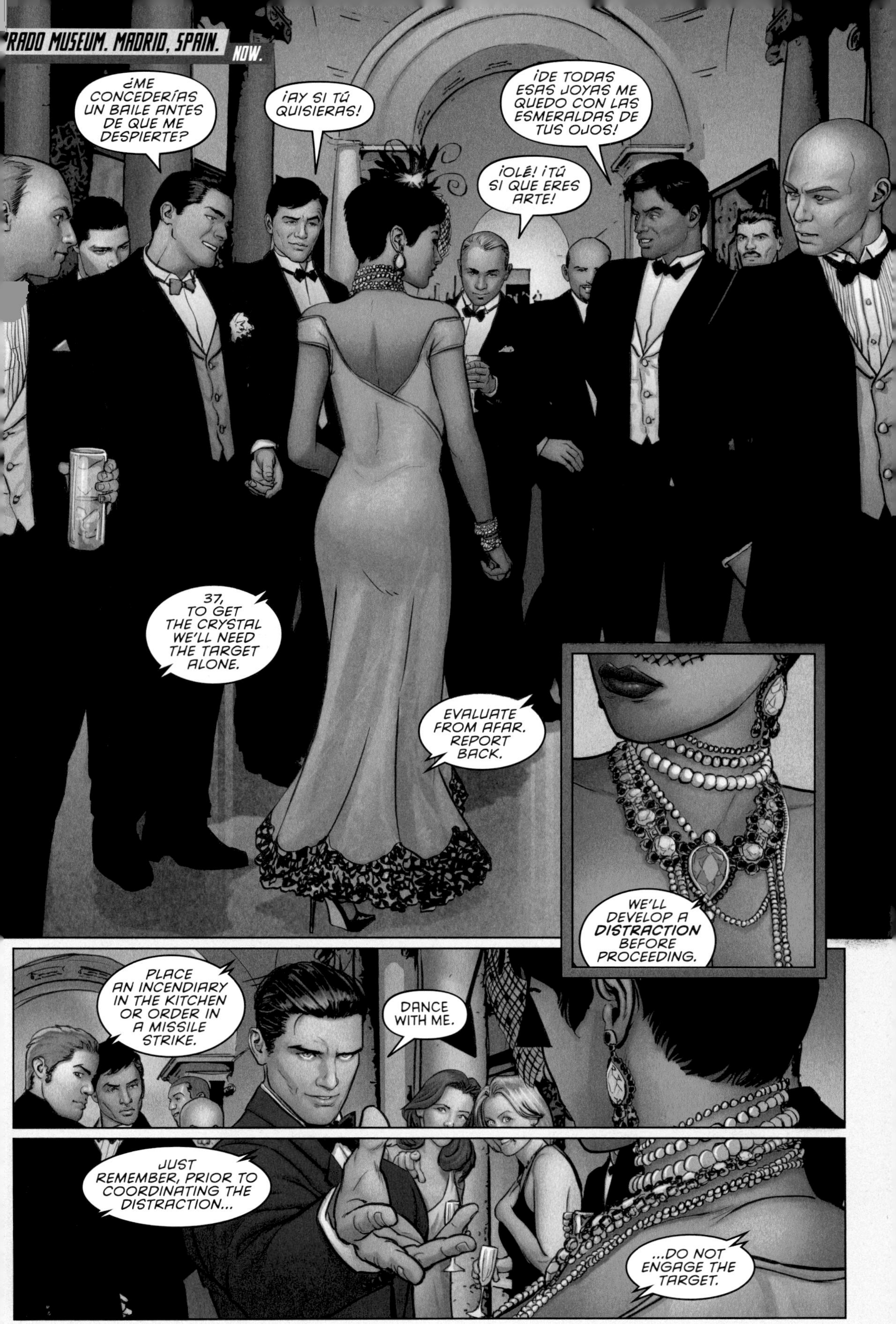

RADO MUSEUM. MADRID, SPAIN.
NOW.
¿ME CONCEDERÍAS UN BAILE ANTES DE QUE ME DESPIERTE?
¡AY SI TÚ QUISIERAS!
¡DE TODAS ESAS JOYAS ME QUEDO CON LAS ESMERALDAS DE TUS OJOS!
¡OLÉ! ¡TÚ SI QUE ERES ARTE!
37, TO GET THE CRYSTAL WE'LL NEED THE TARGET ALONE.
EVALUATE FROM AFAR. REPORT BACK.
WE'LL DEVELOP A DISTRACTION BEFORE PROCEEDING.
PLACE AN INCENDIARY IN THE KITCHEN OR ORDER IN A MISSILE STRIKE.
DANCE WITH ME.
JUST REMEMBER, PRIOR TO COORDINATING THE DISTRACTION...
...DO NOT ENGAGE THE TARGET.

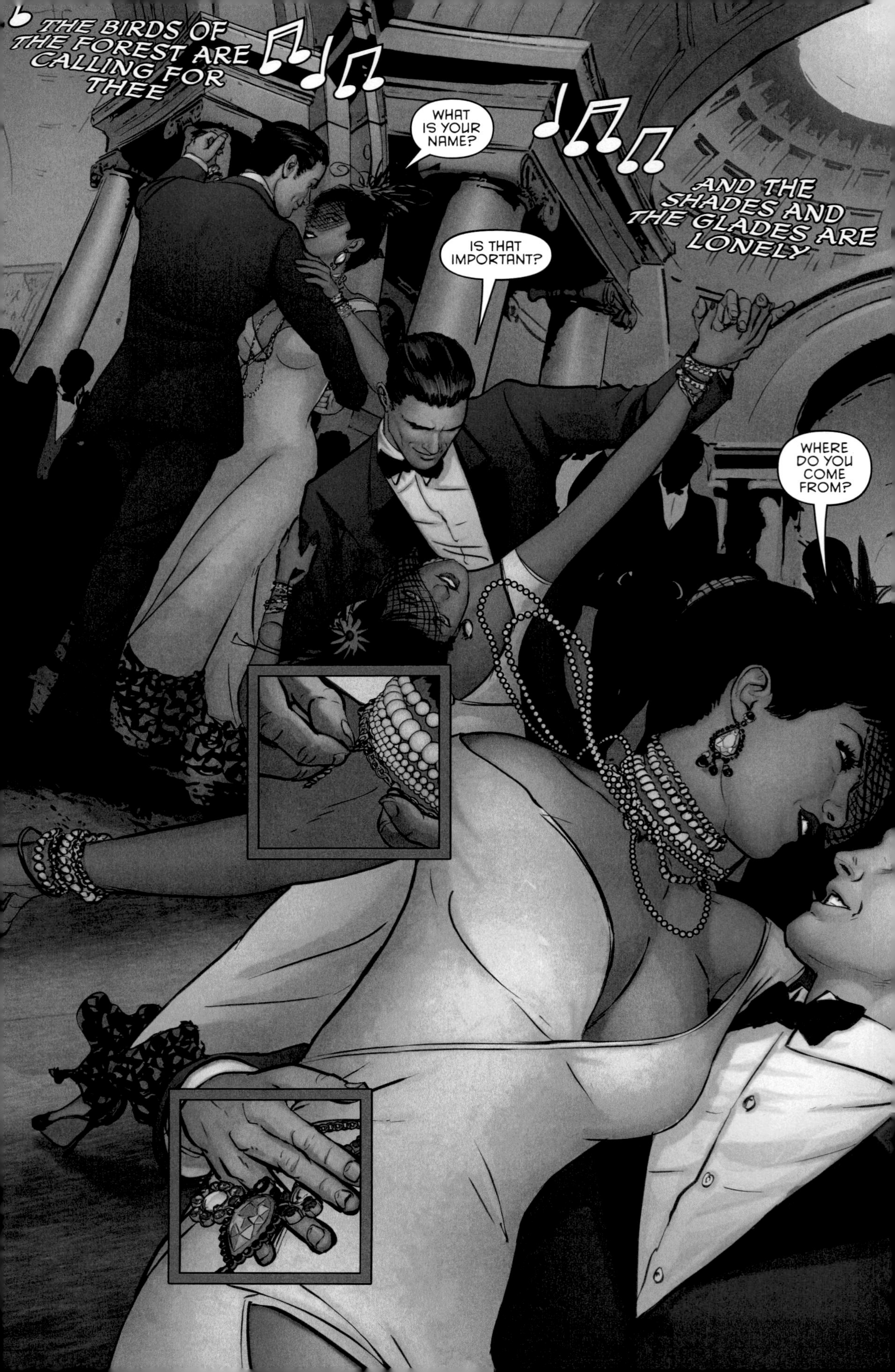
THE BIRDS OF THE FOREST ARE CALLING FOR THEE
WHAT IS YOUR NAME?
IS THAT IMPORTANT?
AND THE SHADES AND THE GLADES ARE LONELY
WHERE DO YOU COME FROM?

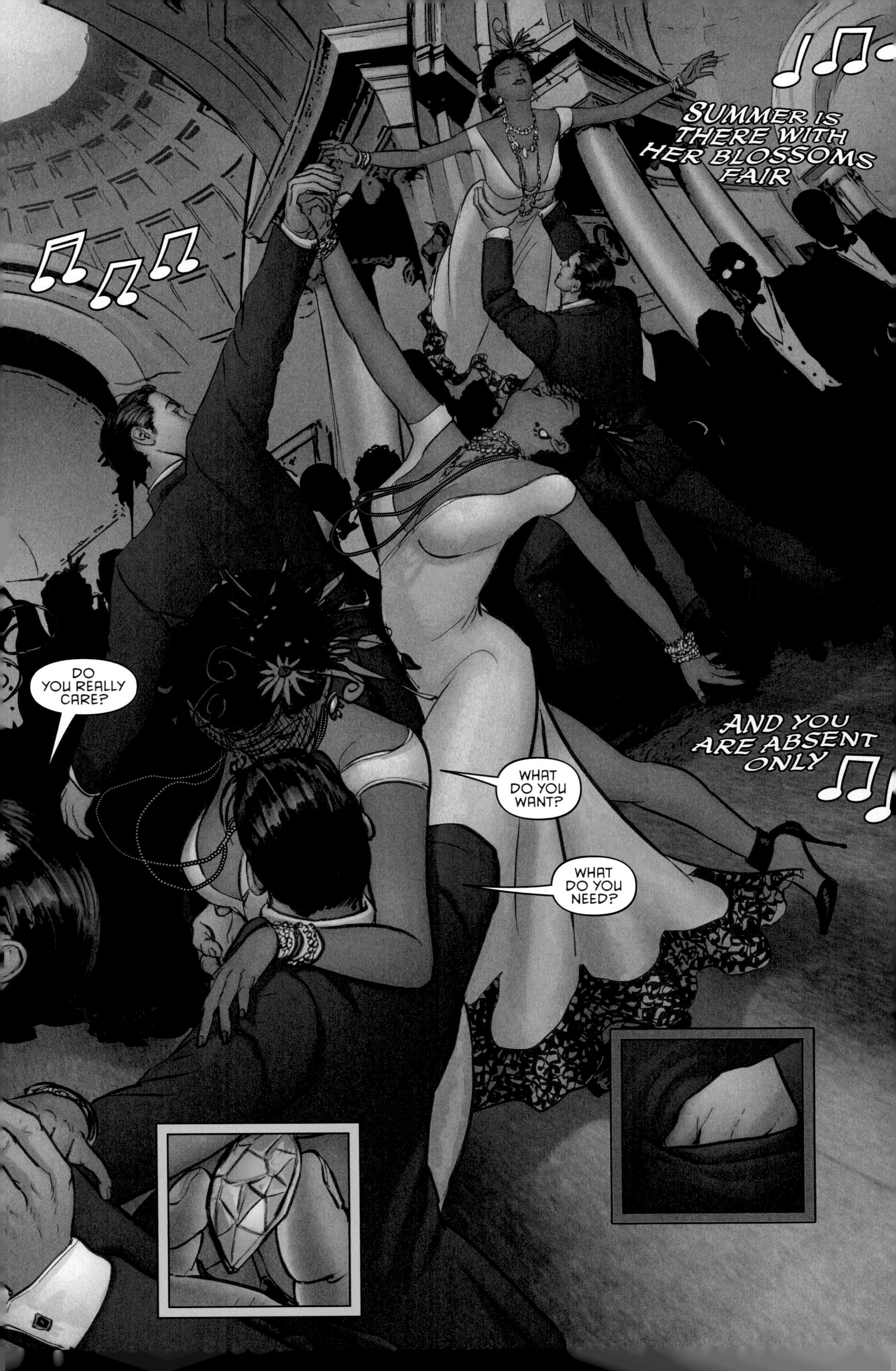
SUMMER IS THERE WITH HER BLOSSOMS FAIR
DO YOU REALLY CARE?
AND YOU ARE ABSENT ONLY
WHAT DO YOU WANT?
WHAT DO YOU NEED?

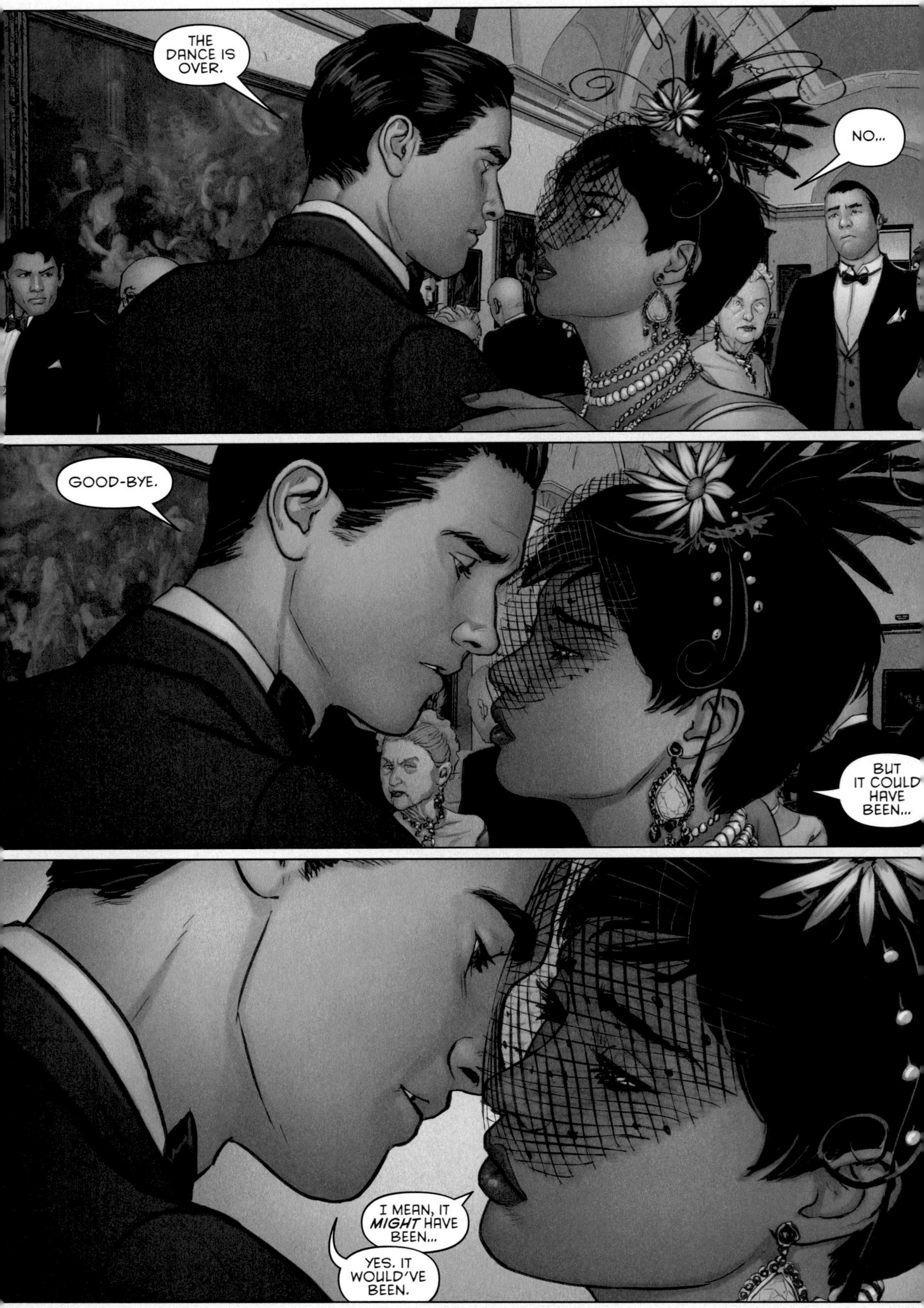
THE DANCE IS OVER.
NO...
GOOD-BYE.
BUT IT COULD HAVE BEEN...
I MEAN, IT *MIGHT* HAVE BEEN...
YES. IT WOULD'VE BEEN.

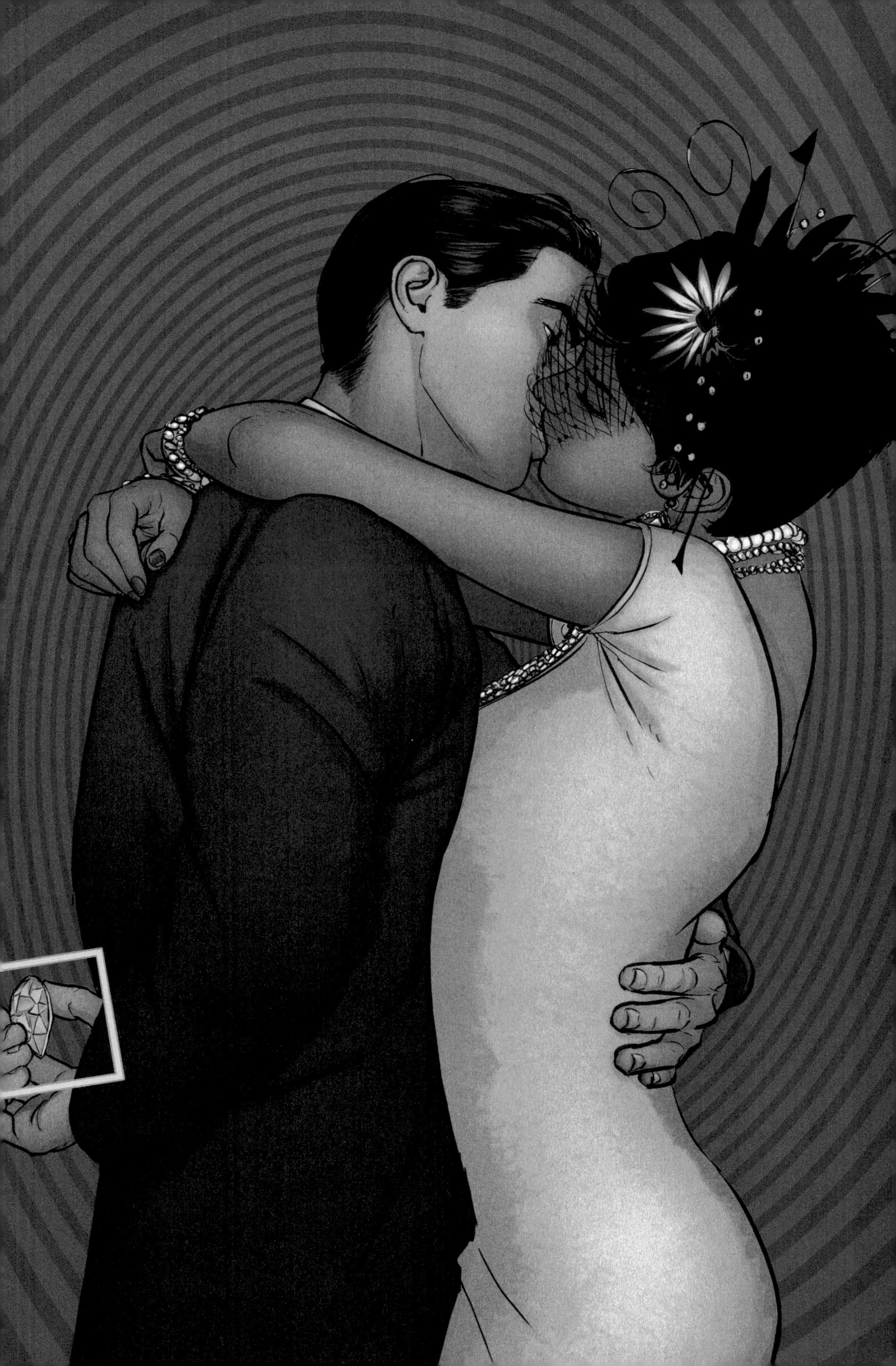

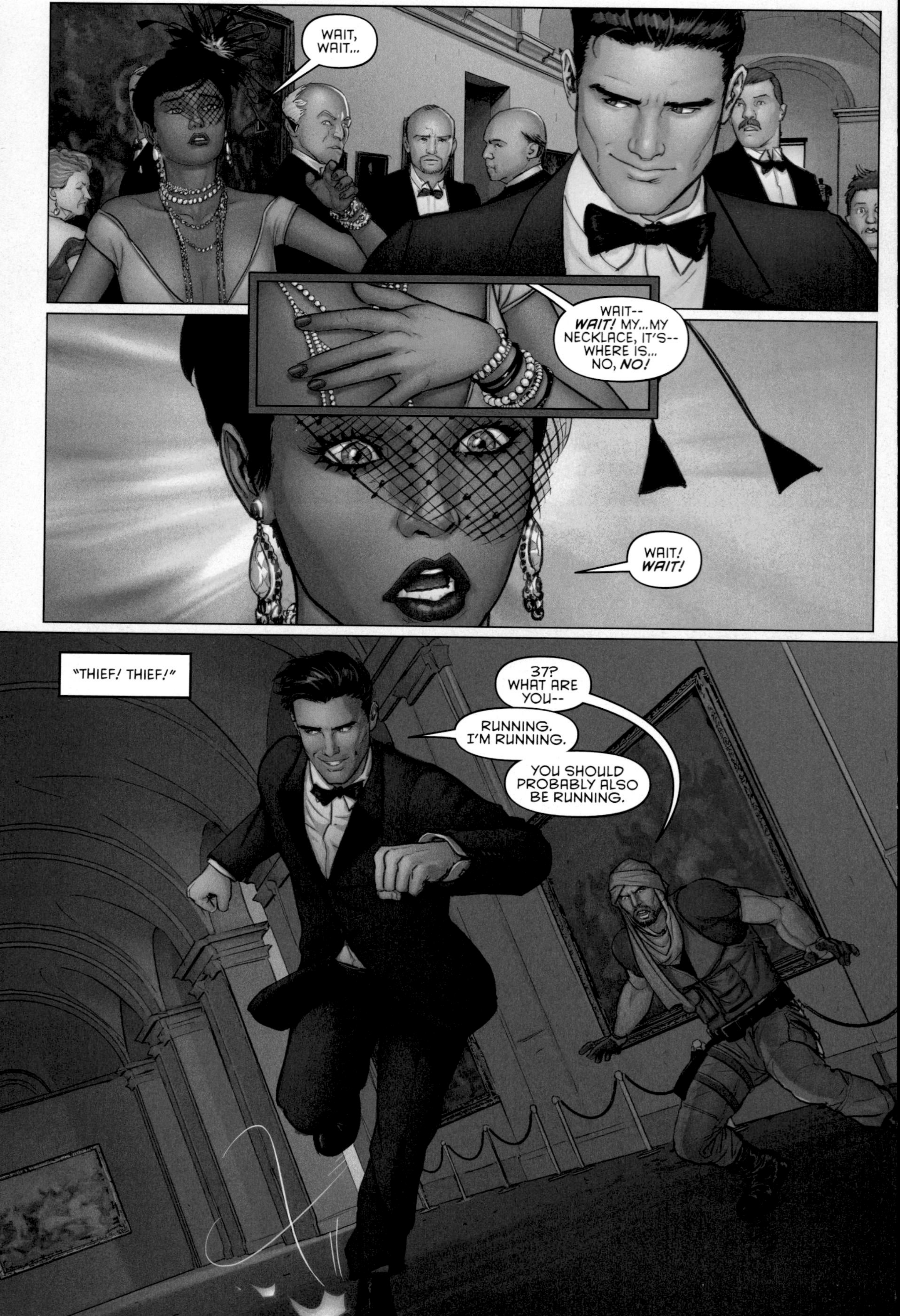
WAIT, WAIT...
WAIT-- WAIT! MY...MY NECKLACE, IT'S-- WHERE IS... NO, NO!
WAIT! WAIT!
"THIEF! THIEF!"
37? WHAT ARE YOU--
RUNNING. I'M RUNNING.
YOU SHOULD PROBABLY ALSO BE RUNNING.

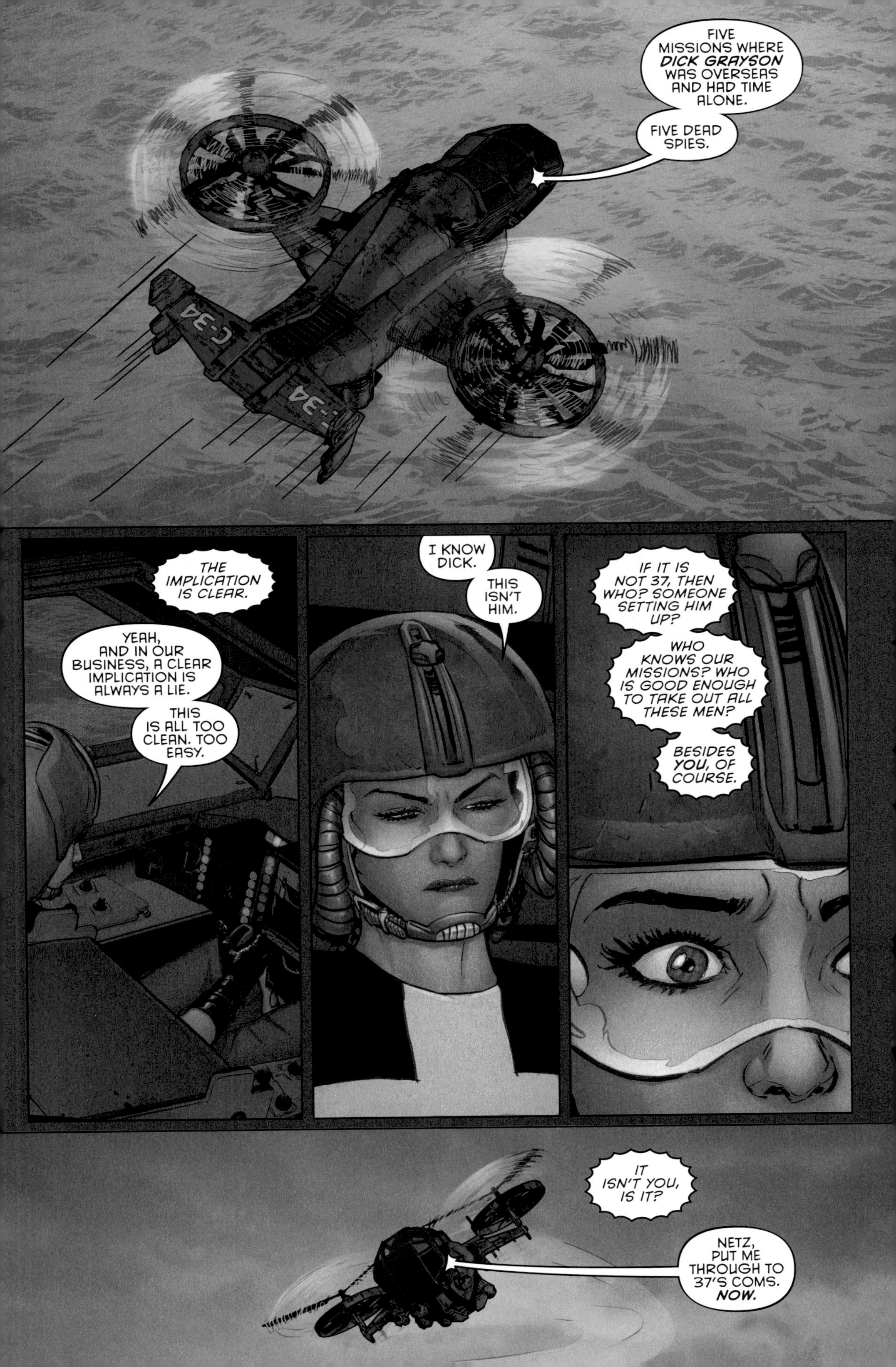
FIVE MISSIONS WHERE DICK GRAYSON WAS OVERSEAS AND HAD TIME ALONE.
FIVE DEAD SPIES.
C-34
C-34
THE IMPLICATION IS CLEAR.
YEAH, AND IN OUR BUSINESS, A CLEAR IMPLICATION IS ALWAYS A LIE.
THIS IS ALL TOO CLEAN. TOO EASY.
I KNOW DICK.
THIS ISN'T HIM.
IF IT IS NOT 37, THEN WHO? SOMEONE SETTING HIM UP?
WHO KNOWS OUR MISSIONS? WHO IS GOOD ENOUGH TO TAKE OUT ALL THESE MEN?
BESIDES YOU, OF COURSE.
IT ISN'T YOU, IS IT?
NETZ, PUT ME THROUGH TO 37'S COMS. NOW.

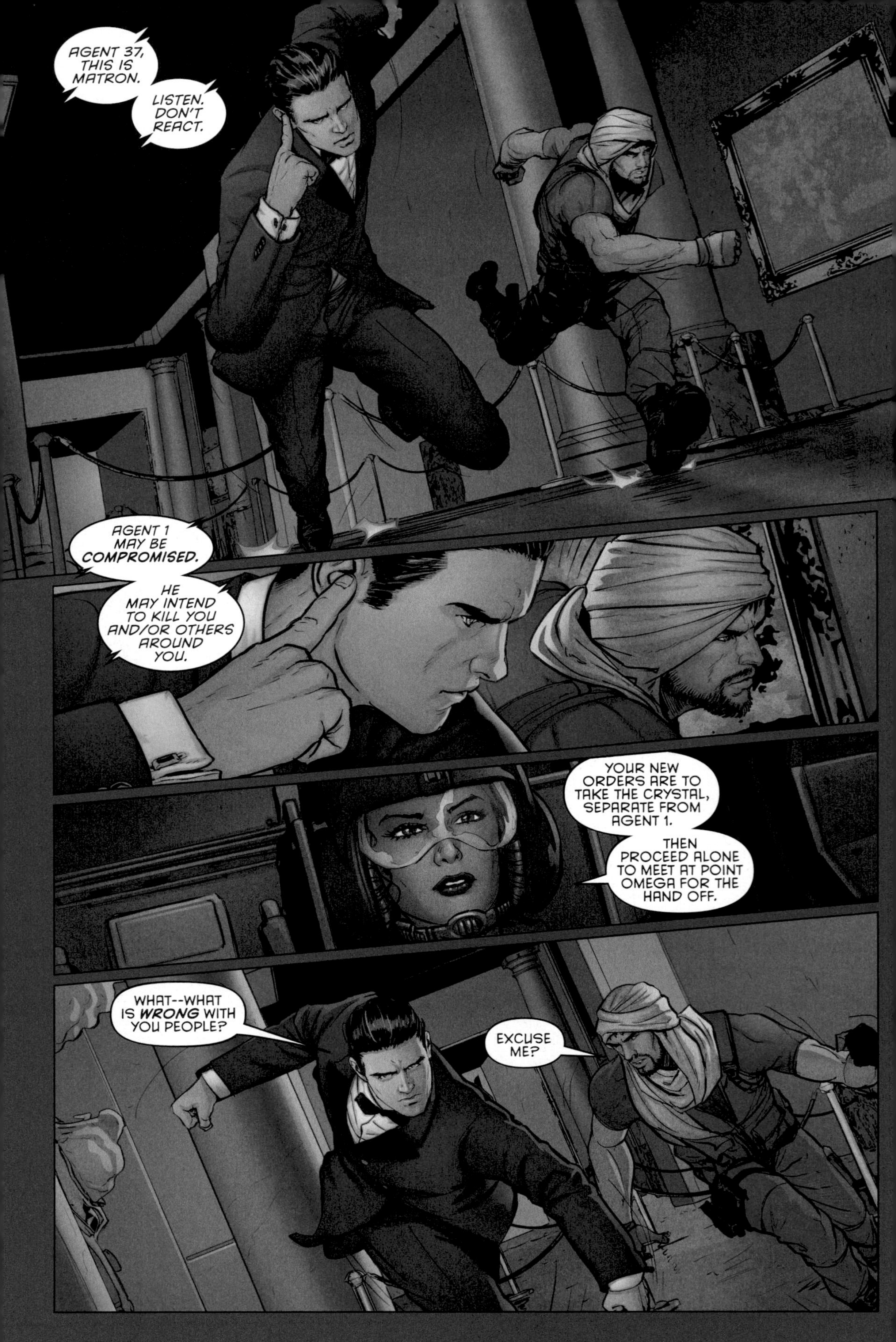

AGENT 37, THIS IS MATRON.
LISTEN. DON'T REACT.
AGENT 1 MAY BE **COMPROMISED.**
HE MAY INTEND TO KILL YOU AND/OR OTHERS AROUND YOU.
YOUR NEW ORDERS ARE TO TAKE THE CRYSTAL, SEPARATE FROM AGENT 1.
THEN PROCEED ALONE TO MEET AT POINT OMEGA FOR THE HAND OFF.
WHAT--WHAT IS ***WRONG*** WITH YOU PEOPLE?
EXCUSE ME?

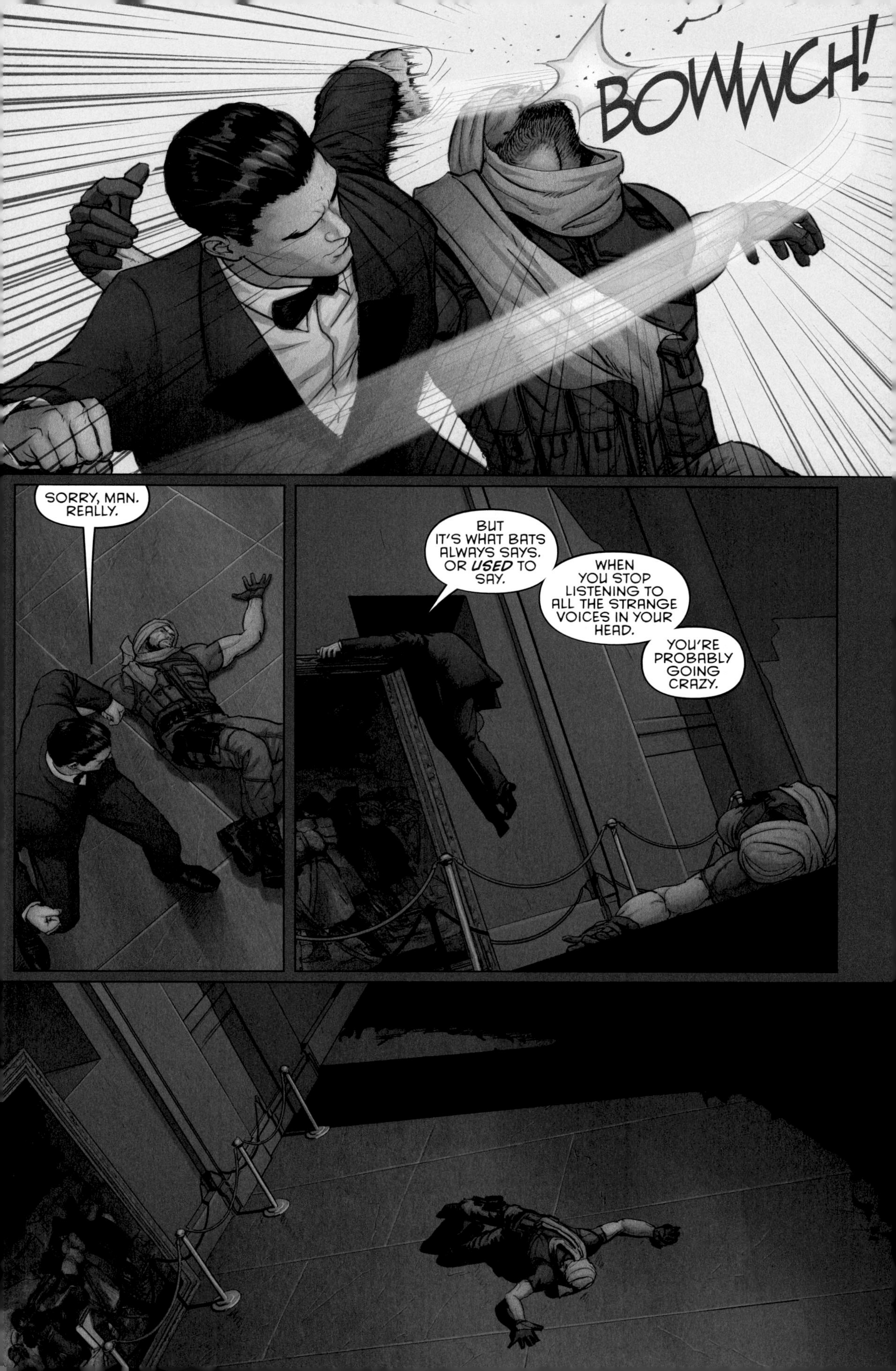
BOWWCH!
SORRY, MAN. REALLY.
BUT IT'S WHAT BATS ALWAYS SAYS. OR *USED* TO SAY.
WHEN YOU STOP LISTENING TO ALL THE STRANGE VOICES IN YOUR HEAD.
YOU'RE PROBABLY GOING CRAZY.

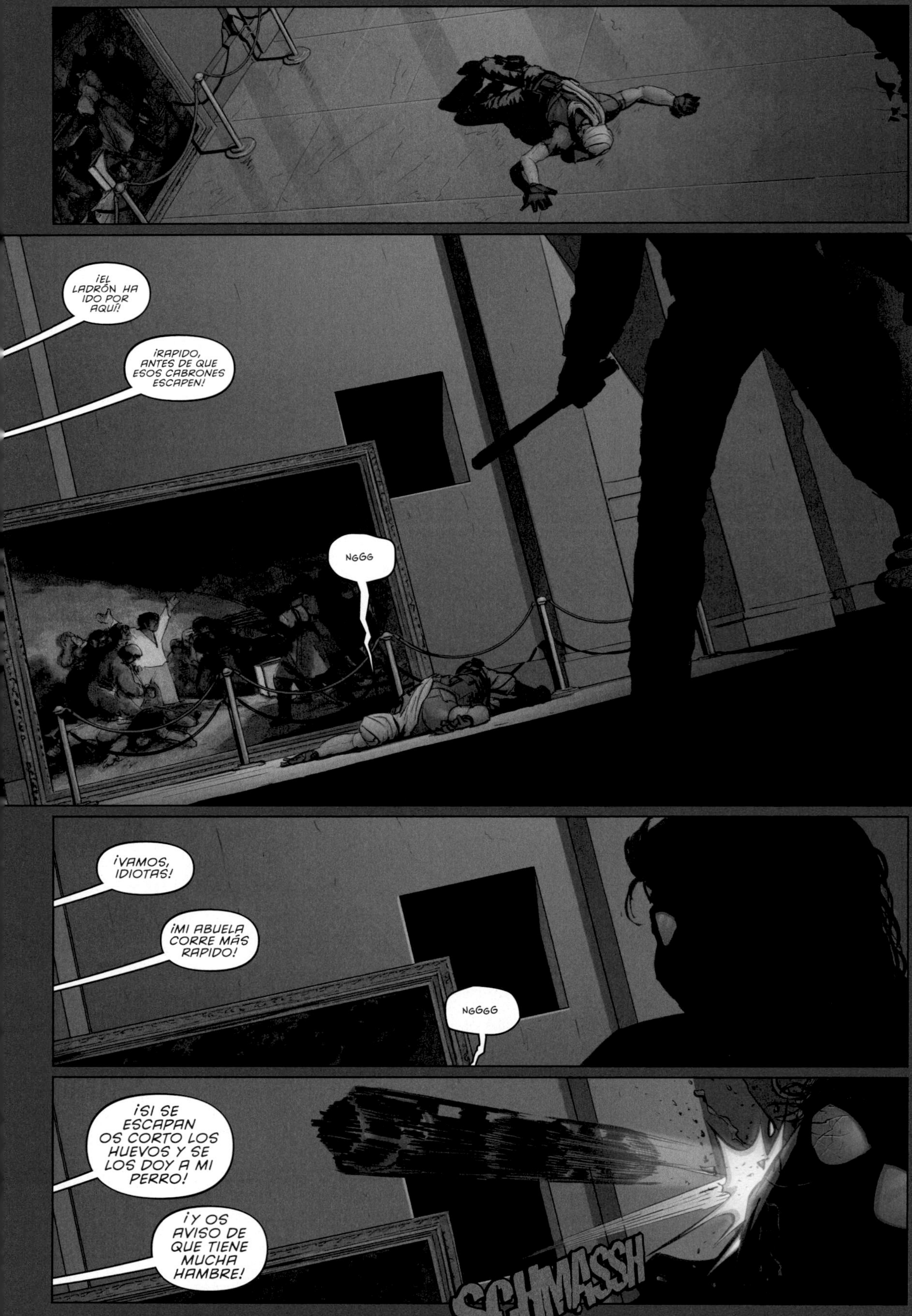

¡EL LADRÓN HA IDO POR AQUÍ!
¡RAPIDO, ANTES DE QUE ESOS CABRONES ESCAPEN!
NGGG
¡VAMOS, IDIOTAS!
¡MI ABUELA CORRE MÁS RAPIDO!
NGGGG
¡SI SE ESCAPAN OS CORTO LOS HUEVOS Y SE LOS DOY A MI PERRO!
¡Y OS AVISO DE QUE TIENE MUCHA HAMBRE!
SCHMASSH

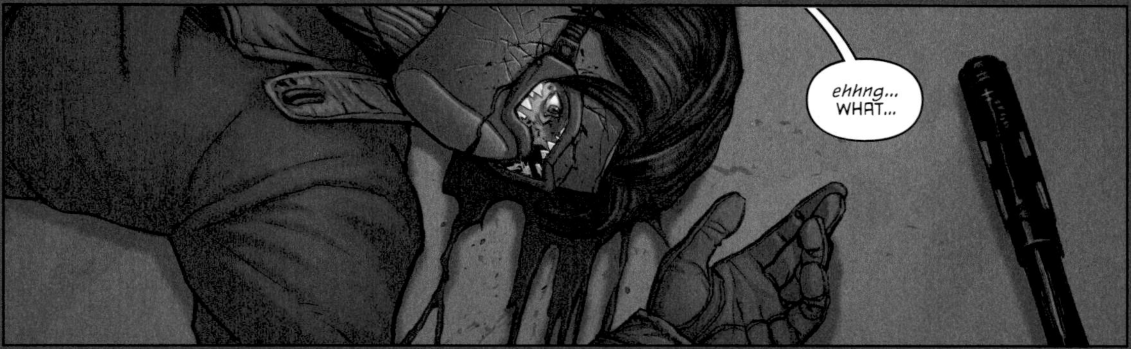
ehhng... WHAT...

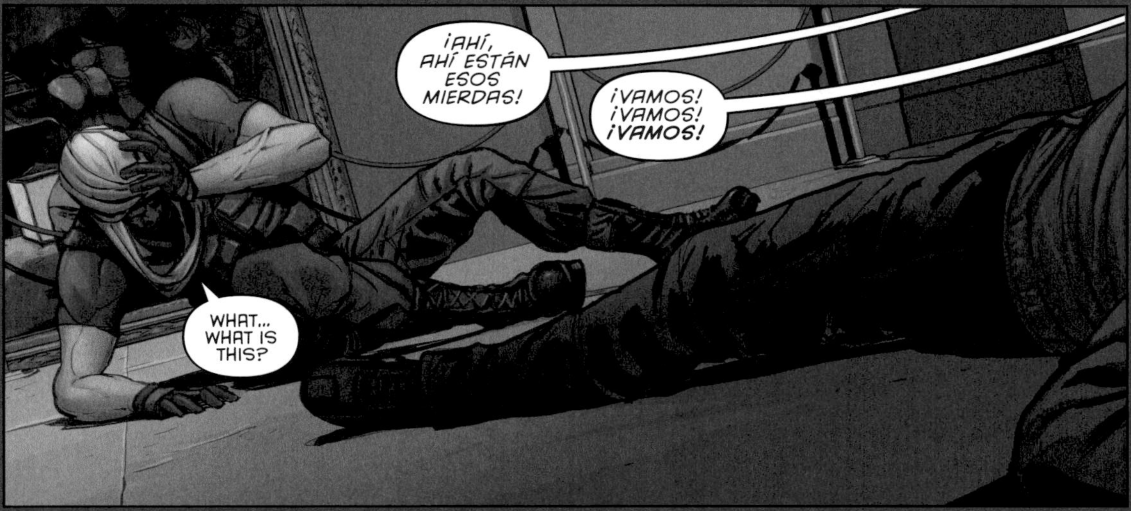
¡AHÍ, AHÍ ESTÁN ESOS MIERDAS!
¡VAMOS! ¡VAMOS! ¡VAMOS!
WHAT... WHAT IS THIS?

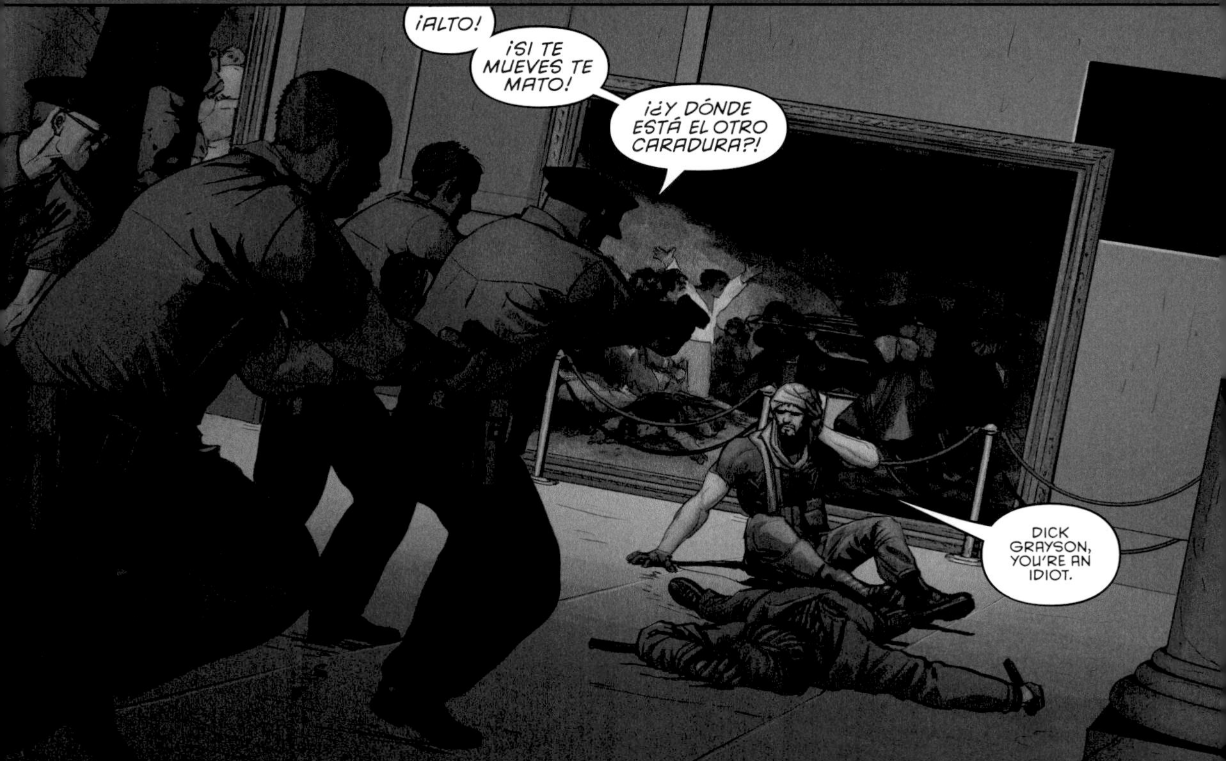
¡ALTO!
¡SI TE MUEVES TE MATO!
¡¿Y DÓNDE ESTÁ EL OTRO CARADURA?!
DICK GRAYSON, YOU'RE AN IDIOT.

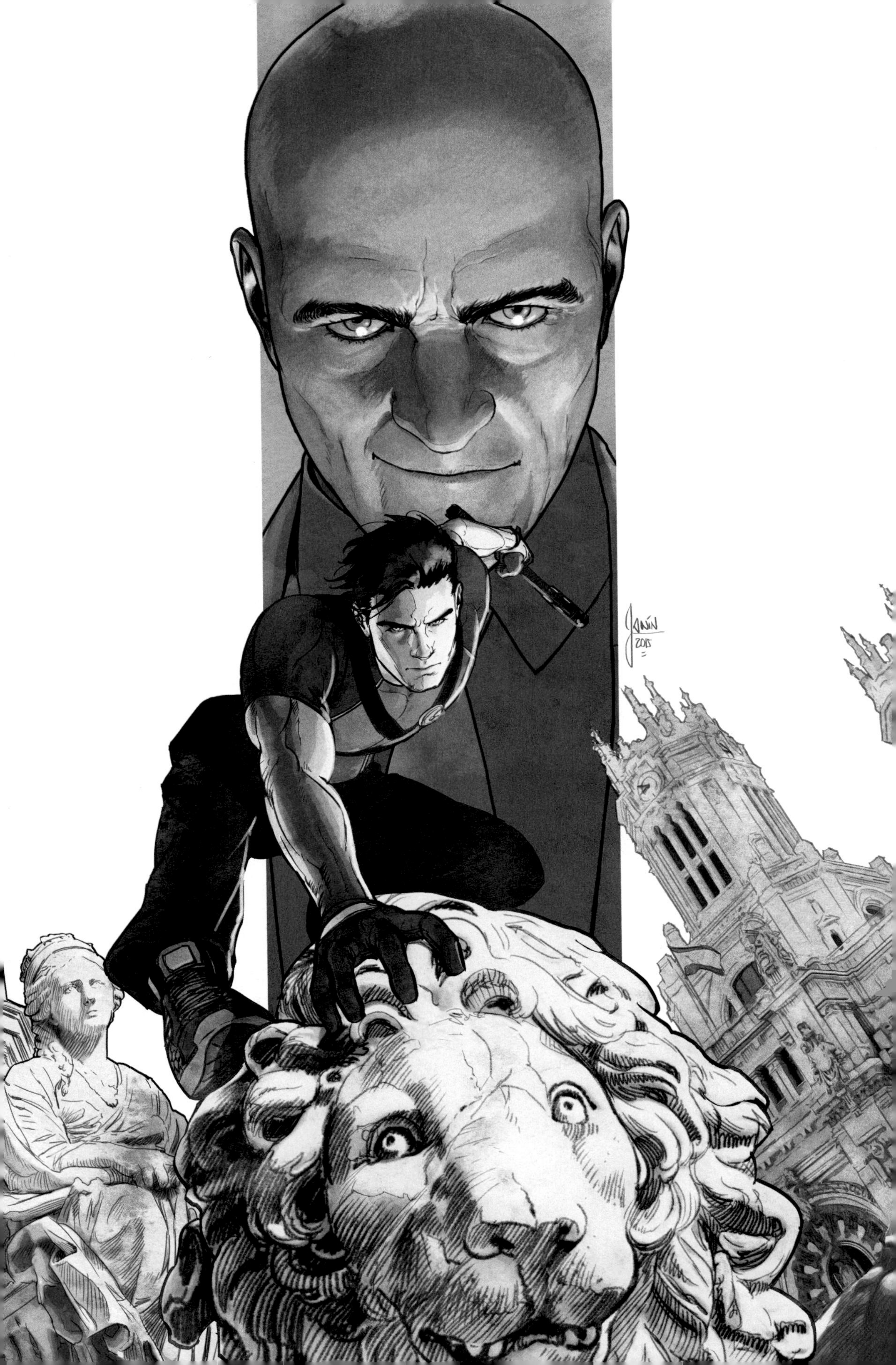
JANÍN
2015

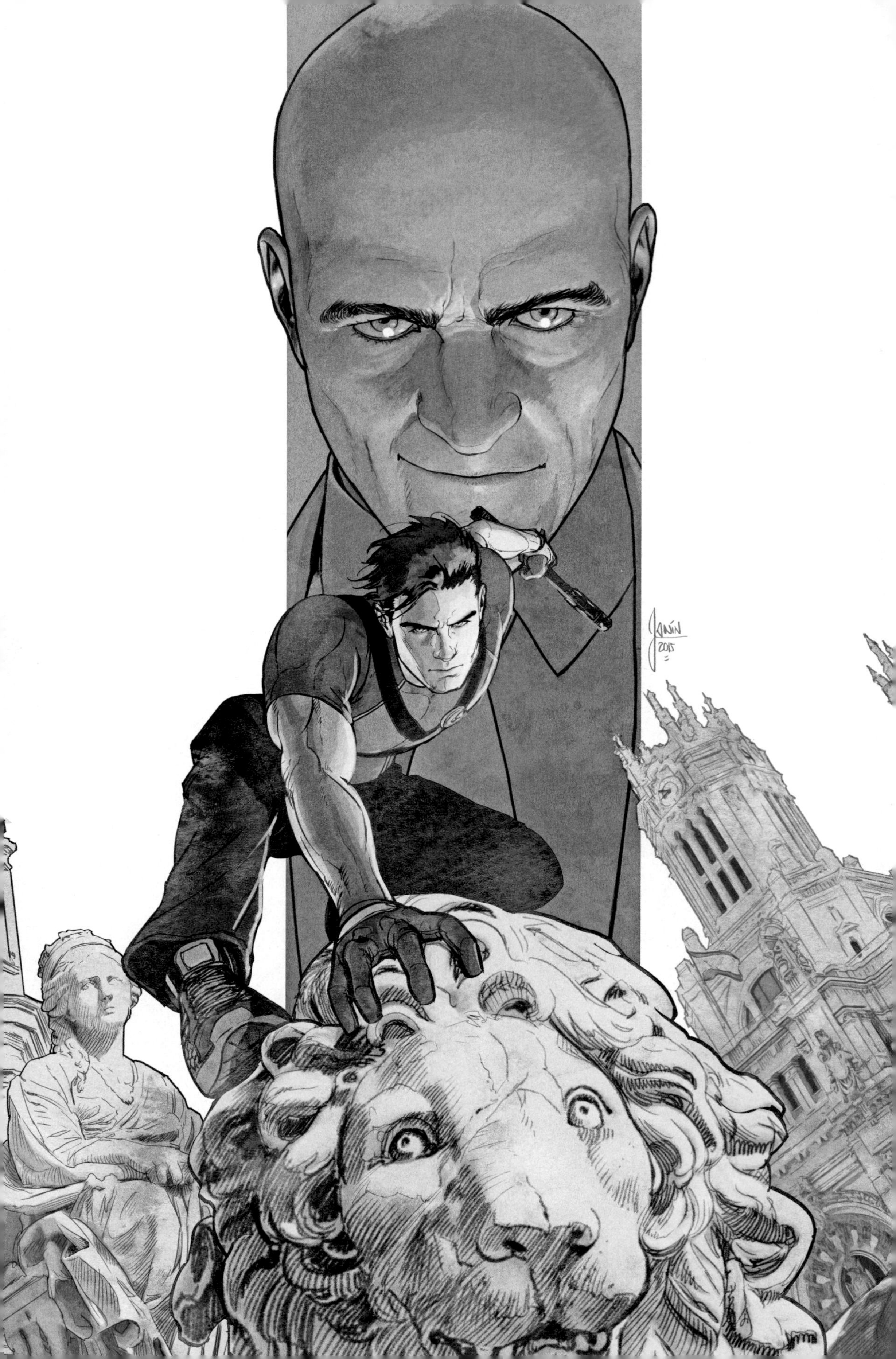

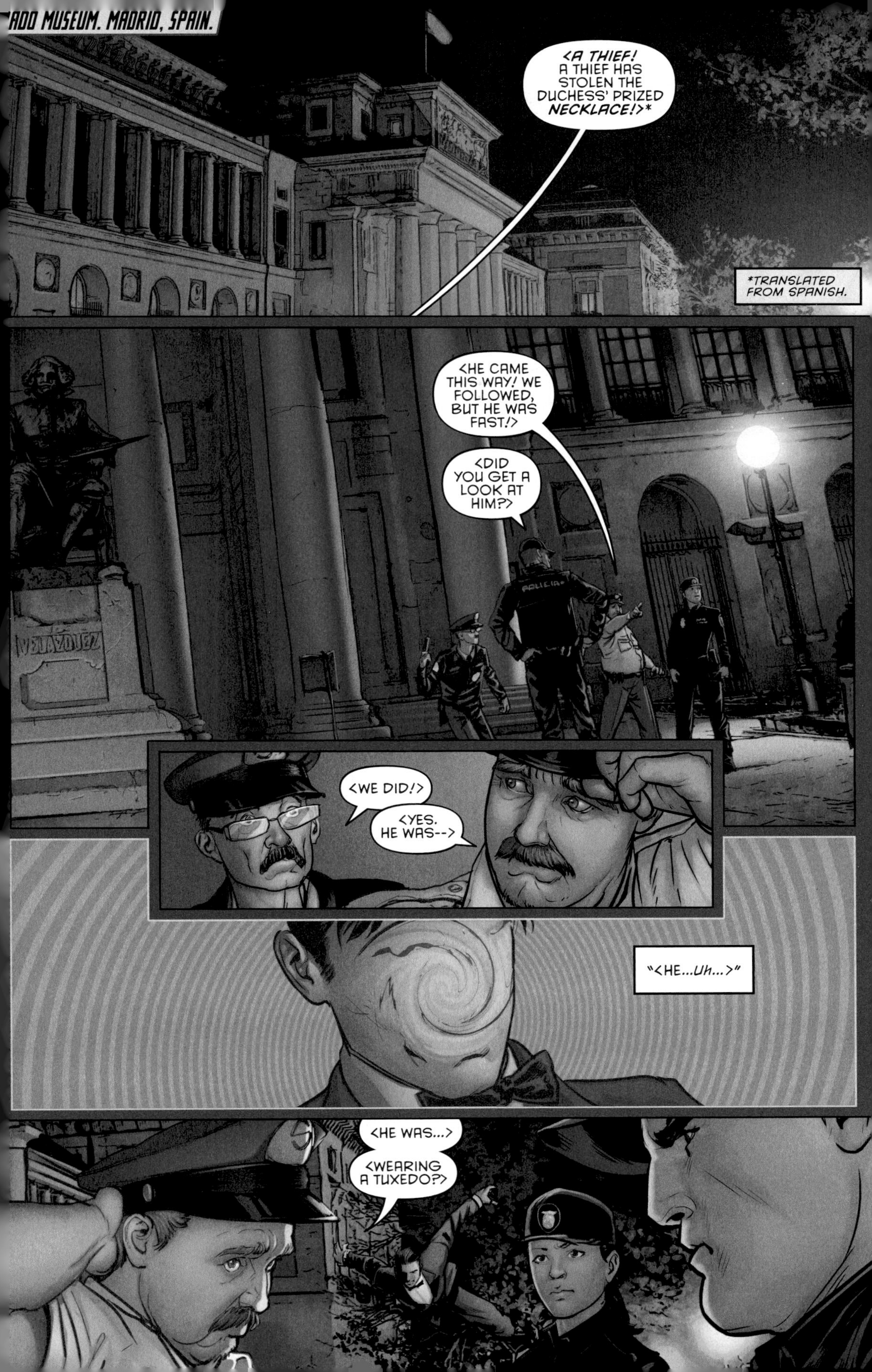

ADO MUSEUM. MADRID, SPAIN.
<A THIEF! A THIEF HAS STOLEN THE DUCHESS' PRIZED NECKLACE!>*
*TRANSLATED FROM SPANISH.
<HE CAME THIS WAY! WE FOLLOWED, BUT HE WAS FAST!>
<DID YOU GET A LOOK AT HIM?>
<WE DID!>
<YES. HE WAS-->
"<HE...Uh...>"
<HE WAS...>
<WEARING A TUXEDO?>

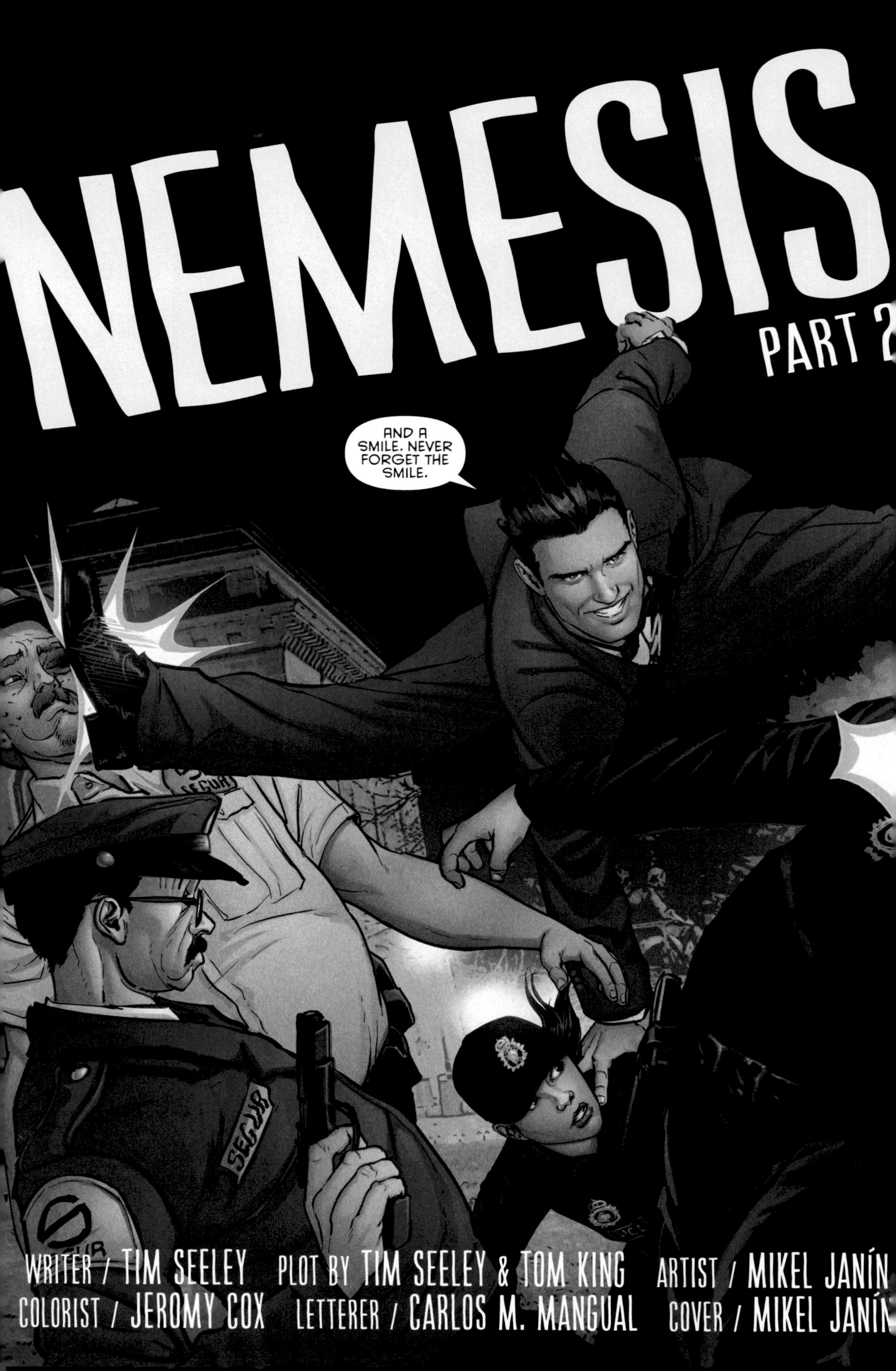
NEMESIS
PART 2
AND A SMILE. NEVER FORGET THE SMILE.
SEGUR
WRITER / TIM SEELEY PLOT BY TIM SEELEY & TOM KING ARTIST / MIKEL JANÍN
COLORIST / JEROMY COX LETTERER / CARLOS M. MANGUAL COVER / MIKEL JANÍN

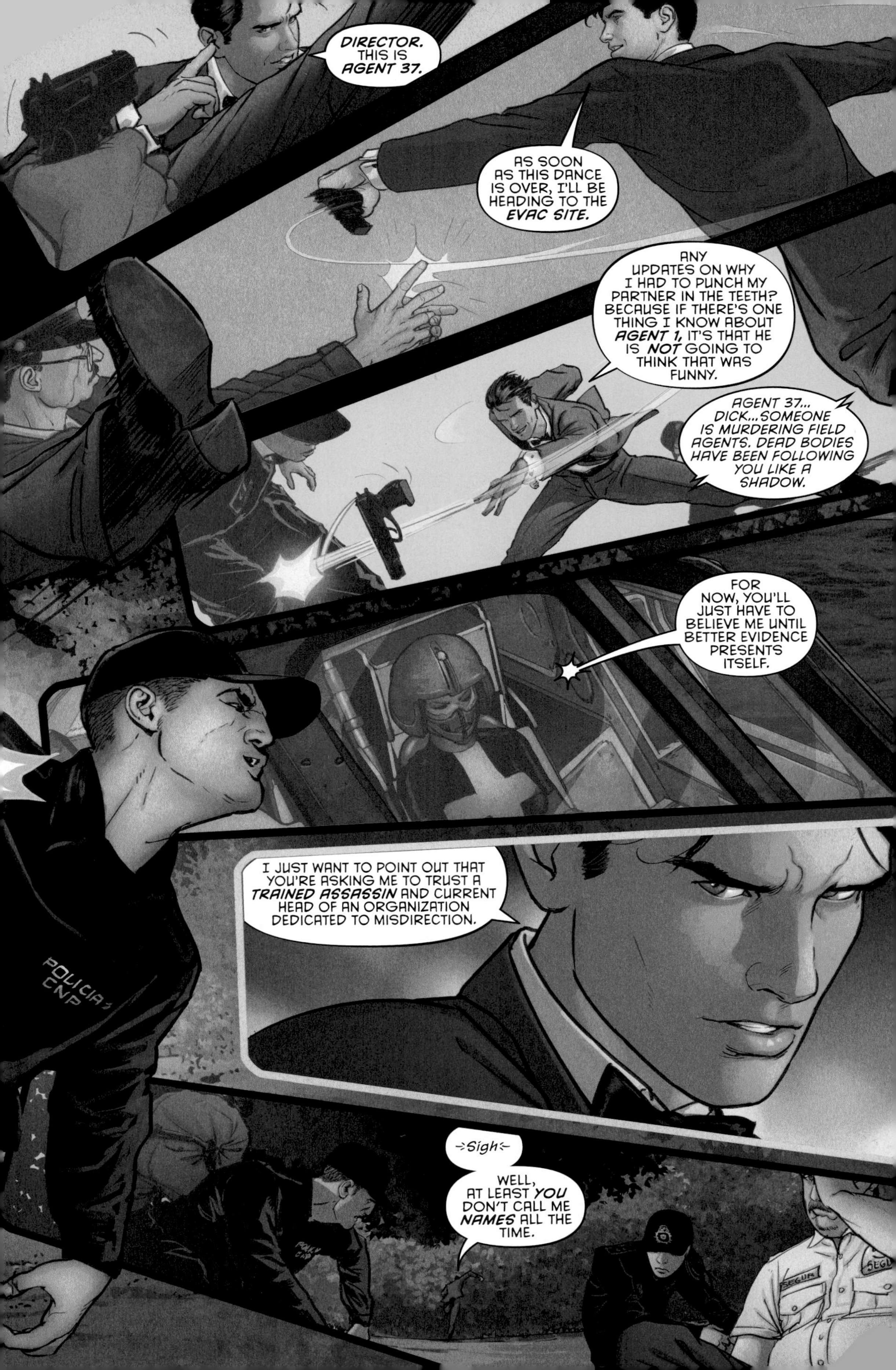
DIRECTOR. THIS IS AGENT 37.
AS SOON AS THIS DANCE IS OVER, I'LL BE HEADING TO THE EVAC SITE.
ANY UPDATES ON WHY I HAD TO PUNCH MY PARTNER IN THE TEETH? BECAUSE IF THERE'S ONE THING I KNOW ABOUT AGENT 1, IT'S THAT HE IS NOT GOING TO THINK THAT WAS FUNNY.
AGENT 37... DICK...SOMEONE IS MURDERING FIELD AGENTS. DEAD BODIES HAVE BEEN FOLLOWING YOU LIKE A SHADOW.
FOR NOW, YOU'LL JUST HAVE TO BELIEVE ME UNTIL BETTER EVIDENCE PRESENTS ITSELF.
POLICIA CNP
I JUST WANT TO POINT OUT THAT YOU'RE ASKING ME TO TRUST A TRAINED ASSASSIN AND CURRENT HEAD OF AN ORGANIZATION DEDICATED TO MISDIRECTION.
Sigh
WELL, AT LEAST YOU DON'T CALL ME NAMES ALL THE TIME.

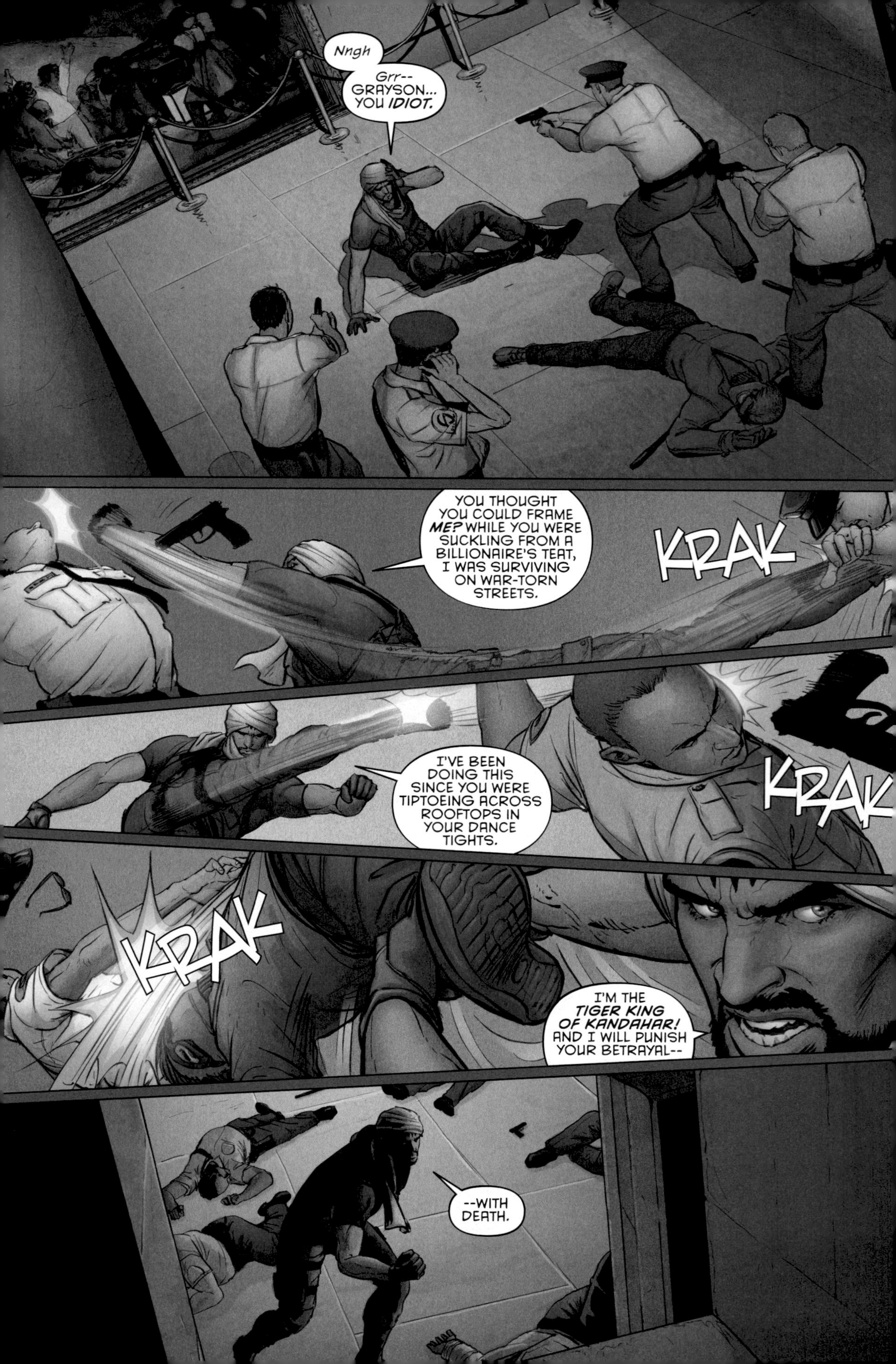
Nngh
Grr-- GRAYSON... YOU IDIOT.
YOU THOUGHT YOU COULD FRAME ME? WHILE YOU WERE SUCKLING FROM A BILLIONAIRE'S TEAT, I WAS SURVIVING ON WAR-TORN STREETS.
KRAK
I'VE BEEN DOING THIS SINCE YOU WERE TIPTOEING ACROSS ROOFTOPS IN YOUR DANCE TIGHTS.
KRAK
KRAK
I'M THE TIGER KING OF KANDAHAR! AND I WILL PUNISH YOUR BETRAYAL--
--WITH DEATH.

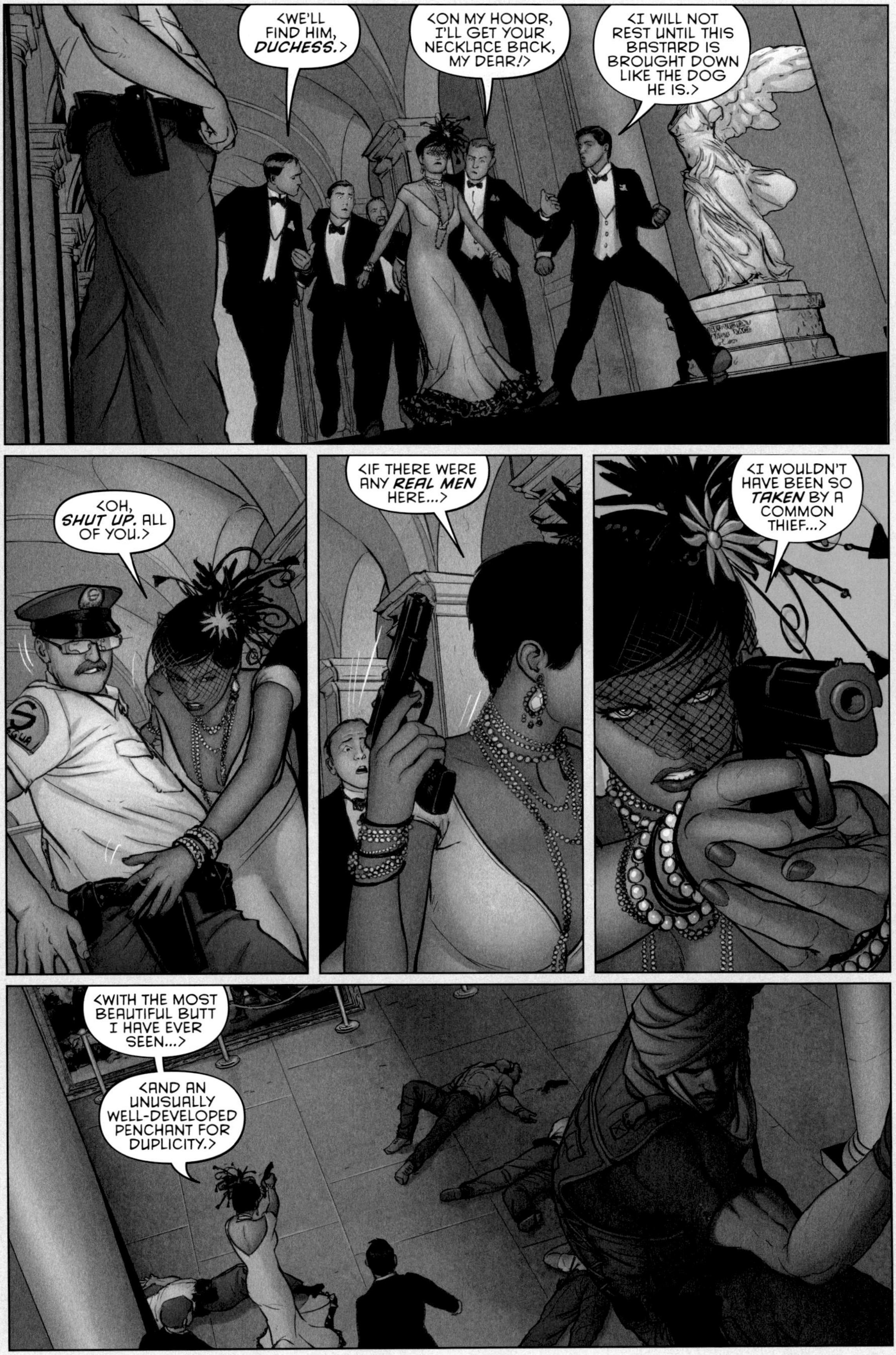
<WE'LL FIND HIM, DUCHESS.>
<ON MY HONOR, I'LL GET YOUR NECKLACE BACK, MY DEAR!>
<I WILL NOT REST UNTIL THIS BASTARD IS BROUGHT DOWN LIKE THE DOG HE IS.>
<OH, SHUT UP. ALL OF YOU.>
<IF THERE WERE ANY REAL MEN HERE...>
<I WOULDN'T HAVE BEEN SO TAKEN BY A COMMON THIEF...>
<WITH THE MOST BEAUTIFUL BUTT I HAVE EVER SEEN...>
<AND AN UNUSUALLY WELL-DEVELOPED PENCHANT FOR DUPLICITY.>

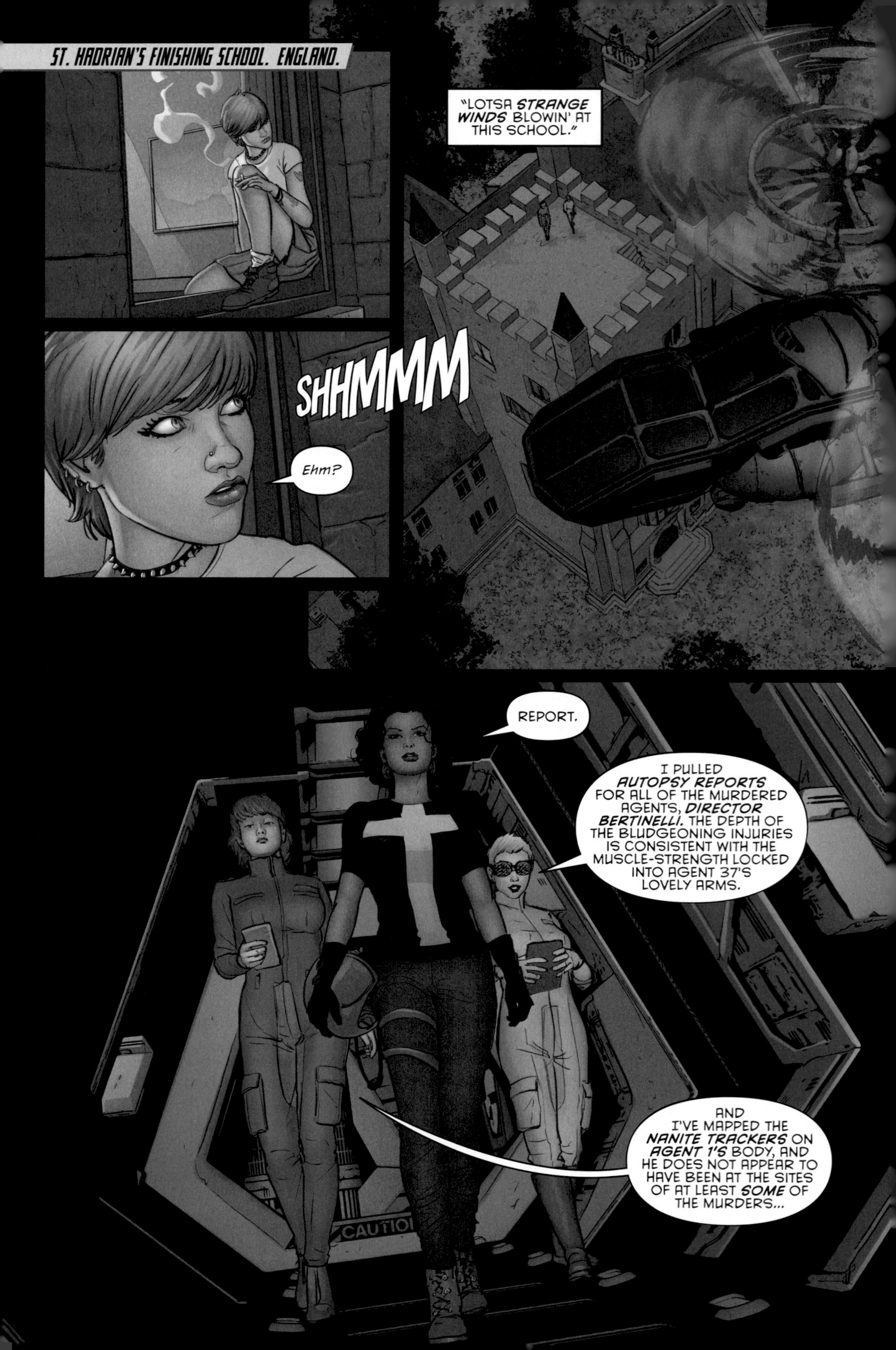
ST. HADRIAN'S FINISHING SCHOOL. ENGLAND.
"LOTSA STRANGE WINDS BLOWIN' AT THIS SCHOOL."
SHHMMM
Ehm?
REPORT.
I PULLED AUTOPSY REPORTS FOR ALL OF THE MURDERED AGENTS, DIRECTOR BERTINELLI. THE DEPTH OF THE BLUDGEONING INJURIES IS CONSISTENT WITH THE MUSCLE-STRENGTH LOCKED INTO AGENT 37'S LOVELY ARMS.
AND I'VE MAPPED THE NANITE TRACKERS ON AGENT 1'S BODY, AND HE DOES NOT APPEAR TO HAVE BEEN AT THE SITES OF AT LEAST SOME OF THE MURDERS...
CAUTION

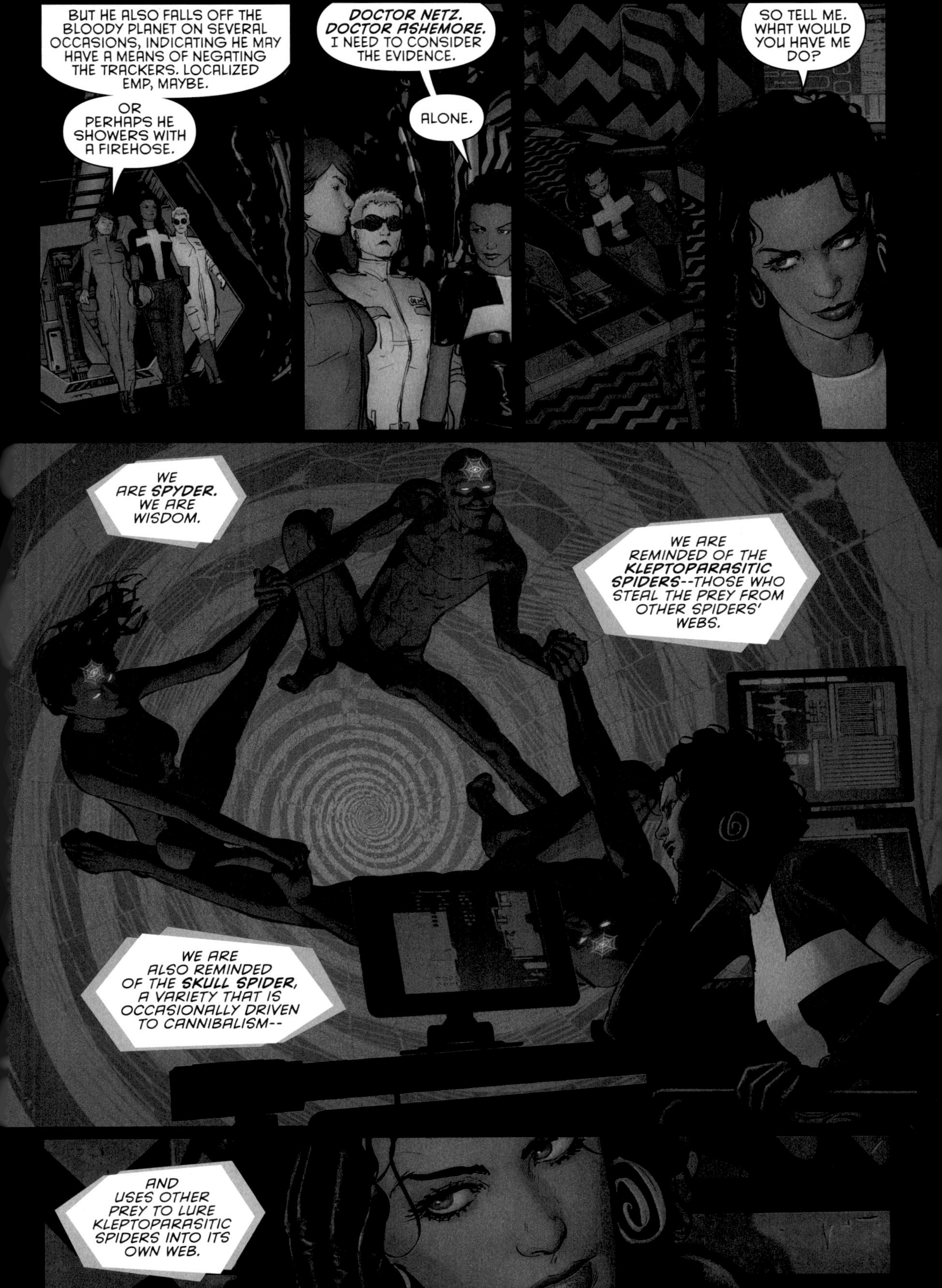
BUT HE ALSO FALLS OFF THE BLOODY PLANET ON SEVERAL OCCASIONS, INDICATING HE MAY HAVE A MEANS OF NEGATING THE TRACKERS. LOCALIZED EMP, MAYBE.
OR PERHAPS HE SHOWERS WITH A FIREHOSE.
DOCTOR NETZ. DOCTOR ASHEMORE. I NEED TO CONSIDER THE EVIDENCE.
ALONE.
SO TELL ME. WHAT WOULD YOU HAVE ME DO?
WE ARE *SPYDER.* WE ARE WISDOM.
WE ARE REMINDED OF THE *KLEPTOPARASITIC SPIDERS*--THOSE WHO STEAL THE PREY FROM OTHER SPIDERS' WEBS.
WE ARE ALSO REMINDED OF THE *SKULL SPIDER,* A VARIETY THAT IS OCCASIONALLY DRIVEN TO CANNIBALISM--
AND USES OTHER PREY TO LURE KLEPTOPARASITIC SPIDERS INTO ITS OWN WEB.

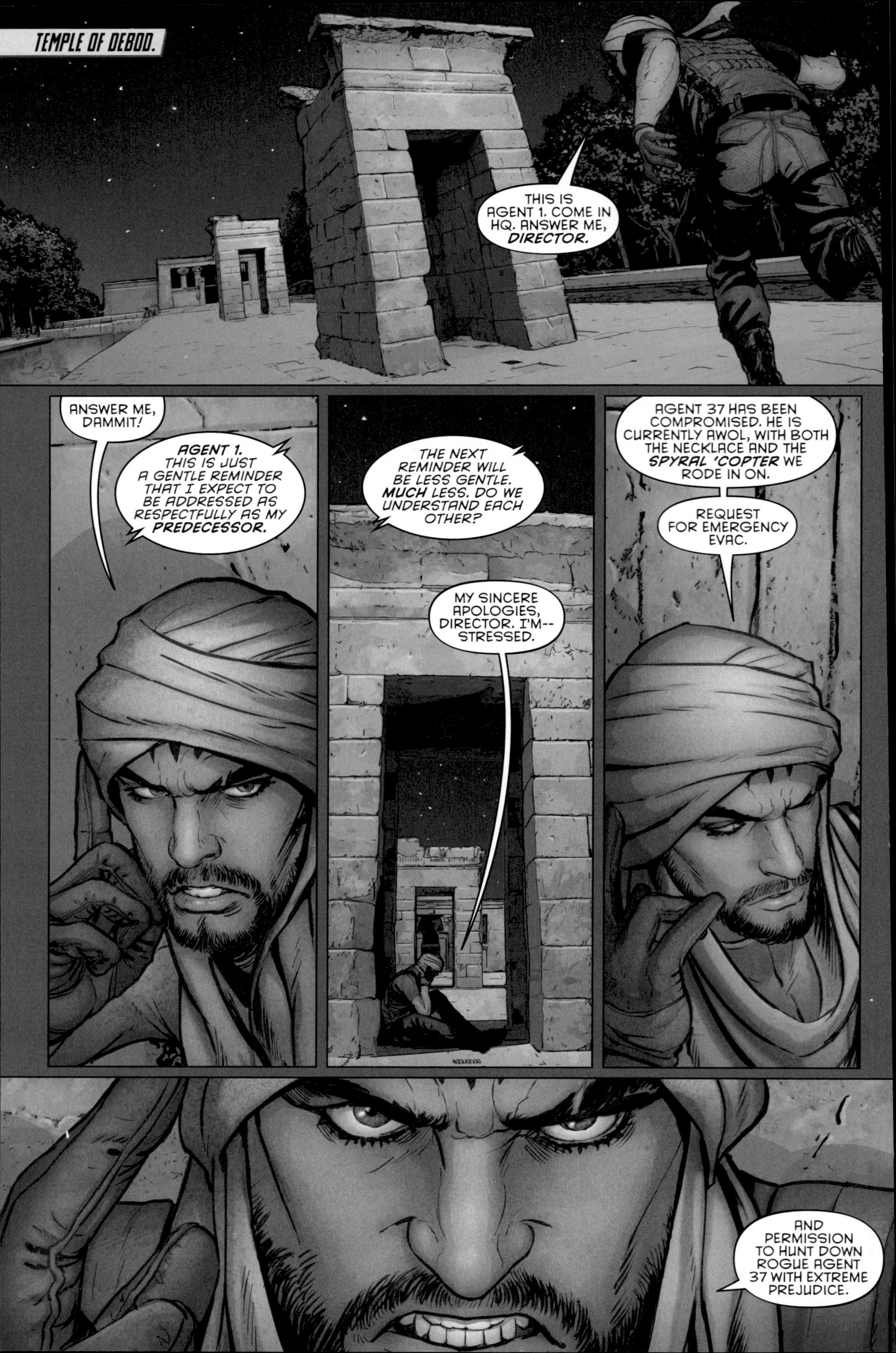
TEMPLE OF DEBOD.
THIS IS AGENT 1. COME IN HQ. ANSWER ME, DIRECTOR.
ANSWER ME, DAMMIT!
AGENT 1. THIS IS JUST A GENTLE REMINDER THAT I EXPECT TO BE ADDRESSED AS RESPECTFULLY AS MY PREDECESSOR.
THE NEXT REMINDER WILL BE LESS GENTLE. MUCH LESS. DO WE UNDERSTAND EACH OTHER?
MY SINCERE APOLOGIES, DIRECTOR. I'M--STRESSED.
AGENT 37 HAS BEEN COMPROMISED. HE IS CURRENTLY AWOL, WITH BOTH THE NECKLACE AND THE SPYRAL 'COPTER WE RODE IN ON.
REQUEST FOR EMERGENCY EVAC.
AND PERMISSION TO HUNT DOWN ROGUE AGENT 37 WITH EXTREME PREJUDICE.

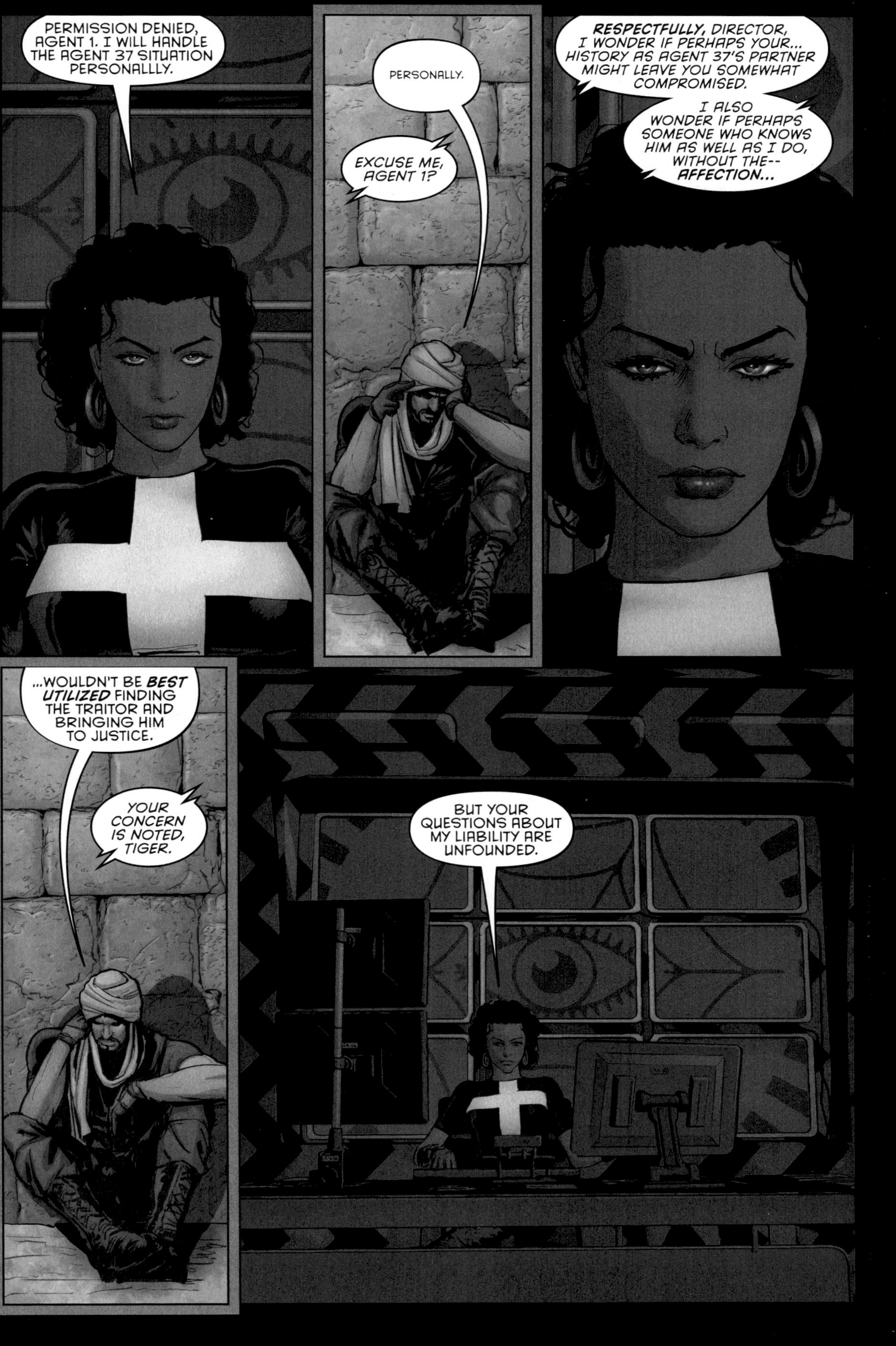
PERMISSION DENIED, AGENT 1. I WILL HANDLE THE AGENT 37 SITUATION PERSONALLLY.
PERSONALLY.
EXCUSE ME, AGENT 1?
RESPECTFULLY, DIRECTOR, I WONDER IF PERHAPS YOUR... HISTORY AS AGENT 37'S PARTNER MIGHT LEAVE YOU SOMEWHAT COMPROMISED.
I ALSO WONDER IF PERHAPS SOMEONE WHO KNOWS HIM AS WELL AS I DO, WITHOUT THE-- AFFECTION...
...WOULDN'T BE BEST UTILIZED FINDING THE TRAITOR AND BRINGING HIM TO JUSTICE.
YOUR CONCERN IS NOTED, TIGER.
BUT YOUR QUESTIONS ABOUT MY LIABILITY ARE UNFOUNDED.

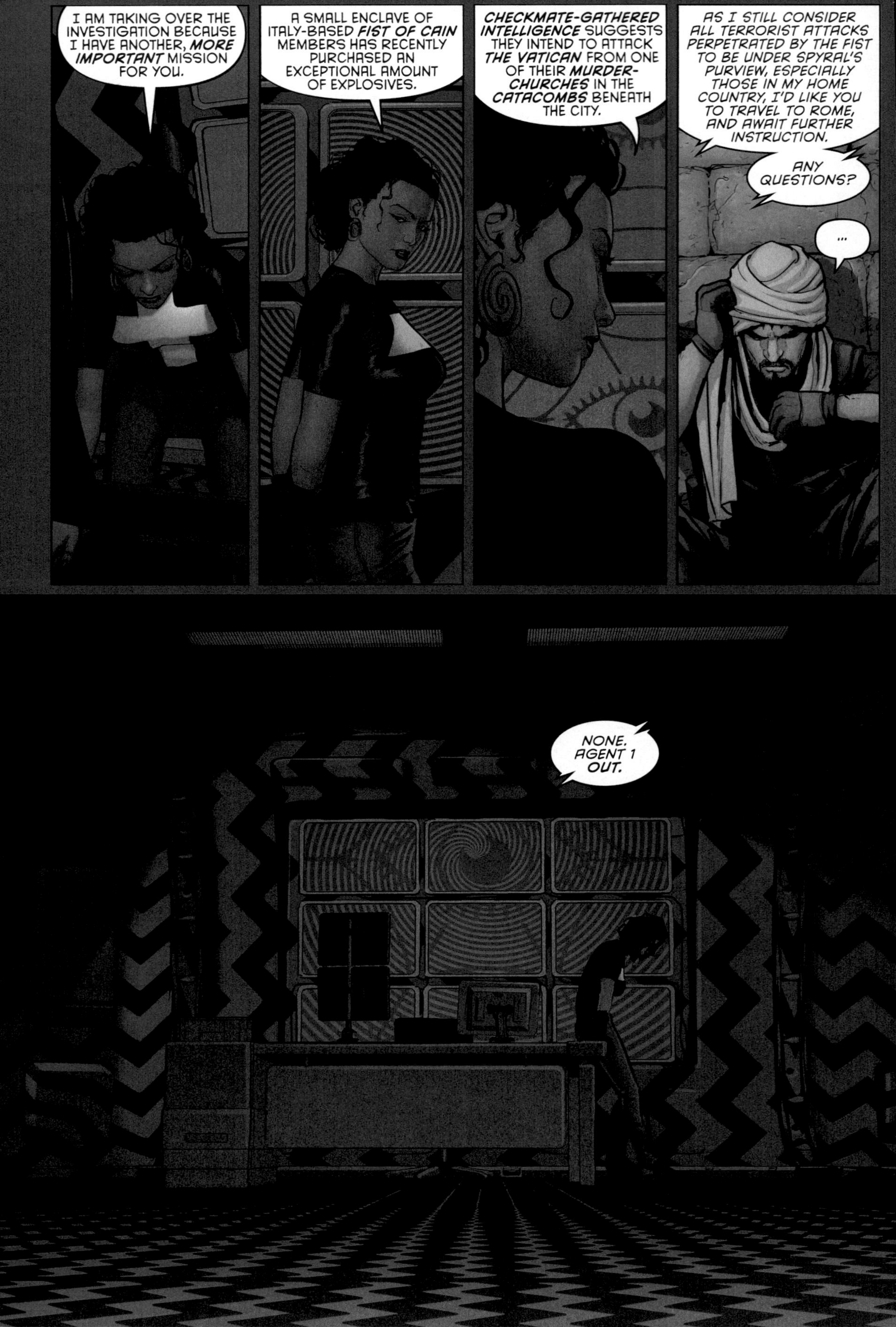
I AM TAKING OVER THE INVESTIGATION BECAUSE I HAVE ANOTHER, ***MORE IMPORTANT*** MISSION FOR YOU.
A SMALL ENCLAVE OF ITALY-BASED ***FIST OF CAIN*** MEMBERS HAS RECENTLY PURCHASED AN EXCEPTIONAL AMOUNT OF EXPLOSIVES.
CHECKMATE-GATHERED INTELLIGENCE SUGGESTS THEY INTEND TO ATTACK ***THE VATICAN*** FROM ONE OF THEIR ***MURDER-CHURCHES*** IN THE ***CATACOMBS*** BENEATH THE CITY.
AS I STILL CONSIDER ALL TERRORIST ATTACKS PERPETRATED BY THE FIST TO BE UNDER SPYRAL'S PURVIEW, ESPECIALLY THOSE IN MY HOME COUNTRY, I'D LIKE YOU TO TRAVEL TO ROME, AND AWAIT FURTHER INSTRUCTION.
ANY QUESTIONS?
...
NONE. AGENT 1 ***OUT.***

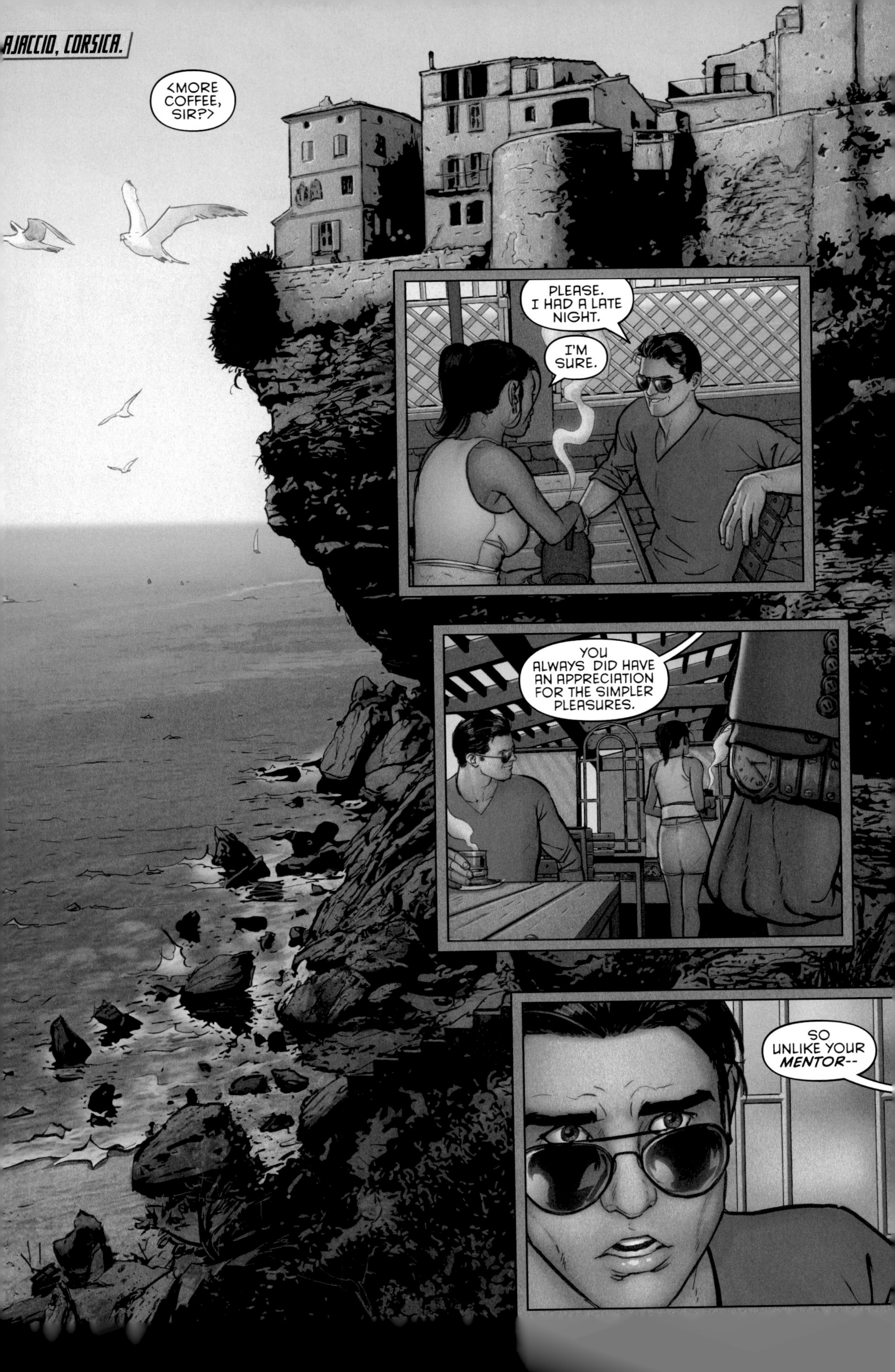
AJACCIO, CORSICA.
<MORE COFFEE, SIR?>
PLEASE. I HAD A LATE NIGHT.
I'M SURE.
YOU ALWAYS DID HAVE AN APPRECIATION FOR THE SIMPLER PLEASURES.
SO UNLIKE YOUR MENTOR--

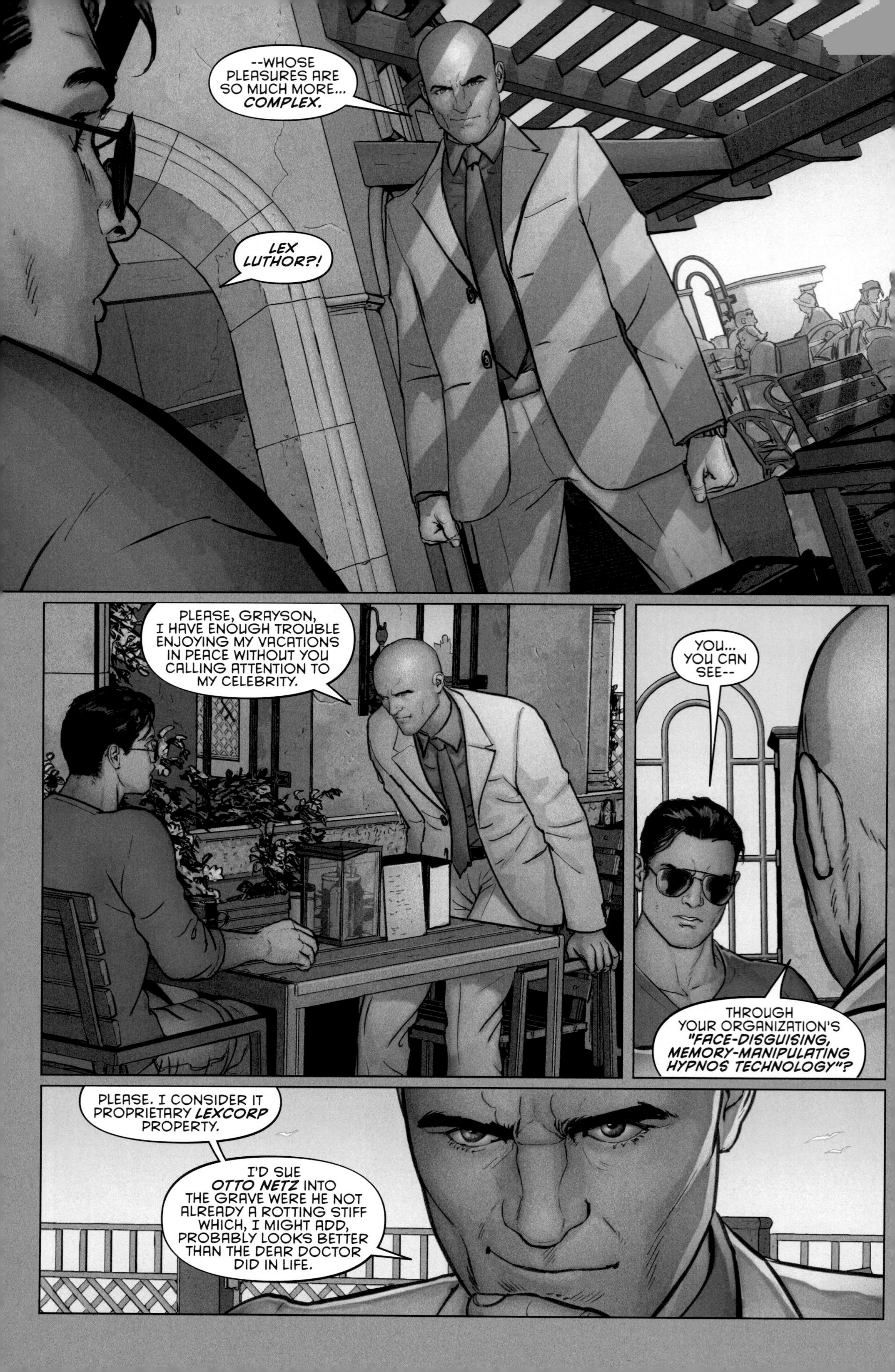
--WHOSE PLEASURES ARE SO MUCH MORE... *COMPLEX.*
LEX LUTHOR?!
PLEASE, GRAYSON, I HAVE ENOUGH TROUBLE ENJOYING MY VACATIONS IN PEACE WITHOUT YOU CALLING ATTENTION TO MY CELEBRITY.
YOU... YOU CAN SEE--
THROUGH YOUR ORGANIZATION'S *"FACE-DISGUISING, MEMORY-MANIPULATING HYPNOS TECHNOLOGY"*?
PLEASE. I CONSIDER IT PROPRIETARY *LEXCORP* PROPERTY.
I'D SUE *OTTO NETZ* INTO THE GRAVE WERE HE NOT ALREADY A ROTTING STIFF WHICH, I MIGHT ADD, PROBABLY LOOKS BETTER THAN THE DEAR DOCTOR DID IN LIFE.

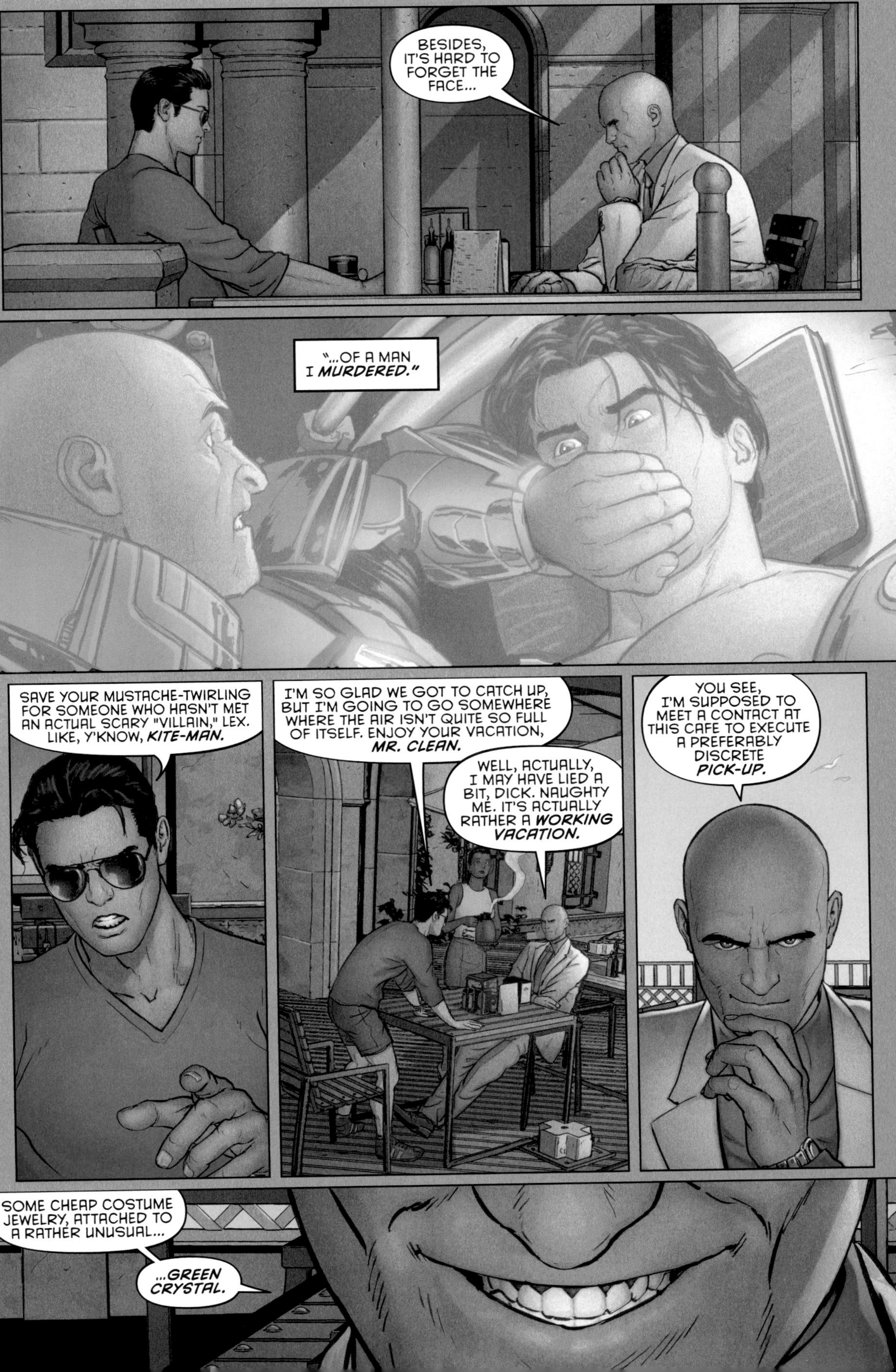
BESIDES, IT'S HARD TO FORGET THE FACE...
"...OF A MAN I MURDERED."
SAVE YOUR MUSTACHE-TWIRLING FOR SOMEONE WHO HASN'T MET AN ACTUAL SCARY "VILLAIN," LEX. LIKE, Y'KNOW, KITE-MAN.
I'M SO GLAD WE GOT TO CATCH UP, BUT I'M GOING TO GO SOMEWHERE WHERE THE AIR ISN'T QUITE SO FULL OF ITSELF. ENJOY YOUR VACATION, MR. CLEAN.
WELL, ACTUALLY, I MAY HAVE LIED A BIT, DICK. NAUGHTY ME. IT'S ACTUALLY RATHER A WORKING VACATION.
YOU SEE, I'M SUPPOSED TO MEET A CONTACT AT THIS CAFE TO EXECUTE A PREFERABLY DISCRETE PICK-UP.
SOME CHEAP COSTUME JEWELRY, ATTACHED TO A RATHER UNUSUAL...
...GREEN CRYSTAL.

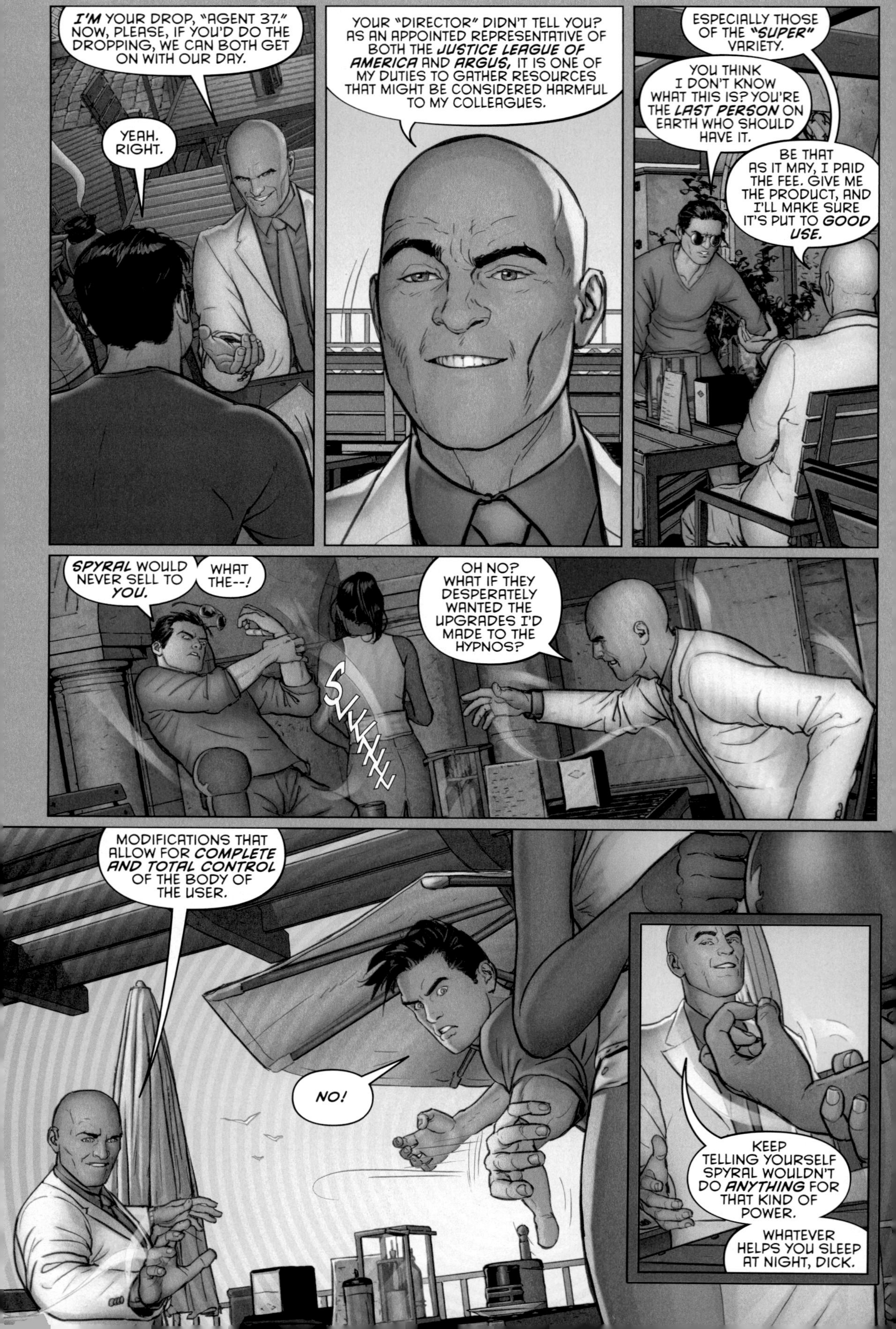
I'M YOUR DROP, "AGENT 37." NOW, PLEASE, IF YOU'D DO THE DROPPING, WE CAN BOTH GET ON WITH OUR DAY.
YEAH. RIGHT.
YOUR "DIRECTOR" DIDN'T TELL YOU? AS AN APPOINTED REPRESENTATIVE OF BOTH THE JUSTICE LEAGUE OF AMERICA AND ARGUS, IT IS ONE OF MY DUTIES TO GATHER RESOURCES THAT MIGHT BE CONSIDERED HARMFUL TO MY COLLEAGUES.
ESPECIALLY THOSE OF THE "SUPER" VARIETY.
YOU THINK I DON'T KNOW WHAT THIS IS? YOU'RE THE LAST PERSON ON EARTH WHO SHOULD HAVE IT.
BE THAT AS IT MAY, I PAID THE FEE. GIVE ME THE PRODUCT, AND I'LL MAKE SURE IT'S PUT TO GOOD USE.
SPYRAL WOULD NEVER SELL TO YOU.
WHAT THE--!
OH NO? WHAT IF THEY DESPERATELY WANTED THE UPGRADES I'D MADE TO THE HYPNOS?
SWHHH
MODIFICATIONS THAT ALLOW FOR COMPLETE AND TOTAL CONTROL OF THE BODY OF THE USER.
NO!
KEEP TELLING YOURSELF SPYRAL WOULDN'T DO ANYTHING FOR THAT KIND OF POWER.
WHATEVER HELPS YOU SLEEP AT NIGHT, DICK.

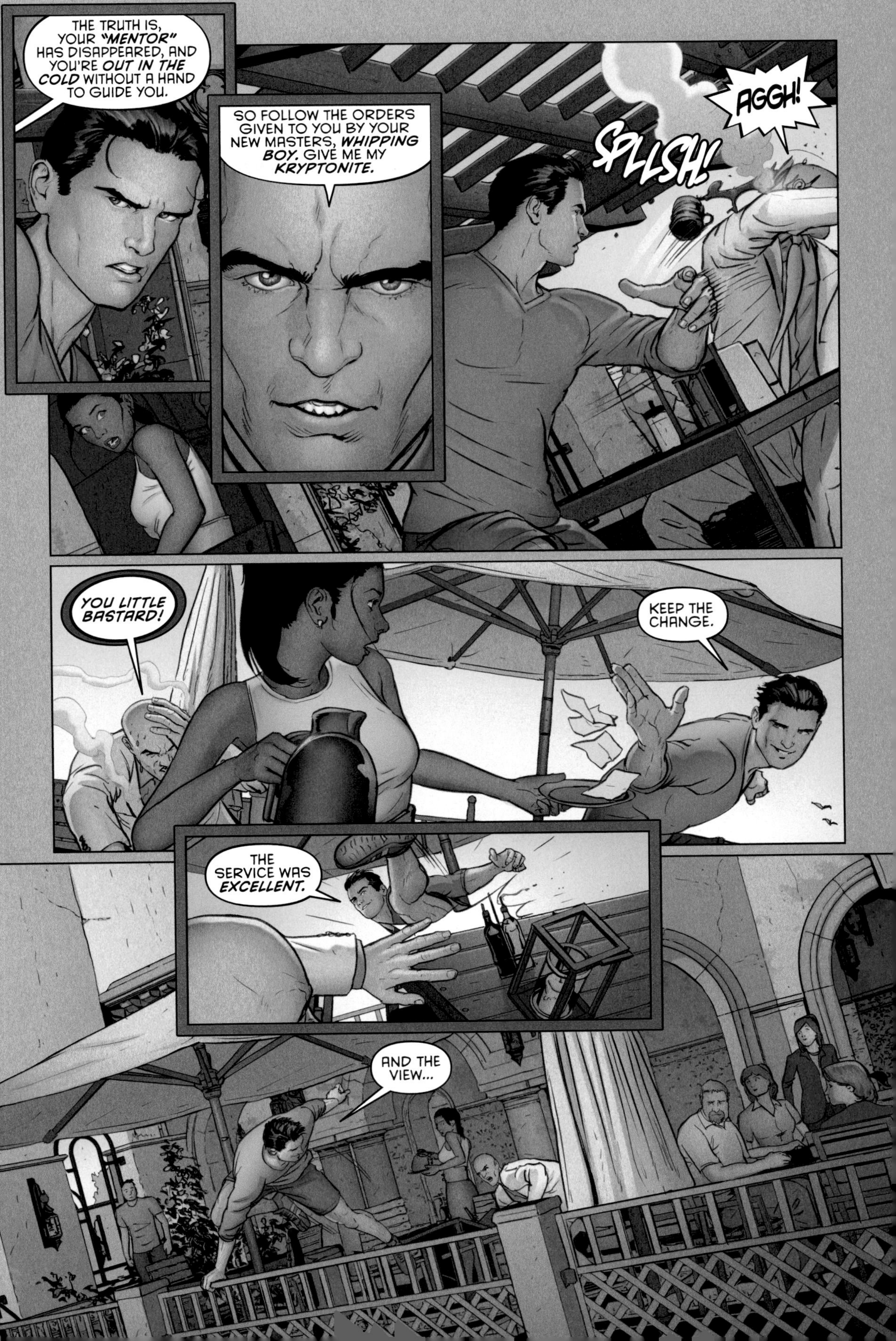
THE TRUTH IS, YOUR "MENTOR" HAS DISAPPEARED, AND YOU'RE OUT IN THE COLD WITHOUT A HAND TO GUIDE YOU.
SO FOLLOW THE ORDERS GIVEN TO YOU BY YOUR NEW MASTERS, WHIPPING BOY. GIVE ME MY KRYPTONITE.
SPLLSH!
AGGH!
YOU LITTLE BASTARD!
KEEP THE CHANGE.
THE SERVICE WAS EXCELLENT.
AND THE VIEW...

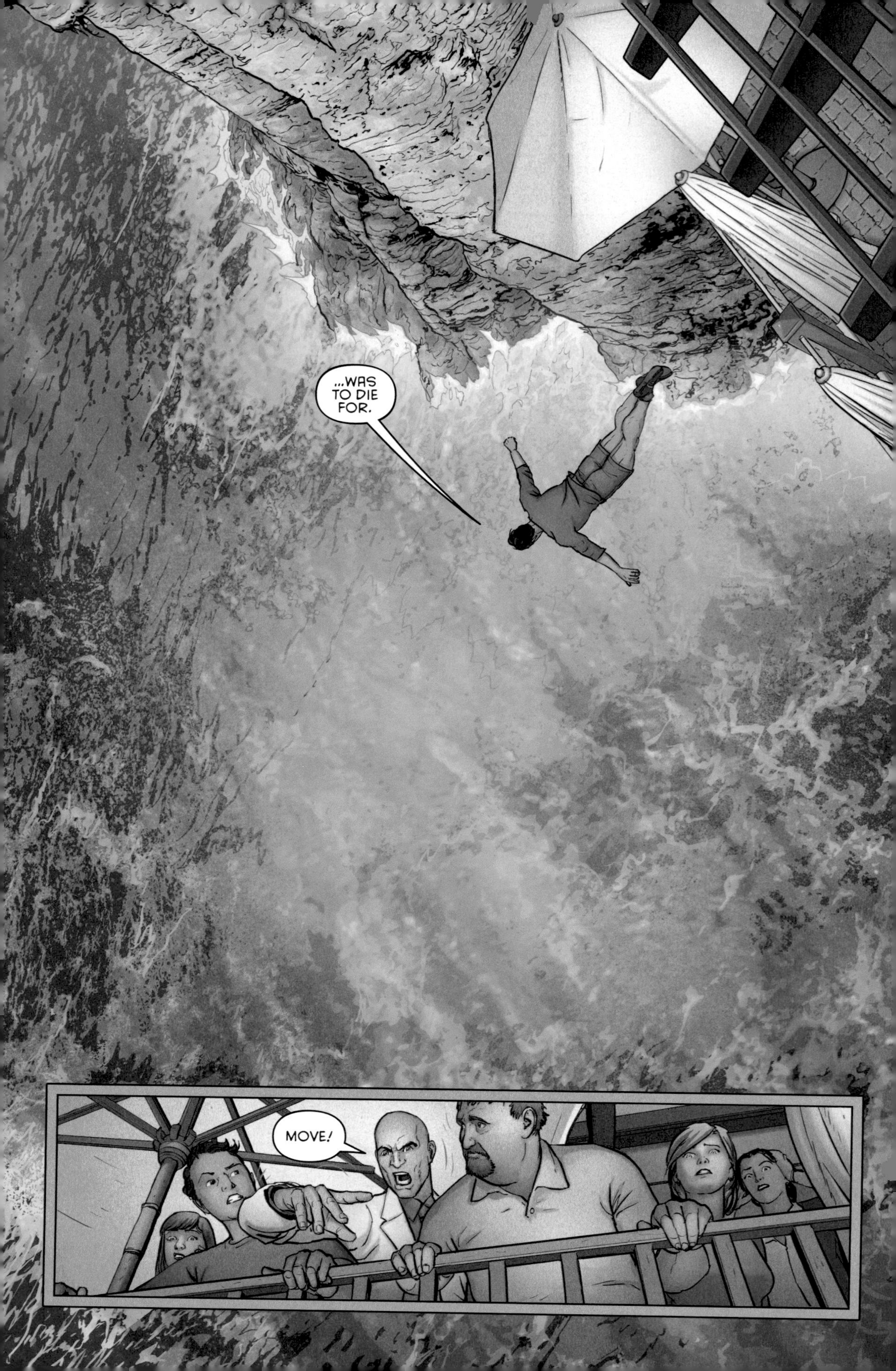
...WAS TO DIE FOR.
MOVE!

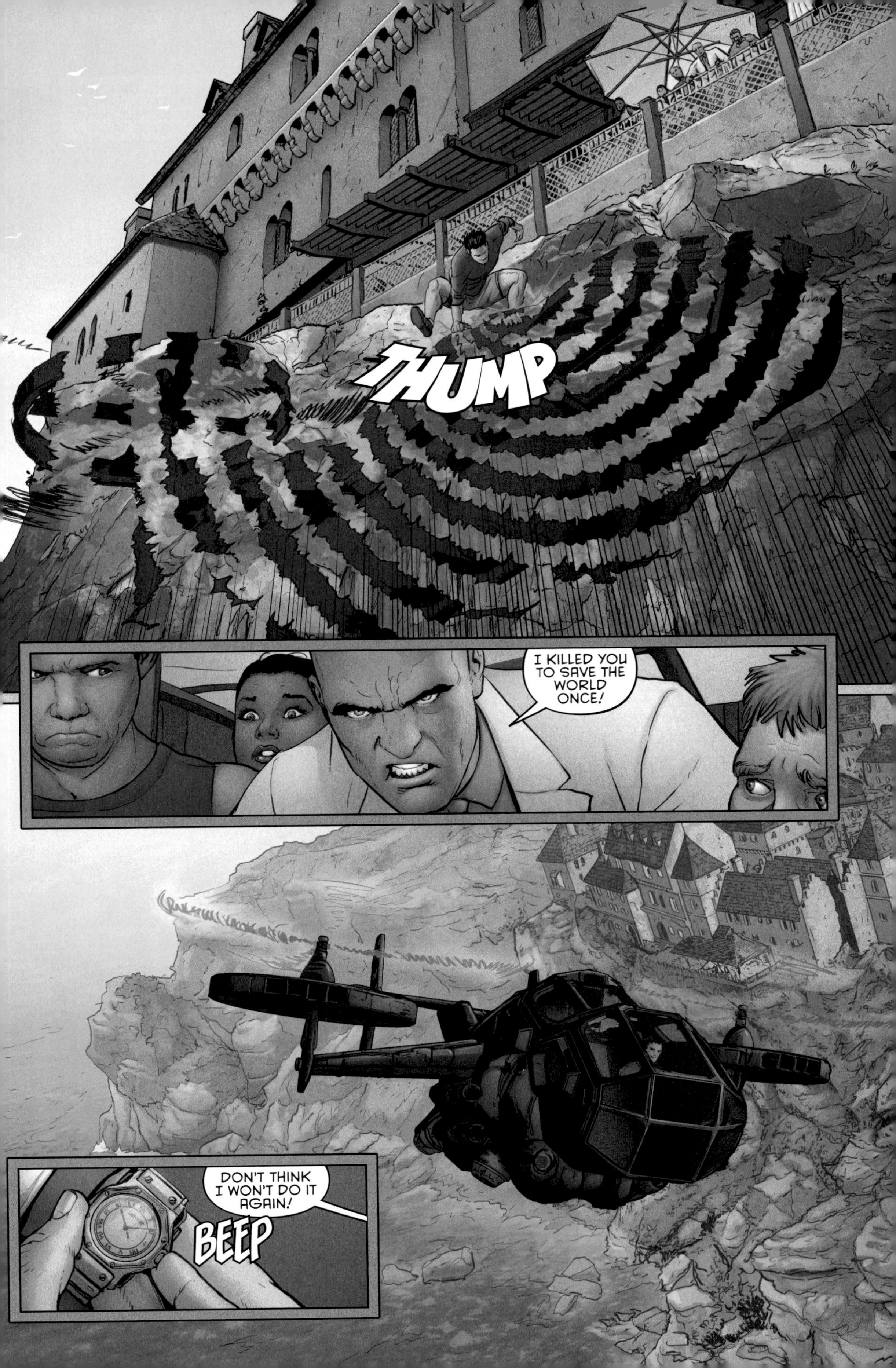
THUMP
I KILLED YOU TO SAVE THE WORLD ONCE!
DON'T THINK I WON'T DO IT AGAIN!
BEEP

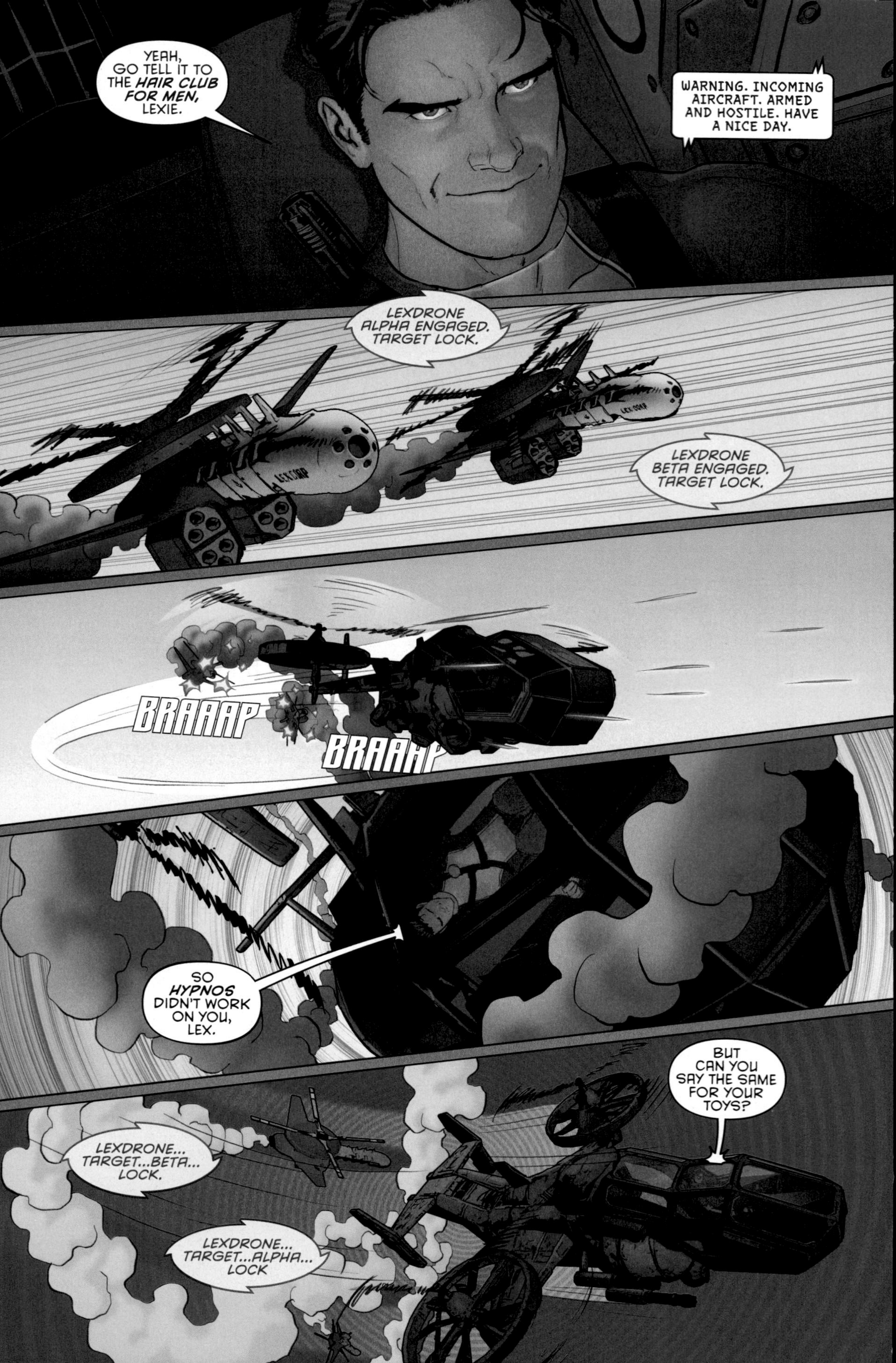
YEAH, GO TELL IT TO THE HAIR CLUB FOR MEN, LEXIE.
WARNING. INCOMING AIRCRAFT. ARMED AND HOSTILE. HAVE A NICE DAY.
LEXDRONE ALPHA ENGAGED. TARGET LOCK.
LEXCORP
LEXDRONE BETA ENGAGED. TARGET LOCK.
BRAAAP
BRAAAP
SO HYPNOS DIDN'T WORK ON YOU, LEX.
BUT CAN YOU SAY THE SAME FOR YOUR TOYS?
LEXDRONE... TARGET...BETA... LOCK.
LEXDRONE... TARGET...ALPHA... LOCK

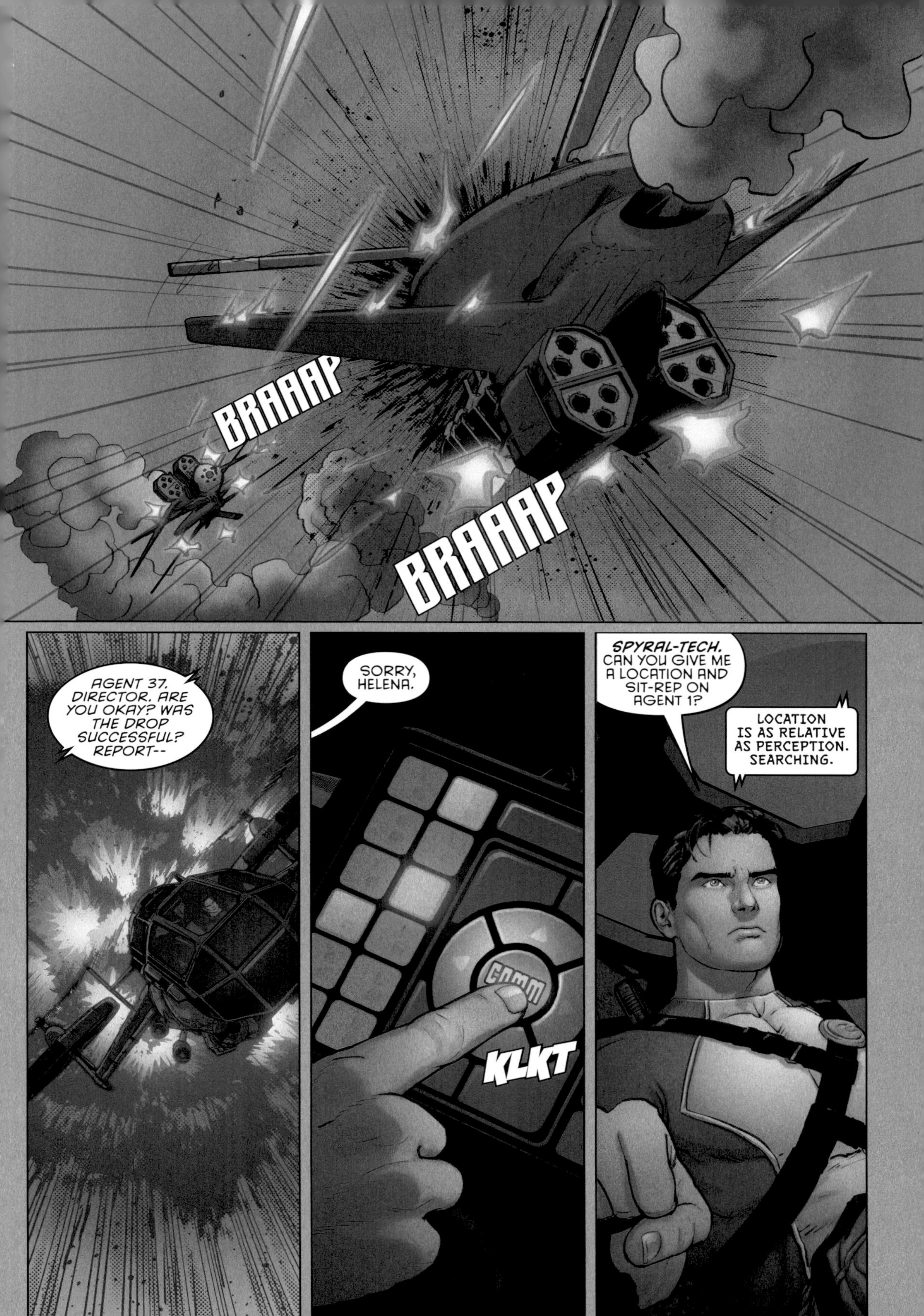
BRAAAP
BRAAAP
AGENT 37. DIRECTOR. ARE YOU OKAY? WAS THE DROP SUCCESSFUL? REPORT--
SORRY, HELENA.
COMM
KLKT
SPYRAL-TECH. CAN YOU GIVE ME A LOCATION AND SIT-REP ON AGENT 1?
LOCATION IS AS RELATIVE AS PERCEPTION. SEARCHING.

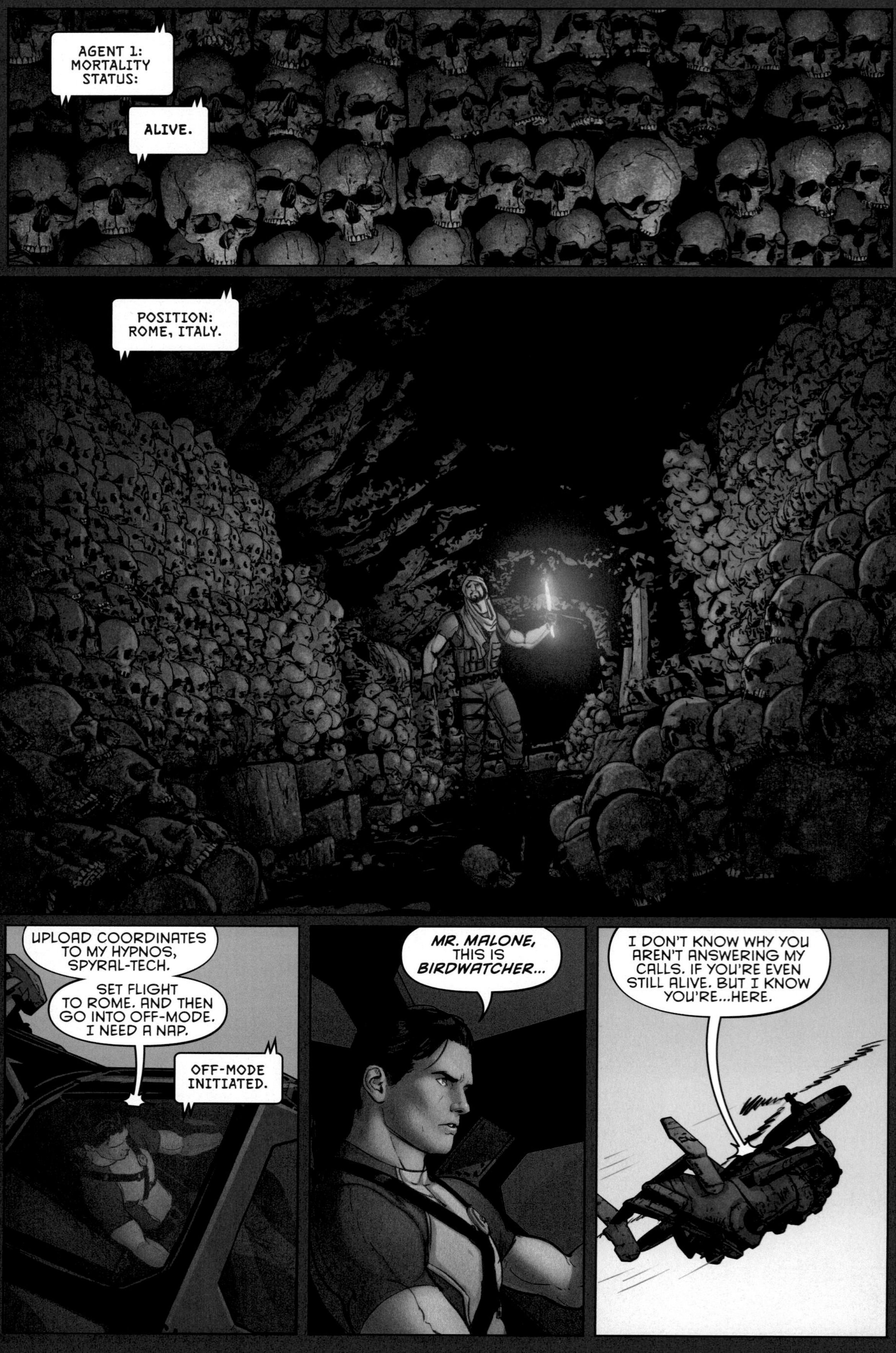
AGENT 1: MORTALITY STATUS:
ALIVE.
POSITION: ROME, ITALY.
UPLOAD COORDINATES TO MY HYPNOS, SPYRAL-TECH.
SET FLIGHT TO ROME. AND THEN GO INTO OFF-MODE. I NEED A NAP.
OFF-MODE INITIATED.
MR. MALONE, THIS IS BIRDWATCHER...
I DON'T KNOW WHY YOU AREN'T ANSWERING MY CALLS. IF YOU'RE EVEN STILL ALIVE. BUT I KNOW YOU'RE...HERE.

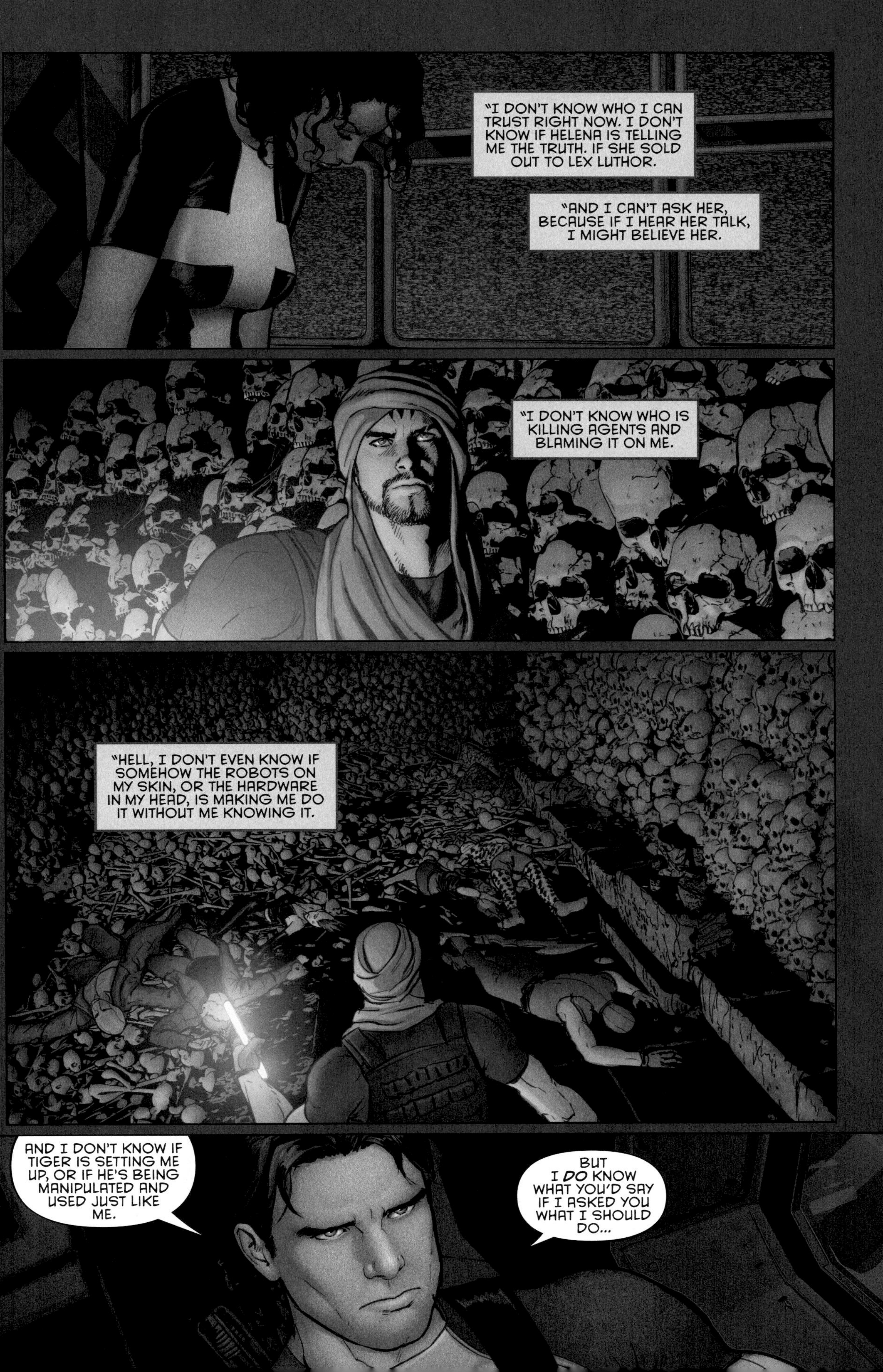
"I DON'T KNOW WHO I CAN TRUST RIGHT NOW. I DON'T KNOW IF HELENA IS TELLING ME THE TRUTH. IF SHE SOLD OUT TO LEX LUTHOR.
"AND I CAN'T ASK HER, BECAUSE IF I HEAR HER TALK, I MIGHT BELIEVE HER.
"I DON'T KNOW WHO IS KILLING AGENTS AND BLAMING IT ON ME.
"HELL, I DON'T EVEN KNOW IF SOMEHOW THE ROBOTS ON MY SKIN, OR THE HARDWARE IN MY HEAD, IS MAKING ME DO IT WITHOUT ME KNOWING IT.
AND I DON'T KNOW IF TIGER IS SETTING ME UP, OR IF HE'S BEING MANIPULATED AND USED JUST LIKE ME.
BUT I DO KNOW WHAT YOU'D SAY IF I ASKED YOU WHAT I SHOULD DO...

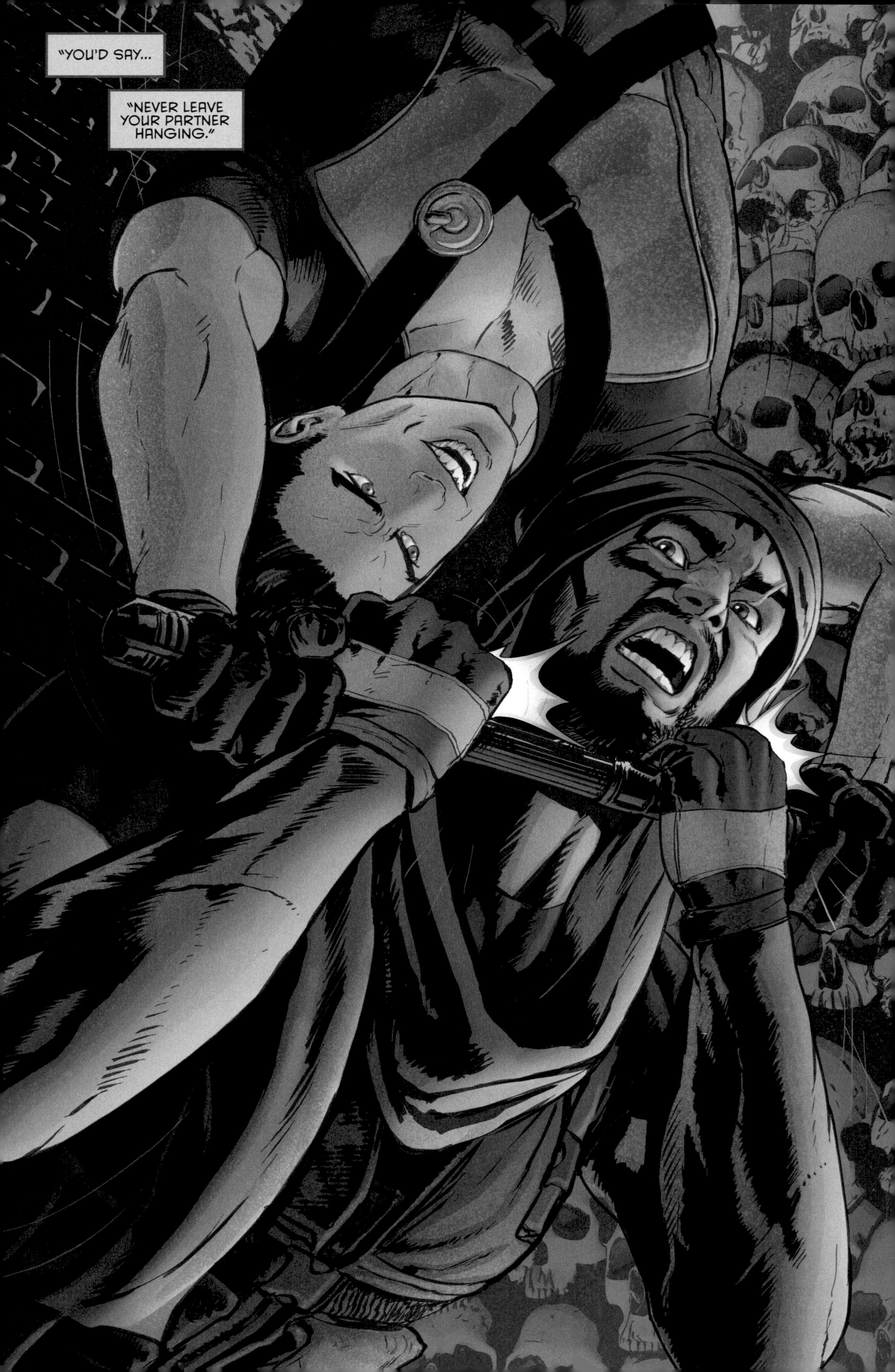
"YOU'D SAY...
"NEVER LEAVE YOUR PARTNER HANGING."

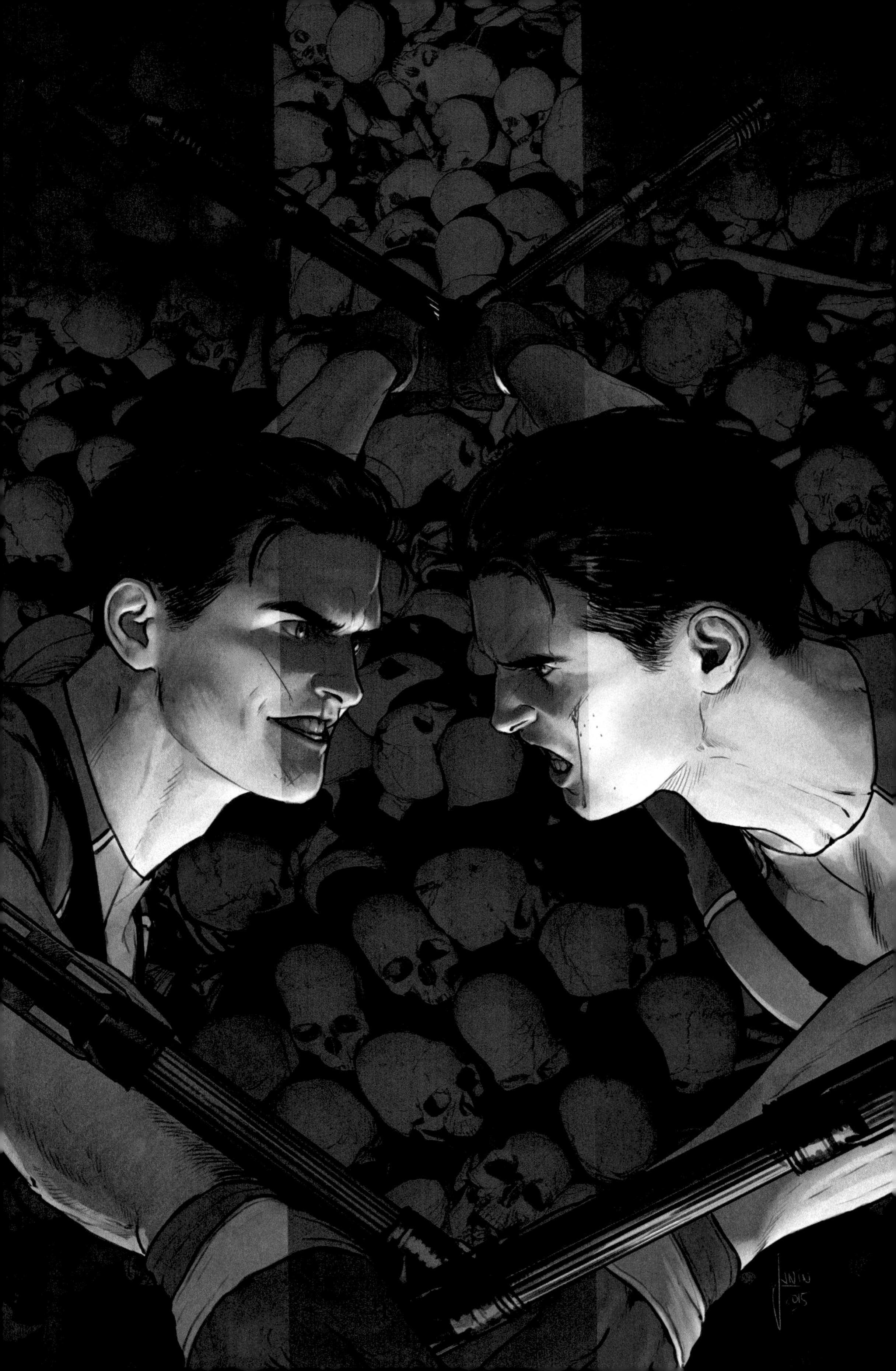

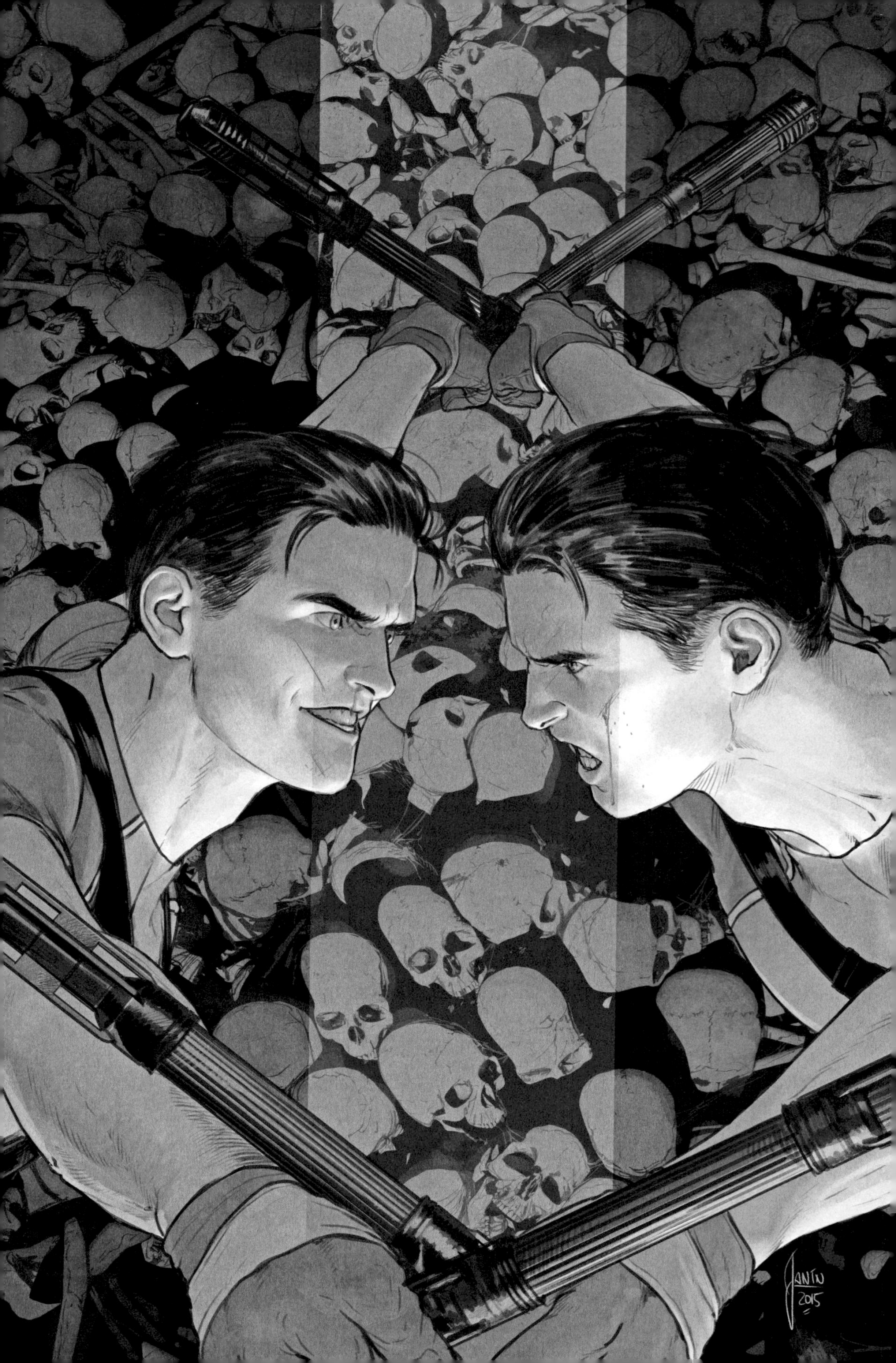

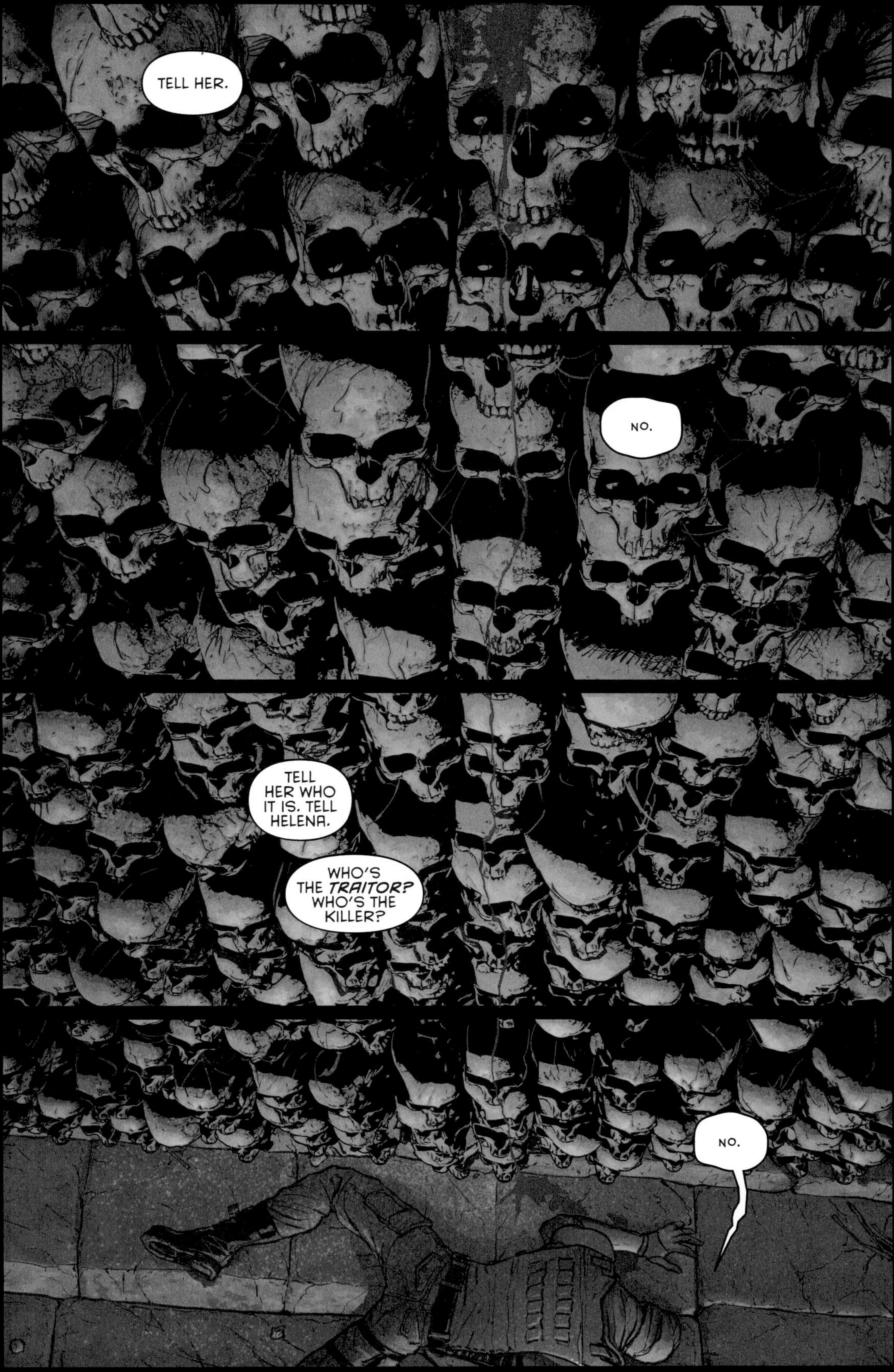
TELL HER.
NO.
TELL HER WHO IT IS. TELL HELENA.
WHO'S THE *TRAITOR?* WHO'S THE KILLER?
NO.

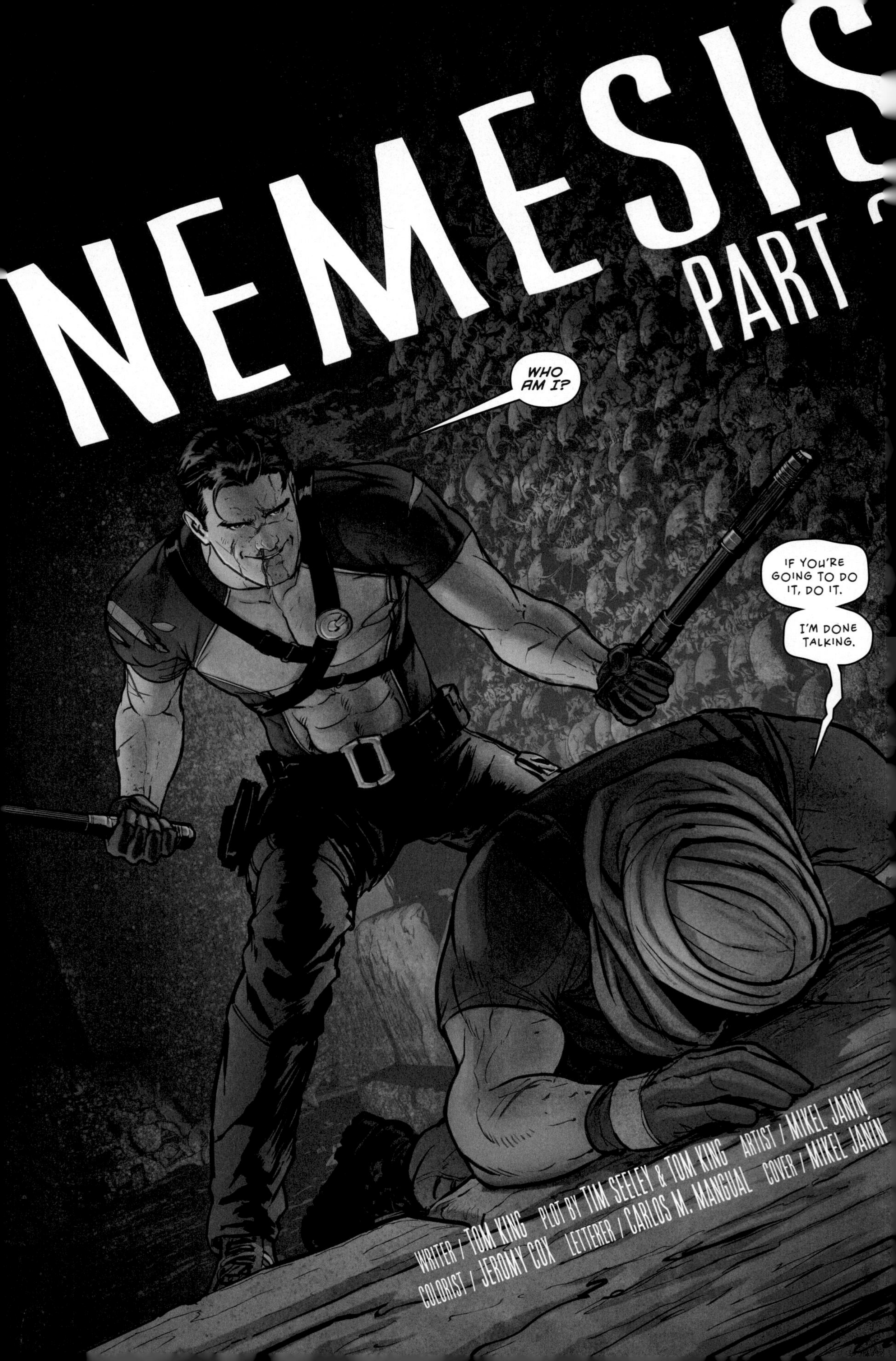
NEMESIS
PART
WHO AM I?
IF YOU'RE GOING TO DO IT, DO IT.
I'M DONE TALKING.
WRITER / TOM KING PLOT BY TIM SEELEY & TOM KING ARTIST / MIKEL JANÍN
COLORIST / JEROMY COX LETTERER / CARLOS M. MANGUAL COVER / MIKEL JANÍN

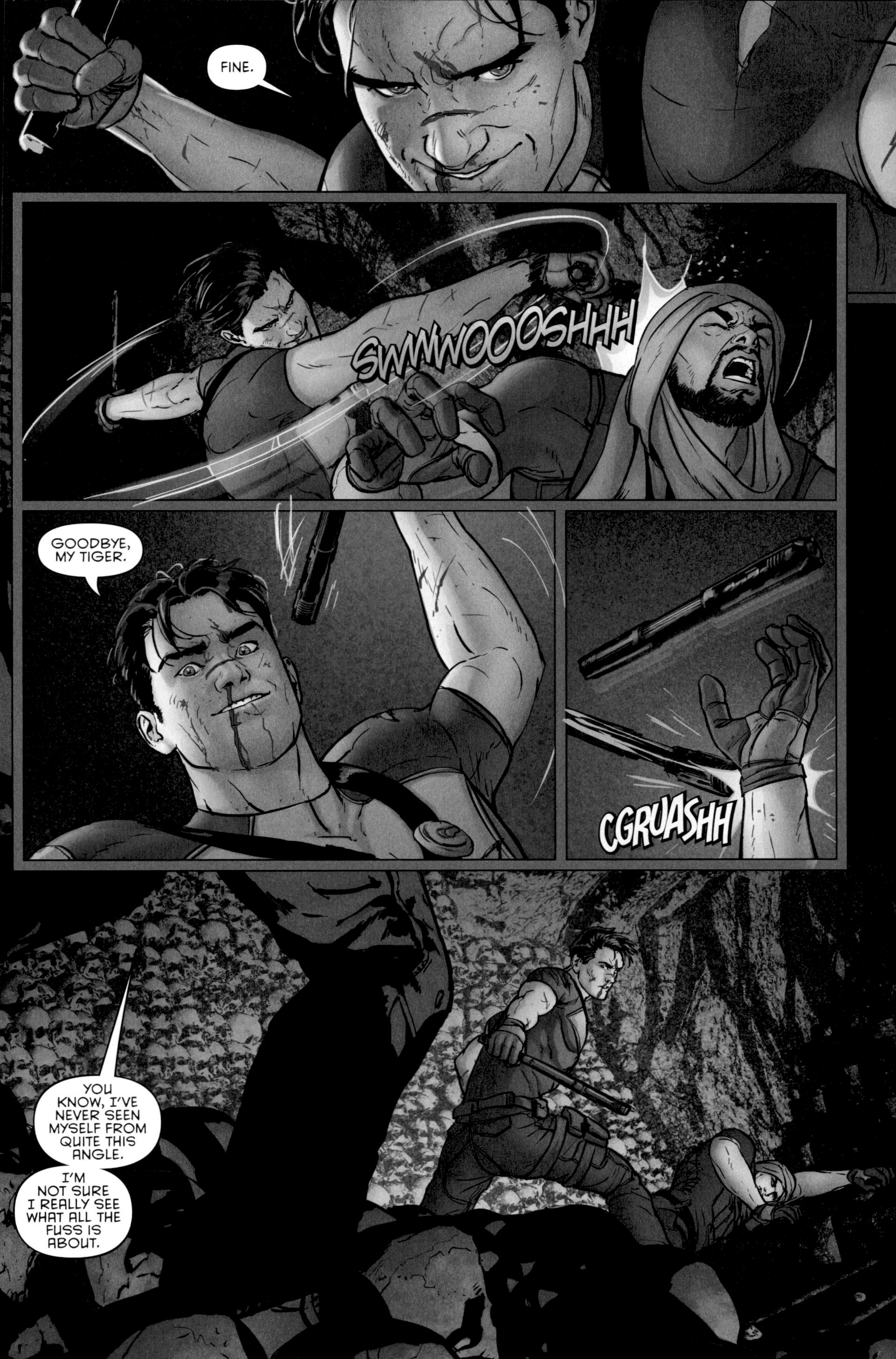
FINE.
SWWWOOOSHHH
GOODBYE, MY TIGER.
CGRUASHH
YOU KNOW, I'VE NEVER SEEN MYSELF FROM QUITE THIS ANGLE.
I'M NOT SURE I REALLY SEE WHAT ALL THE FUSS IS ABOUT.

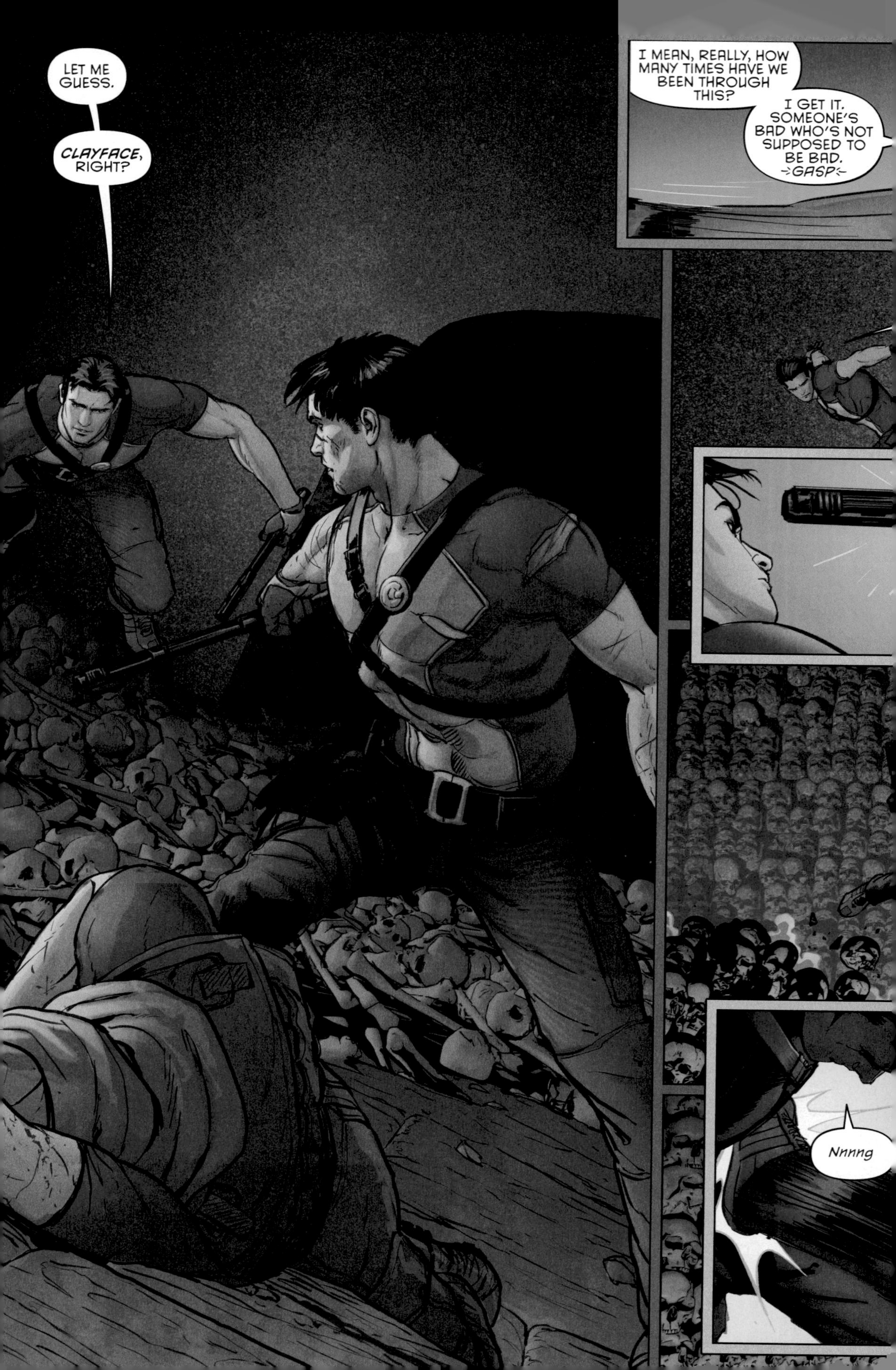
LET ME GUESS.
CLAYFACE, RIGHT?
I MEAN, REALLY, HOW MANY TIMES HAVE WE BEEN THROUGH THIS?
I GET IT. SOMEONE'S BAD WHO'S NOT SUPPOSED TO BE BAD.
GASP
Nnnng

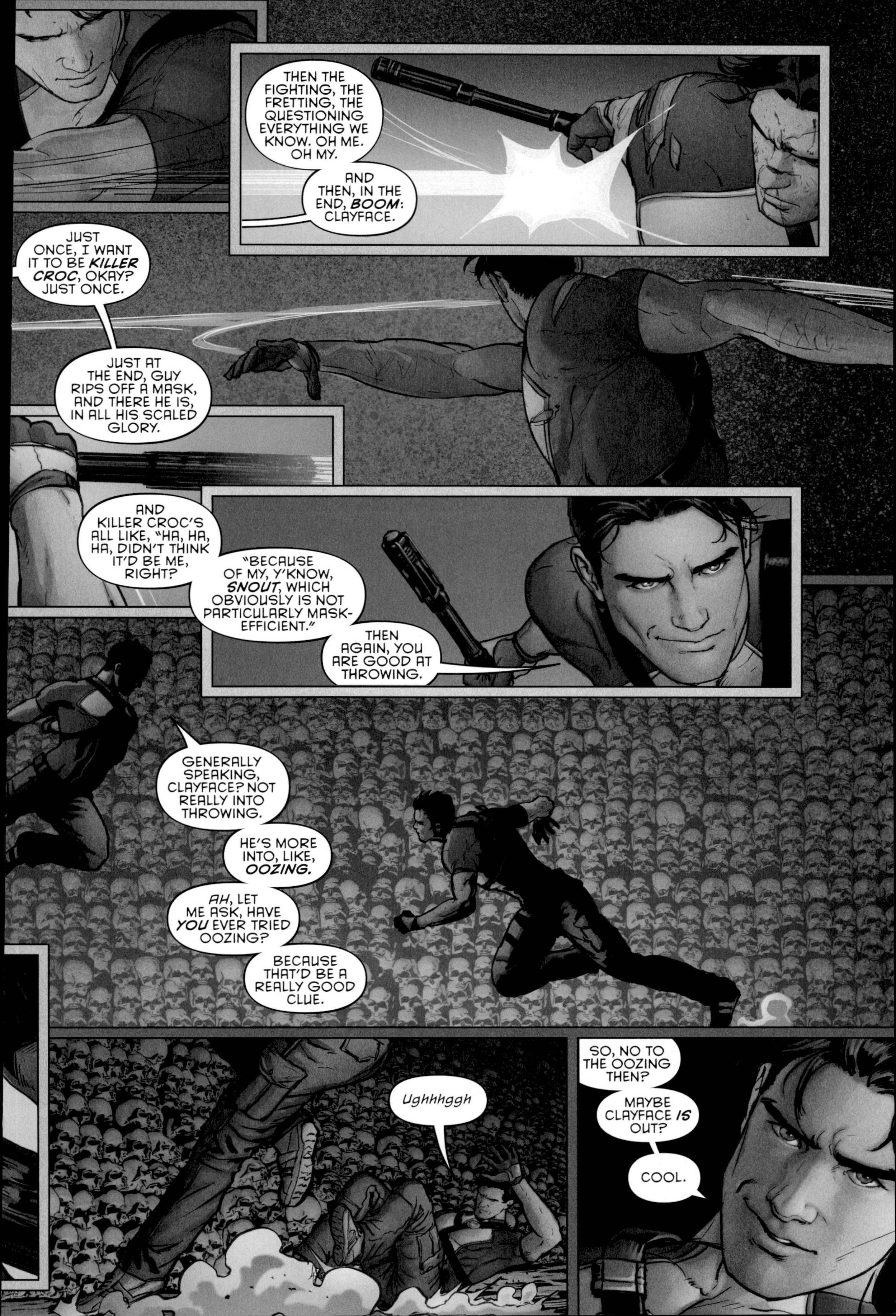
THEN THE FIGHTING, THE FRETTING, THE QUESTIONING EVERYTHING WE KNOW. OH ME. OH MY.
AND THEN, IN THE END, BOOM: CLAYFACE.
JUST ONCE, I WANT IT TO BE KILLER CROC, OKAY? JUST ONCE.
JUST AT THE END, GUY RIPS OFF A MASK, AND THERE HE IS, IN ALL HIS SCALED GLORY.
AND KILLER CROC'S ALL LIKE, "HA, HA, HA, DIDN'T THINK IT'D BE ME, RIGHT?
"BECAUSE OF MY, Y'KNOW, SNOUT, WHICH OBVIOUSLY IS NOT PARTICULARLY MASK-EFFICIENT."
THEN AGAIN, YOU ARE GOOD AT THROWING.
GENERALLY SPEAKING, CLAYFACE? NOT REALLY INTO THROWING.
HE'S MORE INTO, LIKE, OOZING.
AH, LET ME ASK, HAVE YOU EVER TRIED OOZING?
BECAUSE THAT'D BE A REALLY GOOD CLUE.
Ughhhggh
SO, NO TO THE OOZING THEN?
MAYBE CLAYFACE IS OUT?
COOL.

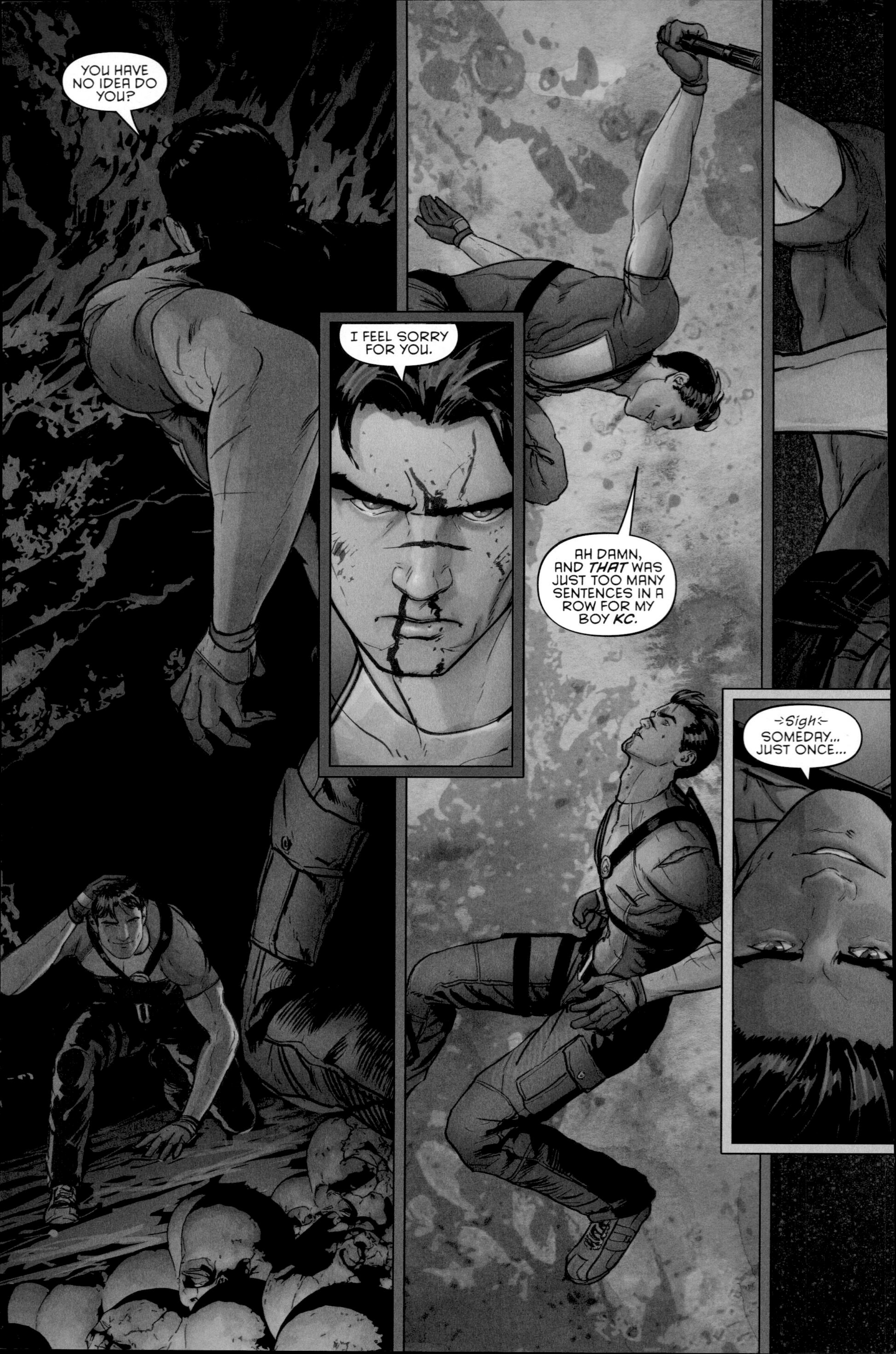
YOU HAVE NO IDEA DO YOU?
I FEEL SORRY FOR YOU.
AH DAMN, AND *THAT* WAS JUST TOO MANY SENTENCES IN A ROW FOR MY BOY *KC*.
Sigh
SOMEDAY... JUST ONCE...

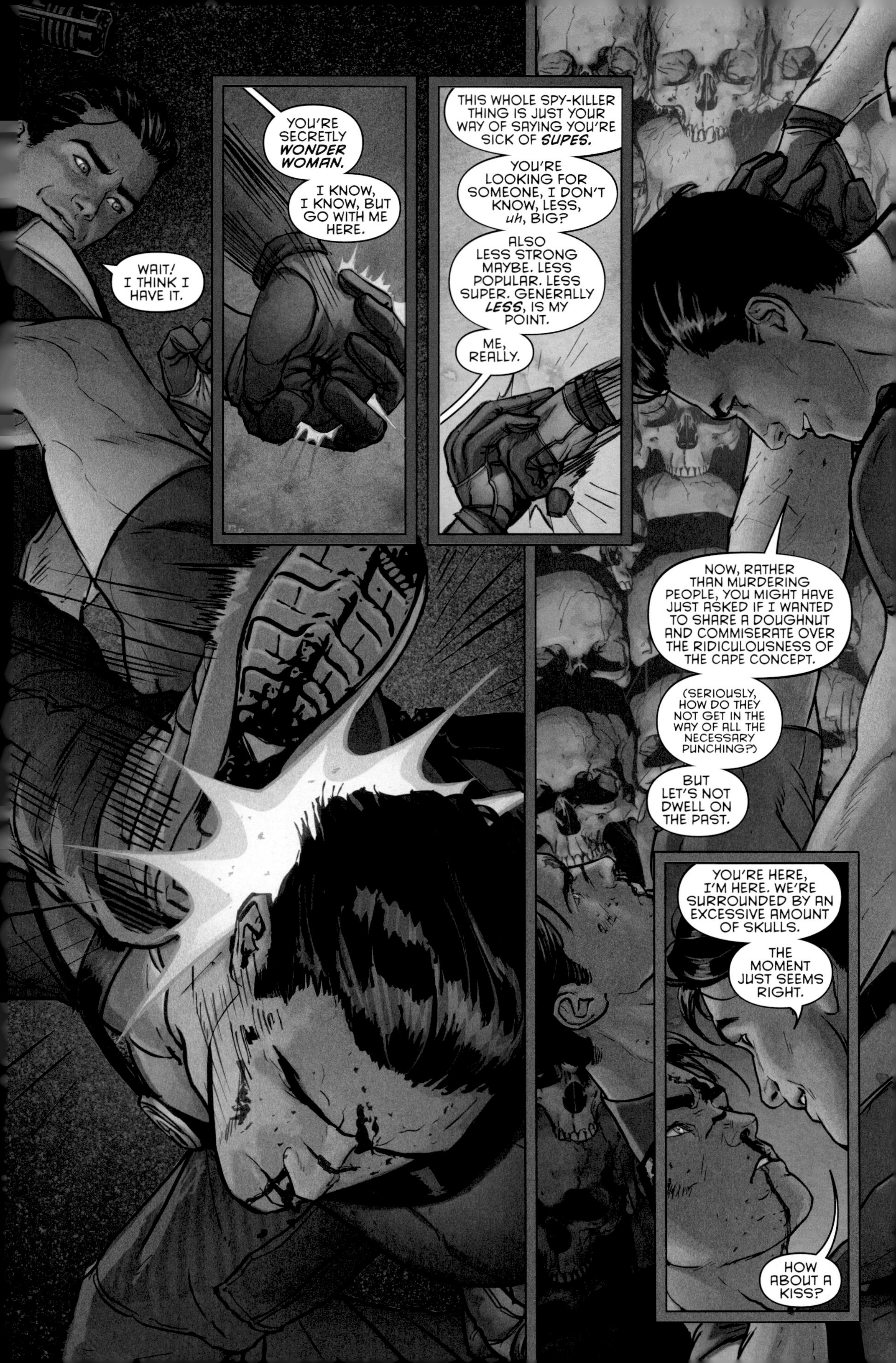
WAIT! I THINK I HAVE IT.
YOU'RE SECRETLY **WONDER WOMAN.**
I KNOW, I KNOW, BUT GO WITH ME HERE.
THIS WHOLE SPY-KILLER THING IS JUST YOUR WAY OF SAYING YOU'RE SICK OF ***SUPES.***
YOU'RE LOOKING FOR SOMEONE, I DON'T KNOW, LESS, *uh*, BIG?
ALSO LESS STRONG MAYBE. LESS POPULAR. LESS SUPER. GENERALLY ***LESS***, IS MY POINT.
ME, REALLY.
NOW, RATHER THAN MURDERING PEOPLE, YOU MIGHT HAVE JUST ASKED IF I WANTED TO SHARE A DOUGHNUT AND COMMISERATE OVER THE RIDICULOUSNESS OF THE CAPE CONCEPT.
(SERIOUSLY, HOW DO THEY NOT GET IN THE WAY OF ALL THE NECESSARY PUNCHING?)
BUT LET'S NOT DWELL ON THE PAST.
YOU'RE HERE, I'M HERE. WE'RE SURROUNDED BY AN EXCESSIVE AMOUNT OF SKULLS.
THE MOMENT JUST SEEMS RIGHT.
HOW ABOUT A KISS?

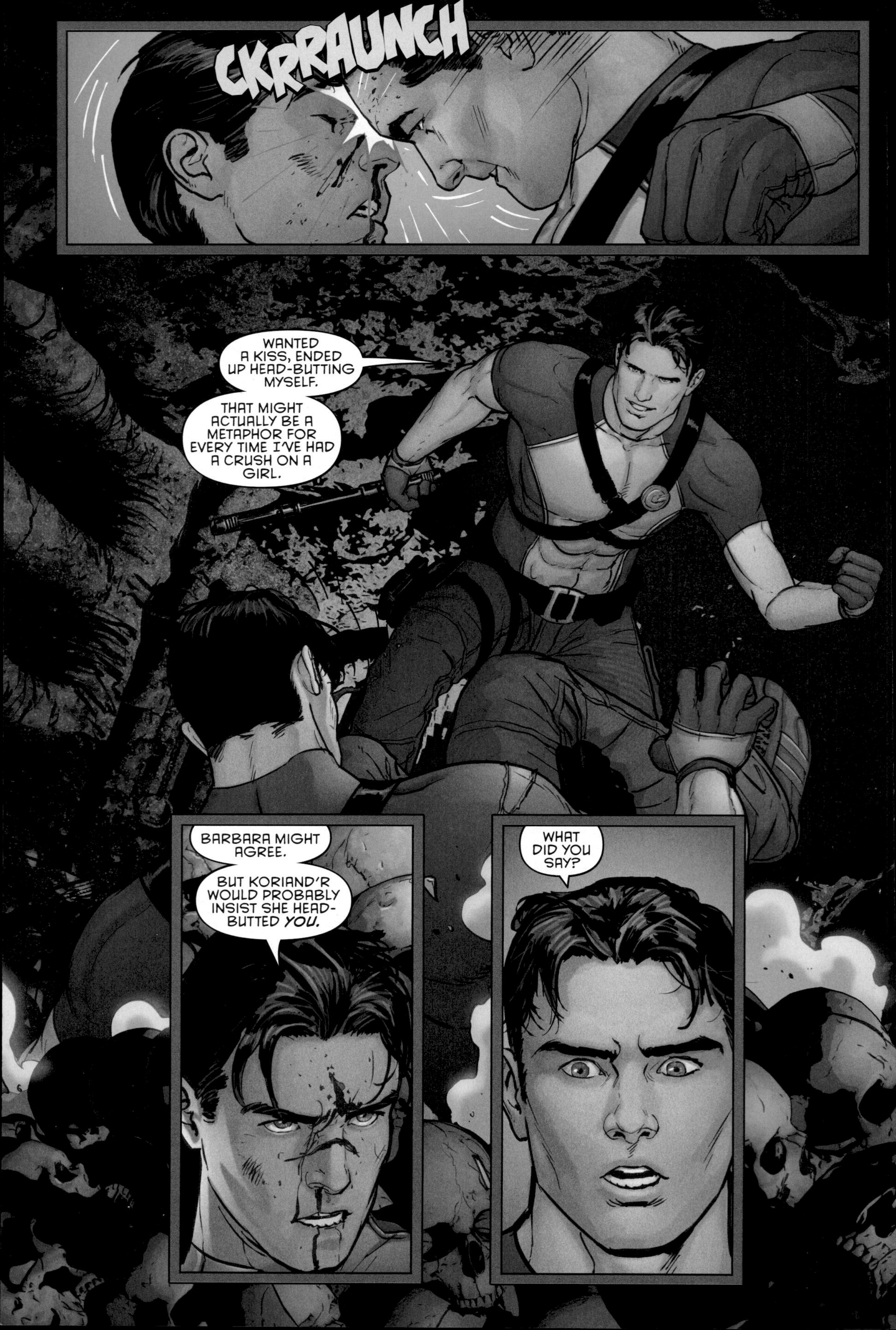
CKRAUNCH
WANTED A KISS, ENDED UP HEAD-BUTTING MYSELF.
THAT MIGHT ACTUALLY BE A METAPHOR FOR EVERY TIME I'VE HAD A CRUSH ON A GIRL.
BARBARA MIGHT AGREE.
BUT KORIAND'R WOULD PROBABLY INSIST SHE HEAD-BUTTED *YOU.*
WHAT DID YOU SAY?

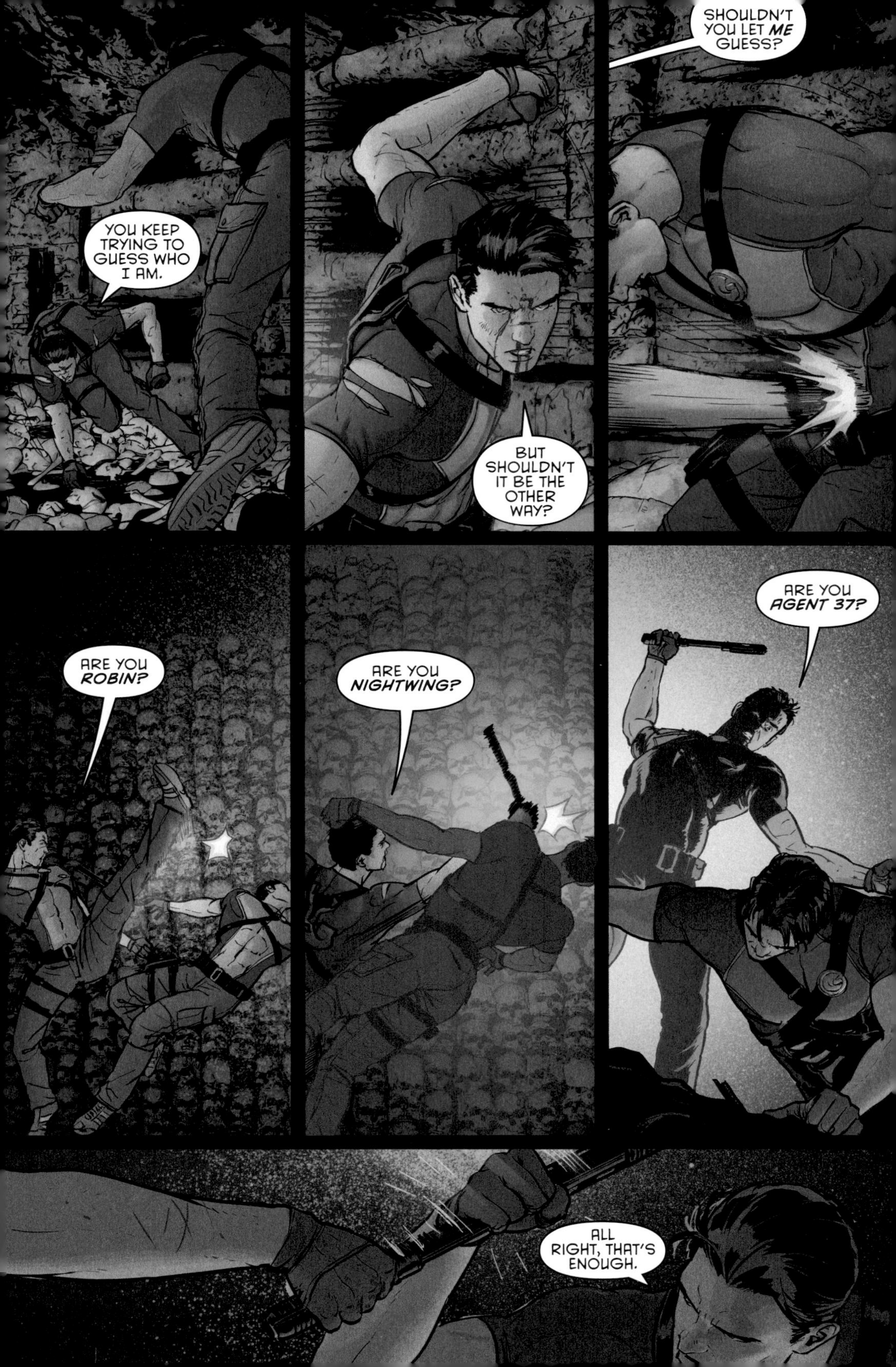
YOU KEEP TRYING TO GUESS WHO I AM.
BUT SHOULDN'T IT BE THE OTHER WAY?
SHOULDN'T YOU LET *ME* GUESS?
ARE YOU *ROBIN?*
ARE YOU *NIGHTWING?*
ARE YOU *AGENT 37?*
ALL RIGHT, THAT'S ENOUGH.

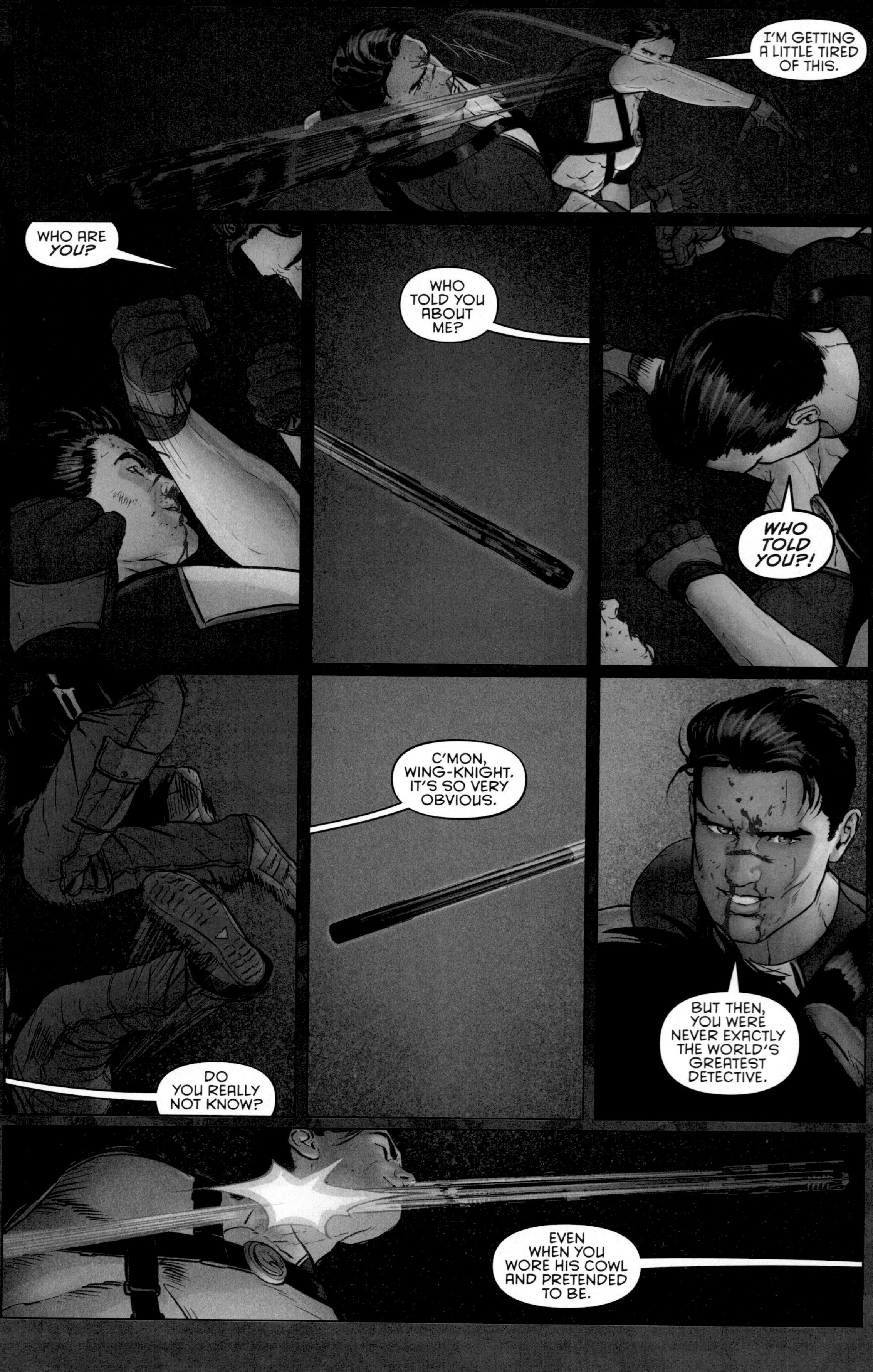
I'M GETTING A LITTLE TIRED OF THIS.
WHO ARE *YOU?*
WHO TOLD YOU ABOUT ME?
WHO TOLD YOU?!
C'MON, WING-KNIGHT. IT'S SO VERY OBVIOUS.
DO YOU REALLY NOT KNOW?
BUT THEN, YOU WERE NEVER EXACTLY THE WORLD'S GREATEST DETECTIVE.
EVEN WHEN YOU WORE HIS COWL AND PRETENDED TO BE.

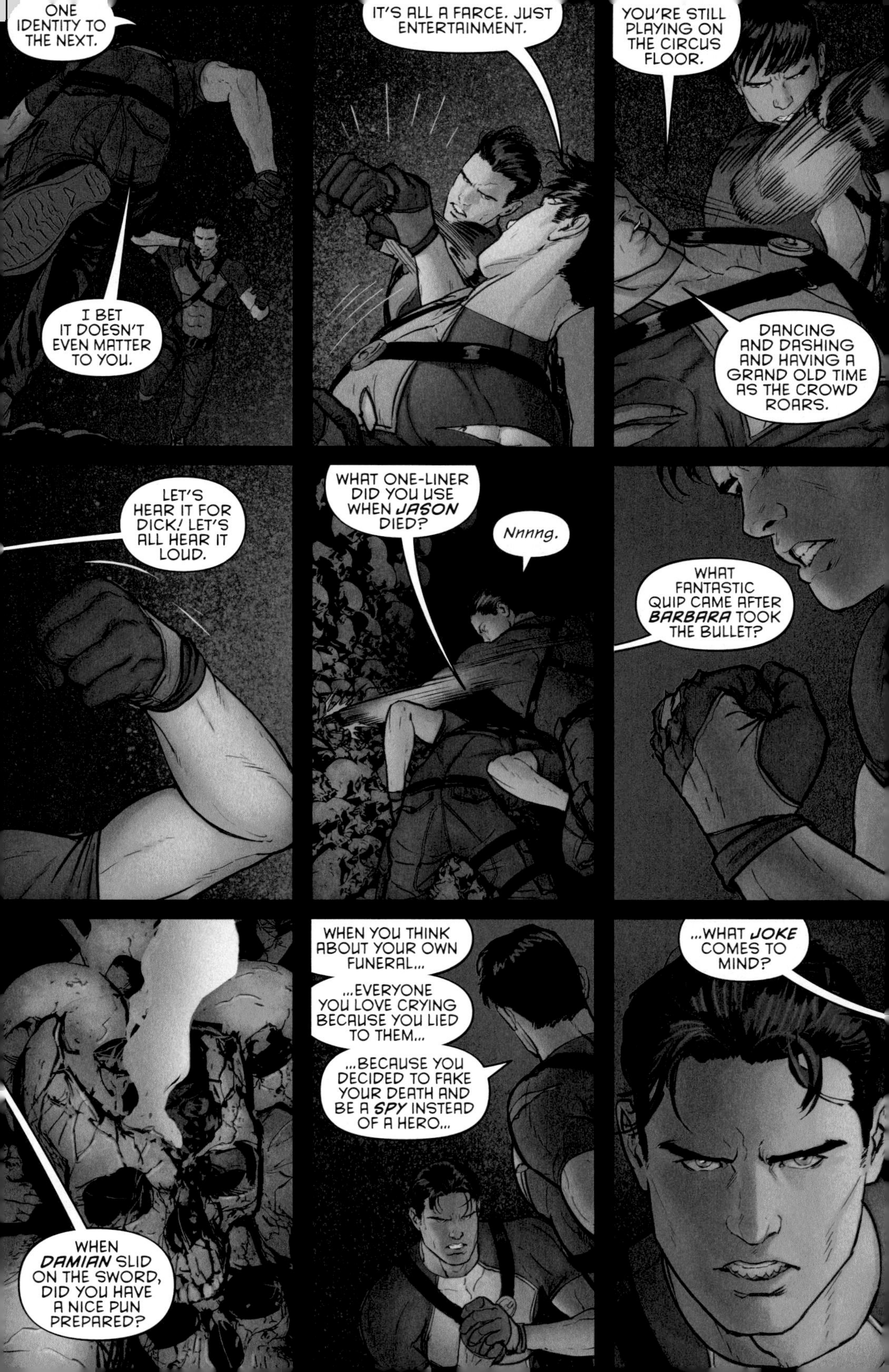
ONE IDENTITY TO THE NEXT.
I BET IT DOESN'T EVEN MATTER TO YOU.
IT'S ALL A FARCE. JUST ENTERTAINMENT.
YOU'RE STILL PLAYING ON THE CIRCUS FLOOR.
DANCING AND DASHING AND HAVING A GRAND OLD TIME AS THE CROWD ROARS.
LET'S HEAR IT FOR DICK! LET'S ALL HEAR IT LOUD.
WHAT ONE-LINER DID YOU USE WHEN JASON DIED?
Nnnng.
WHAT FANTASTIC QUIP CAME AFTER BARBARA TOOK THE BULLET?
WHEN DAMIAN SLID ON THE SWORD, DID YOU HAVE A NICE PUN PREPARED?
WHEN YOU THINK ABOUT YOUR OWN FUNERAL...
...EVERYONE YOU LOVE CRYING BECAUSE YOU LIED TO THEM...
...BECAUSE YOU DECIDED TO FAKE YOUR DEATH AND BE A SPY INSTEAD OF A HERO...
...WHAT JOKE COMES TO MIND?

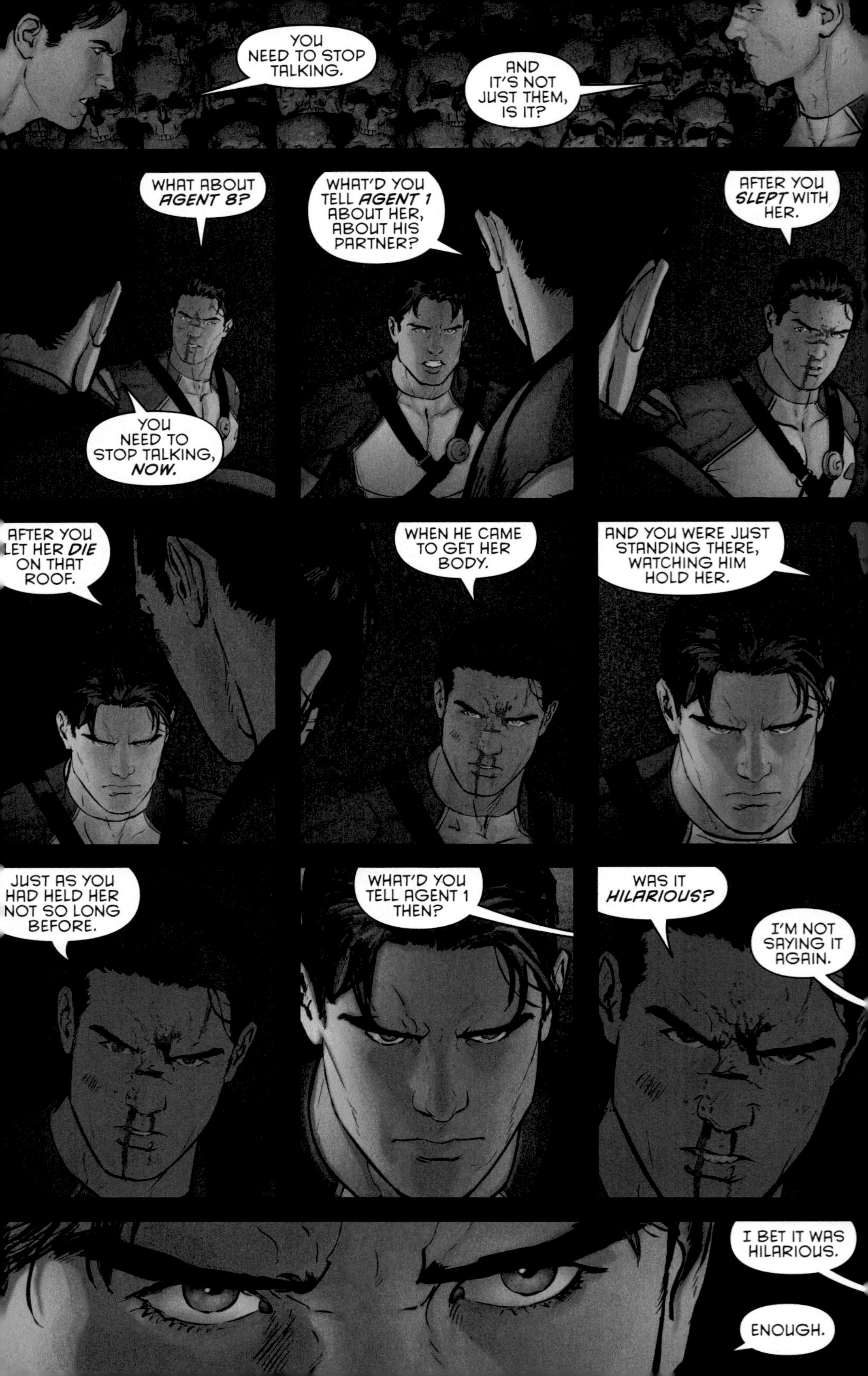
YOU NEED TO STOP TALKING.
AND IT'S NOT JUST THEM, IS IT?
WHAT ABOUT *AGENT 8?*
YOU NEED TO STOP TALKING, *NOW.*
WHAT'D YOU TELL *AGENT 1* ABOUT HER, ABOUT HIS PARTNER?
AFTER YOU *SLEPT* WITH HER.
AFTER YOU LET HER *DIE* ON THAT ROOF.
WHEN HE CAME TO GET HER BODY.
AND YOU WERE JUST STANDING THERE, WATCHING HIM HOLD HER.
JUST AS YOU HAD HELD HER NOT SO LONG BEFORE.
WHAT'D YOU TELL AGENT 1 THEN?
WAS IT *HILARIOUS?*
I'M NOT SAYING IT AGAIN.
I BET IT WAS HILARIOUS.
ENOUGH.

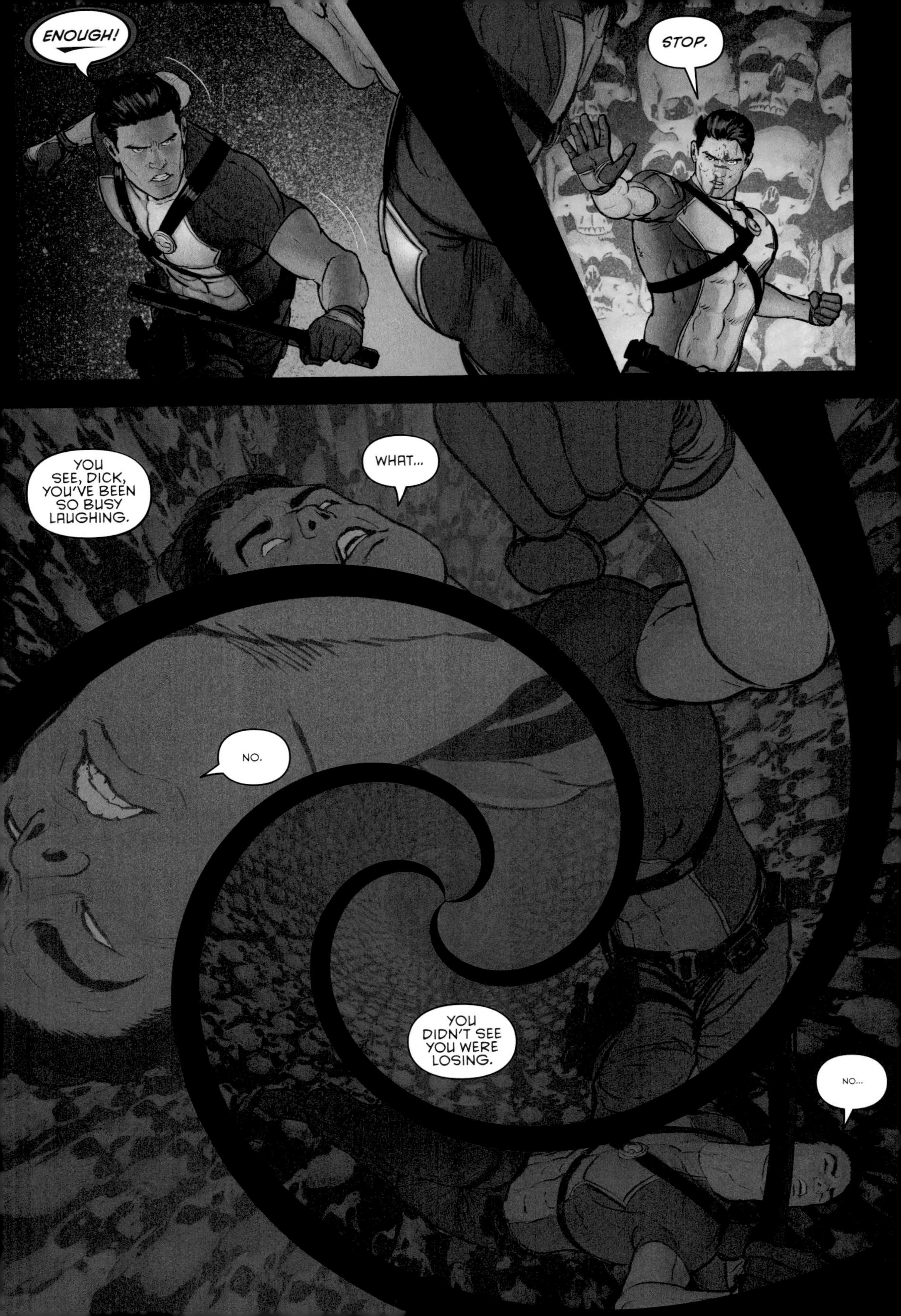
ENOUGH!
STOP.
YOU SEE, DICK, YOU'VE BEEN SO BUSY LAUGHING.
WHAT...
NO.
YOU DIDN'T SEE YOU WERE LOSING.
NO...

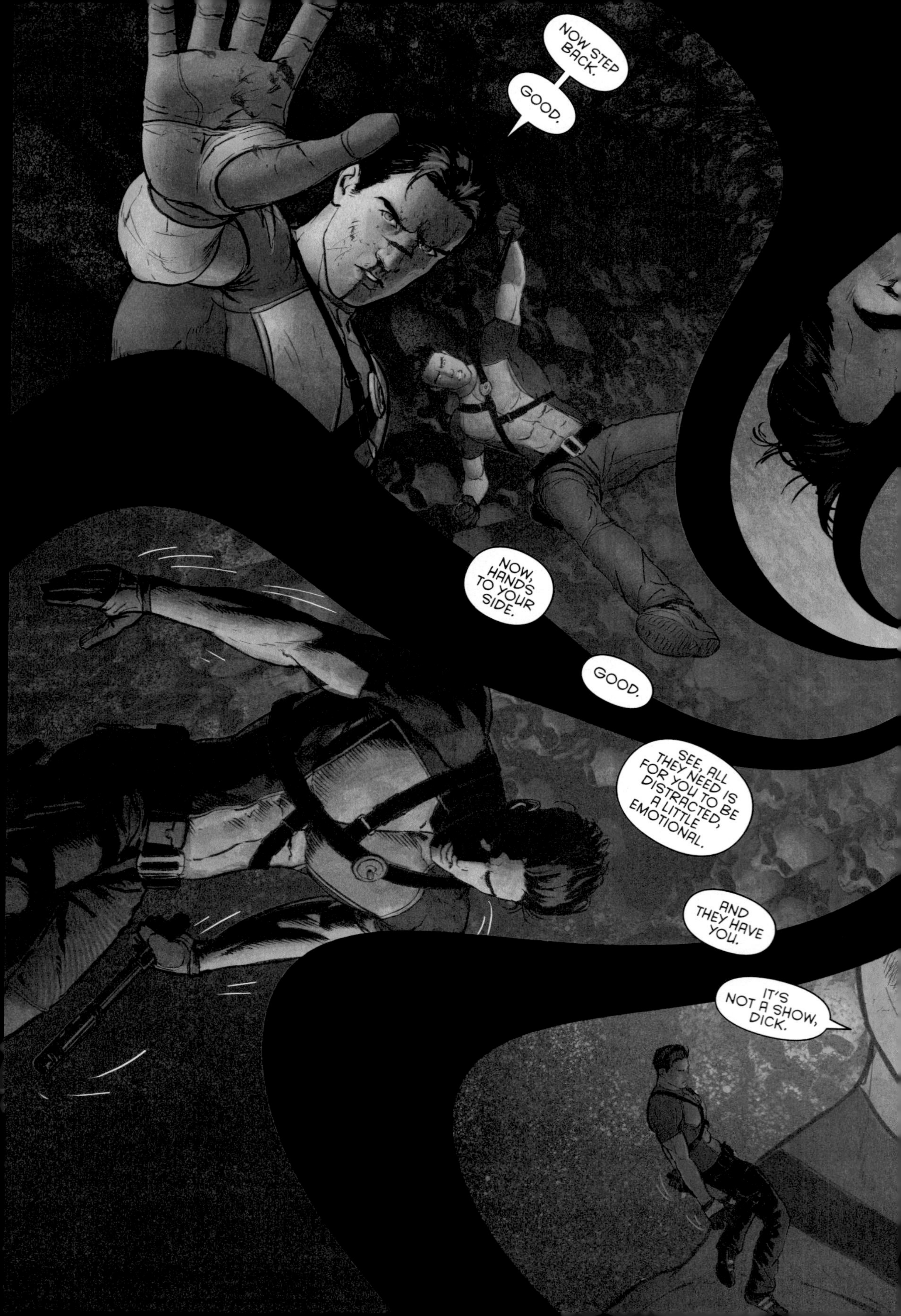
NOW STEP BACK.
GOOD.
NOW, HANDS TO YOUR SIDE.
GOOD.
SEE, ALL THEY NEED IS FOR YOU TO BE DISTRACTED, A LITTLE EMOTIONAL.
AND THEY HAVE YOU.
IT'S NOT A SHOW, DICK.

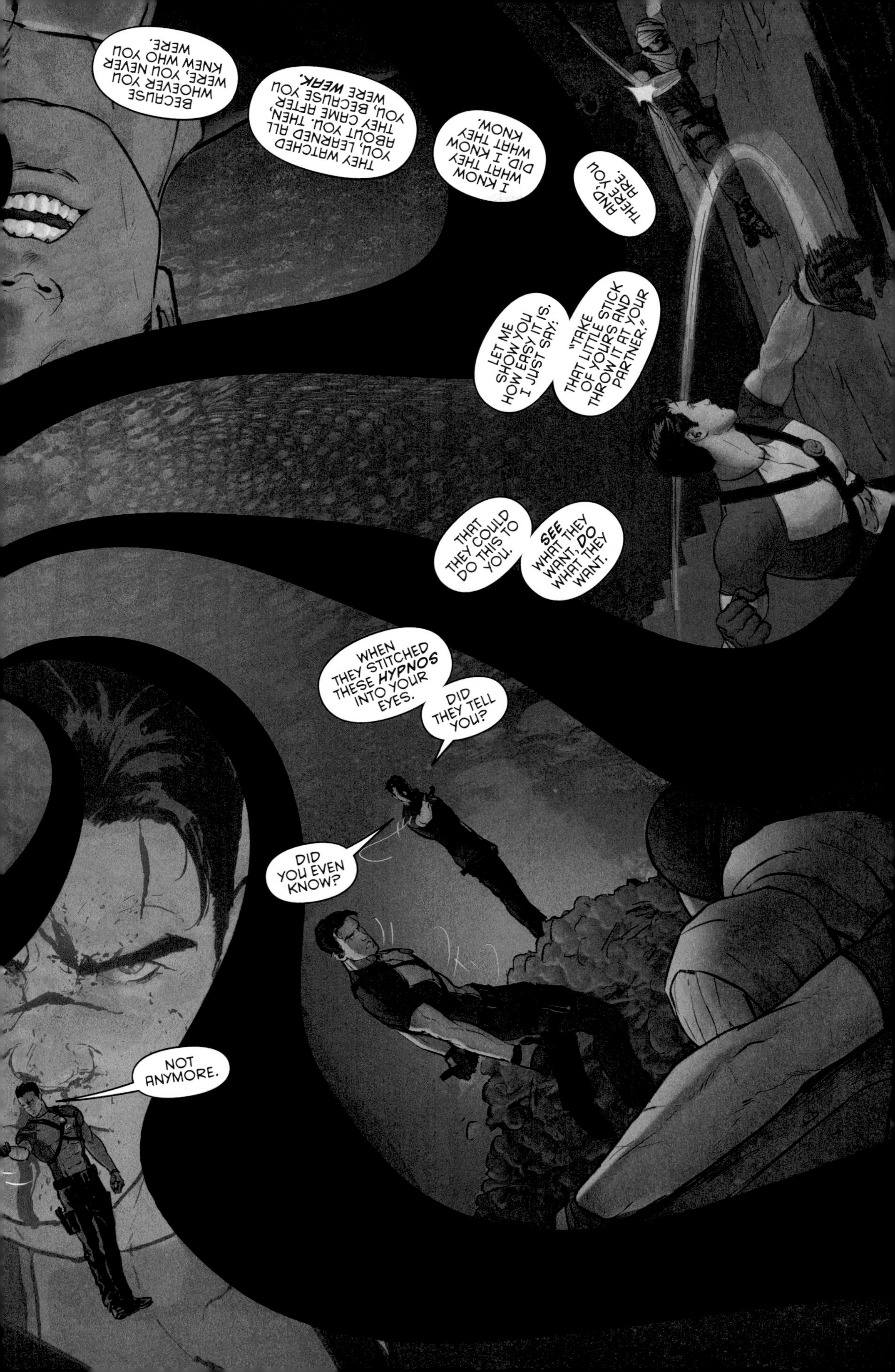
BECAUSE WHOEVER YOU WERE, YOU NEVER KNEW WHO YOU WERE.
THEY WATCHED YOU, LEARNED ALL ABOUT YOU. THEN, THEY CAME AFTER YOU, BECAUSE YOU WERE *WEAK*.
I KNOW WHAT THEY DID. I KNOW WHAT THEY KNOW.
AND, THERE YOU ARE.
LET ME SHOW YOU HOW EASY IT IS. I JUST SAY:
"TAKE THAT LITTLE STICK OF YOURS AND THROW IT AT YOUR PARTNER."
SEE WHAT THEY WANT, *DO* WHAT THEY WANT.
THAT THEY COULD DO THIS TO YOU.
WHEN THEY STITCHED THESE *HYPNOS* INTO YOUR EYES.
DID THEY TELL YOU?
DID YOU EVEN KNOW?
NOT ANYMORE.

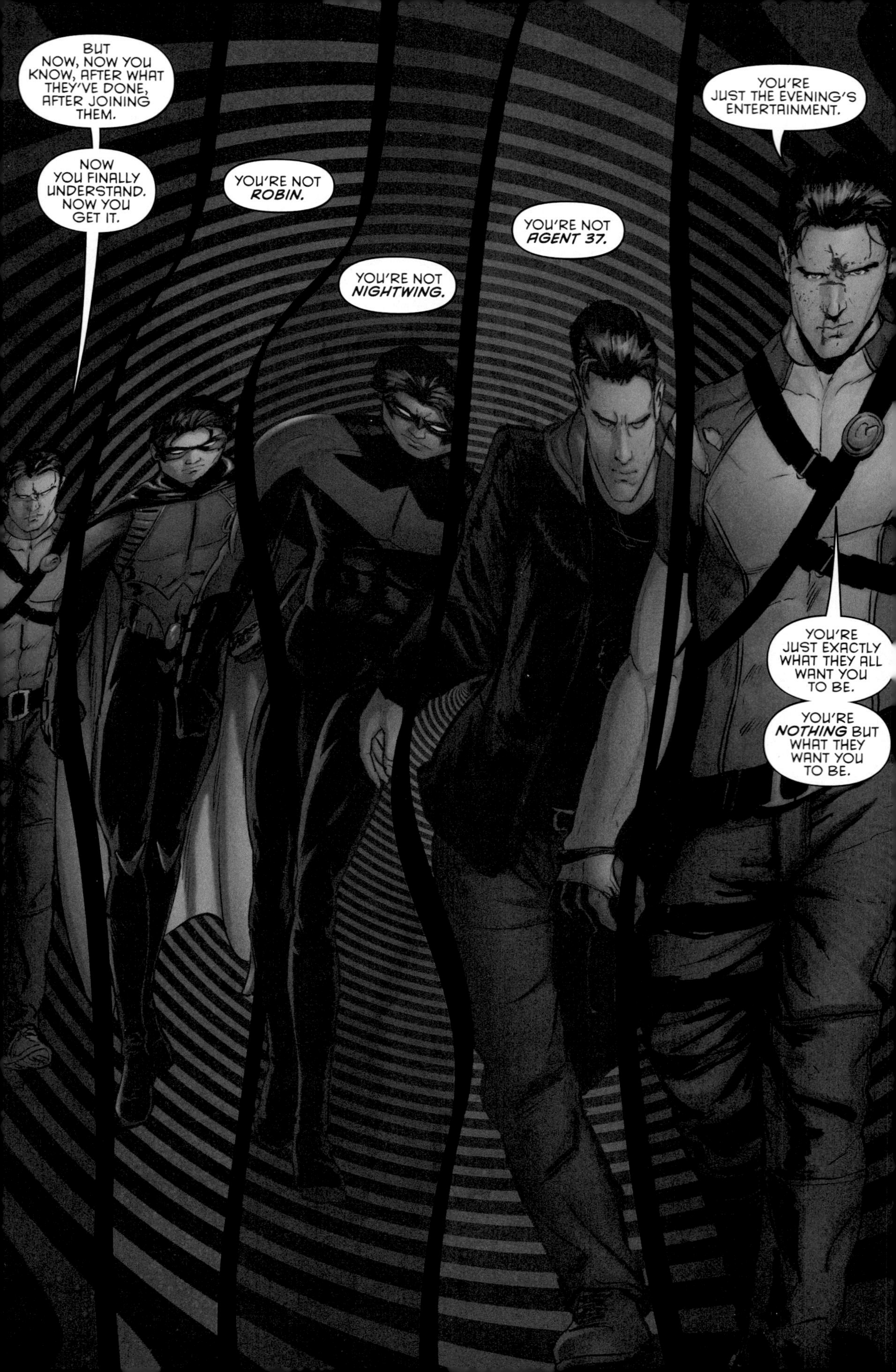
BUT NOW, NOW YOU KNOW, AFTER WHAT THEY'VE DONE, AFTER JOINING THEM.
NOW YOU FINALLY UNDERSTAND. NOW YOU GET IT.
YOU'RE NOT *ROBIN.*
YOU'RE NOT *NIGHTWING.*
YOU'RE NOT *AGENT 37.*
YOU'RE JUST THE EVENING'S ENTERTAINMENT.
YOU'RE JUST EXACTLY WHAT THEY ALL WANT YOU TO BE.
YOU'RE *NOTHING* BUT WHAT THEY WANT YOU TO BE.

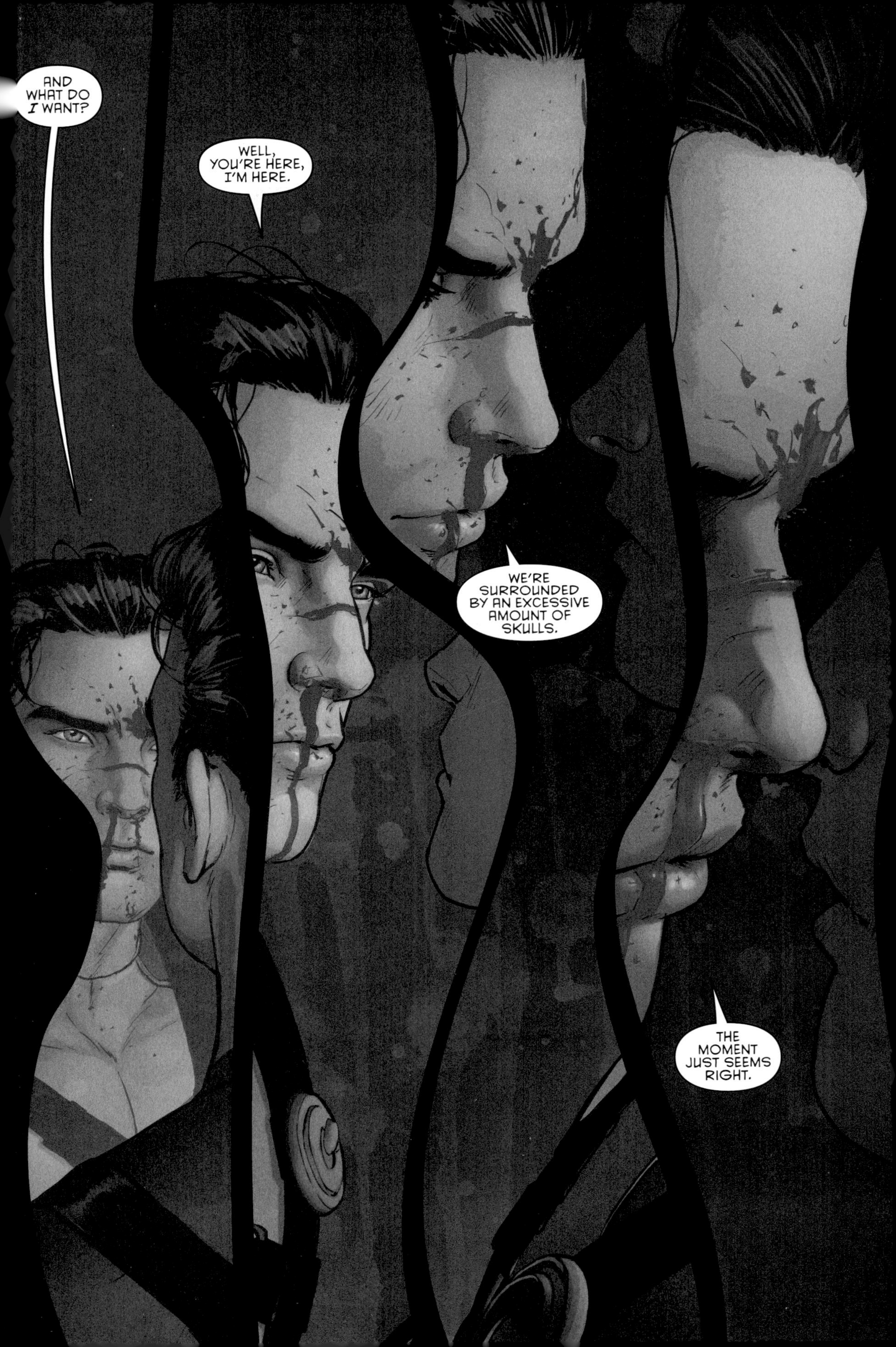
AND WHAT DO *I* WANT?
WELL, YOU'RE HERE, I'M HERE.
WE'RE SURROUNDED BY AN EXCESSIVE AMOUNT OF SKULLS.
THE MOMENT JUST SEEMS RIGHT.

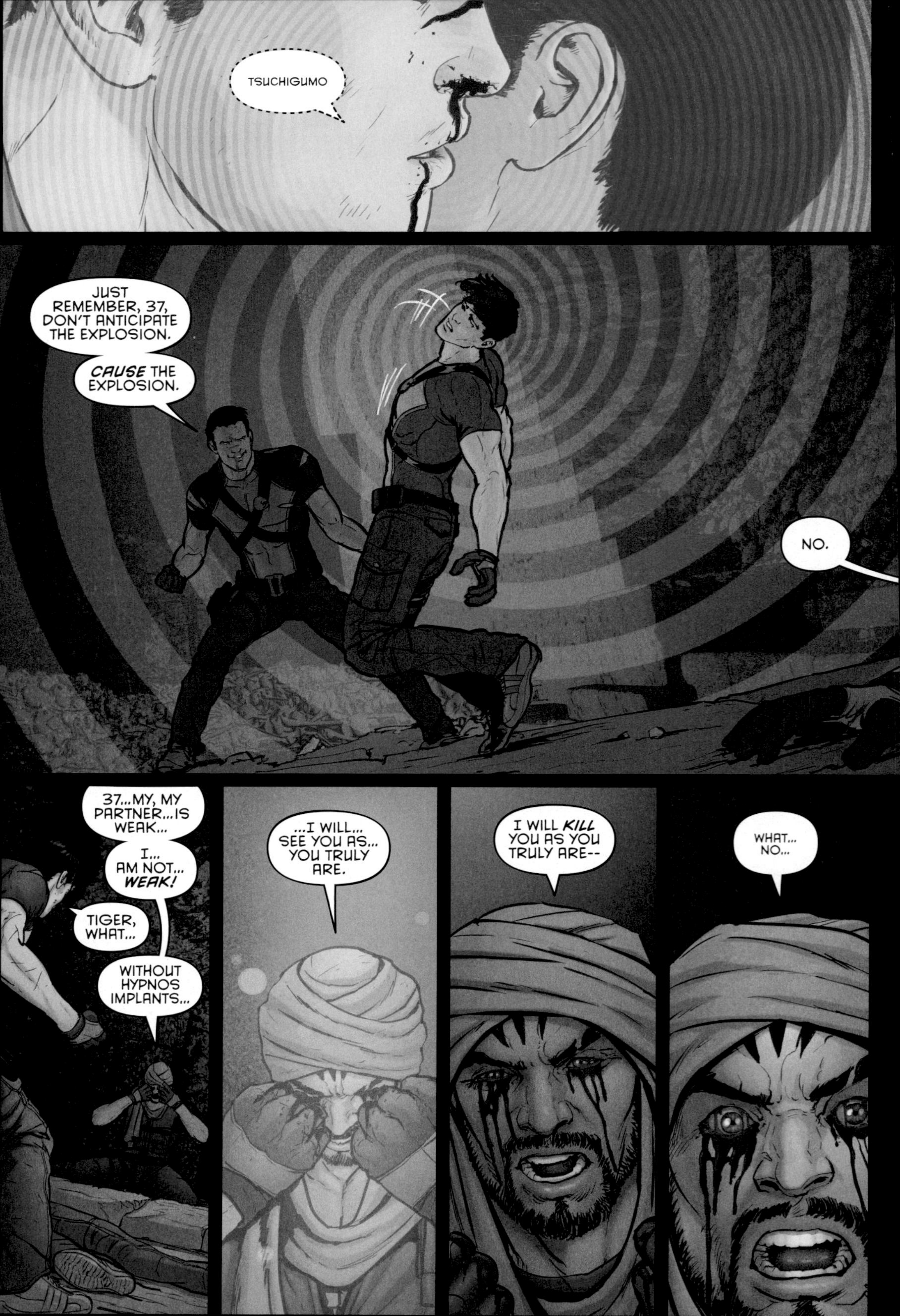
TSUCHIGUMO
JUST REMEMBER, 37, DON'T ANTICIPATE THE EXPLOSION.
CAUSE THE EXPLOSION.
NO.
37...MY, MY PARTNER...IS WEAK...
I... AM NOT... *WEAK!*
TIGER, WHAT...
WITHOUT HYPNOS IMPLANTS...
...I WILL... SEE YOU AS... YOU TRULY ARE.
I WILL *KILL* YOU AS YOU TRULY ARE--
WHAT... NO...

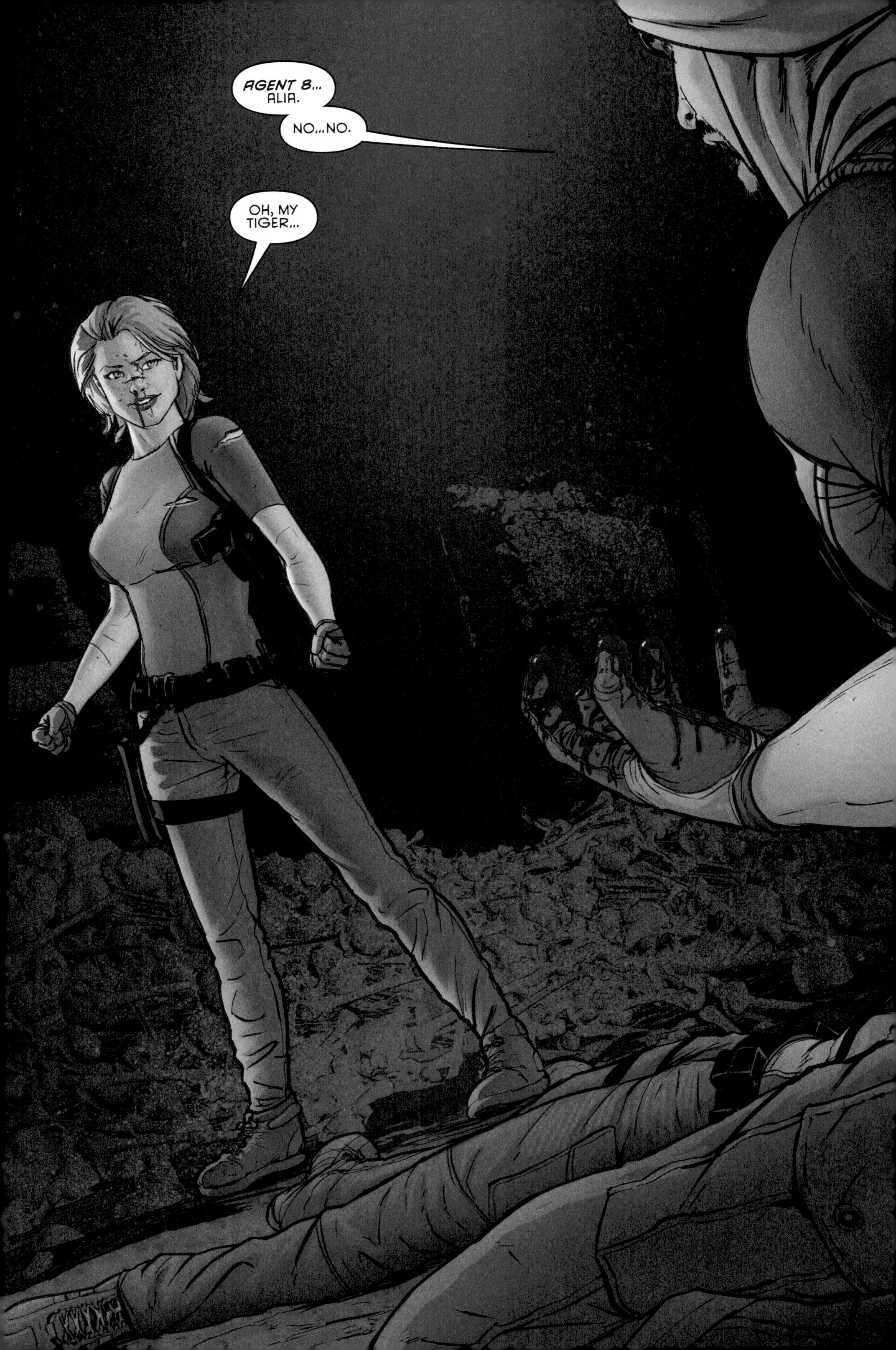
AGENT 8... ALIA.
NO...NO.
OH, MY TIGER...

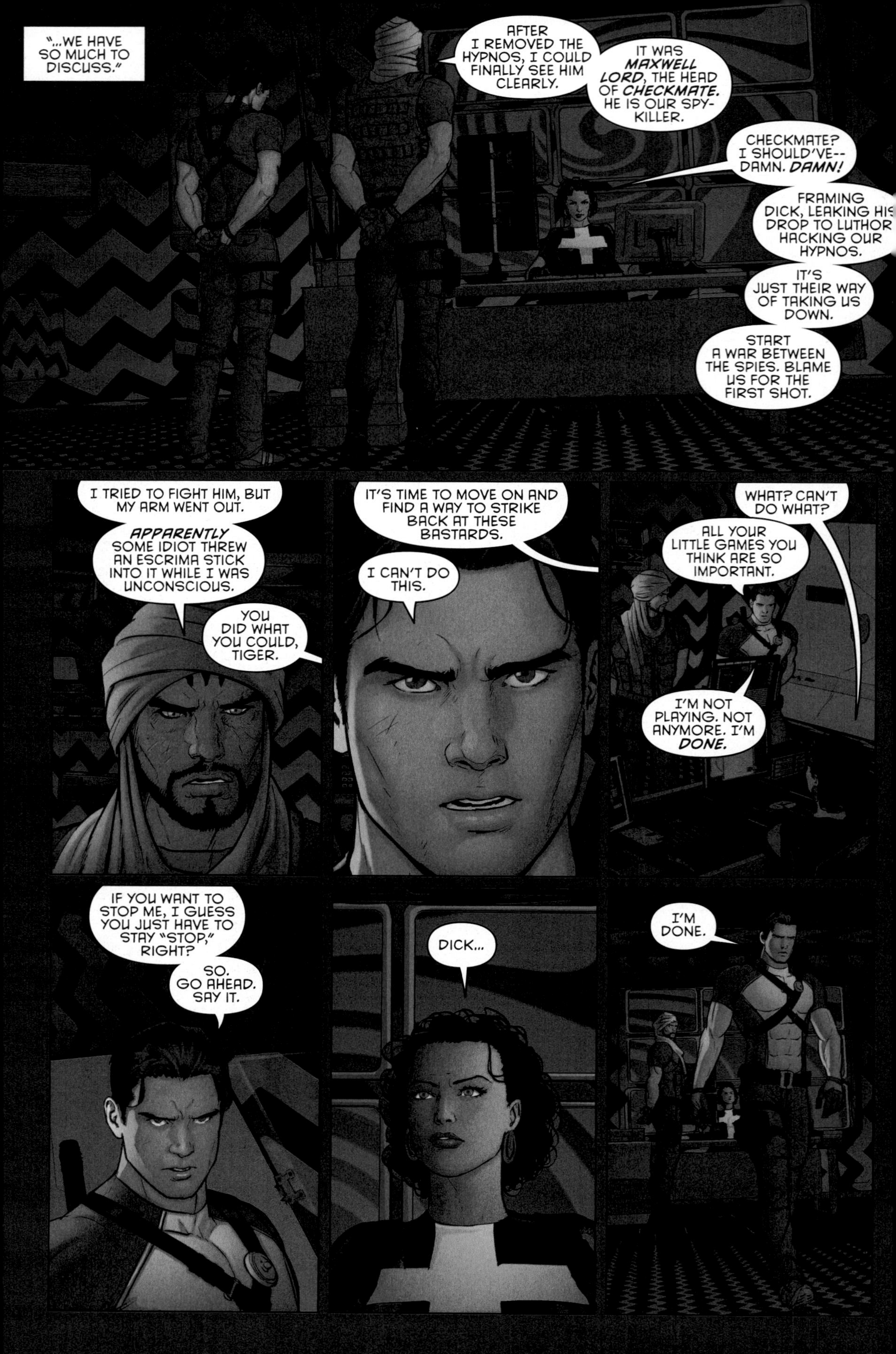
"...WE HAVE SO MUCH TO DISCUSS."
AFTER I REMOVED THE HYPNOS, I COULD FINALLY SEE HIM CLEARLY.
IT WAS *MAXWELL LORD*, THE HEAD OF *CHECKMATE.* HE IS OUR SPY-KILLER.
CHECKMATE? I SHOULD'VE-- DAMN. *DAMN!*
FRAMING DICK, LEAKING HIS DROP TO LUTHOR HACKING OUR HYPNOS.
IT'S JUST THEIR WAY OF TAKING US DOWN.
START A WAR BETWEEN THE SPIES. BLAME US FOR THE FIRST SHOT.
I TRIED TO FIGHT HIM, BUT MY ARM WENT OUT.
APPARENTLY SOME IDIOT THREW AN ESCRIMA STICK INTO IT WHILE I WAS UNCONSCIOUS.
YOU DID WHAT YOU COULD, TIGER.
IT'S TIME TO MOVE ON AND FIND A WAY TO STRIKE BACK AT THESE BASTARDS.
I CAN'T DO THIS.
WHAT? CAN'T DO WHAT?
ALL YOUR LITTLE GAMES YOU THINK ARE SO IMPORTANT.
I'M NOT PLAYING. NOT ANYMORE. I'M *DONE.*
IF YOU WANT TO STOP ME, I GUESS YOU JUST HAVE TO STAY "STOP," RIGHT?
SO. GO AHEAD. SAY IT.
DICK...
I'M DONE.

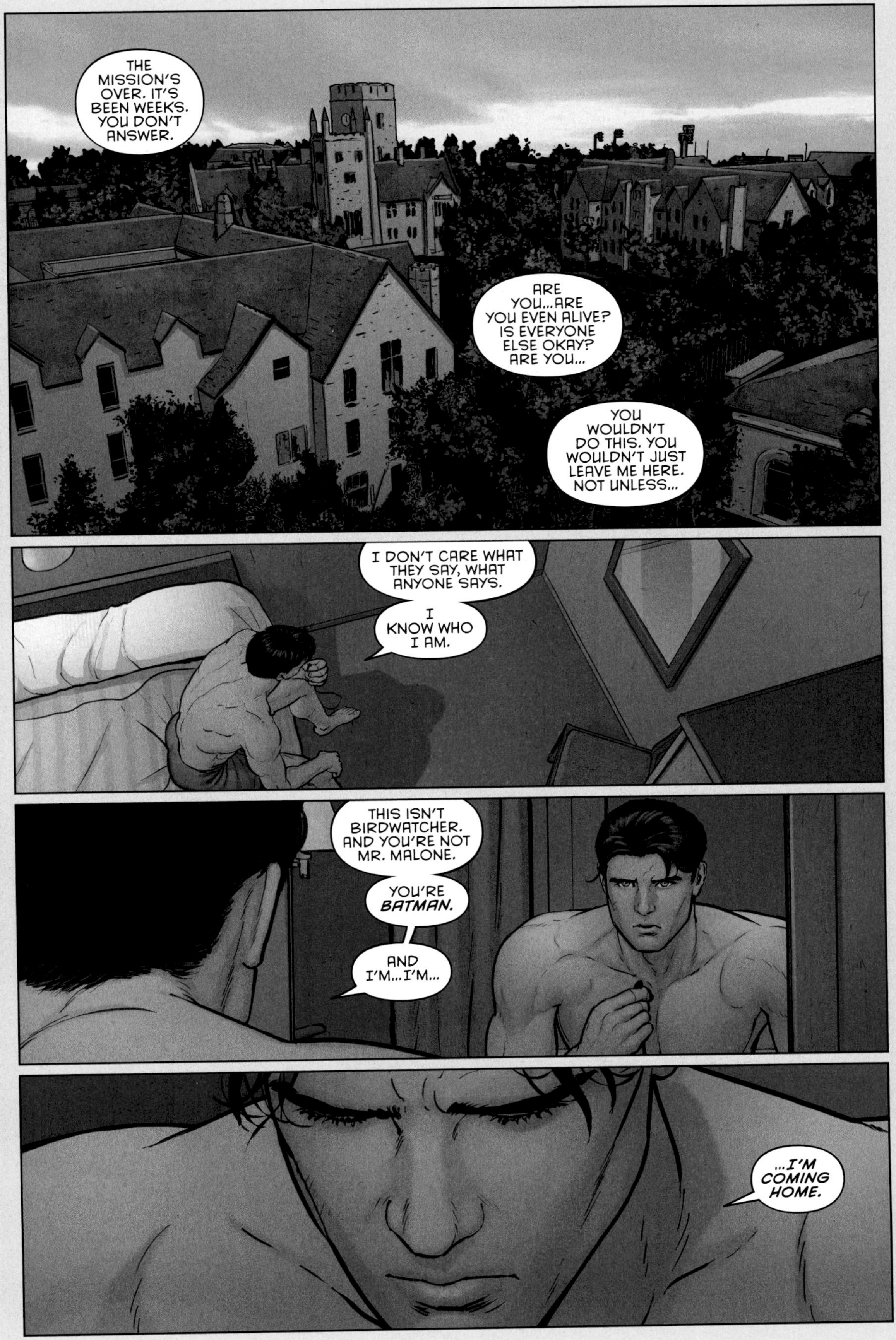
THE MISSION'S OVER. IT'S BEEN WEEKS. YOU DON'T ANSWER.
ARE YOU...ARE YOU EVEN ALIVE? IS EVERYONE ELSE OKAY? ARE YOU...
YOU WOULDN'T DO THIS. YOU WOULDN'T JUST LEAVE ME HERE. NOT UNLESS...
I DON'T CARE WHAT THEY SAY, WHAT ANYONE SAYS.
I KNOW WHO I AM.
THIS ISN'T BIRDWATCHER. AND YOU'RE NOT MR. MALONE.
YOU'RE BATMAN.
AND I'M...I'M...
...I'M COMING HOME.

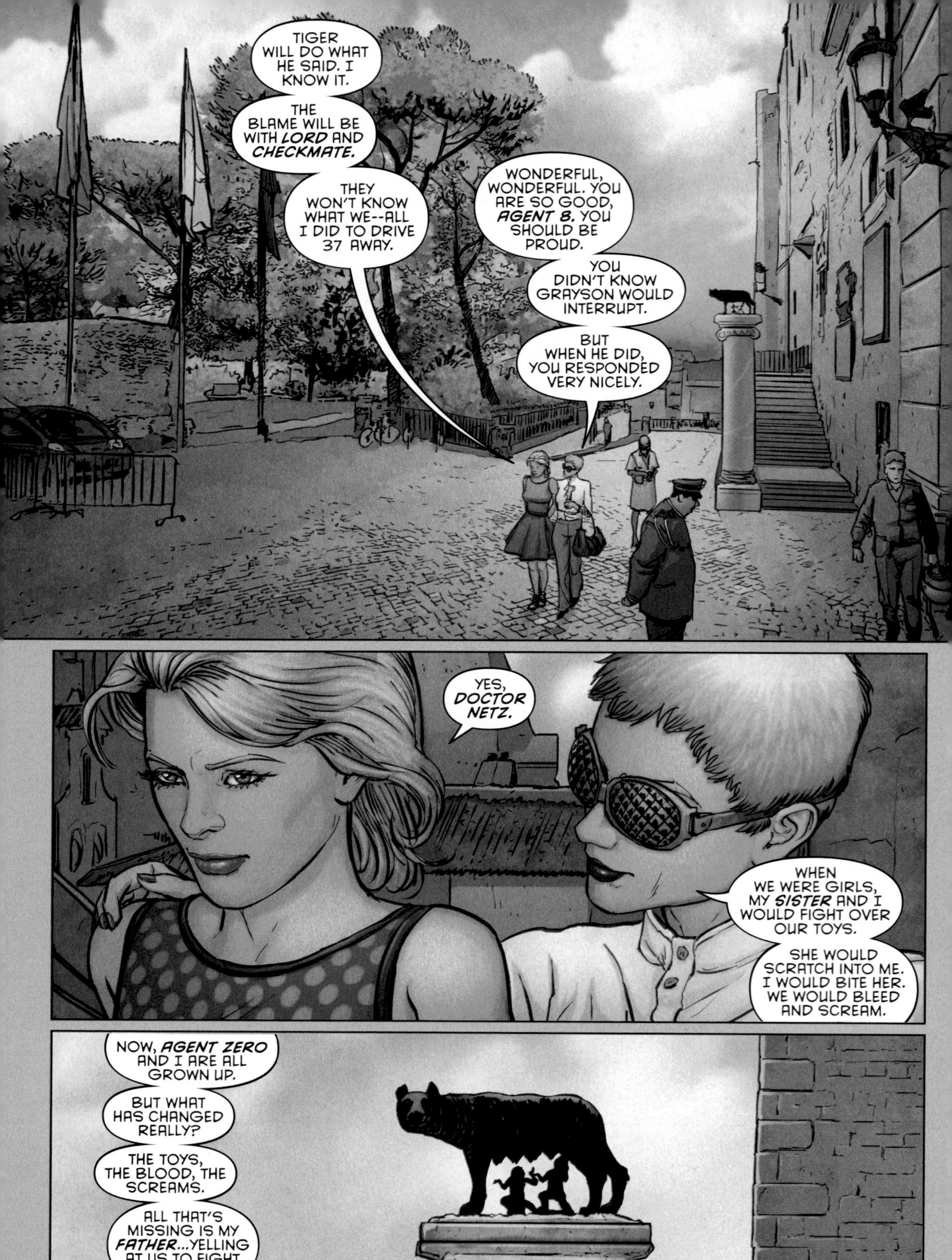
TIGER WILL DO WHAT HE SAID. I KNOW IT.
THE BLAME WILL BE WITH LORD AND CHECKMATE.
THEY WON'T KNOW WHAT WE--ALL I DID TO DRIVE 37 AWAY.
WONDERFUL, WONDERFUL. YOU ARE SO GOOD, AGENT 8. YOU SHOULD BE PROUD.
YOU DIDN'T KNOW GRAYSON WOULD INTERRUPT.
BUT WHEN HE DID, YOU RESPONDED VERY NICELY.
YES, DOCTOR NETZ.
WHEN WE WERE GIRLS, MY SISTER AND I WOULD FIGHT OVER OUR TOYS.
SHE WOULD SCRATCH INTO ME. I WOULD BITE HER. WE WOULD BLEED AND SCREAM.
NOW, AGENT ZERO AND I ARE ALL GROWN UP.
BUT WHAT HAS CHANGED REALLY?
THE TOYS, THE BLOOD, THE SCREAMS.
ALL THAT'S MISSING IS MY FATHER...YELLING AT US TO FIGHT HARDER.

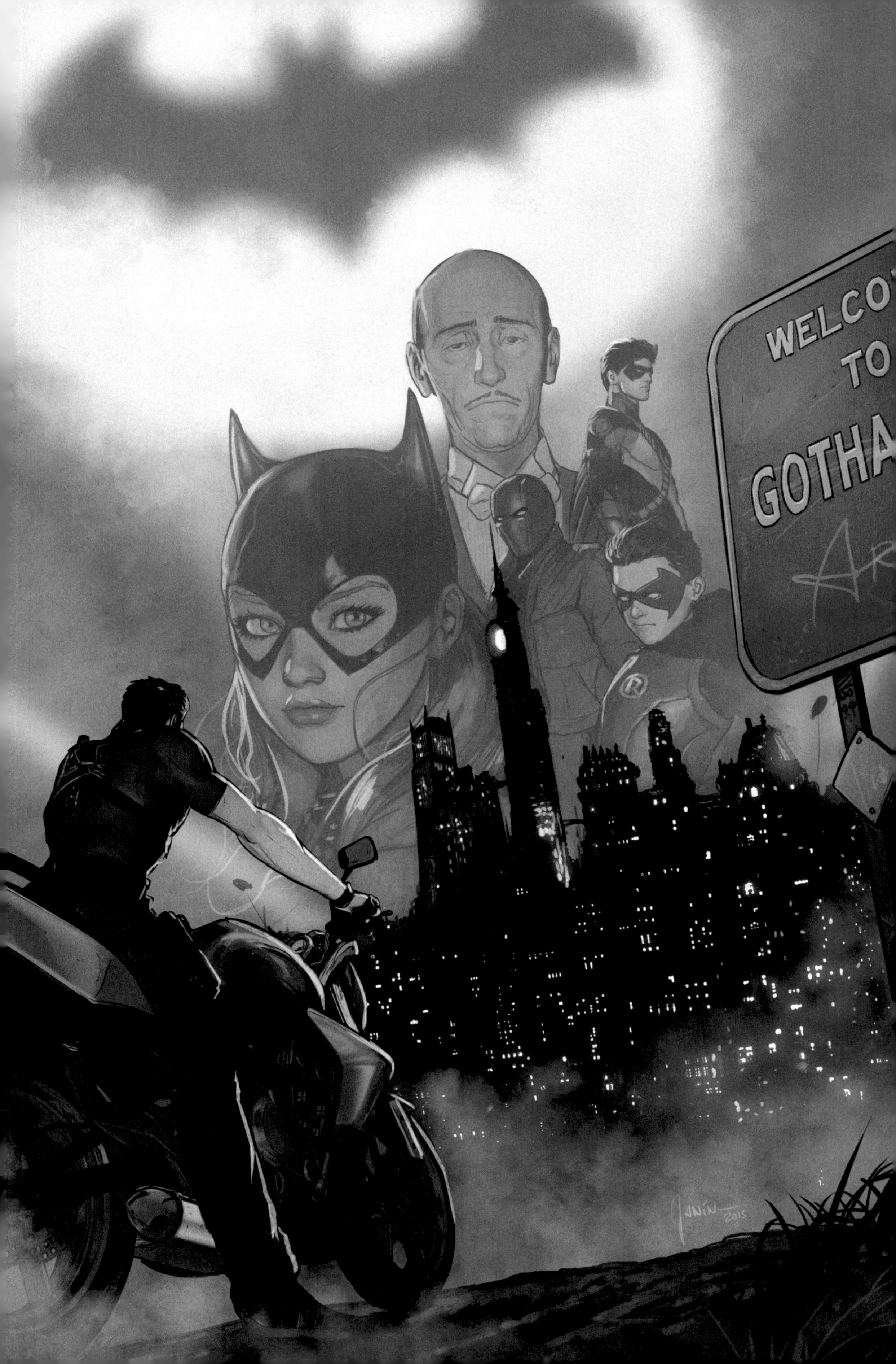
WELCO
TO
GOTHA

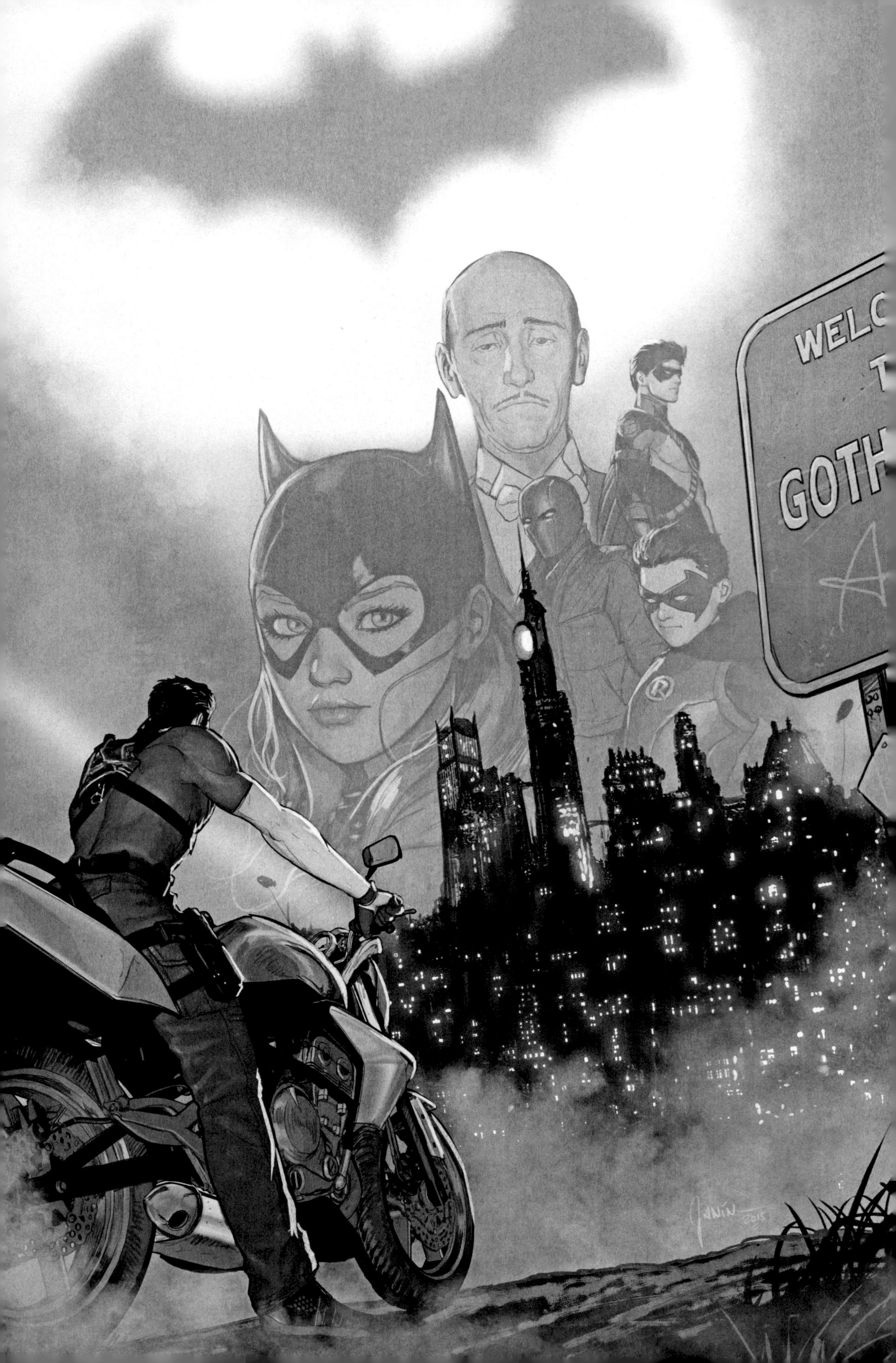
WELC
GOTH

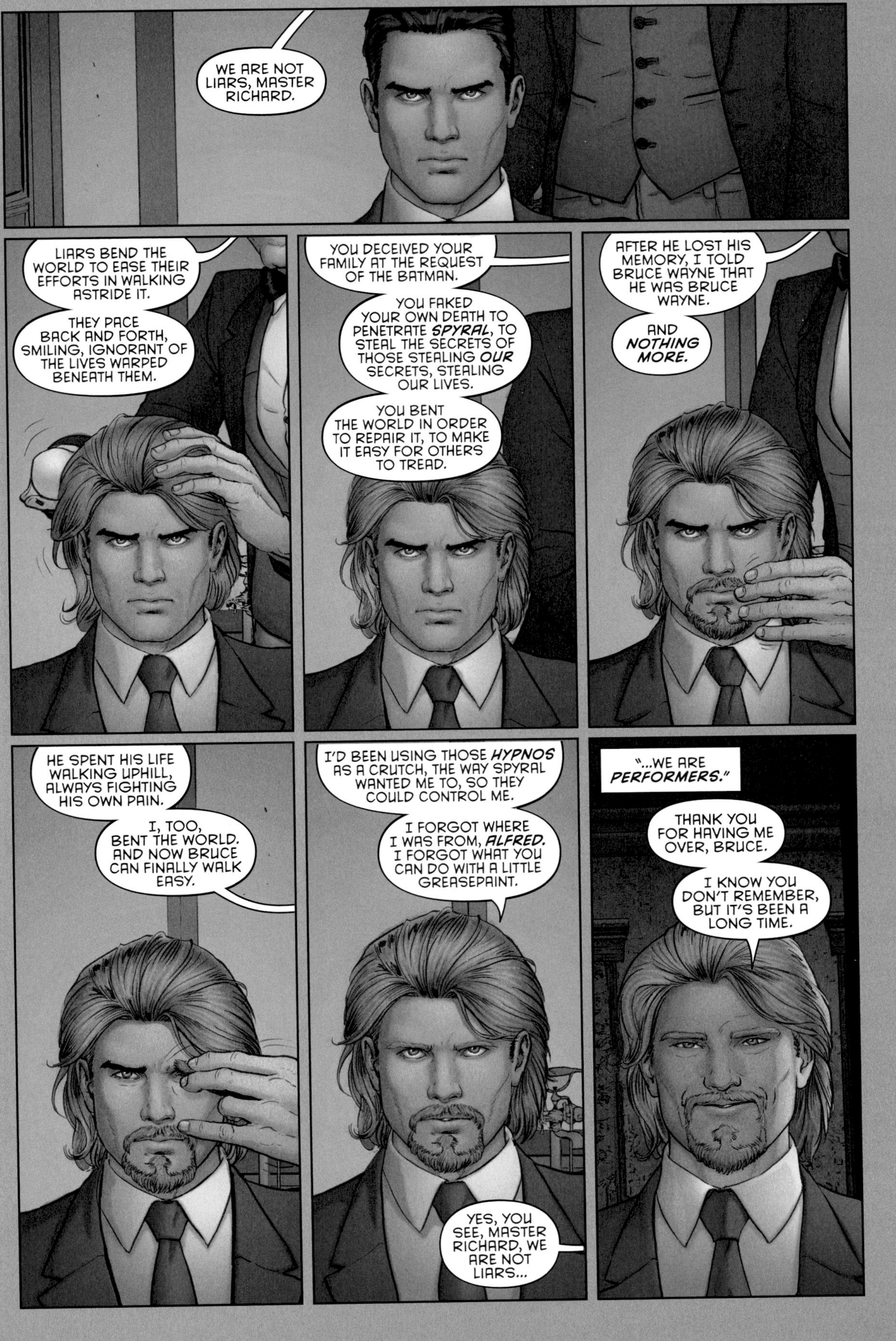
WE ARE NOT LIARS, MASTER RICHARD.
LIARS BEND THE WORLD TO EASE THEIR EFFORTS IN WALKING ASTRIDE IT.
THEY PACE BACK AND FORTH, SMILING, IGNORANT OF THE LIVES WARPED BENEATH THEM.
YOU DECEIVED YOUR FAMILY AT THE REQUEST OF THE BATMAN.
YOU FAKED YOUR OWN DEATH TO PENETRATE SPYRAL, TO STEAL THE SECRETS OF THOSE STEALING OUR SECRETS, STEALING OUR LIVES.
YOU BENT THE WORLD IN ORDER TO REPAIR IT, TO MAKE IT EASY FOR OTHERS TO TREAD.
AFTER HE LOST HIS MEMORY, I TOLD BRUCE WAYNE THAT HE WAS BRUCE WAYNE.
AND NOTHING MORE.
HE SPENT HIS LIFE WALKING UPHILL, ALWAYS FIGHTING HIS OWN PAIN.
I, TOO, BENT THE WORLD. AND NOW BRUCE CAN FINALLY WALK EASY.
I'D BEEN USING THOSE HYPNOS AS A CRUTCH, THE WAY SPYRAL WANTED ME TO, SO THEY COULD CONTROL ME.
I FORGOT WHERE I WAS FROM, ALFRED. I FORGOT WHAT YOU CAN DO WITH A LITTLE GREASEPAINT.
YES, YOU SEE, MASTER RICHARD, WE ARE NOT LIARS...
"...WE ARE PERFORMERS."
THANK YOU FOR HAVING ME OVER, BRUCE.
I KNOW YOU DON'T REMEMBER, BUT IT'S BEEN A LONG TIME.

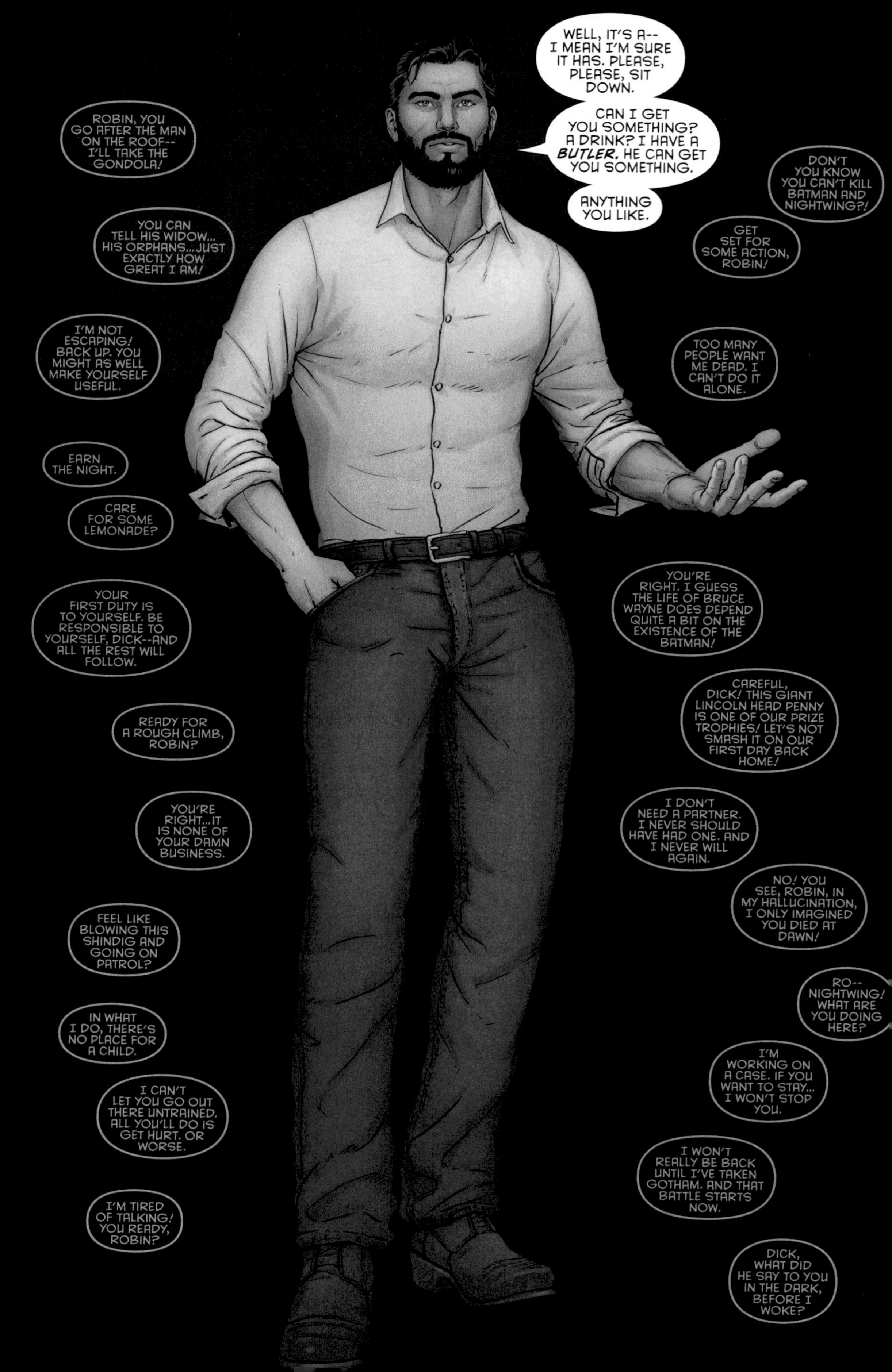
WELL, IT'S A-- I MEAN I'M SURE IT HAS. PLEASE, PLEASE, SIT DOWN.
CAN I GET YOU SOMETHING? A DRINK? I HAVE A *BUTLER.* HE CAN GET YOU SOMETHING.
ANYTHING YOU LIKE.
ROBIN, YOU GO AFTER THE MAN ON THE ROOF-- I'LL TAKE THE GONDOLA!
YOU CAN TELL HIS WIDOW... HIS ORPHANS...JUST EXACTLY HOW GREAT I AM!
I'M NOT ESCAPING! BACK UP. YOU MIGHT AS WELL MAKE YOURSELF USEFUL.
EARN THE NIGHT.
CARE FOR SOME LEMONADE?
YOUR FIRST DUTY IS TO YOURSELF. BE RESPONSIBLE TO YOURSELF, DICK--AND ALL THE REST WILL FOLLOW.
READY FOR A ROUGH CLIMB, ROBIN?
YOU'RE RIGHT...IT IS NONE OF YOUR DAMN BUSINESS.
FEEL LIKE BLOWING THIS SHINDIG AND GOING ON PATROL?
IN WHAT I DO, THERE'S NO PLACE FOR A CHILD.
I CAN'T LET YOU GO OUT THERE UNTRAINED. ALL YOU'LL DO IS GET HURT. OR WORSE.
I'M TIRED OF TALKING! YOU READY, ROBIN?
DON'T YOU KNOW YOU CAN'T KILL BATMAN AND NIGHTWING?!
GET SET FOR SOME ACTION, ROBIN!
TOO MANY PEOPLE WANT ME DEAD. I CAN'T DO IT ALONE.
YOU'RE RIGHT. I GUESS THE LIFE OF BRUCE WAYNE DOES DEPEND QUITE A BIT ON THE EXISTENCE OF THE BATMAN!
CAREFUL, DICK! THIS GIANT LINCOLN HEAD PENNY IS ONE OF OUR PRIZE TROPHIES! LET'S NOT SMASH IT ON OUR FIRST DAY BACK HOME!
I DON'T NEED A PARTNER. I NEVER SHOULD HAVE HAD ONE. AND I NEVER WILL AGAIN.
NO! YOU SEE, ROBIN, IN MY HALLUCINATION, I ONLY IMAGINED YOU DIED AT DAWN!
RO-- NIGHTWING! WHAT ARE YOU DOING HERE?
I'M WORKING ON A CASE. IF YOU WANT TO STAY... I WON'T STOP YOU.
I WON'T REALLY BE BACK UNTIL I'VE TAKEN GOTHAM. AND THAT BATTLE STARTS NOW.
DICK, WHAT DID HE SAY TO YOU IN THE DARK, BEFORE I WOKE?

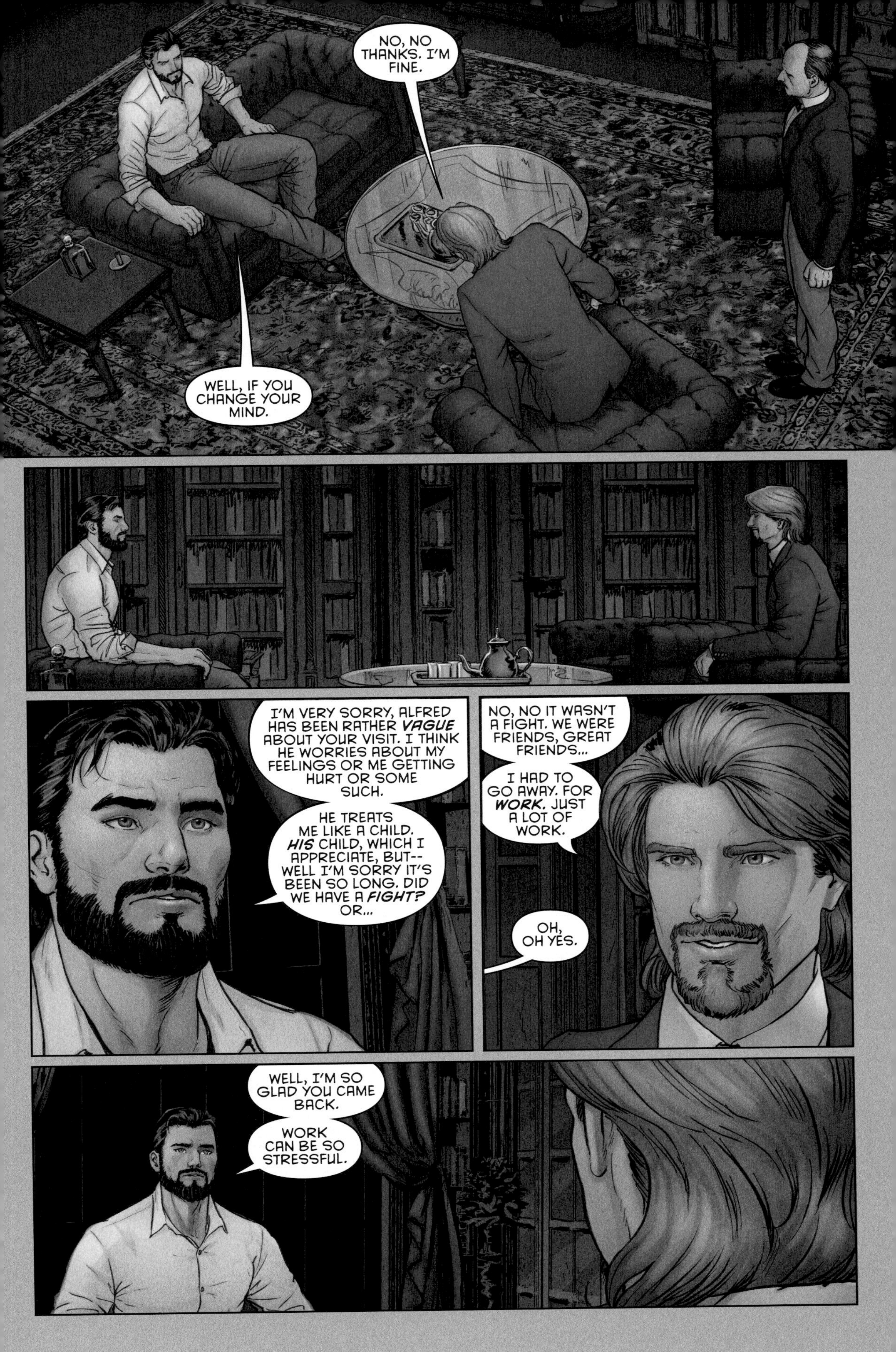

NO, NO THANKS. I'M FINE.
WELL, IF YOU CHANGE YOUR MIND.
I'M VERY SORRY, ALFRED HAS BEEN RATHER *VAGUE* ABOUT YOUR VISIT. I THINK HE WORRIES ABOUT MY FEELINGS OR ME GETTING HURT OR SOME SUCH.
HE TREATS ME LIKE A CHILD. *HIS* CHILD, WHICH I APPRECIATE, BUT-- WELL I'M SORRY IT'S BEEN SO LONG. DID WE HAVE A *FIGHT?* OR...
NO, NO IT WASN'T A FIGHT. WE WERE FRIENDS, GREAT FRIENDS...
I HAD TO GO AWAY. FOR *WORK.* JUST A LOT OF WORK.
OH, OH YES.
WELL, I'M SO GLAD YOU CAME BACK.
WORK CAN BE SO STRESSFUL.

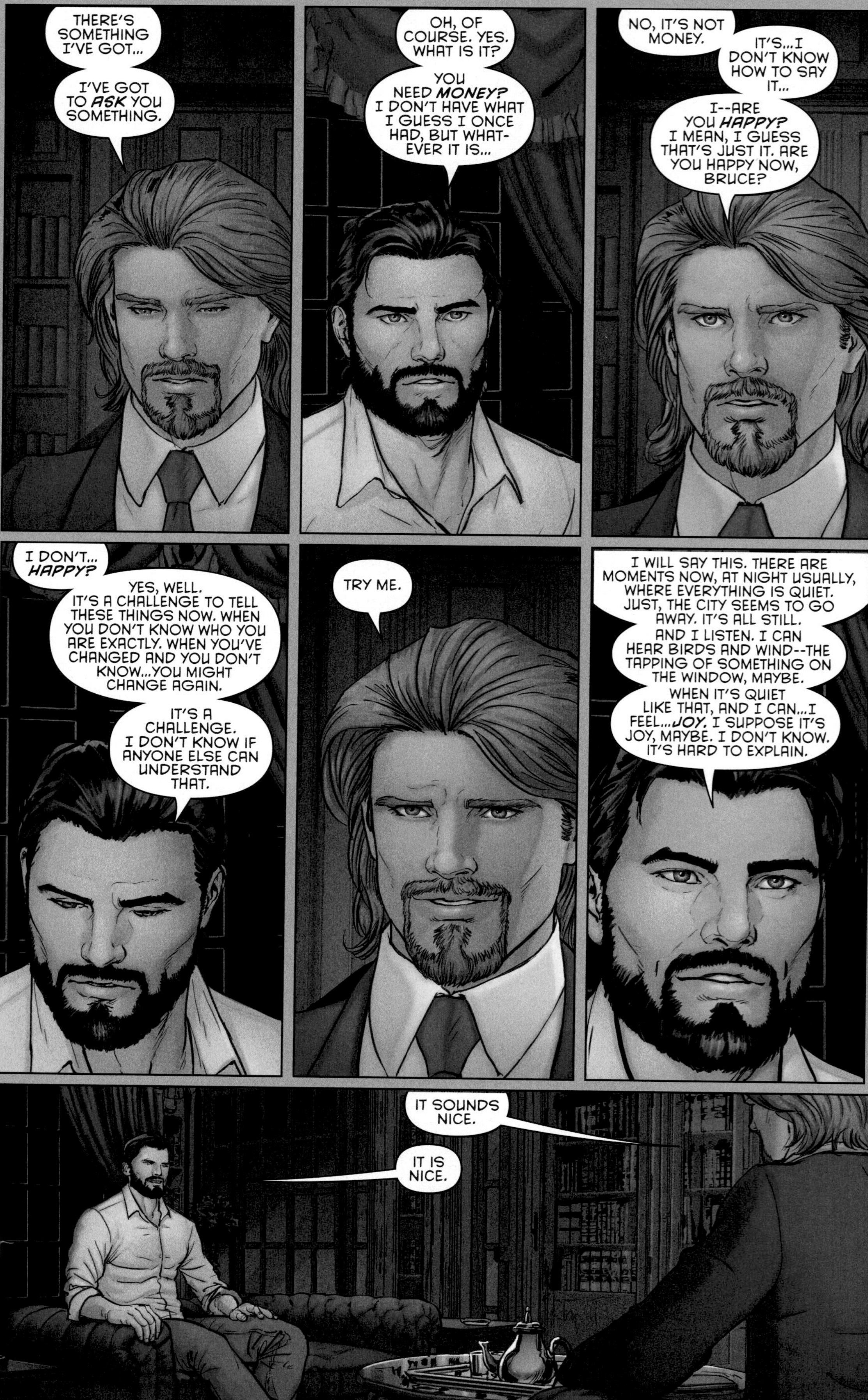
THERE'S SOMETHING I'VE GOT...
I'VE GOT TO ASK YOU SOMETHING.
OH, OF COURSE. YES. WHAT IS IT?
YOU NEED MONEY? I DON'T HAVE WHAT I GUESS I ONCE HAD, BUT WHATEVER IT IS...
NO, IT'S NOT MONEY.
IT'S...I DON'T KNOW HOW TO SAY IT...
I--ARE YOU HAPPY? I MEAN, I GUESS THAT'S JUST IT. ARE YOU HAPPY NOW, BRUCE?
I DON'T... HAPPY?
YES, WELL. IT'S A CHALLENGE TO TELL THESE THINGS NOW. WHEN YOU DON'T KNOW WHO YOU ARE EXACTLY. WHEN YOU'VE CHANGED AND YOU DON'T KNOW...YOU MIGHT CHANGE AGAIN.
IT'S A CHALLENGE. I DON'T KNOW IF ANYONE ELSE CAN UNDERSTAND THAT.
TRY ME.
I WILL SAY THIS. THERE ARE MOMENTS NOW, AT NIGHT USUALLY, WHERE EVERYTHING IS QUIET. JUST, THE CITY SEEMS TO GO AWAY. IT'S ALL STILL.
AND I LISTEN. I CAN HEAR BIRDS AND WIND--THE TAPPING OF SOMETHING ON THE WINDOW, MAYBE.
WHEN IT'S QUIET LIKE THAT, AND I CAN...I FEEL...JOY. I SUPPOSE IT'S JOY, MAYBE. I DON'T KNOW. IT'S HARD TO EXPLAIN.
IT SOUNDS NICE.
IT IS NICE.

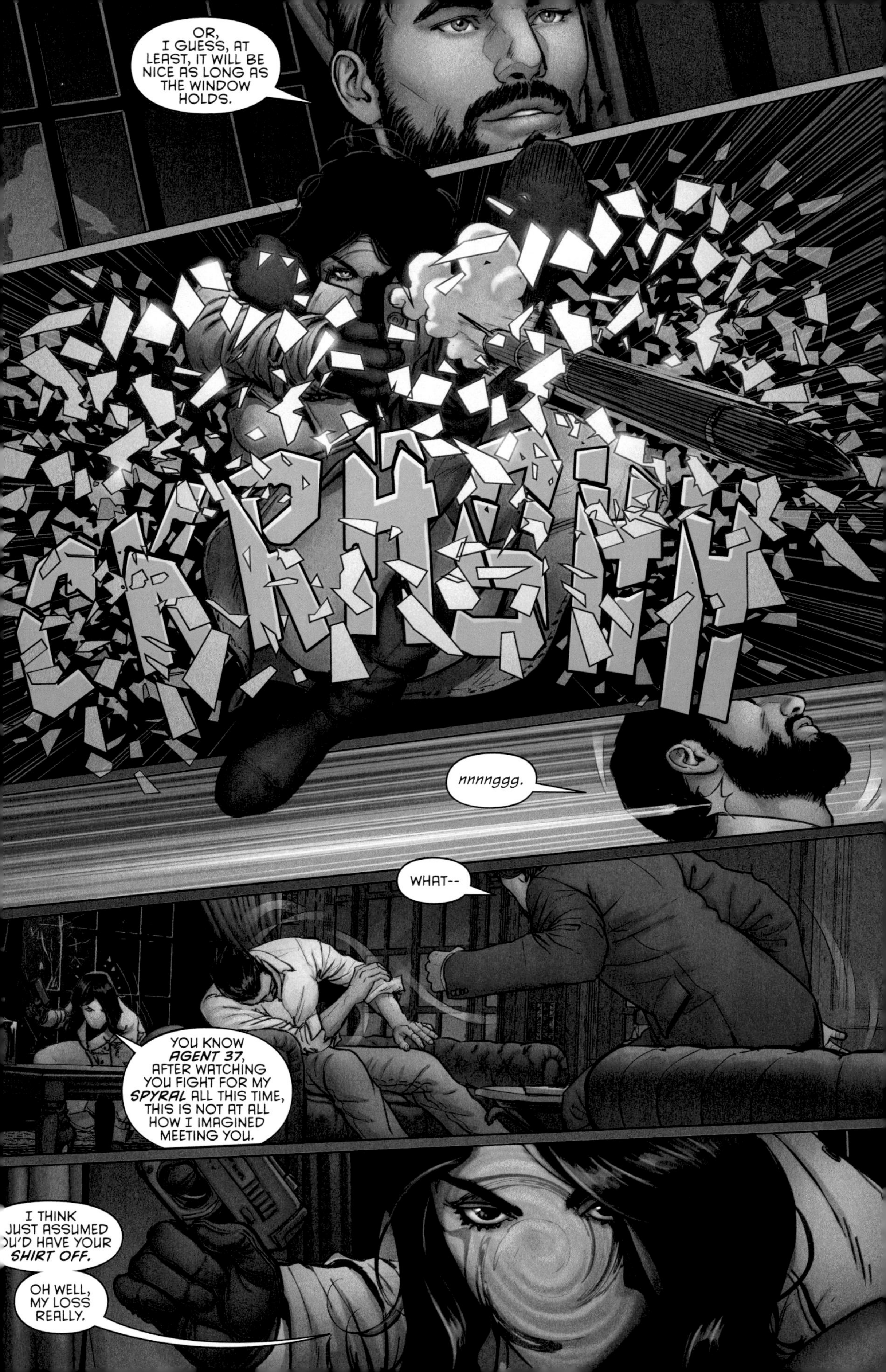
OR, I GUESS, AT LEAST, IT WILL BE NICE AS LONG AS THE WINDOW HOLDS.
CRASSH!!
nnnnggg.
WHAT--
YOU KNOW AGENT 37, AFTER WATCHING YOU FIGHT FOR MY SPYRAL ALL THIS TIME, THIS IS NOT AT ALL HOW I IMAGINED MEETING YOU.
I THINK JUST ASSUMED YOU'D HAVE YOUR SHIRT OFF.
OH WELL, MY LOSS REALLY.

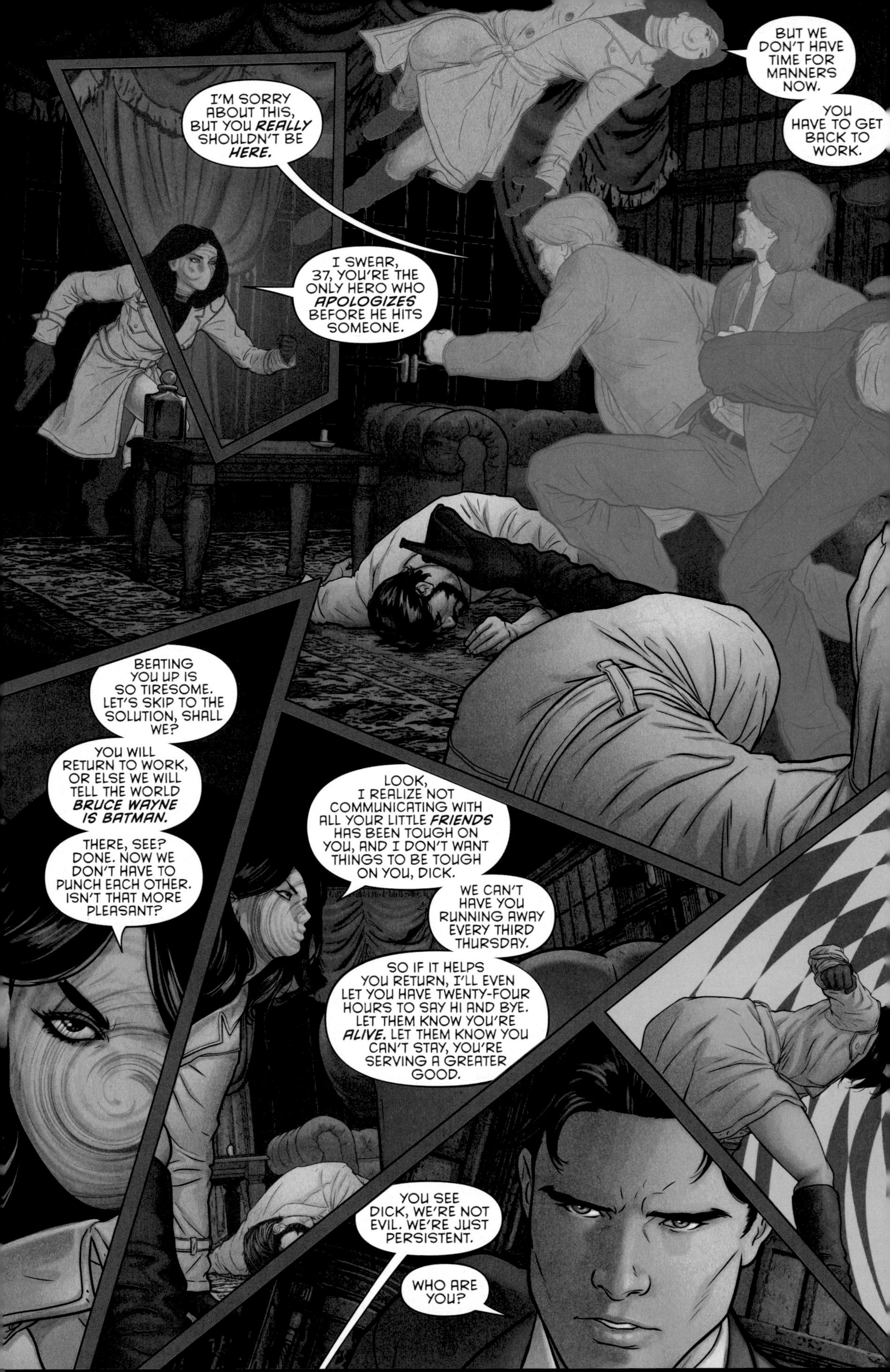
BUT WE DON'T HAVE TIME FOR MANNERS NOW.
YOU HAVE TO GET BACK TO WORK.
I'M SORRY ABOUT THIS, BUT YOU REALLY SHOULDN'T BE HERE.
I SWEAR, 37, YOU'RE THE ONLY HERO WHO APOLOGIZES BEFORE HE HITS SOMEONE.
BEATING YOU UP IS SO TIRESOME. LET'S SKIP TO THE SOLUTION, SHALL WE?
YOU WILL RETURN TO WORK, OR ELSE WE WILL TELL THE WORLD BRUCE WAYNE IS BATMAN.
THERE, SEE? DONE. NOW WE DON'T HAVE TO PUNCH EACH OTHER. ISN'T THAT MORE PLEASANT?
LOOK, I REALIZE NOT COMMUNICATING WITH ALL YOUR LITTLE FRIENDS HAS BEEN TOUGH ON YOU, AND I DON'T WANT THINGS TO BE TOUGH ON YOU, DICK.
WE CAN'T HAVE YOU RUNNING AWAY EVERY THIRD THURSDAY.
SO IF IT HELPS YOU RETURN, I'LL EVEN LET YOU HAVE TWENTY-FOUR HOURS TO SAY HI AND BYE. LET THEM KNOW YOU'RE ALIVE. LET THEM KNOW YOU CAN'T STAY, YOU'RE SERVING A GREATER GOOD.
YOU SEE DICK, WE'RE NOT EVIL. WE'RE JUST PERSISTENT.
WHO ARE YOU?

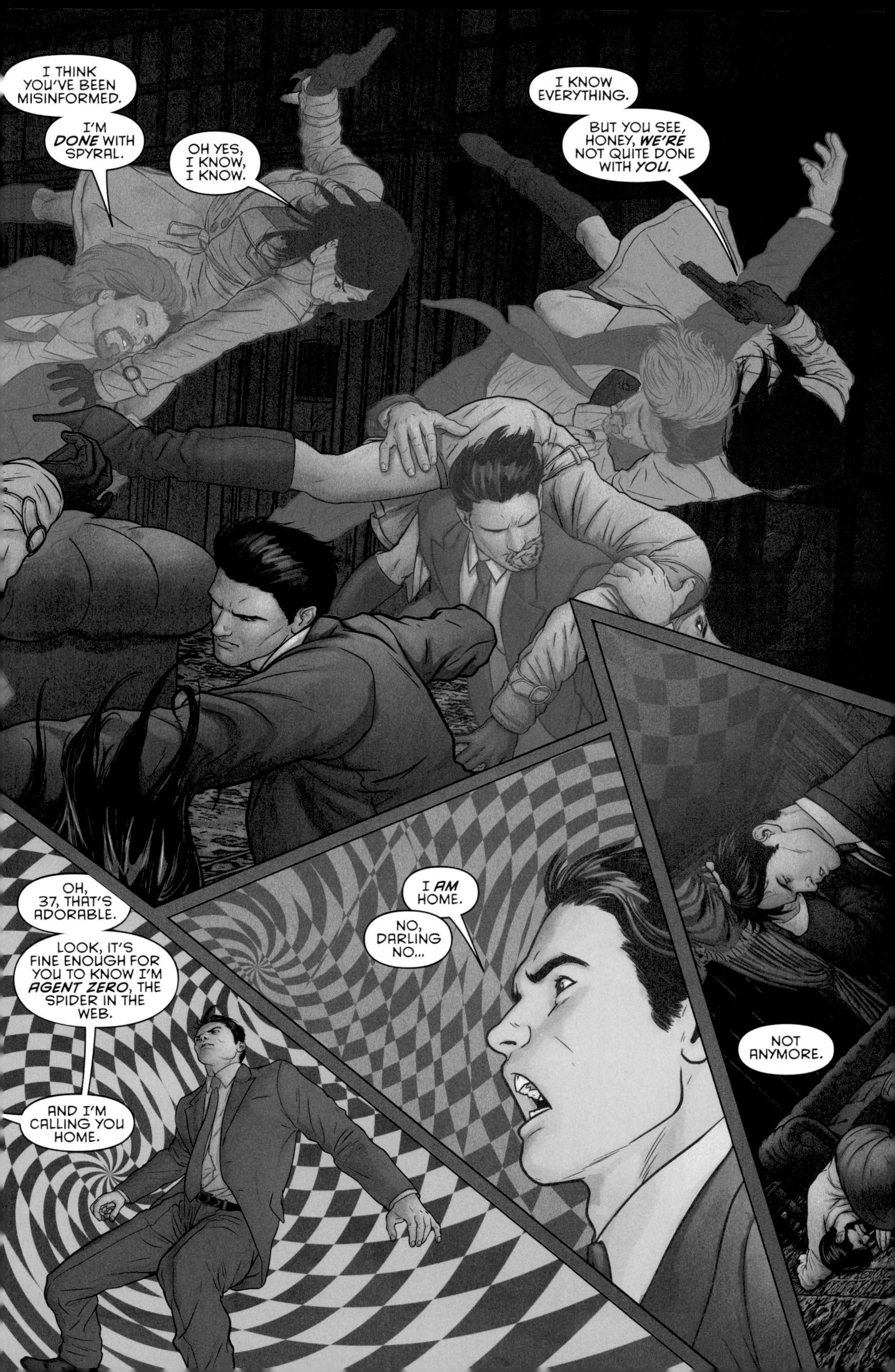

I THINK YOU'VE BEEN MISINFORMED.
I'M *DONE* WITH SPYRAL.
OH YES, I KNOW, I KNOW.
I KNOW EVERYTHING.
BUT YOU SEE, HONEY, *WE'RE* NOT QUITE DONE WITH *YOU.*
OH, 37, THAT'S ADORABLE.
LOOK, IT'S FINE ENOUGH FOR YOU TO KNOW I'M *AGENT ZERO*, THE SPIDER IN THE WEB.
AND I'M CALLING YOU HOME.
I *AM* HOME.
NO, DARLING NO...
NOT ANYMORE.

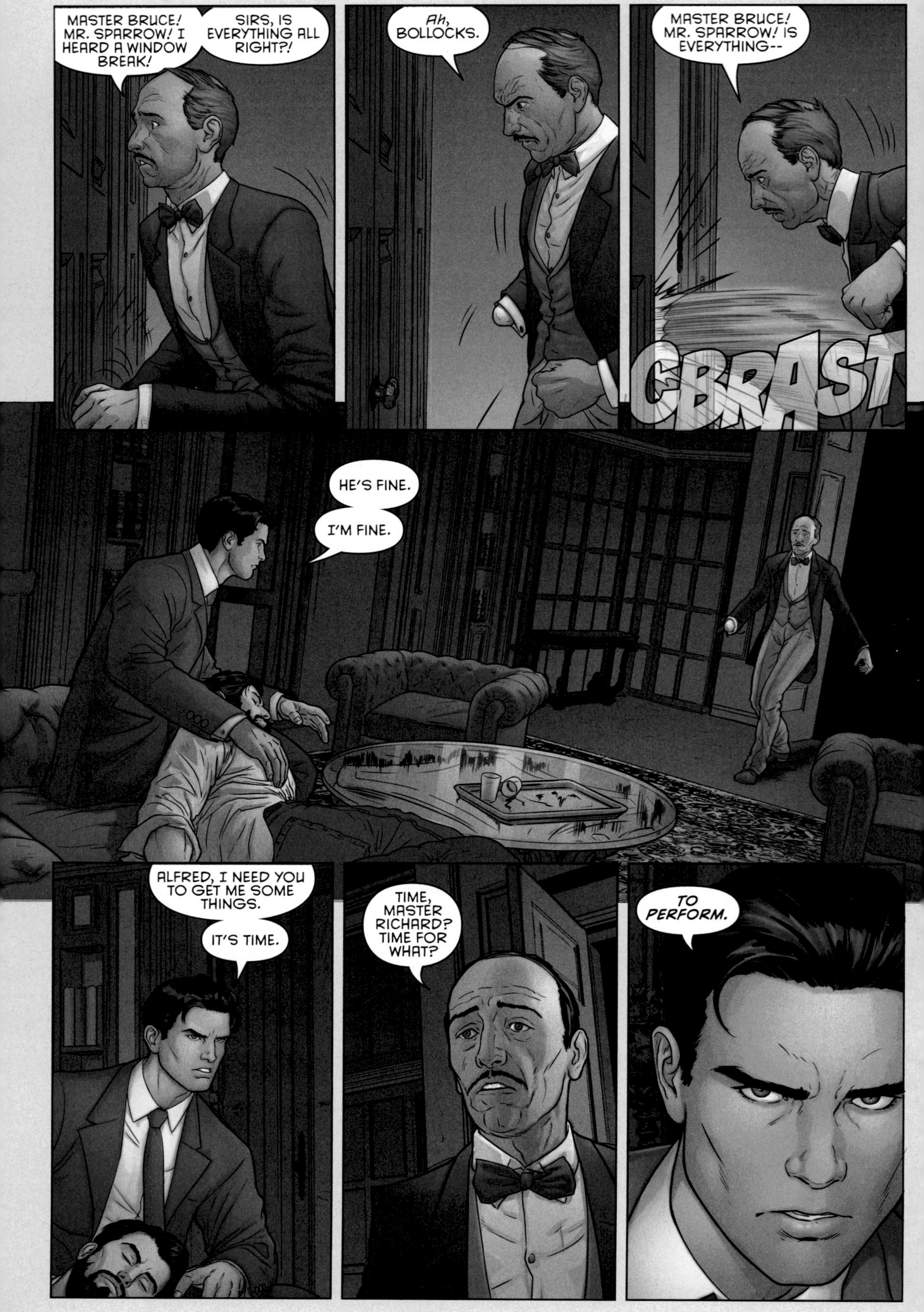
MASTER BRUCE! MR. SPARROW! I HEARD A WINDOW BREAK!
SIRS, IS EVERYTHING ALL RIGHT?!
Ah, BOLLOCKS.
MASTER BRUCE! MR. SPARROW! IS EVERYTHING--
CBRAST
HE'S FINE.
I'M FINE.
ALFRED, I NEED YOU TO GET ME SOME THINGS.
IT'S TIME.
TIME, MASTER RICHARD? TIME FOR WHAT?
TO PERFORM.

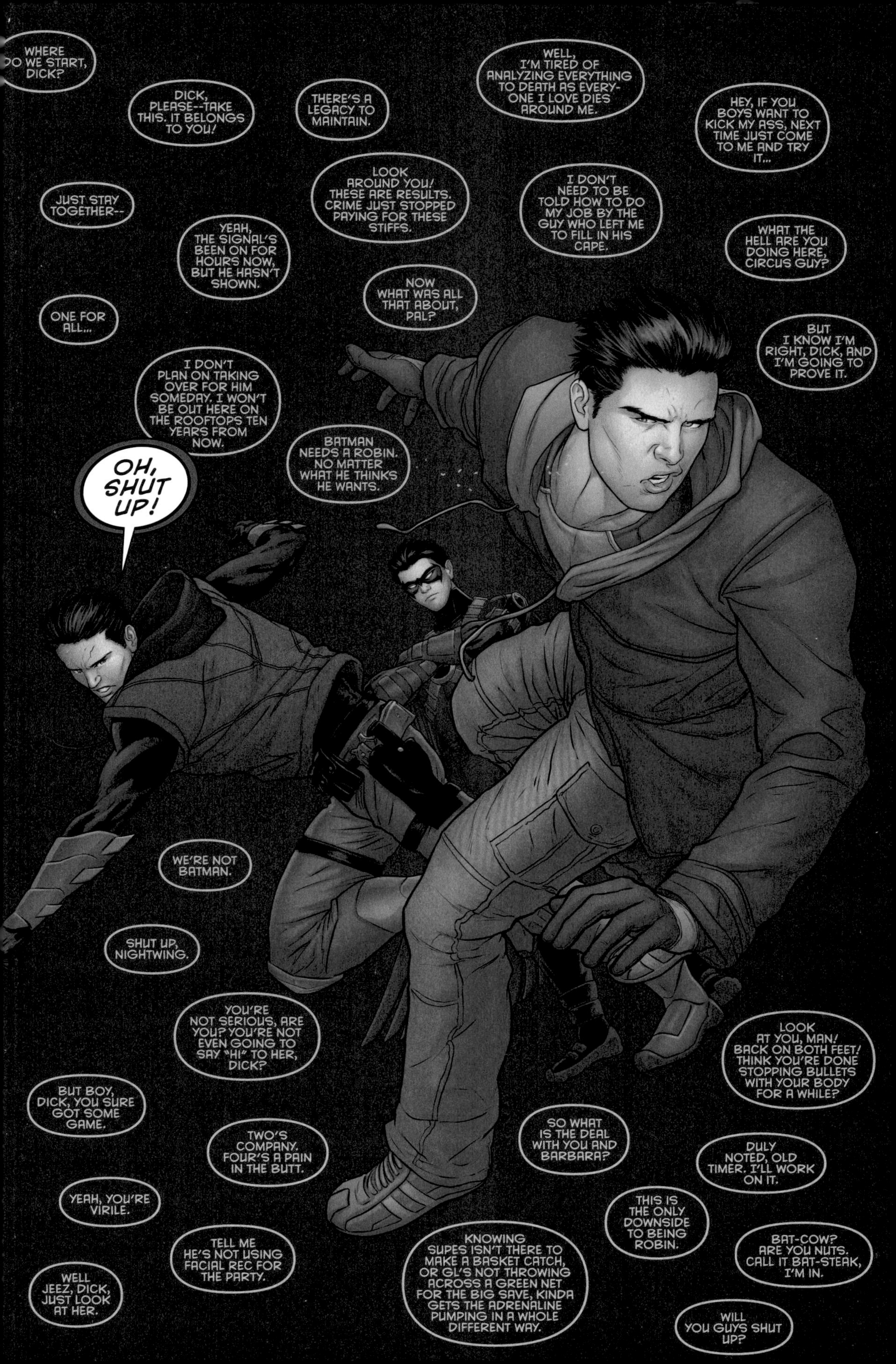

WHERE DO WE START, DICK?
DICK, PLEASE--TAKE THIS. IT BELONGS TO YOU!
THERE'S A LEGACY TO MAINTAIN.
WELL, I'M TIRED OF ANALYZING EVERYTHING TO DEATH AS EVERY-ONE I LOVE DIES AROUND ME.
HEY, IF YOU BOYS WANT TO KICK MY ASS, NEXT TIME JUST COME TO ME AND TRY IT...
JUST STAY TOGETHER--
LOOK AROUND YOU! THESE ARE RESULTS. CRIME JUST STOPPED PAYING FOR THESE STIFFS.
I DON'T NEED TO BE TOLD HOW TO DO MY JOB BY THE GUY WHO LEFT ME TO FILL IN HIS CAPE.
YEAH, THE SIGNAL'S BEEN ON FOR HOURS NOW, BUT HE HASN'T SHOWN.
WHAT THE HELL ARE YOU DOING HERE, CIRCUS GUY?
NOW WHAT WAS ALL THAT ABOUT, PAL?
ONE FOR ALL...
BUT I KNOW I'M RIGHT, DICK, AND I'M GOING TO PROVE IT.
I DON'T PLAN ON TAKING OVER FOR HIM SOMEDAY. I WON'T BE OUT HERE ON THE ROOFTOPS TEN YEARS FROM NOW.
BATMAN NEEDS A ROBIN. NO MATTER WHAT HE THINKS HE WANTS.
OH, SHUT UP!
WE'RE NOT BATMAN.
SHUT UP, NIGHTWING.
YOU'RE NOT SERIOUS, ARE YOU? YOU'RE NOT EVEN GOING TO SAY "HI" TO HER, DICK?
LOOK AT YOU, MAN! BACK ON BOTH FEET! THINK YOU'RE DONE STOPPING BULLETS WITH YOUR BODY FOR A WHILE?
BUT BOY, DICK, YOU SURE GOT SOME GAME.
TWO'S COMPANY. FOUR'S A PAIN IN THE BUTT.
SO WHAT IS THE DEAL WITH YOU AND BARBARA?
DULY NOTED, OLD TIMER. I'LL WORK ON IT.
YEAH, YOU'RE VIRILE.
THIS IS THE ONLY DOWNSIDE TO BEING ROBIN.
TELL ME HE'S NOT USING FACIAL REC FOR THE PARTY.
KNOWING SUPES ISN'T THERE TO MAKE A BASKET CATCH, OR GL'S NOT THROWING ACROSS A GREEN NET FOR THE BIG SAVE, KINDA GETS THE ADRENALINE PUMPING IN A WHOLE DIFFERENT WAY.
BAT-COW? ARE YOU NUTS. CALL IT BAT-STEAK, I'M IN.
WELL JEEZ, DICK, JUST LOOK AT HER.
WILL YOU GUYS SHUT UP?

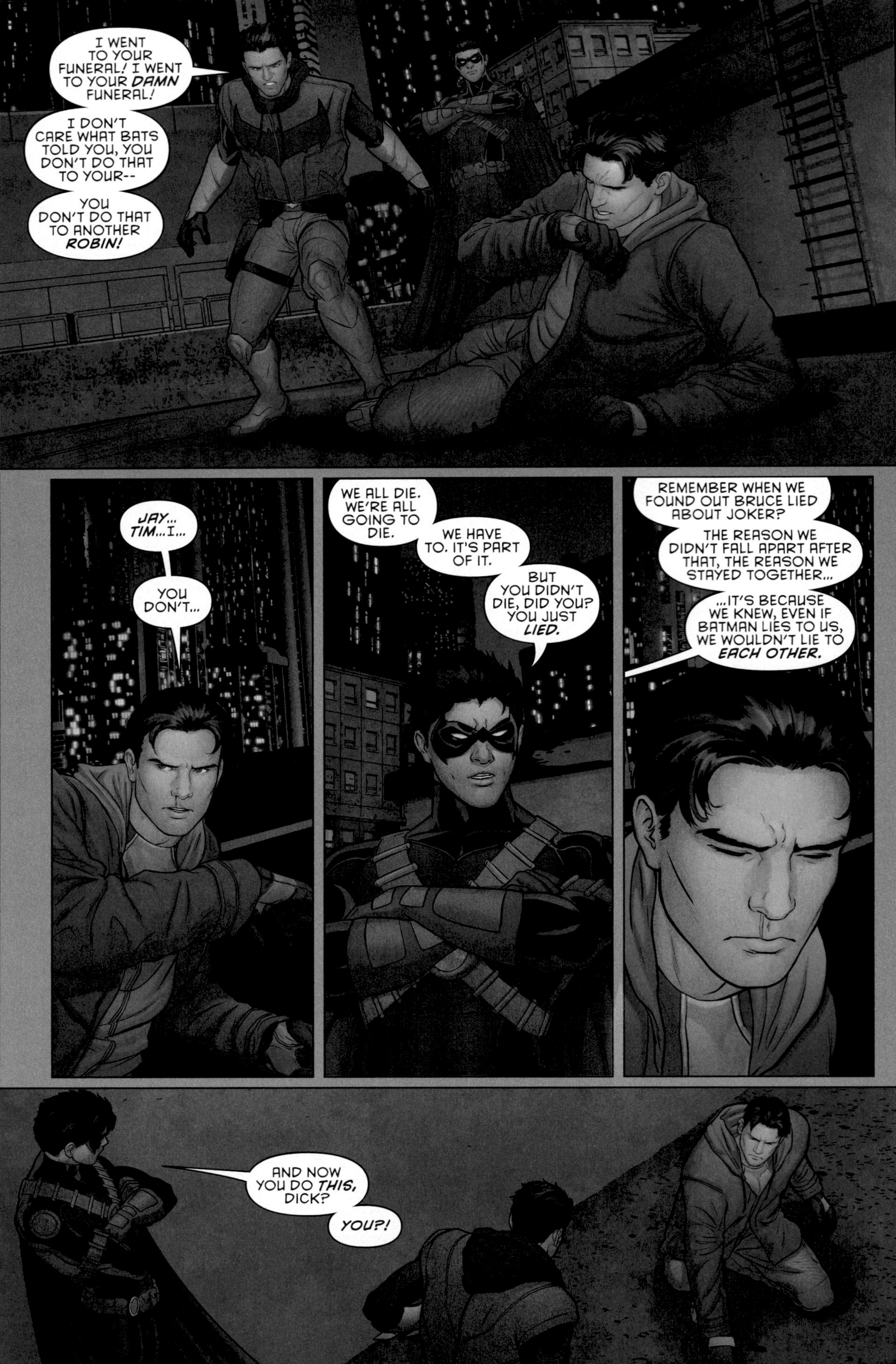
I WENT TO YOUR FUNERAL! I WENT TO YOUR DAMN FUNERAL!
I DON'T CARE WHAT BATS TOLD YOU, YOU DON'T DO THAT TO YOUR--
YOU DON'T DO THAT TO ANOTHER ROBIN!
JAY... TIM...I...
YOU DON'T...
WE ALL DIE. WE'RE ALL GOING TO DIE.
WE HAVE TO. IT'S PART OF IT.
BUT YOU DIDN'T DIE, DID YOU? YOU JUST LIED.
REMEMBER WHEN WE FOUND OUT BRUCE LIED ABOUT JOKER?
THE REASON WE DIDN'T FALL APART AFTER THAT, THE REASON WE STAYED TOGETHER...
...IT'S BECAUSE WE KNEW, EVEN IF BATMAN LIES TO US, WE WOULDN'T LIE TO EACH OTHER.
AND NOW YOU DO THIS, DICK?
YOU?!

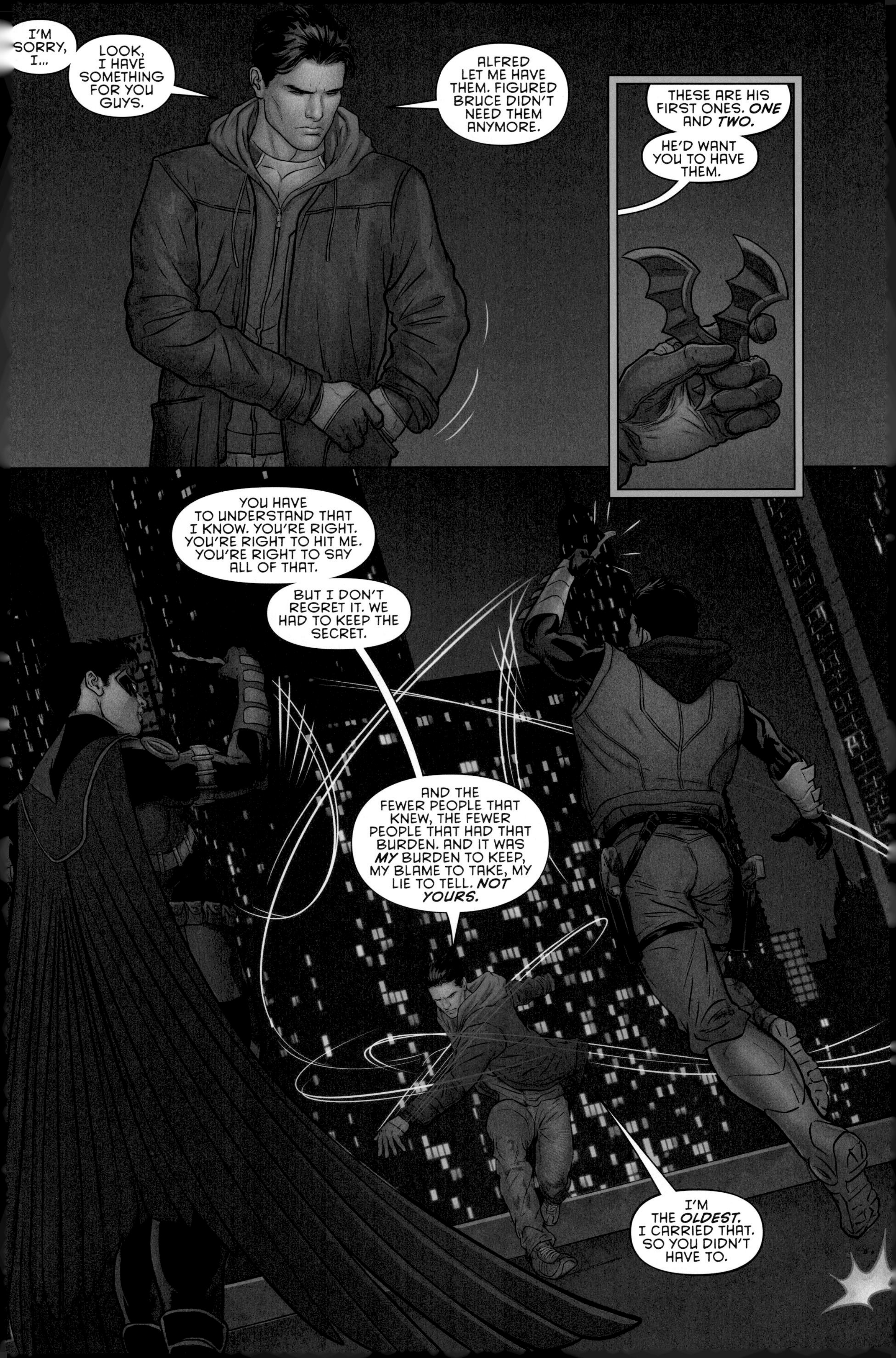
I'M SORRY, I...
LOOK, I HAVE SOMETHING FOR YOU GUYS.
ALFRED LET ME HAVE THEM. FIGURED BRUCE DIDN'T NEED THEM ANYMORE.
THESE ARE HIS FIRST ONES. *ONE* AND *TWO.*
HE'D WANT YOU TO HAVE THEM.
YOU HAVE TO UNDERSTAND THAT I KNOW. YOU'RE RIGHT. YOU'RE RIGHT TO HIT ME. YOU'RE RIGHT TO SAY ALL OF THAT.
BUT I DON'T REGRET IT. WE HAD TO KEEP THE SECRET.
AND THE FEWER PEOPLE THAT KNEW, THE FEWER PEOPLE THAT HAD THAT BURDEN. AND IT WAS *MY* BURDEN TO KEEP, MY BLAME TO TAKE, MY LIE TO TELL. *NOT YOURS.*
I'M THE *OLDEST.* I CARRIED THAT. SO YOU DIDN'T HAVE TO.

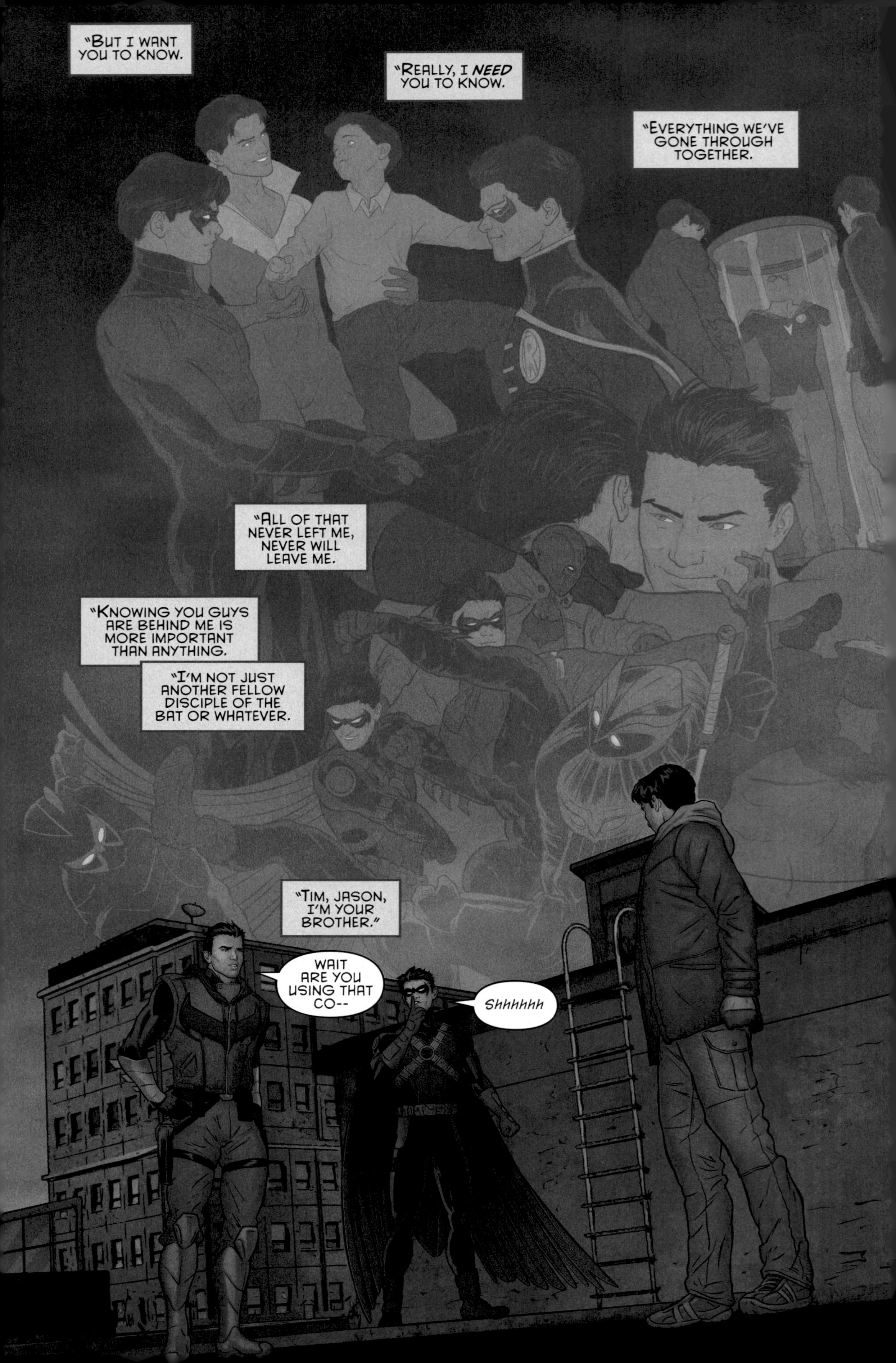
"But I want you to know.
"Really, I *need* you to know.
"Everything we've gone through together.
"All of that never left me, never will leave me.
"Knowing you guys are behind me is more important than anything.
"I'm not just another fellow disciple of the bat or whatever.
"Tim, Jason, I'm your brother."
Wait are you using that co--
Shhhhhh

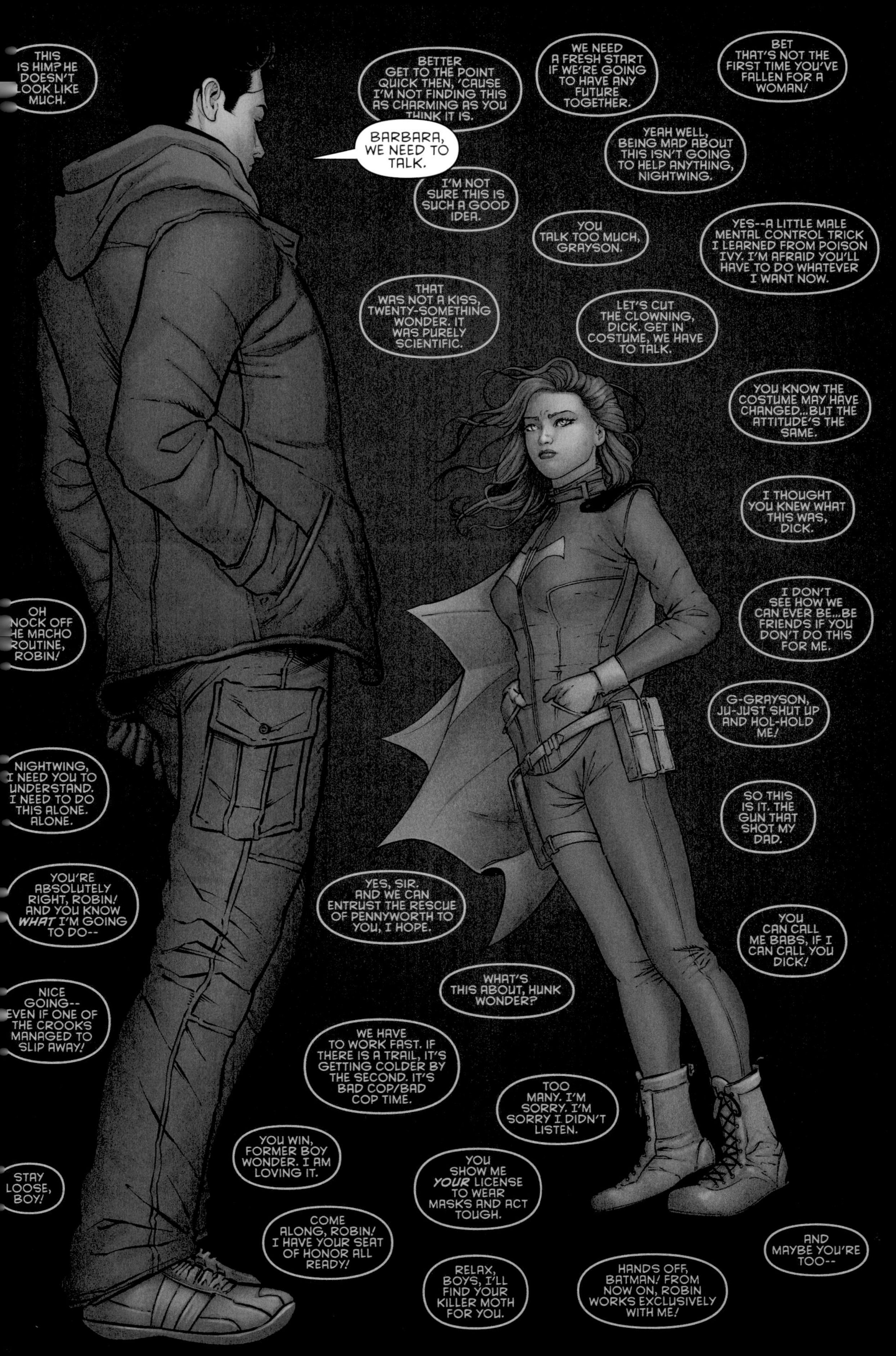

THIS IS HIM? HE DOESN'T OOK LIKE MUCH.
BETTER GET TO THE POINT QUICK THEN, 'CAUSE I'M NOT FINDING THIS AS CHARMING AS YOU THINK IT IS.
WE NEED A FRESH START IF WE'RE GOING TO HAVE ANY FUTURE TOGETHER.
BET THAT'S NOT THE FIRST TIME YOU'VE FALLEN FOR A WOMAN!
BARBARA, WE NEED TO TALK.
YEAH WELL, BEING MAD ABOUT THIS ISN'T GOING TO HELP ANYTHING, NIGHTWING.
I'M NOT SURE THIS IS SUCH A GOOD IDEA.
YOU TALK TOO MUCH, GRAYSON.
YES--A LITTLE MALE MENTAL CONTROL TRICK I LEARNED FROM POISON IVY. I'M AFRAID YOU'LL HAVE TO DO WHATEVER I WANT NOW.
THAT WAS NOT A KISS, TWENTY-SOMETHING WONDER. IT WAS PURELY SCIENTIFIC.
LET'S CUT THE CLOWNING, DICK. GET IN COSTUME, WE HAVE TO TALK.
YOU KNOW THE COSTUME MAY HAVE CHANGED...BUT THE ATTITUDE'S THE SAME.
I THOUGHT YOU KNEW WHAT THIS WAS, DICK.
OH NOCK OFF HE MACHO ROUTINE, ROBIN!
I DON'T SEE HOW WE CAN EVER BE...BE FRIENDS IF YOU DON'T DO THIS FOR ME.
G-GRAYSON, JU-JUST SHUT UP AND HOL-HOLD ME!
NIGHTWING, I NEED YOU TO UNDERSTAND. I NEED TO DO THIS ALONE. ALONE.
SO THIS IS IT. THE GUN THAT SHOT MY DAD.
YOU'RE ABSOLUTELY RIGHT, ROBIN! AND YOU KNOW *WHAT* I'M GOING TO DO--
YES, SIR. AND WE CAN ENTRUST THE RESCUE OF PENNYWORTH TO YOU, I HOPE.
YOU CAN CALL ME BABS, IF I CAN CALL YOU DICK!
WHAT'S THIS ABOUT, HUNK WONDER?
NICE GOING-- EVEN IF ONE OF THE CROOKS MANAGED TO SLIP AWAY!
WE HAVE TO WORK FAST. IF THERE IS A TRAIL, IT'S GETTING COLDER BY THE SECOND. IT'S BAD COP/BAD COP TIME.
TOO MANY. I'M SORRY. I'M SORRY I DIDN'T LISTEN.
YOU WIN, FORMER BOY WONDER. I AM LOVING IT.
STAY LOOSE, BOY!
YOU SHOW ME *YOUR* LICENSE TO WEAR MASKS AND ACT TOUGH.
COME ALONG, ROBIN! I HAVE YOUR SEAT OF HONOR ALL READY!
AND MAYBE YOU'RE TOO--
RELAX, BOYS, I'LL FIND YOUR KILLER MOTH FOR YOU.
HANDS OFF, BATMAN! FROM NOW ON, ROBIN WORKS EXCLUSIVELY WITH ME!

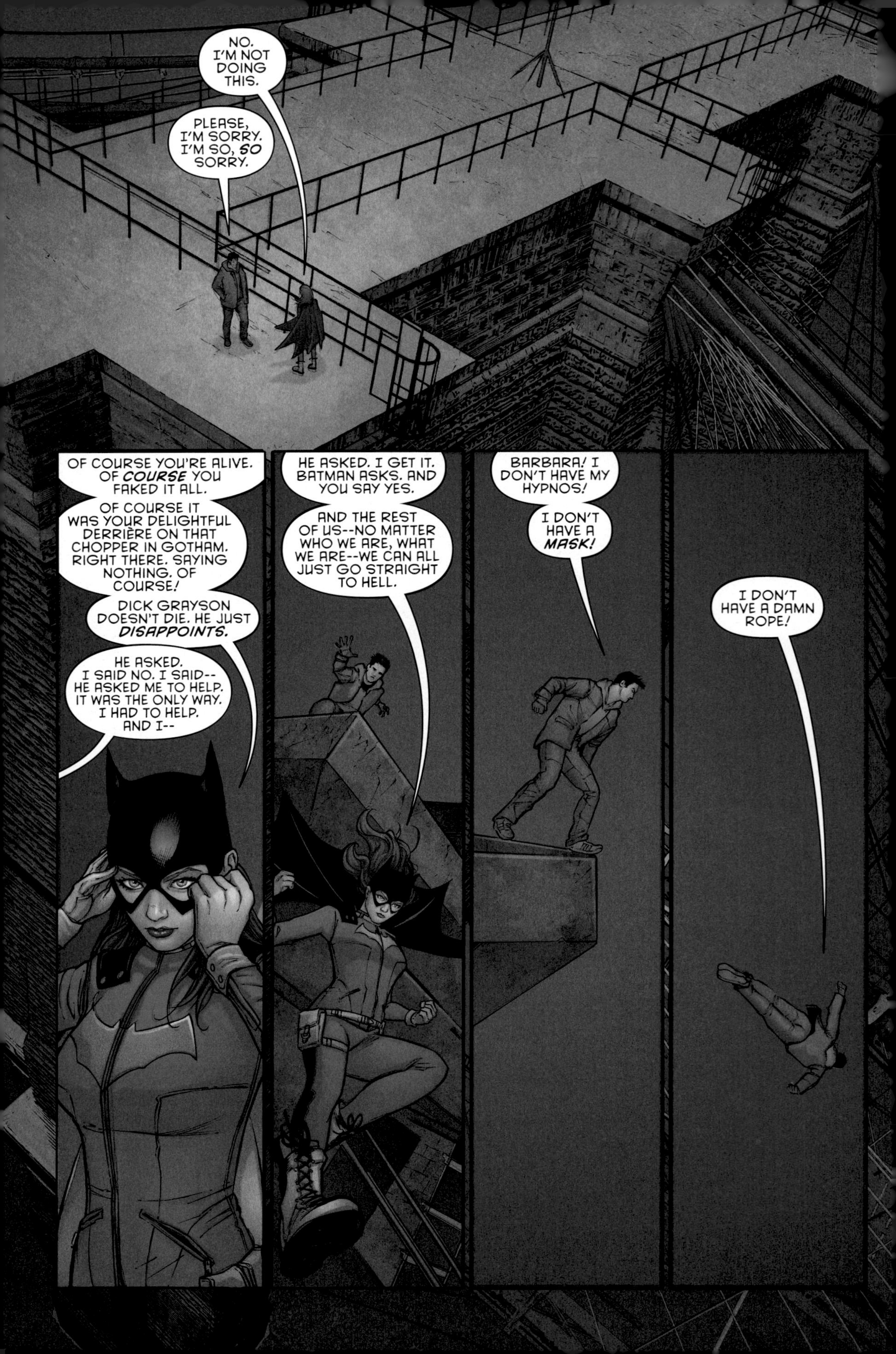
NO. I'M NOT DOING THIS.
PLEASE, I'M SORRY. I'M SO, SO SORRY.
OF COURSE YOU'RE ALIVE. OF COURSE YOU FAKED IT ALL.
OF COURSE IT WAS YOUR DELIGHTFUL DERRIÈRE ON THAT CHOPPER IN GOTHAM. RIGHT THERE. SAYING NOTHING. OF COURSE!
DICK GRAYSON DOESN'T DIE. HE JUST DISAPPOINTS.
HE ASKED. I SAID NO. I SAID-- HE ASKED ME TO HELP. IT WAS THE ONLY WAY. I HAD TO HELP. AND I--
HE ASKED. I GET IT. BATMAN ASKS. AND YOU SAY YES.
AND THE REST OF US--NO MATTER WHO WE ARE, WHAT WE ARE--WE CAN ALL JUST GO STRAIGHT TO HELL.
BARBARA! I DON'T HAVE MY HYPNOS!
I DON'T HAVE A MASK!
I DON'T HAVE A DAMN ROPE!

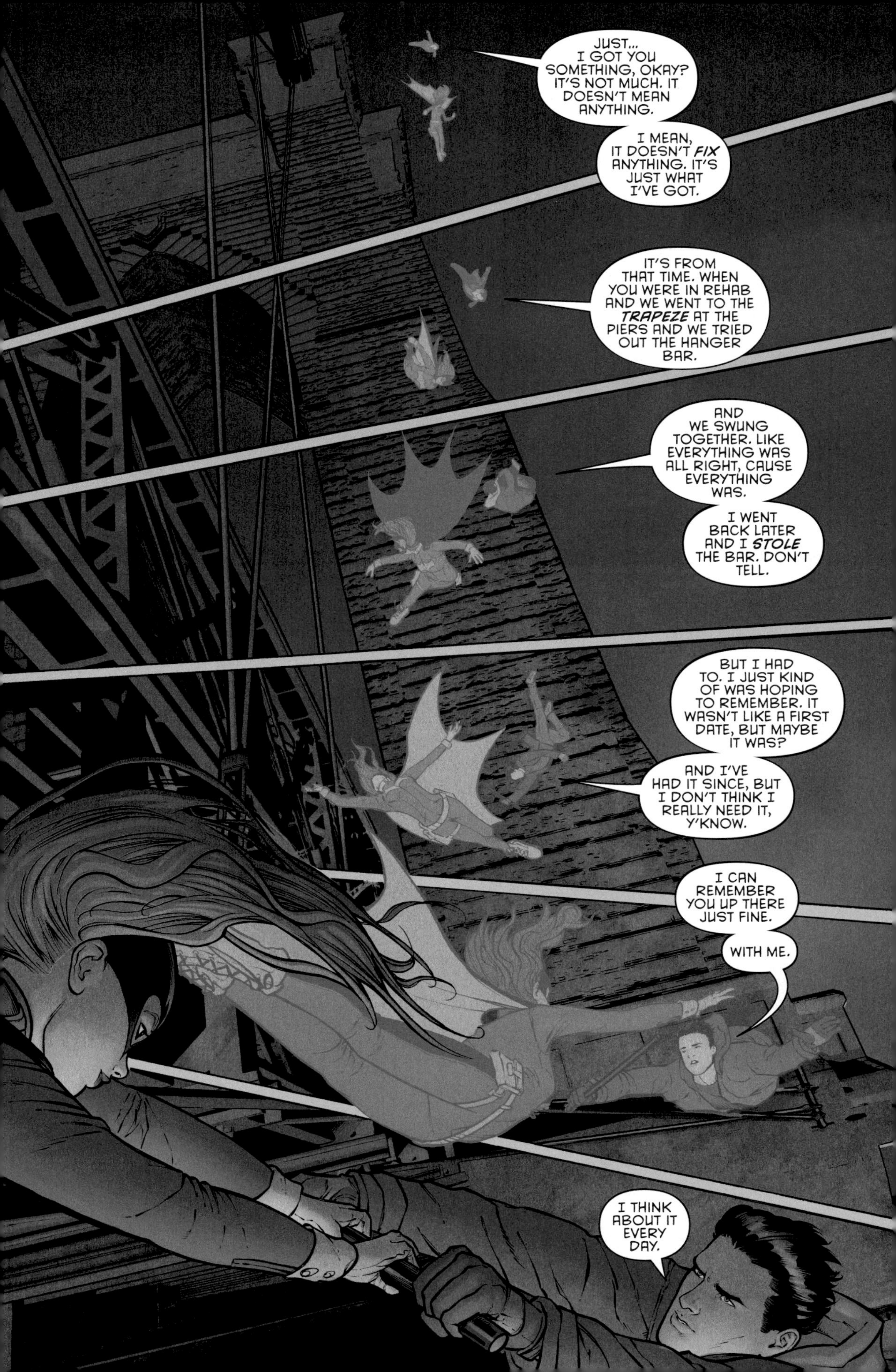
JUST... I GOT YOU SOMETHING, OKAY? IT'S NOT MUCH. IT DOESN'T MEAN ANYTHING.
I MEAN, IT DOESN'T FIX ANYTHING. IT'S JUST WHAT I'VE GOT.
IT'S FROM THAT TIME. WHEN YOU WERE IN REHAB AND WE WENT TO THE TRAPEZE AT THE PIERS AND WE TRIED OUT THE HANGER BAR.
AND WE SWUNG TOGETHER. LIKE EVERYTHING WAS ALL RIGHT, CAUSE EVERYTHING WAS.
I WENT BACK LATER AND I STOLE THE BAR. DON'T TELL.
BUT I HAD TO. I JUST KIND OF WAS HOPING TO REMEMBER. IT WASN'T LIKE A FIRST DATE, BUT MAYBE IT WAS?
AND I'VE HAD IT SINCE, BUT I DON'T THINK I REALLY NEED IT, Y'KNOW.
I CAN REMEMBER YOU UP THERE JUST FINE.
WITH ME.
I THINK ABOUT IT EVERY DAY.

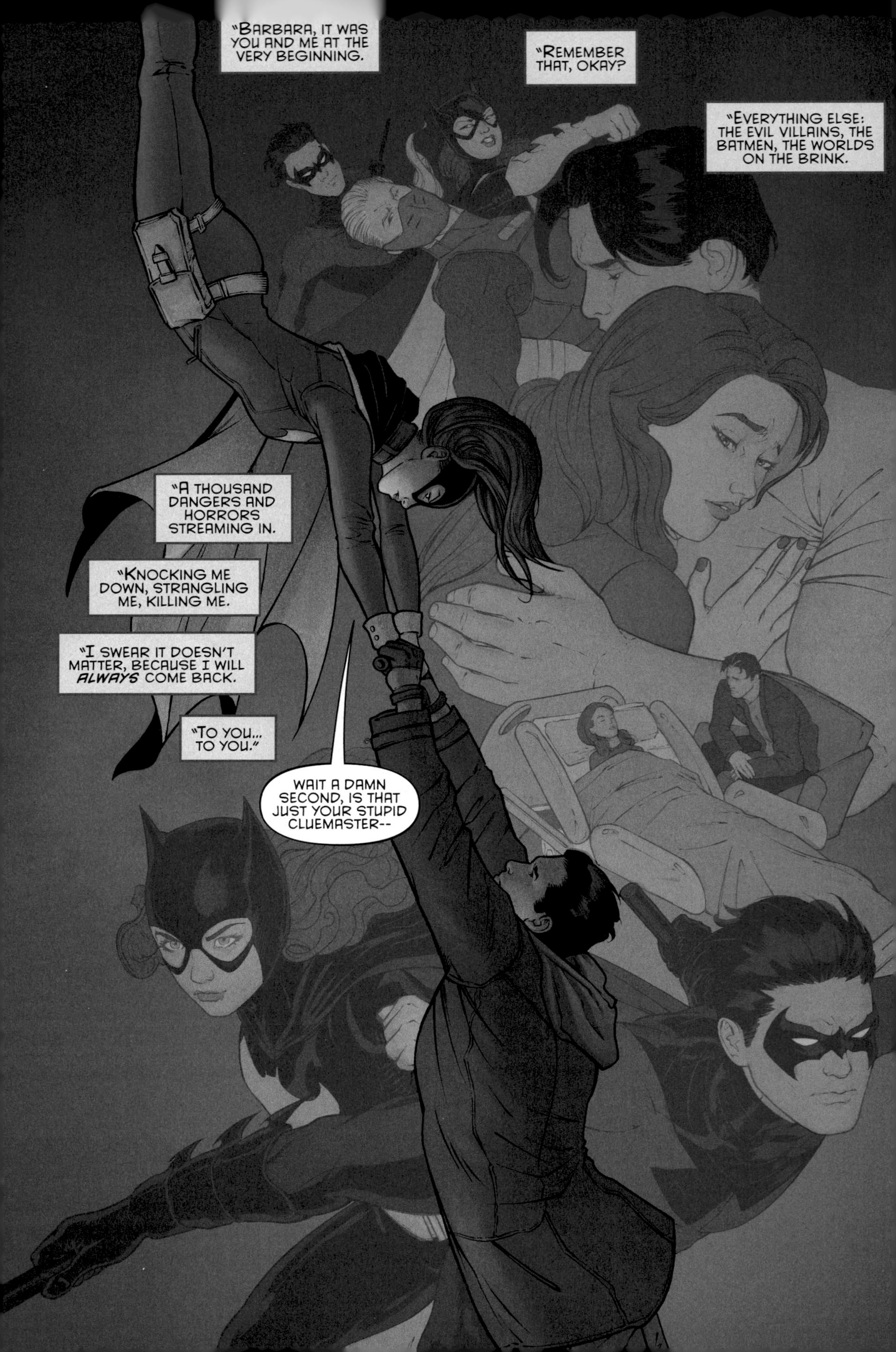
"BARBARA, IT WAS YOU AND ME AT THE VERY BEGINNING.
"REMEMBER THAT, OKAY?
"EVERYTHING ELSE: THE EVIL VILLAINS, THE BATMEN, THE WORLDS ON THE BRINK.
"A THOUSAND DANGERS AND HORRORS STREAMING IN.
"KNOCKING ME DOWN, STRANGLING ME, KILLING ME.
"I SWEAR IT DOESN'T MATTER, BECAUSE I WILL *ALWAYS* COME BACK.
"TO YOU... TO YOU."
WAIT A DAMN SECOND, IS THAT JUST YOUR STUPID CLUEMASTER--

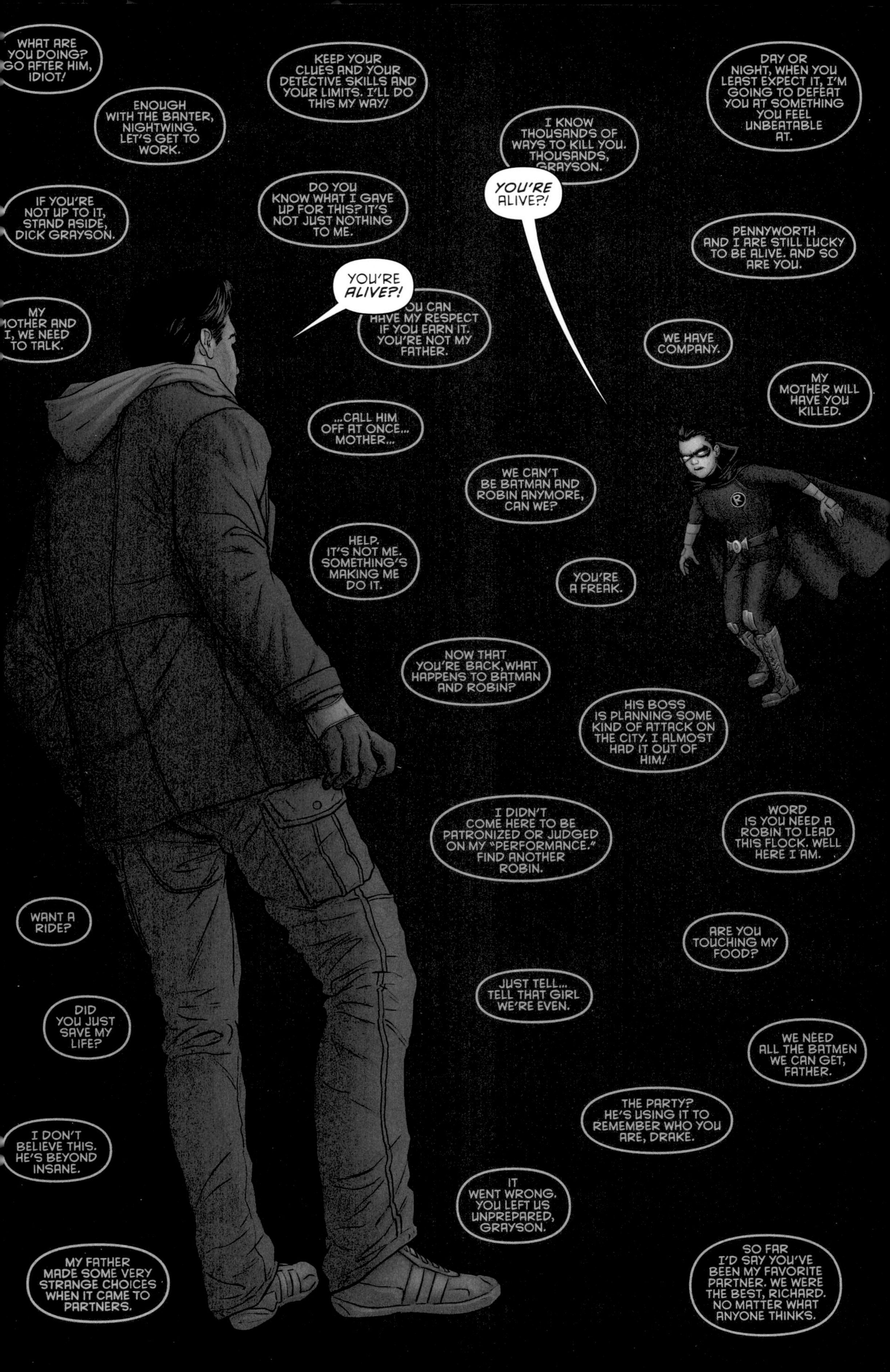
WHAT ARE YOU DOING? GO AFTER HIM, IDIOT!
KEEP YOUR CLUES AND YOUR DETECTIVE SKILLS AND YOUR LIMITS. I'LL DO THIS MY WAY!
DAY OR NIGHT, WHEN YOU LEAST EXPECT IT, I'M GOING TO DEFEAT YOU AT SOMETHING YOU FEEL UNBEATABLE AT.
ENOUGH WITH THE BANTER, NIGHTWING. LET'S GET TO WORK.
I KNOW THOUSANDS OF WAYS TO KILL YOU. THOUSANDS, GRAYSON.
YOU'RE ALIVE?!
IF YOU'RE NOT UP TO IT, STAND ASIDE, DICK GRAYSON.
DO YOU KNOW WHAT I GAVE UP FOR THIS? IT'S NOT JUST NOTHING TO ME.
PENNYWORTH AND I ARE STILL LUCKY TO BE ALIVE. AND SO ARE YOU.
YOU'RE ALIVE?!
MY MOTHER AND I, WE NEED TO TALK.
OU CAN HAVE MY RESPECT IF YOU EARN IT. YOU'RE NOT MY FATHER.
WE HAVE COMPANY.
MY MOTHER WILL HAVE YOU KILLED.
...CALL HIM OFF AT ONCE... MOTHER...
WE CAN'T BE BATMAN AND ROBIN ANYMORE, CAN WE?
HELP. IT'S NOT ME. SOMETHING'S MAKING ME DO IT.
YOU'RE A FREAK.
NOW THAT YOU'RE BACK, WHAT HAPPENS TO BATMAN AND ROBIN?
HIS BOSS IS PLANNING SOME KIND OF ATTACK ON THE CITY. I ALMOST HAD IT OUT OF HIM!
I DIDN'T COME HERE TO BE PATRONIZED OR JUDGED ON MY "PERFORMANCE." FIND ANOTHER ROBIN.
WORD IS YOU NEED A ROBIN TO LEAD THIS FLOCK. WELL HERE I AM.
WANT A RIDE?
ARE YOU TOUCHING MY FOOD?
JUST TELL... TELL THAT GIRL WE'RE EVEN.
DID YOU JUST SAVE MY LIFE?
WE NEED ALL THE BATMEN WE CAN GET, FATHER.
THE PARTY? HE'S USING IT TO REMEMBER WHO YOU ARE, DRAKE.
I DON'T BELIEVE THIS. HE'S BEYOND INSANE.
IT WENT WRONG. YOU LEFT US UNPREPARED, GRAYSON.
MY FATHER MADE SOME VERY STRANGE CHOICES WHEN IT CAME TO PARTNERS.
SO FAR I'D SAY YOU'VE BEEN MY FAVORITE PARTNER. WE WERE THE BEST, RICHARD. NO MATTER WHAT ANYONE THINKS.

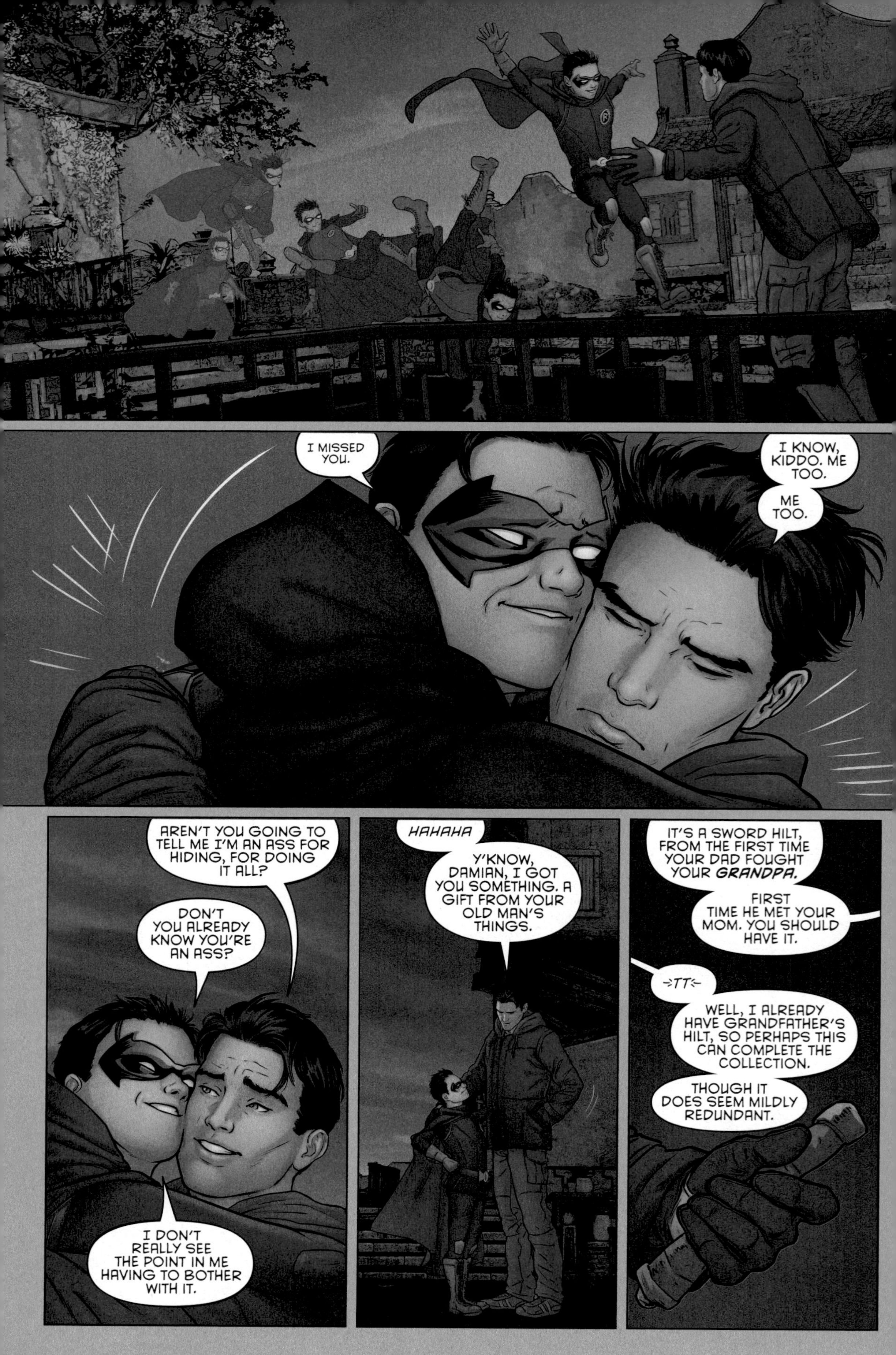
I MISSED YOU.
I KNOW, KIDDO. ME TOO.
ME TOO.
AREN'T YOU GOING TO TELL ME I'M AN ASS FOR HIDING, FOR DOING IT ALL?
DON'T YOU ALREADY KNOW YOU'RE AN ASS?
I DON'T REALLY SEE THE POINT IN ME HAVING TO BOTHER WITH IT.
HAHAHA
Y'KNOW, DAMIAN, I GOT YOU SOMETHING. A GIFT FROM YOUR OLD MAN'S THINGS.
IT'S A SWORD HILT, FROM THE FIRST TIME YOUR DAD FOUGHT YOUR GRANDPA.
FIRST TIME HE MET YOUR MOM. YOU SHOULD HAVE IT.
TT
WELL, I ALREADY HAVE GRANDFATHER'S HILT, SO PERHAPS THIS CAN COMPLETE THE COLLECTION.
THOUGH IT DOES SEEM MILDLY REDUNDANT.

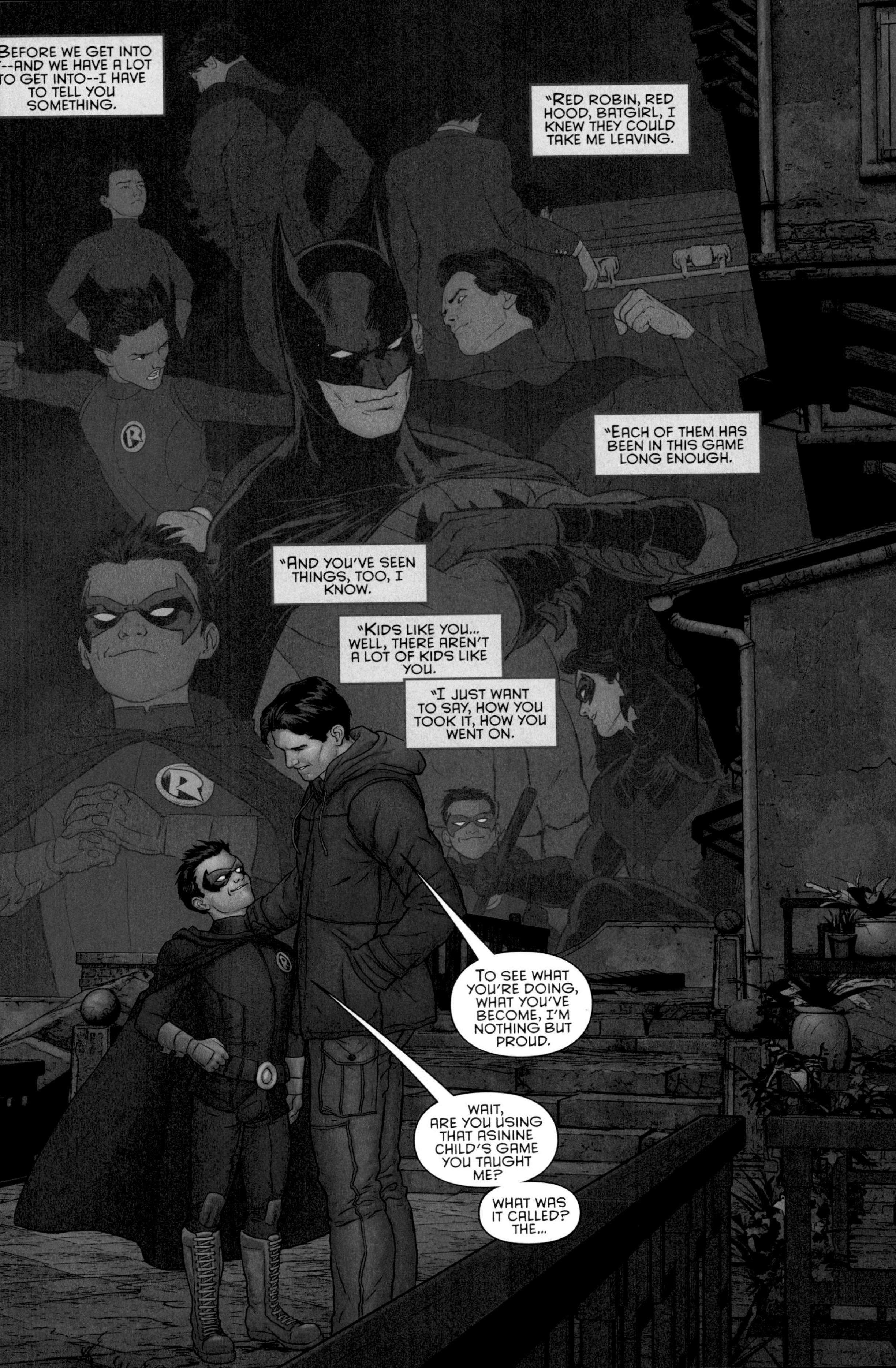
BEFORE WE GET INTO IT--AND WE HAVE A LOT TO GET INTO--I HAVE TO TELL YOU SOMETHING.
"RED ROBIN, RED HOOD, BATGIRL, I KNEW THEY COULD TAKE ME LEAVING.
"EACH OF THEM HAS BEEN IN THIS GAME LONG ENOUGH.
"AND YOU'VE SEEN THINGS, TOO, I KNOW.
"KIDS LIKE YOU... WELL, THERE AREN'T A LOT OF KIDS LIKE YOU.
"I JUST WANT TO SAY, HOW YOU TOOK IT, HOW YOU WENT ON.
TO SEE WHAT YOU'RE DOING, WHAT YOU'VE BECOME, I'M NOTHING BUT PROUD.
WAIT, ARE YOU USING THAT ASININE CHILD'S GAME YOU TAUGHT ME?
WHAT WAS IT CALLED? THE...

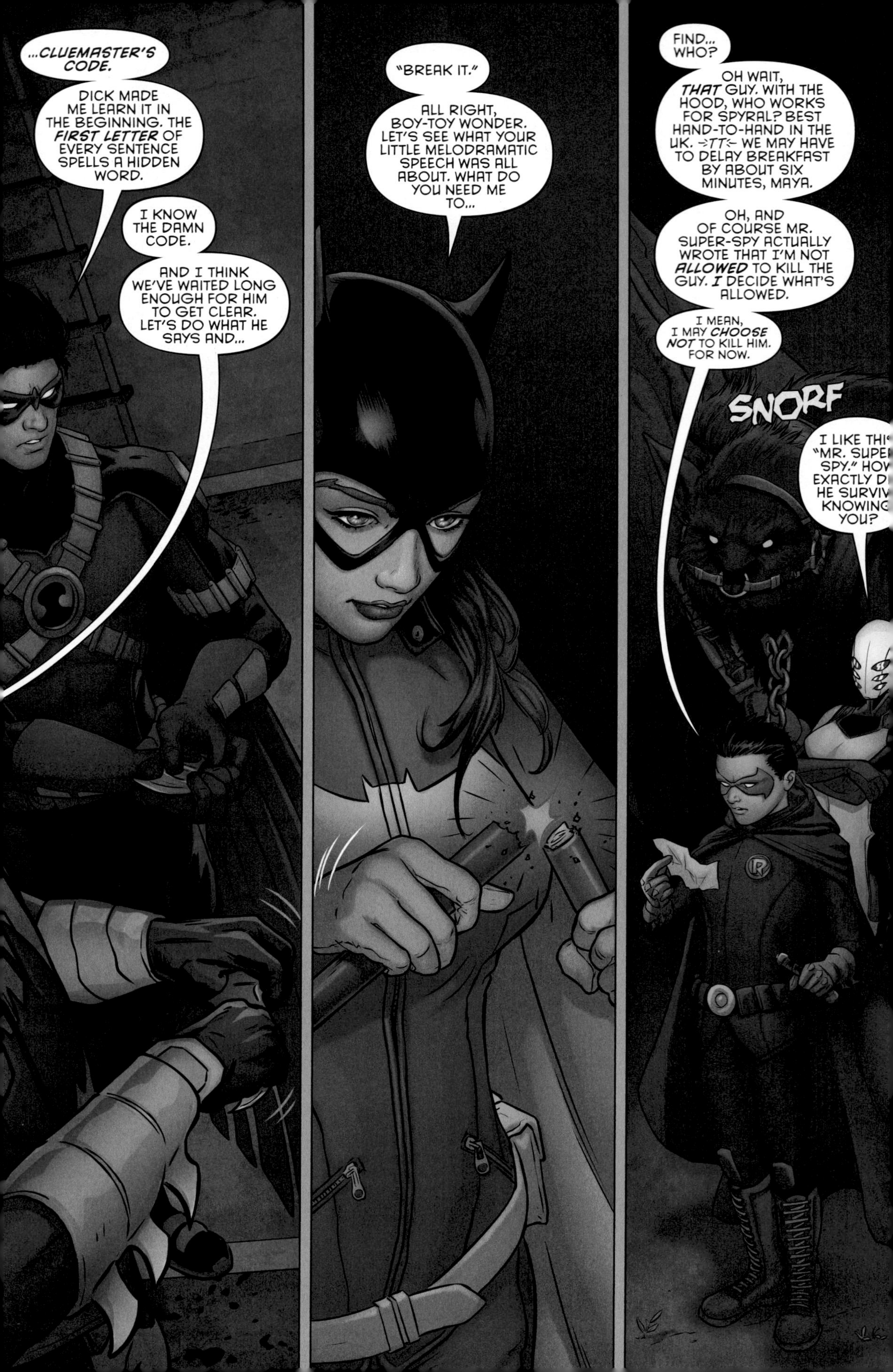

...CLUEMASTER'S CODE.
DICK MADE ME LEARN IT IN THE BEGINNING. THE FIRST LETTER OF EVERY SENTENCE SPELLS A HIDDEN WORD.
I KNOW THE DAMN CODE.
AND I THINK WE'VE WAITED LONG ENOUGH FOR HIM TO GET CLEAR. LET'S DO WHAT HE SAYS AND...
"BREAK IT."
ALL RIGHT, BOY-TOY WONDER. LET'S SEE WHAT YOUR LITTLE MELODRAMATIC SPEECH WAS ALL ABOUT. WHAT DO YOU NEED ME TO...
FIND... WHO?
OH WAIT, THAT GUY. WITH THE HOOD, WHO WORKS FOR SPYRAL? BEST HAND-TO-HAND IN THE UK. -TT- WE MAY HAVE TO DELAY BREAKFAST BY ABOUT SIX MINUTES, MAYA.
OH, AND OF COURSE MR. SUPER-SPY ACTUALLY WROTE THAT I'M NOT ALLOWED TO KILL THE GUY. I DECIDE WHAT'S ALLOWED.
I MEAN, I MAY CHOOSE NOT TO KILL HIM. FOR NOW.
SNORF

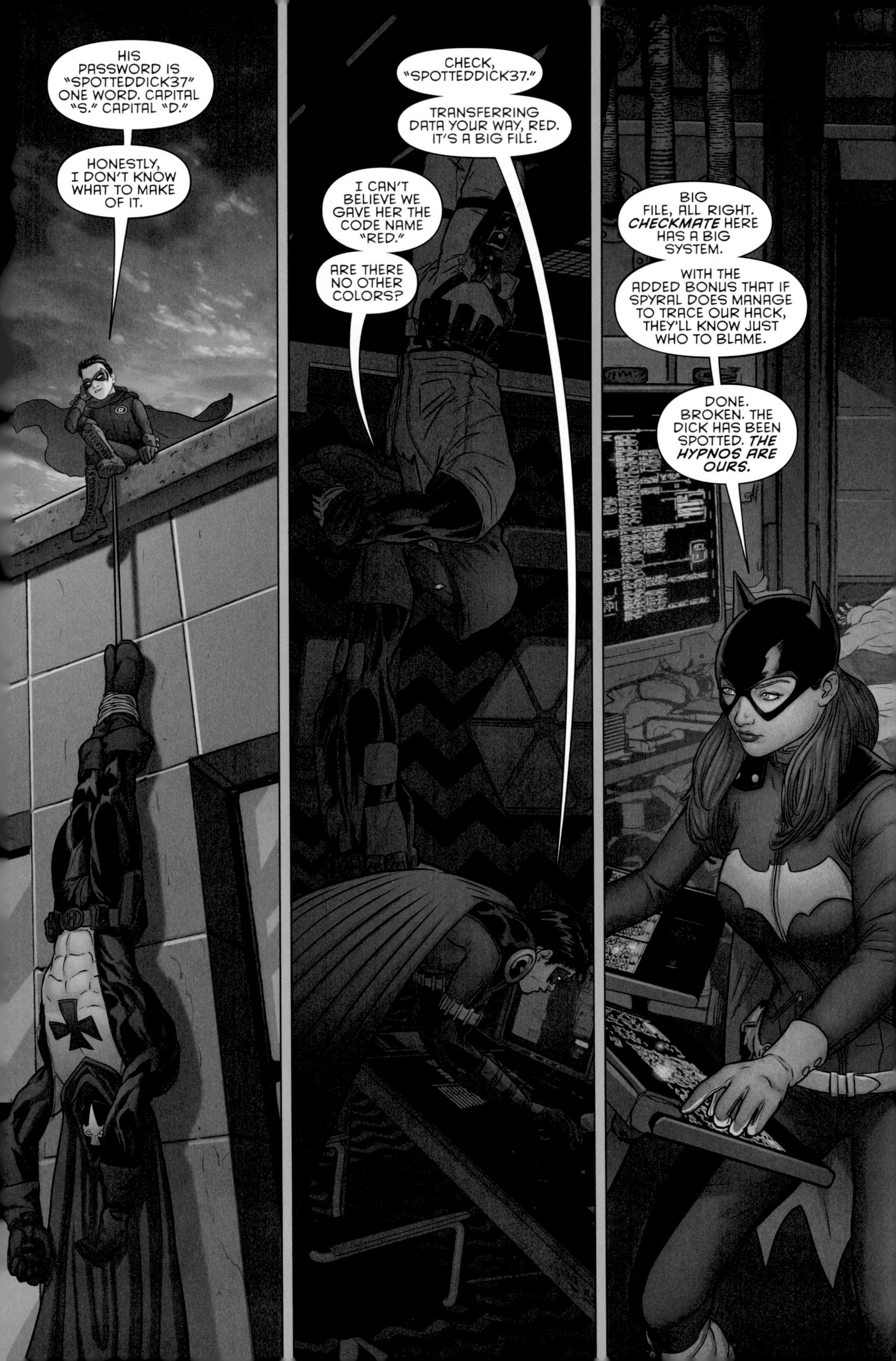

HIS PASSWORD IS "SPOTTEDDICK37" ONE WORD. CAPITAL "S." CAPITAL "D."
HONESTLY, I DON'T KNOW WHAT TO MAKE OF IT.
CHECK, "SPOTTEDDICK37."
TRANSFERRING DATA YOUR WAY, RED. IT'S A BIG FILE.
I CAN'T BELIEVE WE GAVE HER THE CODE NAME "RED."
ARE THERE NO OTHER COLORS?
BIG FILE, ALL RIGHT. CHECKMATE HERE HAS A BIG SYSTEM.
WITH THE ADDED BONUS THAT IF SPYRAL DOES MANAGE TO TRACE OUR HACK, THEY'LL KNOW JUST WHO TO BLAME.
DONE. BROKEN. THE DICK HAS BEEN SPOTTED. THE HYPNOS ARE OURS.

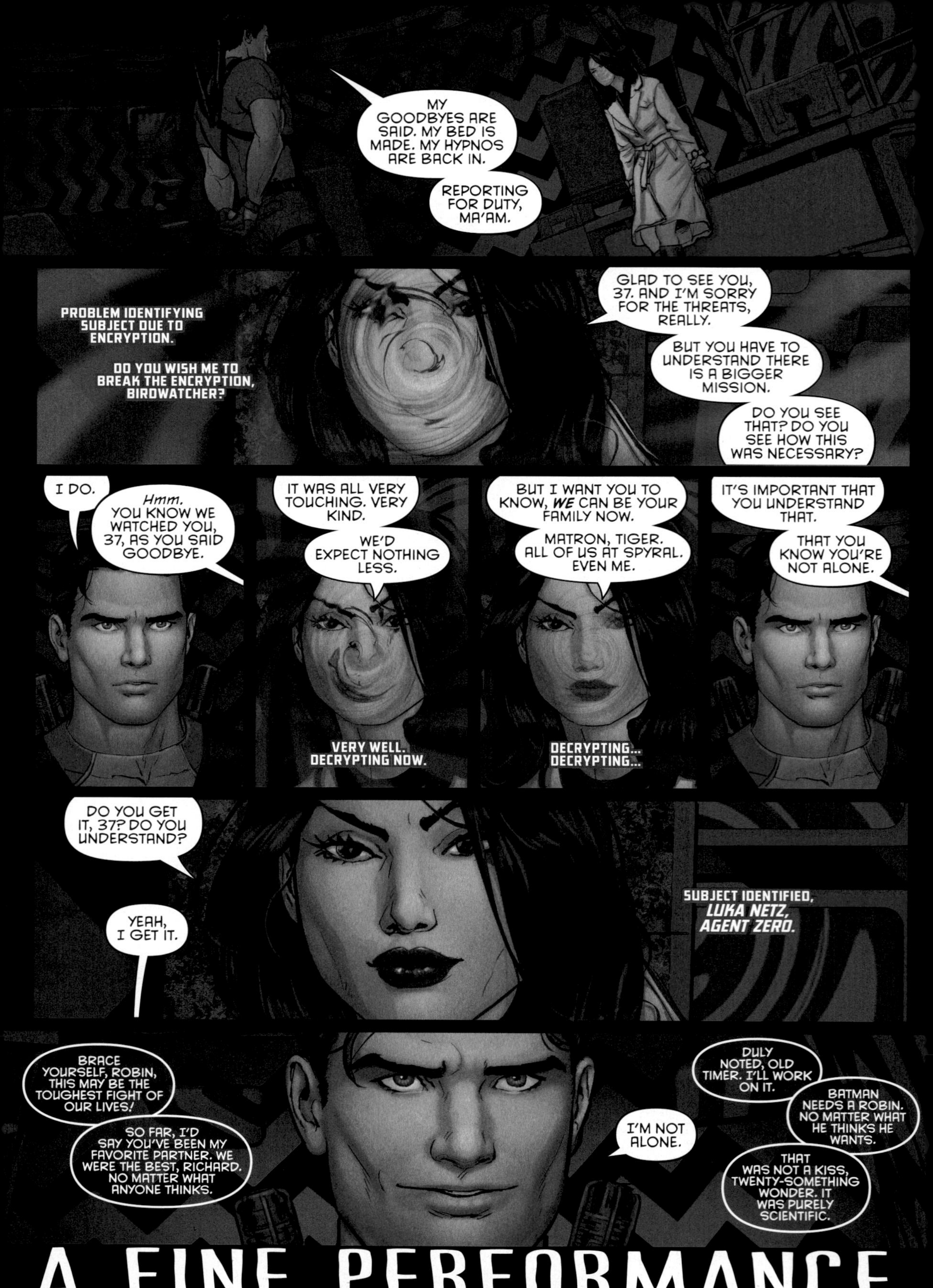

MY GOODBYES ARE SAID. MY BED IS MADE. MY HYPNOS ARE BACK IN.
REPORTING FOR DUTY, MA'AM.
PROBLEM IDENTIFYING SUBJECT DUE TO ENCRYPTION.
DO YOU WISH ME TO BREAK THE ENCRYPTION, BIRDWATCHER?
GLAD TO SEE YOU, 37. AND I'M SORRY FOR THE THREATS, REALLY.
BUT YOU HAVE TO UNDERSTAND THERE IS A BIGGER MISSION.
DO YOU SEE THAT? DO YOU SEE HOW THIS WAS NECESSARY?
I DO.
Hmm. YOU KNOW WE WATCHED YOU, 37, AS YOU SAID GOODBYE.
IT WAS ALL VERY TOUCHING. VERY KIND.
WE'D EXPECT NOTHING LESS.
VERY WELL. DECRYPTING NOW.
BUT I WANT YOU TO KNOW, *WE* CAN BE YOUR FAMILY NOW.
MATRON, TIGER. ALL OF US AT SPYRAL. EVEN ME.
DECRYPTING... DECRYPTING...
IT'S IMPORTANT THAT YOU UNDERSTAND THAT.
THAT YOU KNOW YOU'RE NOT ALONE.
DO YOU GET IT, 37? DO YOU UNDERSTAND?
YEAH, I GET IT.
SUBJECT IDENTIFIED, *LUKA NETZ, AGENT ZERO.*
BRACE YOURSELF, ROBIN, THIS MAY BE THE TOUGHEST FIGHT OF OUR LIVES!
SO FAR, I'D SAY YOU'VE BEEN MY FAVORITE PARTNER. WE WERE THE BEST, RICHARD. NO MATTER WHAT ANYONE THINKS.
I'M NOT ALONE.
DULY NOTED, OLD TIMER. I'LL WORK ON IT.
BATMAN NEEDS A ROBIN. NO MATTER WHAT HE THINKS HE WANTS.
THAT WAS NOT A KISS, TWENTY-SOMETHING WONDER. IT WAS PURELY SCIENTIFIC.

A FINE PERFORMANCE

SCRIPT / TOM KING PLOT BY TIM SEELEY & TOM KING PENCILS & GREYTONES / MIKEL JANÍN INKS / MIKEL JANÍN, HUGO PETRUS & JUAN CASTRO
COLORIST / JEROMY COX LETTERER / CARLOS M. MANGUAL COVER / MIKEL JANÍN

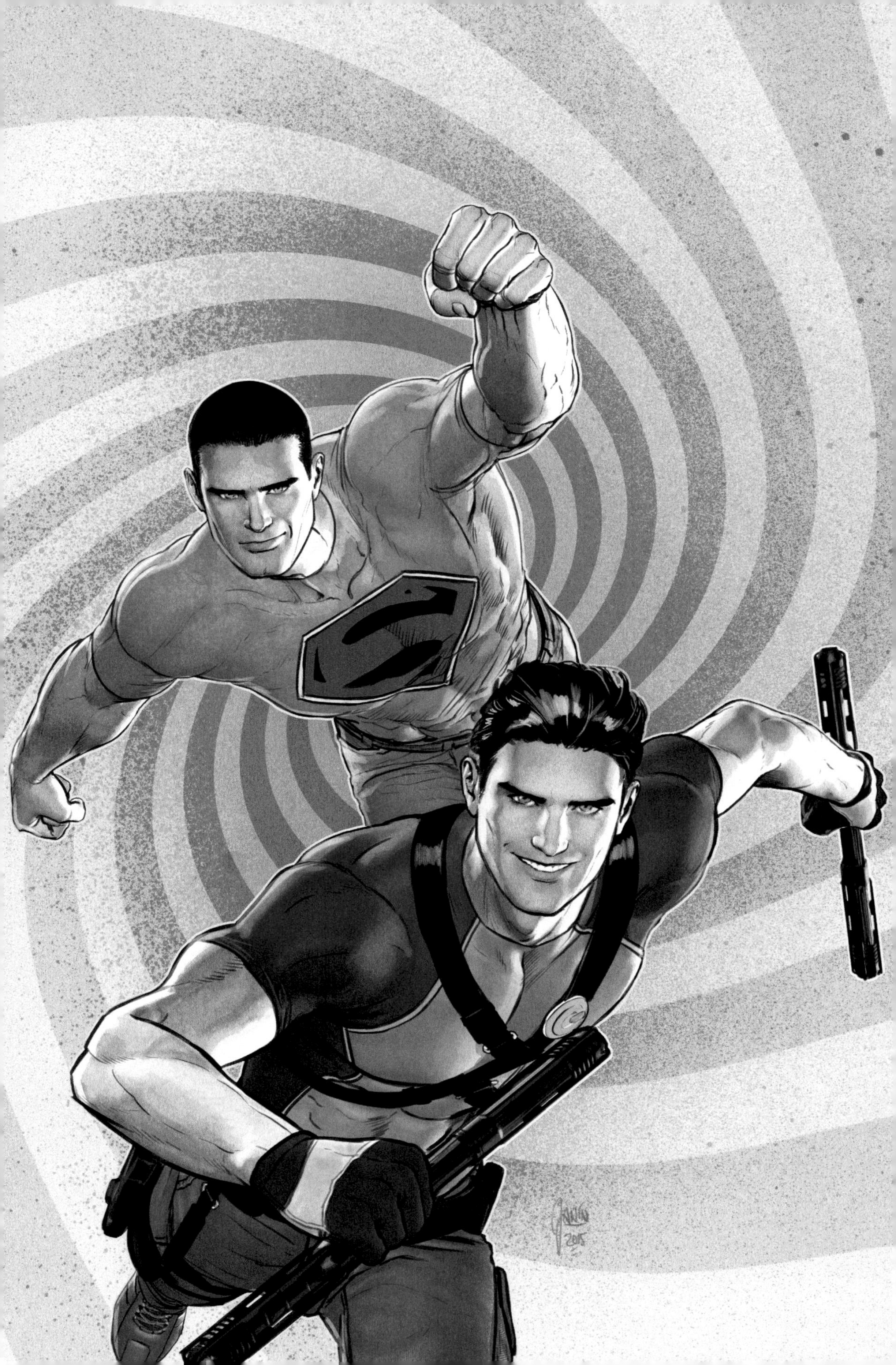

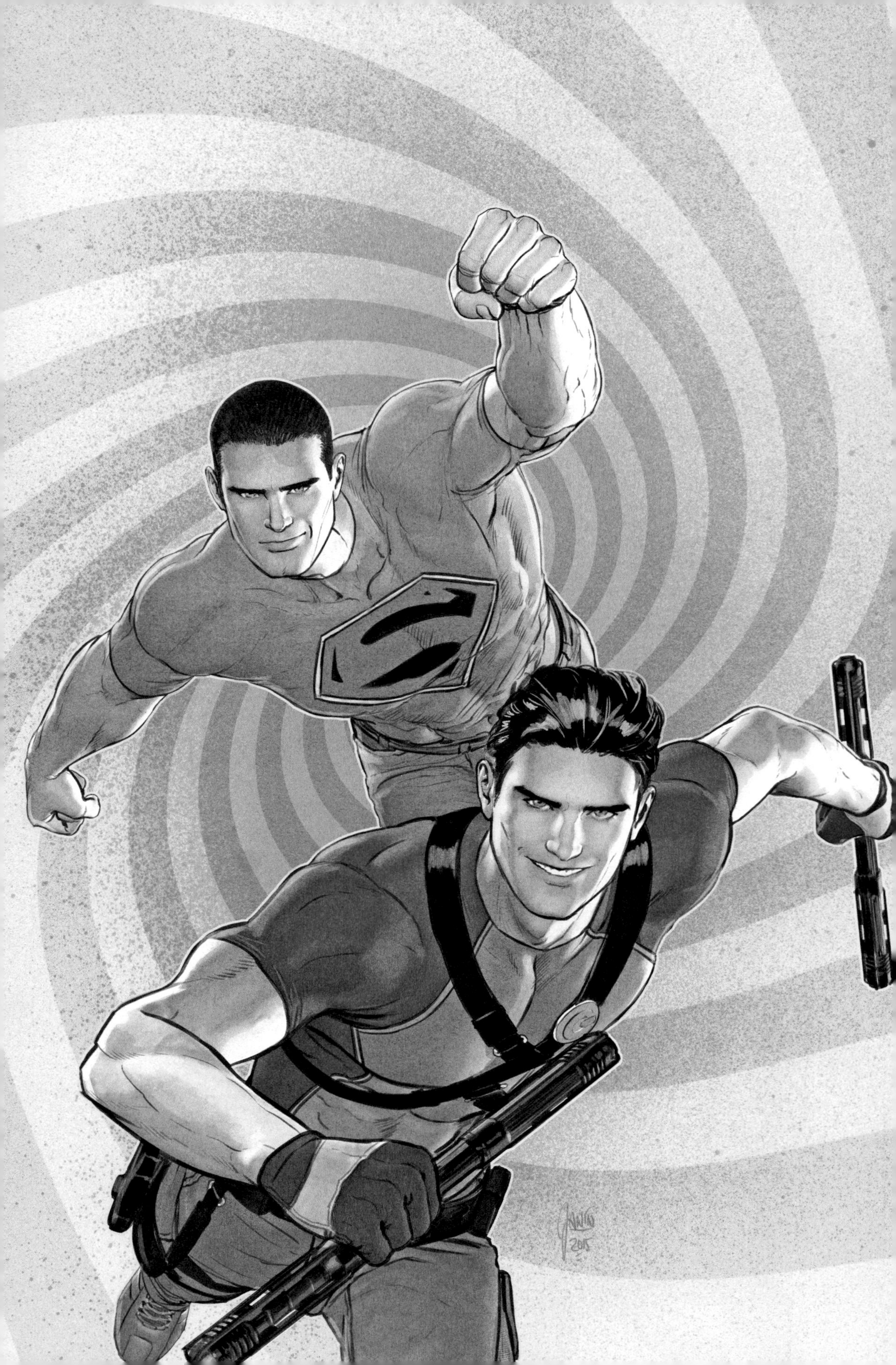

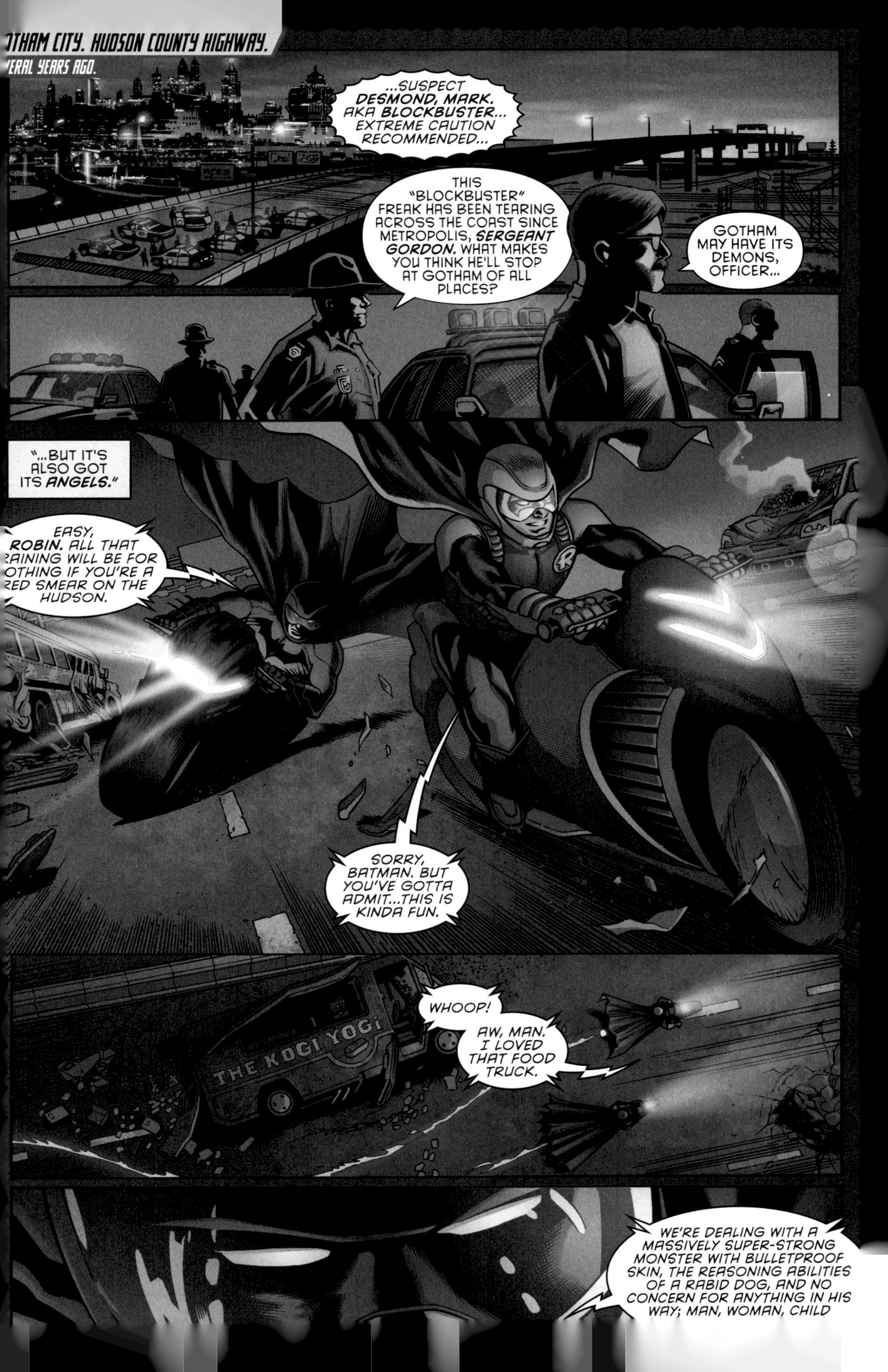

OTHAM CITY. HUDSON COUNTY HIGHWAY.
VERAL YEARS AGO.
...SUSPECT DESMOND, MARK. AKA BLOCKBUSTER... EXTREME CAUTION RECOMMENDED...
THIS "BLOCKBUSTER" FREAK HAS BEEN TEARING ACROSS THE COAST SINCE METROPOLIS, SERGEANT GORDON. WHAT MAKES YOU THINK HE'LL STOP AT GOTHAM OF ALL PLACES?
GOTHAM MAY HAVE ITS DEMONS, OFFICER...
"...BUT IT'S ALSO GOT ITS ANGELS."
EASY, ROBIN. ALL THAT RAINING WILL BE FOR OTHING IF YOU'RE A RED SMEAR ON THE HUDSON.
SORRY, BATMAN. BUT YOU'VE GOTTA ADMIT...THIS IS KINDA FUN.
THE KOGI YOGi
WHOOP!
AW, MAN. I LOVED THAT FOOD TRUCK.
WE'RE DEALING WITH A MASSIVELY SUPER-STRONG MONSTER WITH BULLETPROOF SKIN, THE REASONING ABILITIES OF A RABID DOG, AND NO CONCERN FOR ANYTHING IN HIS WAY; MAN, WOMAN, CHILD

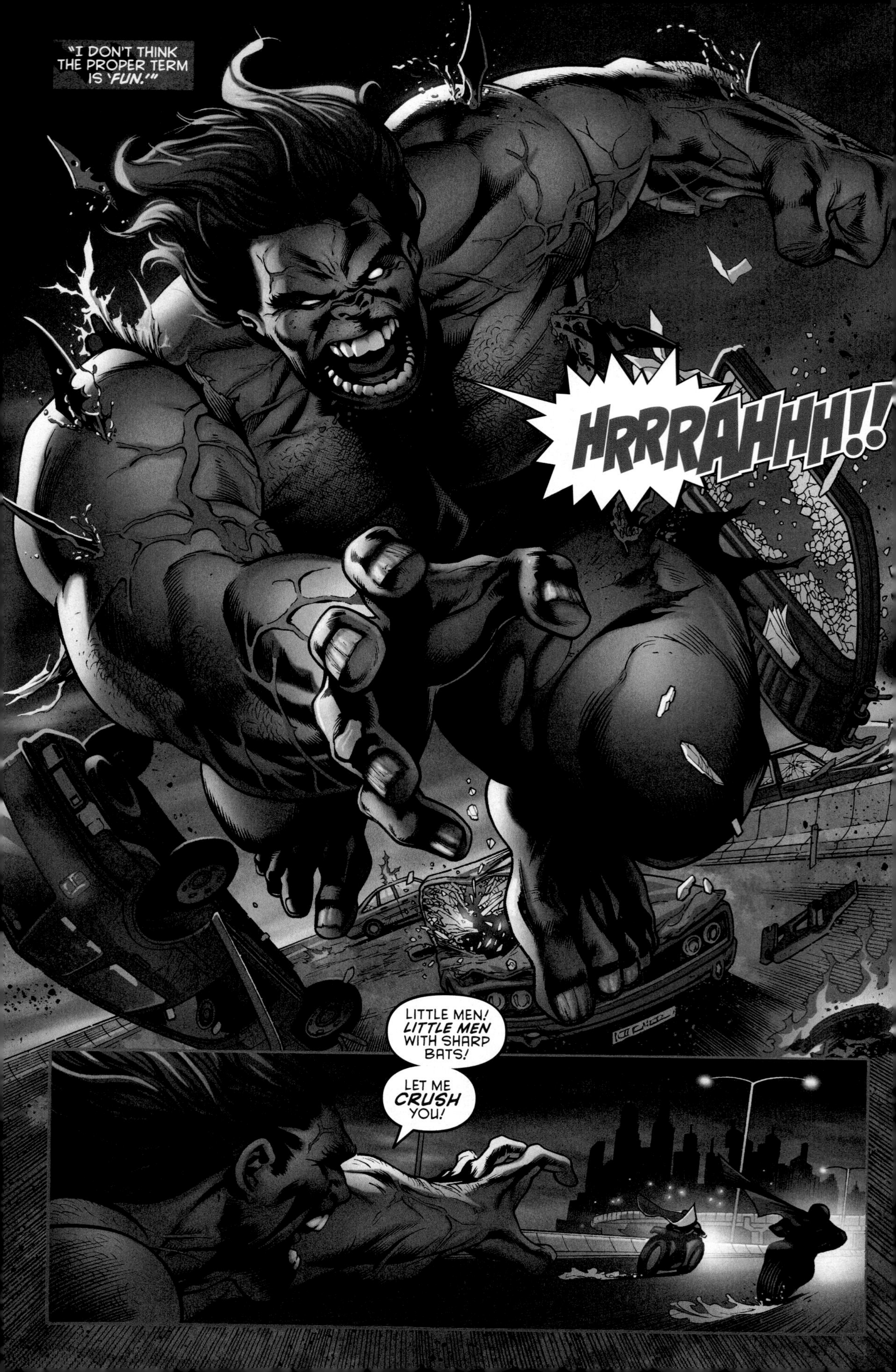
"I DON'T THINK THE PROPER TERM IS 'FUN.'"
HRRRAHHH!!
LITTLE MEN! LITTLE MEN WITH SHARP BATS!
LET ME CRUSH YOU!

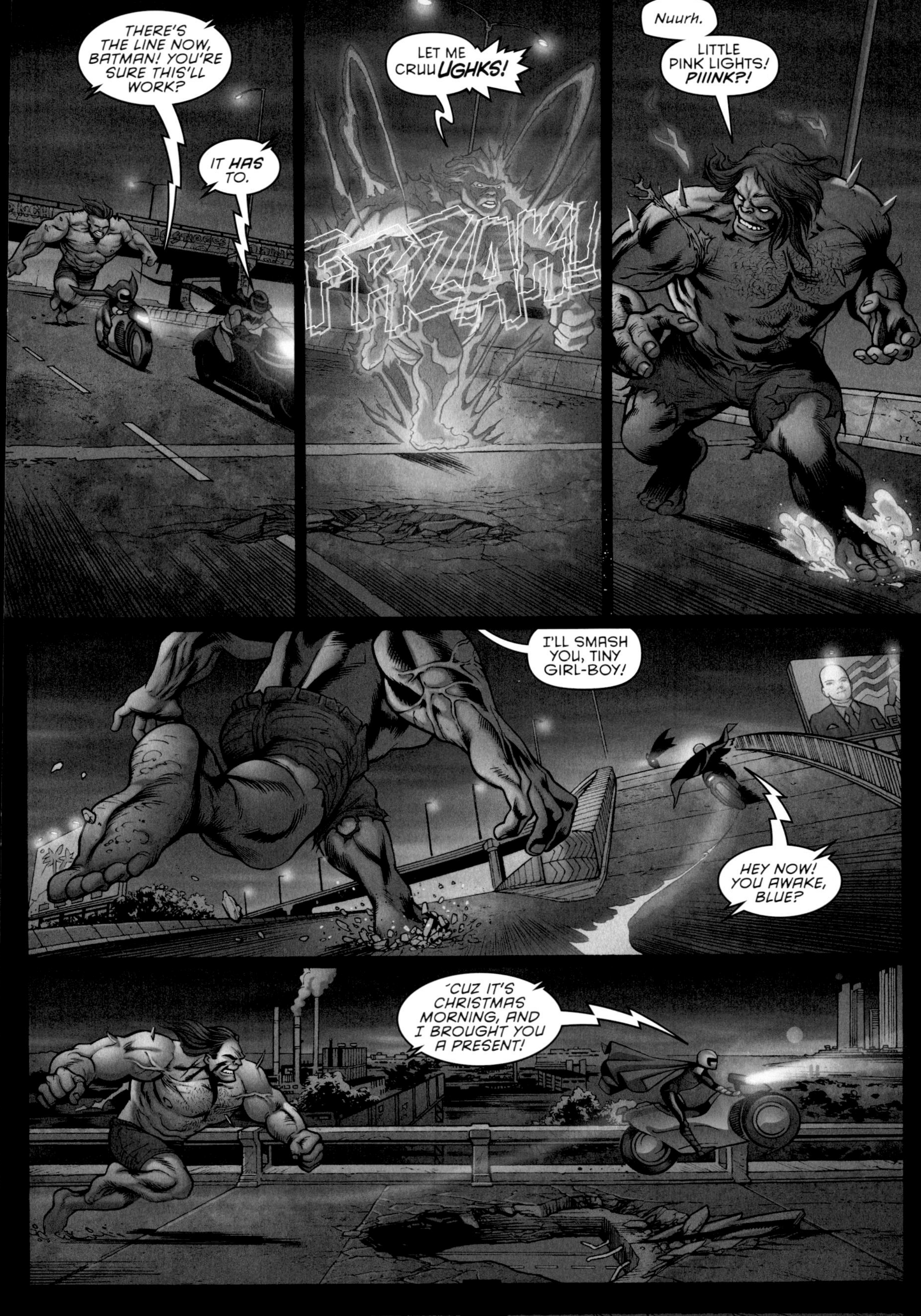
THERE'S THE LINE NOW, BATMAN! YOU'RE SURE THIS'LL WORK?
IT HAS TO.
LET ME CRUUUGHKS!
Nuurh.
LITTLE PINK LIGHTS! PIIINK?!
I'LL SMASH YOU, TINY GIRL-BOY!
HEY NOW! YOU AWAKE, BLUE?
'CUZ IT'S CHRISTMAS MORNING, AND I BROUGHT YOU A PRESENT!

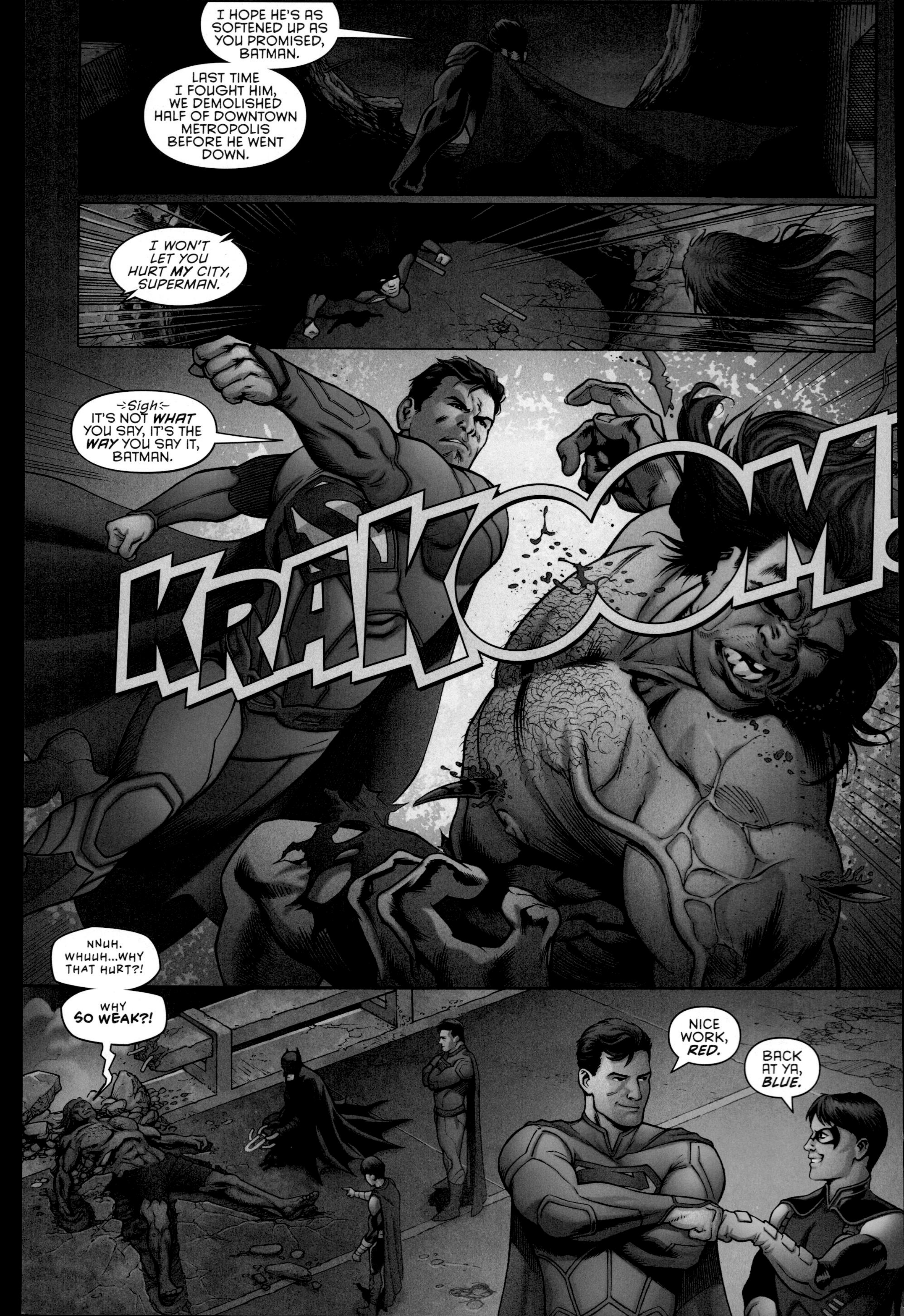
I HOPE HE'S AS SOFTENED UP AS YOU PROMISED, BATMAN.
LAST TIME I FOUGHT HIM, WE DEMOLISHED HALF OF DOWNTOWN METROPOLIS BEFORE HE WENT DOWN.
I WON'T LET YOU HURT MY CITY, SUPERMAN.
Sigh
IT'S NOT WHAT YOU SAY, IT'S THE WAY YOU SAY IT, BATMAN.
KRAKOOM!
NNUH. WHUUH...WHY THAT HURT?!
WHY SO WEAK?!
NICE WORK, RED.
BACK AT YA, BLUE.

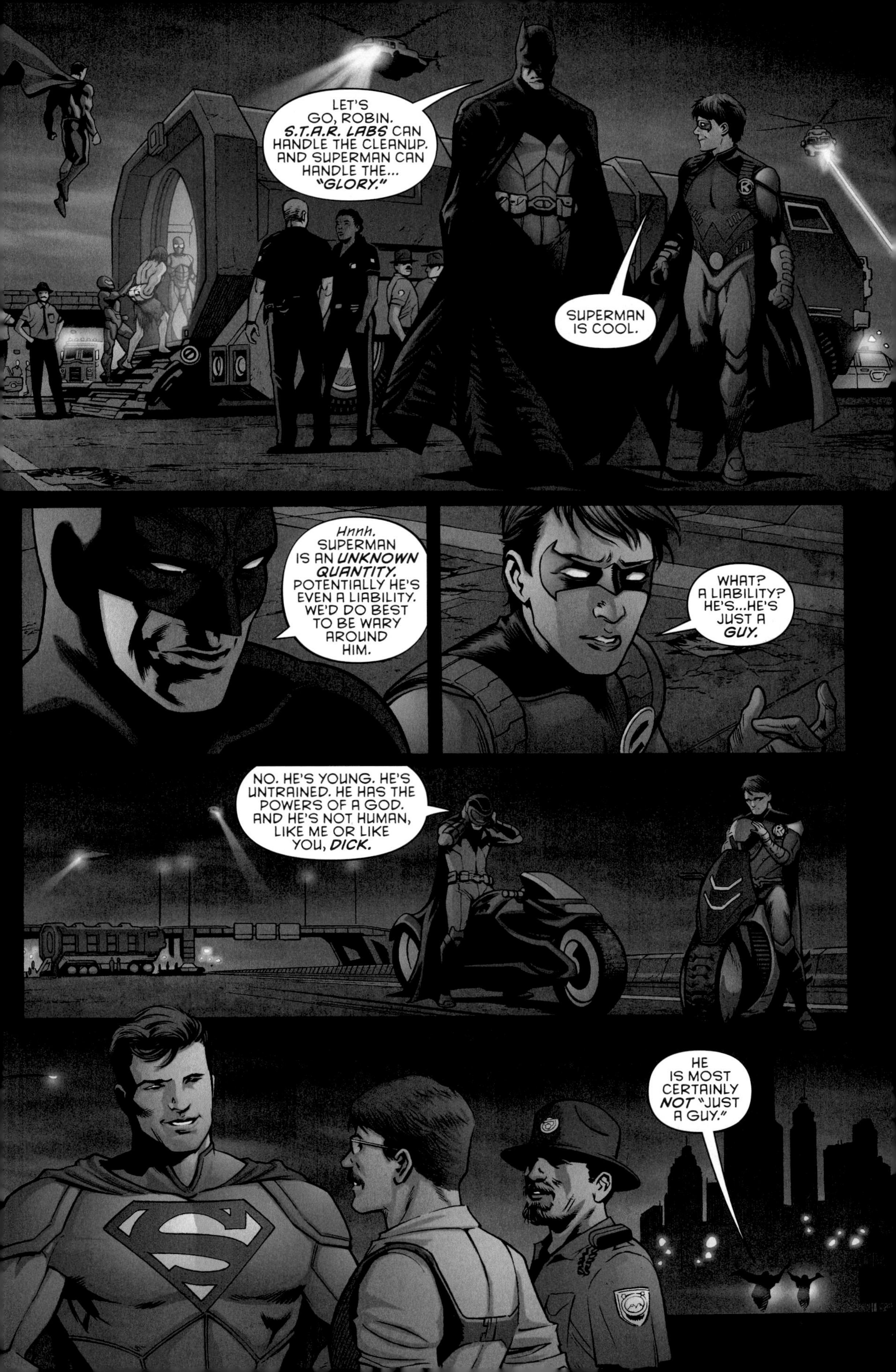

LET'S GO, ROBIN. *S.T.A.R. LABS* CAN HANDLE THE CLEANUP. AND SUPERMAN CAN HANDLE THE... *"GLORY."*
SUPERMAN IS COOL.
Hnnh. SUPERMAN IS AN *UNKNOWN QUANTITY.* POTENTIALLY HE'S EVEN A LIABILITY. WE'D DO BEST TO BE WARY AROUND HIM.
WHAT? A LIABILITY? HE'S...HE'S JUST A *GUY.*
NO. HE'S YOUNG. HE'S UNTRAINED. HE HAS THE POWERS OF A GOD. AND HE'S NOT HUMAN, LIKE ME OR LIKE YOU, *DICK.*
HE IS MOST CERTAINLY *NOT* "JUST A GUY."

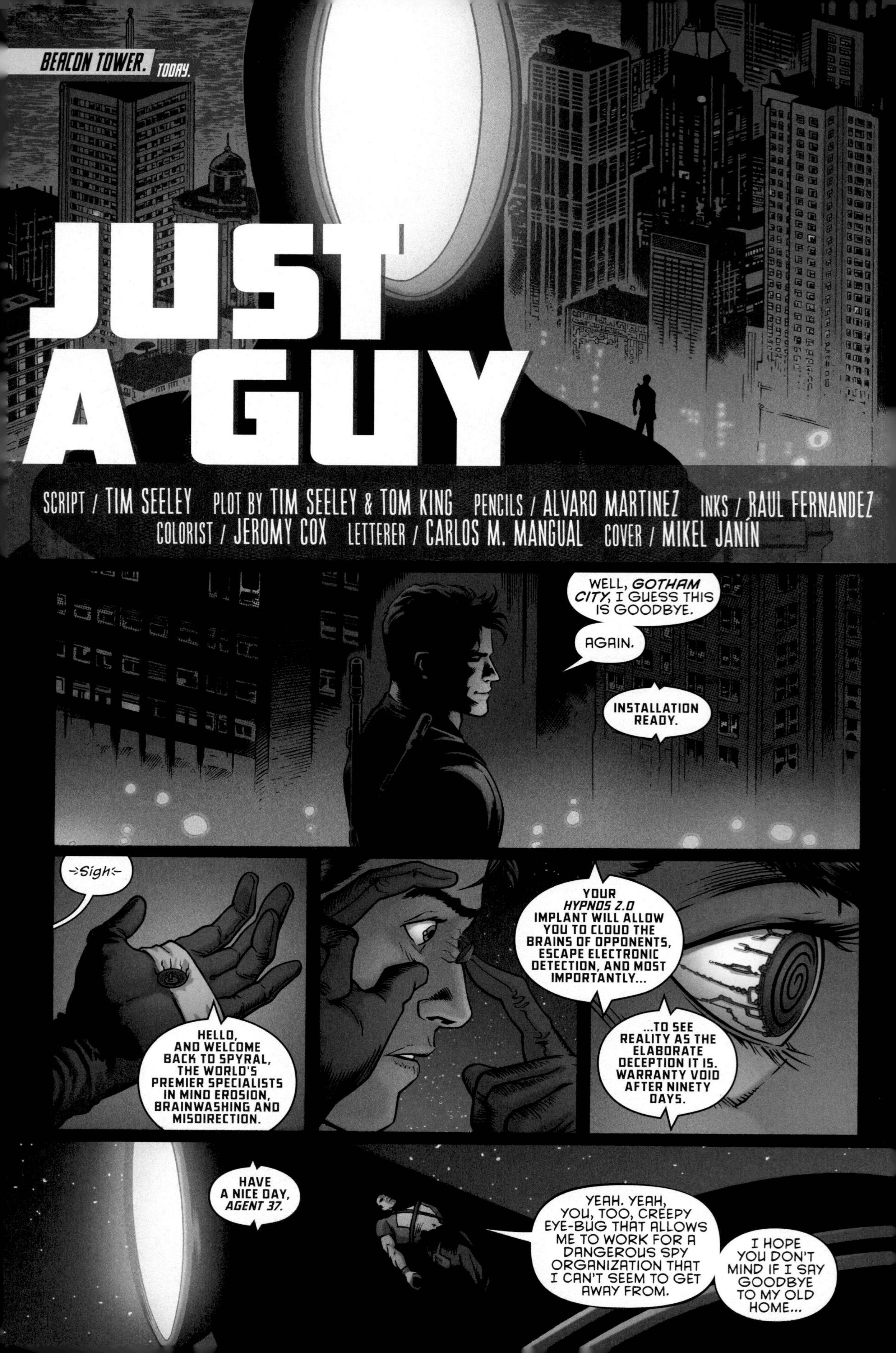

BEACON TOWER. TODAY.
JUST A GUY
SCRIPT / TIM SEELEY PLOT BY TIM SEELEY & TOM KING PENCILS / ALVARO MARTINEZ INKS / RAUL FERNANDEZ
COLORIST / JEROMY COX LETTERER / CARLOS M. MANGUAL COVER / MIKEL JANÍN
WELL, GOTHAM CITY, I GUESS THIS IS GOODBYE.
AGAIN.
INSTALLATION READY.
>Sigh<
HELLO, AND WELCOME BACK TO SPYRAL, THE WORLD'S PREMIER SPECIALISTS IN MIND EROSION, BRAINWASHING AND MISDIRECTION.
YOUR HYPNOS 2.0 IMPLANT WILL ALLOW YOU TO CLOUD THE BRAINS OF OPPONENTS, ESCAPE ELECTRONIC DETECTION, AND MOST IMPORTANTLY...
...TO SEE REALITY AS THE ELABORATE DECEPTION IT IS. WARRANTY VOID AFTER NINETY DAYS.
HAVE A NICE DAY, AGENT 37.
YEAH. YEAH, YOU, TOO, CREEPY EYE-BUG THAT ALLOWS ME TO WORK FOR A DANGEROUS SPY ORGANIZATION THAT I CAN'T SEEM TO GET AWAY FROM.
I HOPE YOU DON'T MIND IF I SAY GOODBYE TO MY OLD HOME...

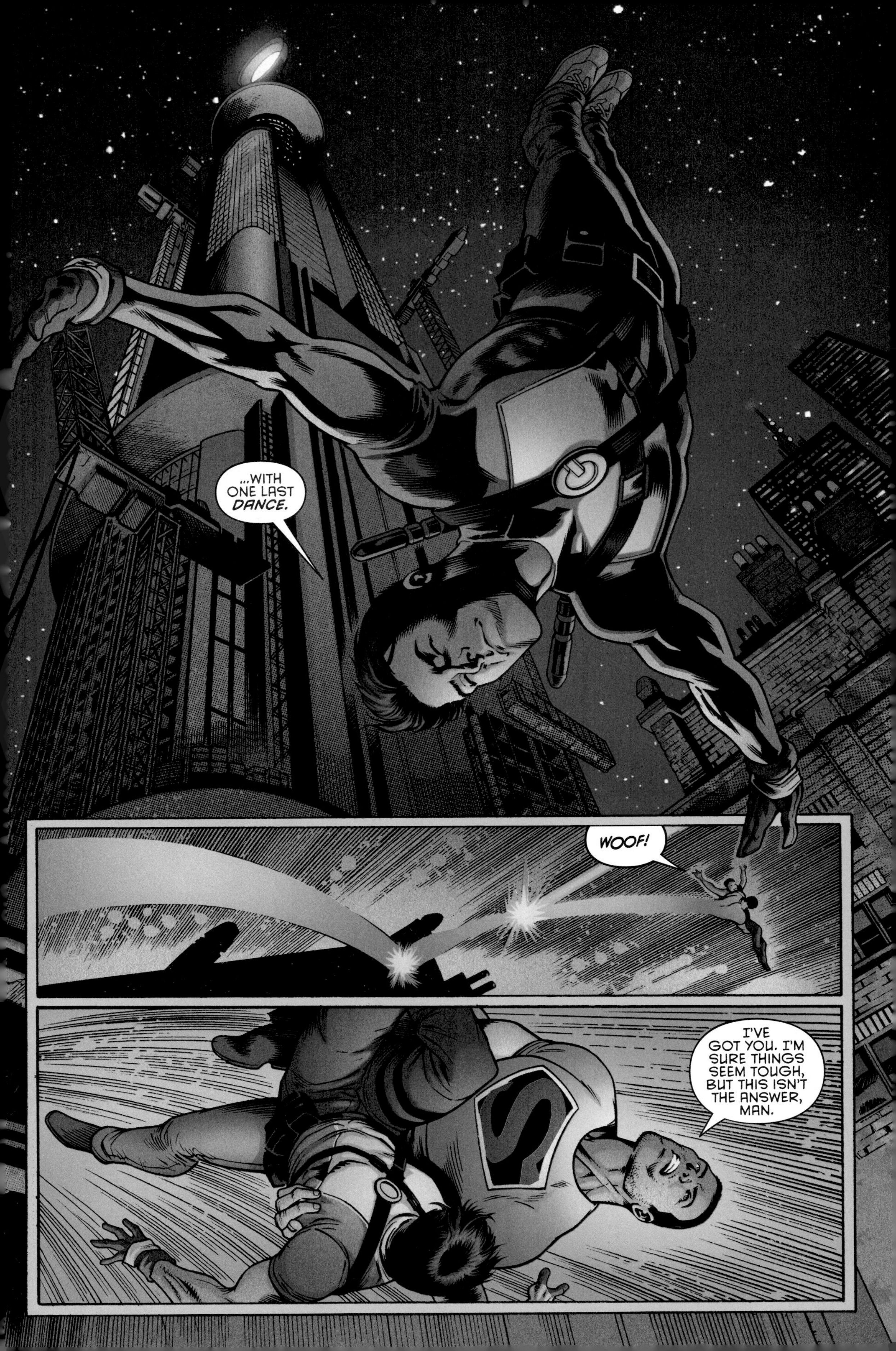
...WITH ONE LAST DANCE.
WOOF!
I'VE GOT YOU. I'M SURE THINGS SEEM TOUGH, BUT THIS ISN'T THE ANSWER, MAN.

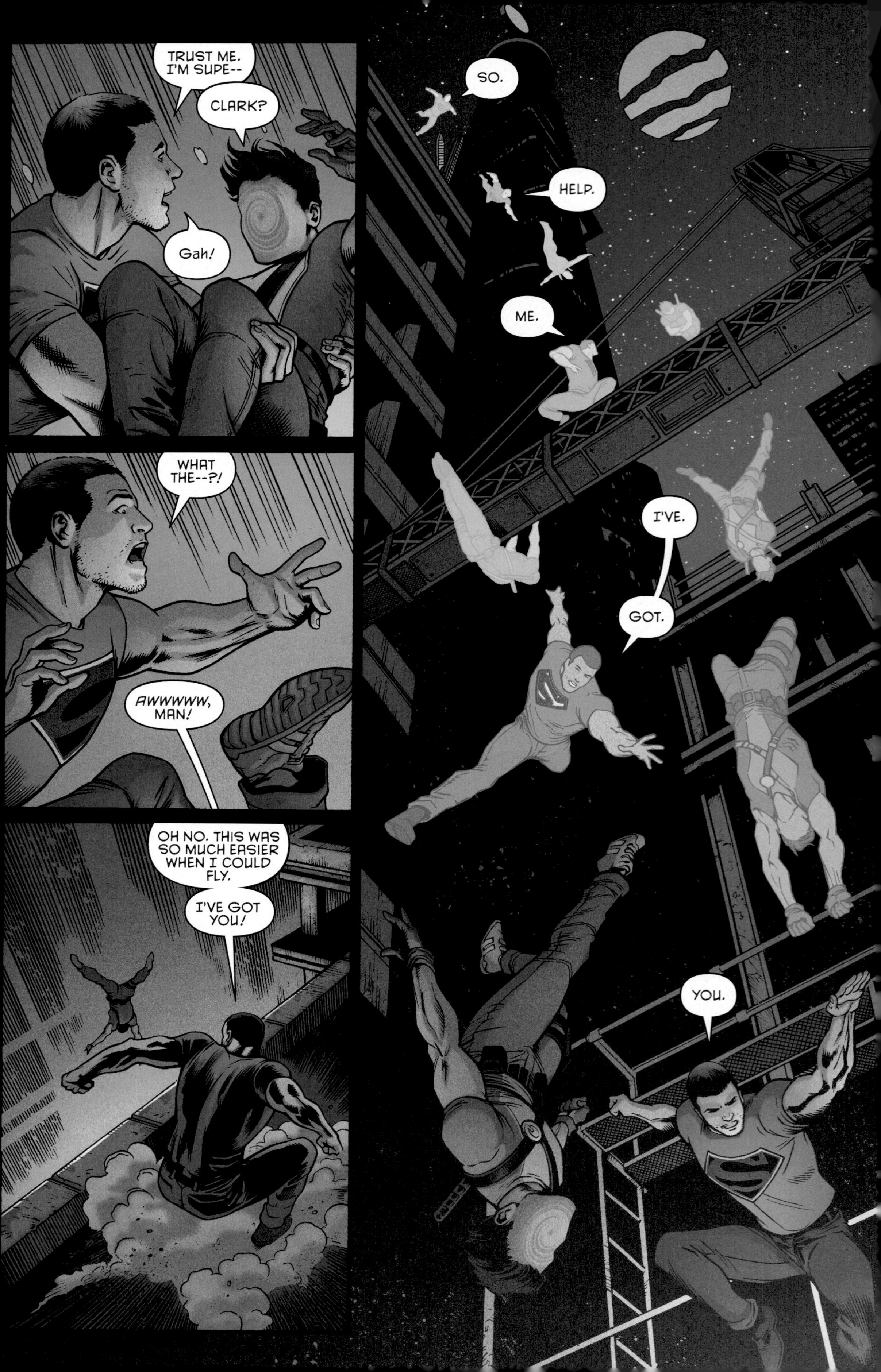
TRUST ME. I'M SUPE--
CLARK?
Gah!
WHAT THE--?!
AWWWWW, MAN!
OH NO. THIS WAS SO MUCH EASIER WHEN I COULD FLY.
I'VE GOT YOU!
SO.
HELP.
ME.
I'VE.
GOT.
YOU.

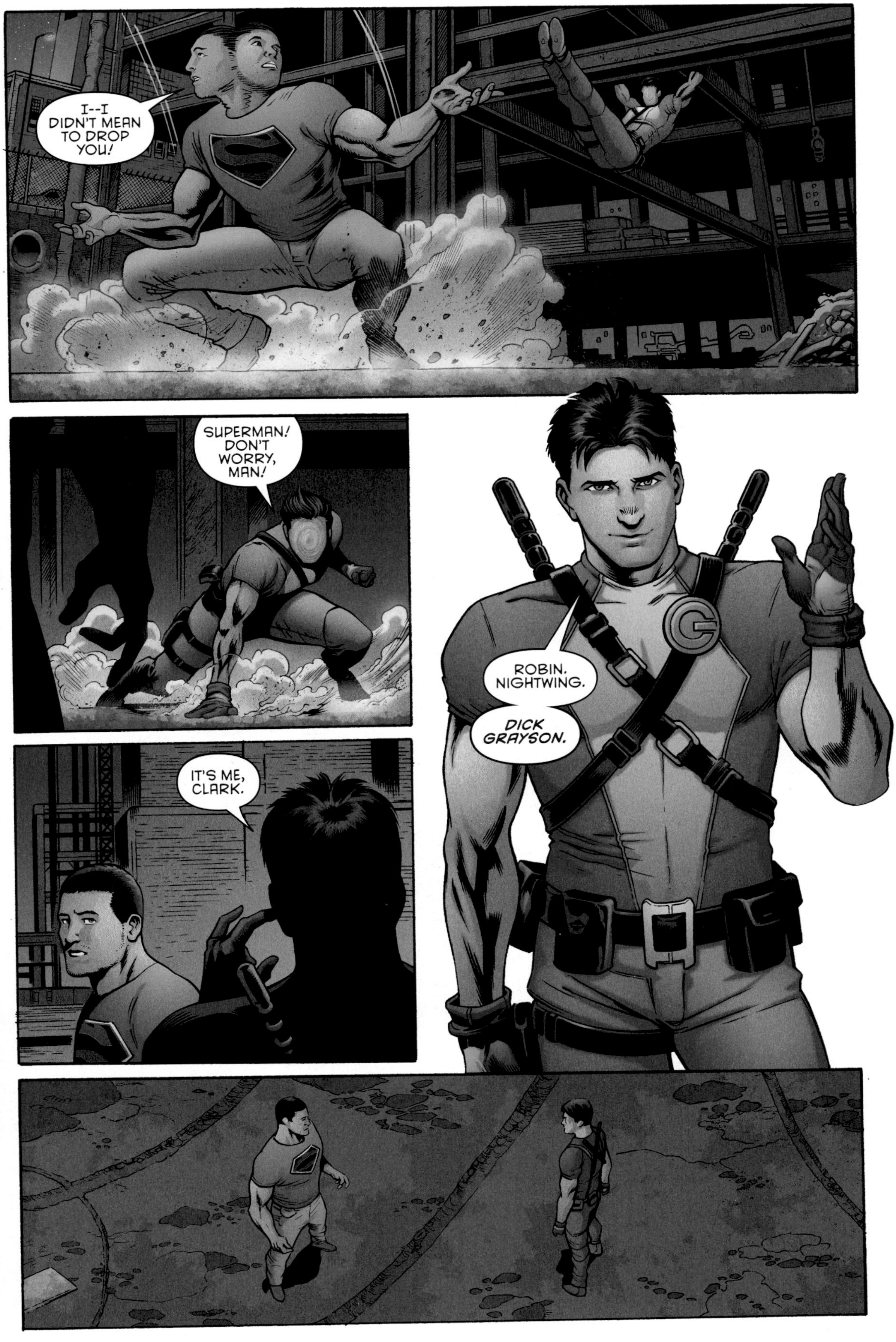
I--I DIDN'T MEAN TO DROP YOU!
SUPERMAN! DON'T WORRY, MAN!
IT'S ME, CLARK.
ROBIN. NIGHTWING.
DICK GRAYSON.

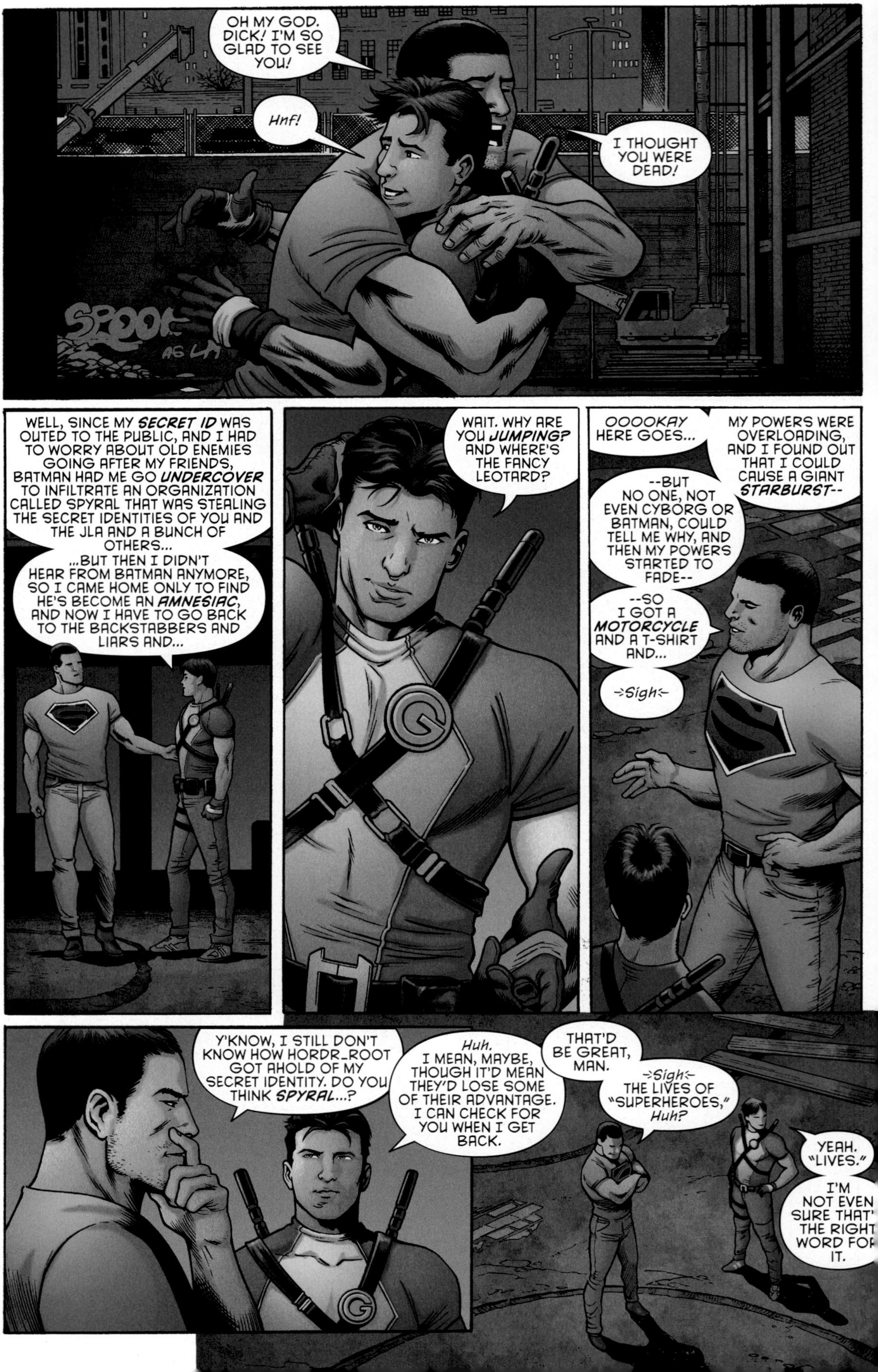
OH MY GOD. DICK! I'M SO GLAD TO SEE YOU!
Hnf!
I THOUGHT YOU WERE DEAD!
WELL, SINCE MY SECRET ID WAS OUTED TO THE PUBLIC, AND I HAD TO WORRY ABOUT OLD ENEMIES GOING AFTER MY FRIENDS, BATMAN HAD ME GO UNDERCOVER TO INFILTRATE AN ORGANIZATION CALLED SPYRAL THAT WAS STEALING THE SECRET IDENTITIES OF YOU AND THE JLA AND A BUNCH OF OTHERS...
...BUT THEN I DIDN'T HEAR FROM BATMAN ANYMORE, SO I CAME HOME ONLY TO FIND HE'S BECOME AN AMNESIAC, AND NOW I HAVE TO GO BACK TO THE BACKSTABBERS AND LIARS AND...
WAIT. WHY ARE YOU JUMPING? AND WHERE'S THE FANCY LEOTARD?
OOOOKAY HERE GOES...
MY POWERS WERE OVERLOADING, AND I FOUND OUT THAT I COULD CAUSE A GIANT STARBURST--
--BUT NO ONE, NOT EVEN CYBORG OR BATMAN, COULD TELL ME WHY, AND THEN MY POWERS STARTED TO FADE--
--SO I GOT A MOTORCYCLE AND A T-SHIRT AND...
Sigh
Y'KNOW, I STILL DON'T KNOW HOW HORDR_ROOT GOT AHOLD OF MY SECRET IDENTITY. DO YOU THINK SPYRAL...?
Huh. I MEAN, MAYBE, THOUGH IT'D MEAN THEY'D LOSE SOME OF THEIR ADVANTAGE. I CAN CHECK FOR YOU WHEN I GET BACK.
THAT'D BE GREAT, MAN.
Sigh THE LIVES OF "SUPERHEROES," HUH?
YEAH. "LIVES."
I'M NOT EVEN SURE THAT' THE RIGHT WORD FOR IT.

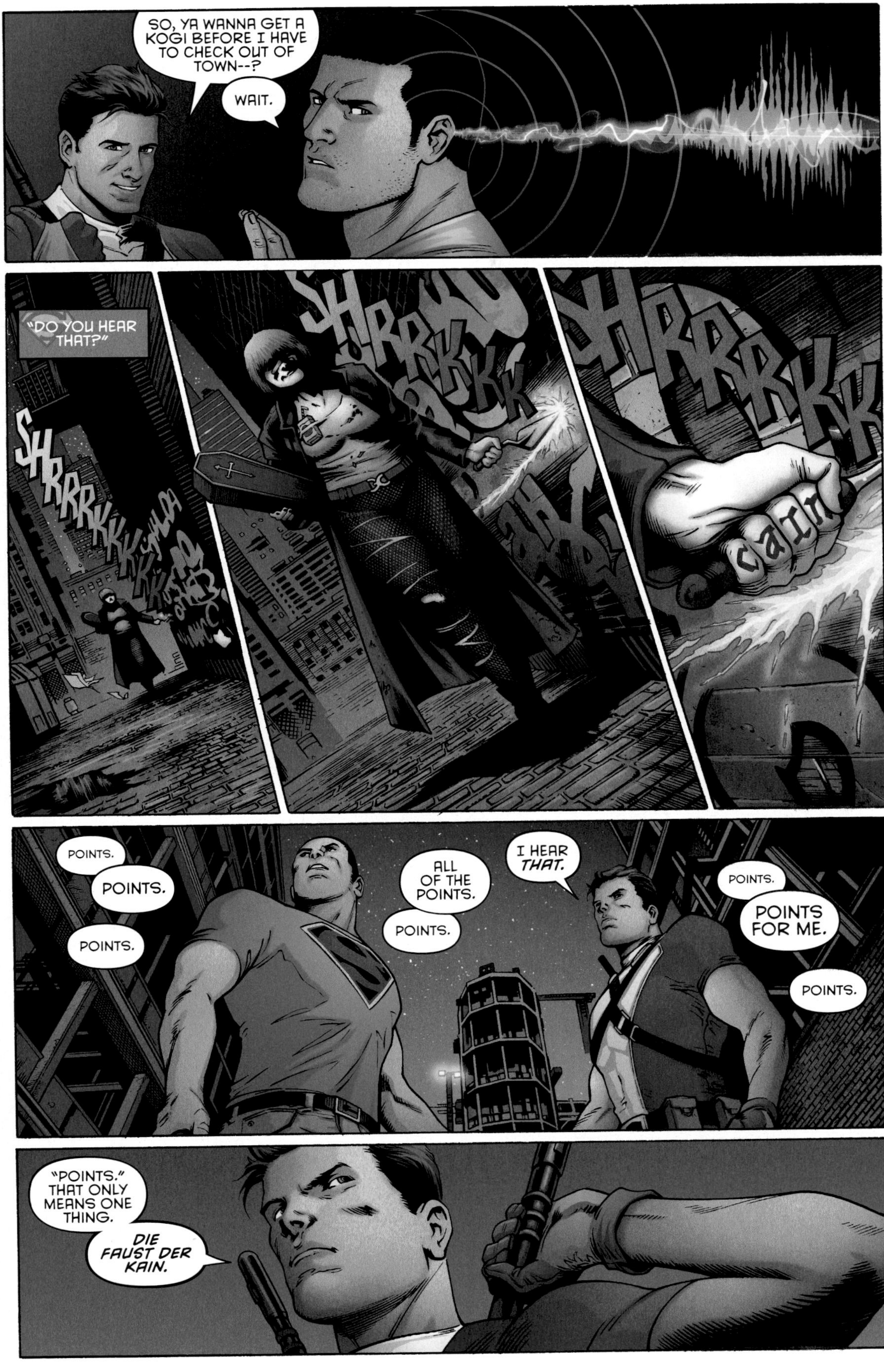

SO, YA WANNA GET A KOGI BEFORE I HAVE TO CHECK OUT OF TOWN--?
WAIT.
"DO YOU HEAR THAT?"
cain
POINTS.
POINTS.
POINTS.
ALL OF THE POINTS.
POINTS.
I HEAR THAT.
POINTS.
POINTS FOR ME.
POINTS.
"POINTS." THAT ONLY MEANS ONE THING.
DIE FAUST DER KAIN.

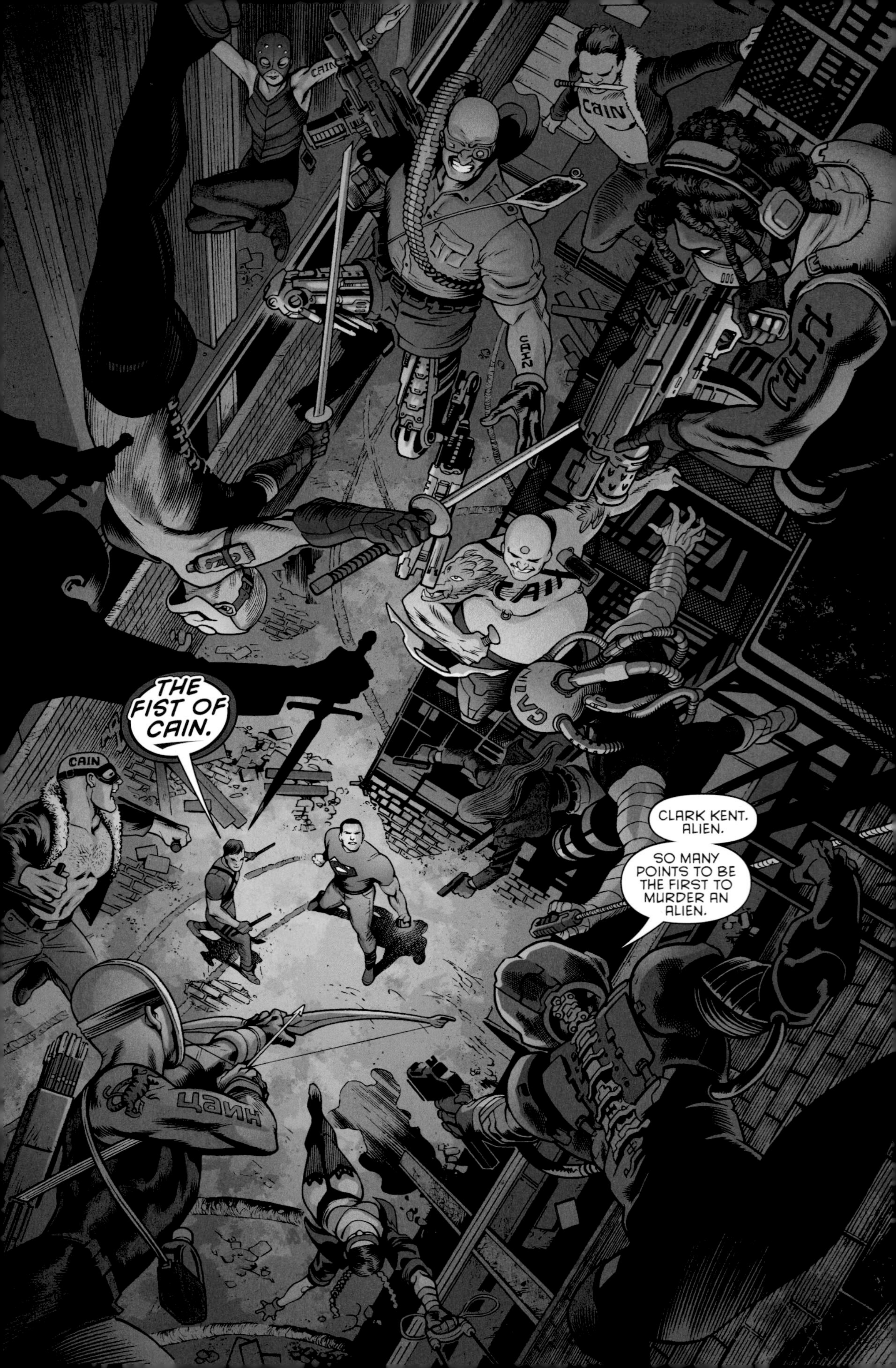
THE FIST OF CAIN.
CLARK KENT. ALIEN.
SO MANY POINTS TO BE THE FIRST TO MURDER AN ALIEN.

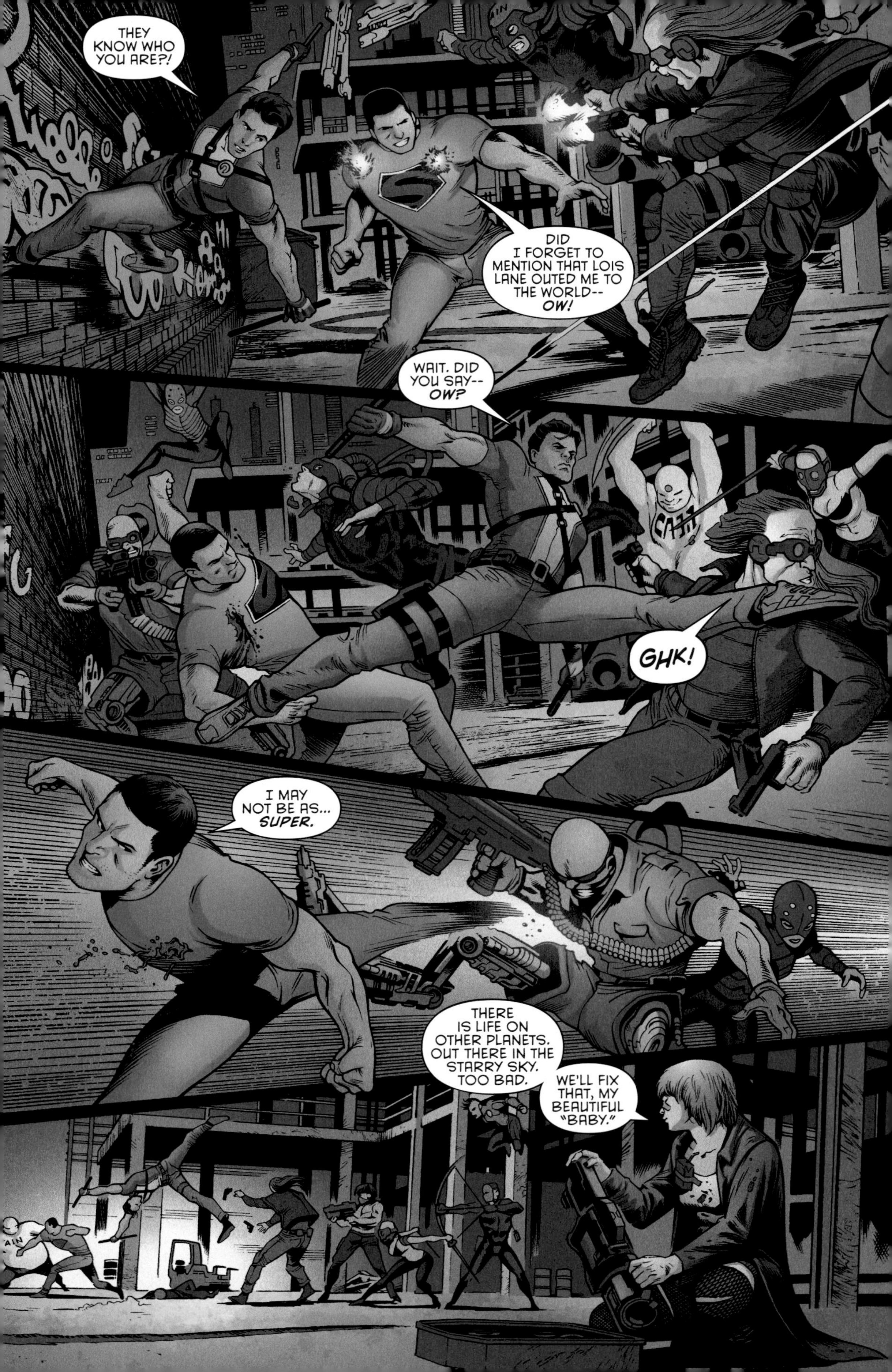

THEY KNOW WHO YOU ARE?!
DID I FORGET TO MENTION THAT LOIS LANE OUTED ME TO THE WORLD-- OW!
WAIT. DID YOU SAY-- OW?
GHK!
I MAY NOT BE AS... SUPER.
THERE IS LIFE ON OTHER PLANETS. OUT THERE IN THE STARRY SKY. TOO BAD.
WE'LL FIX THAT, MY BEAUTIFUL "BABY."

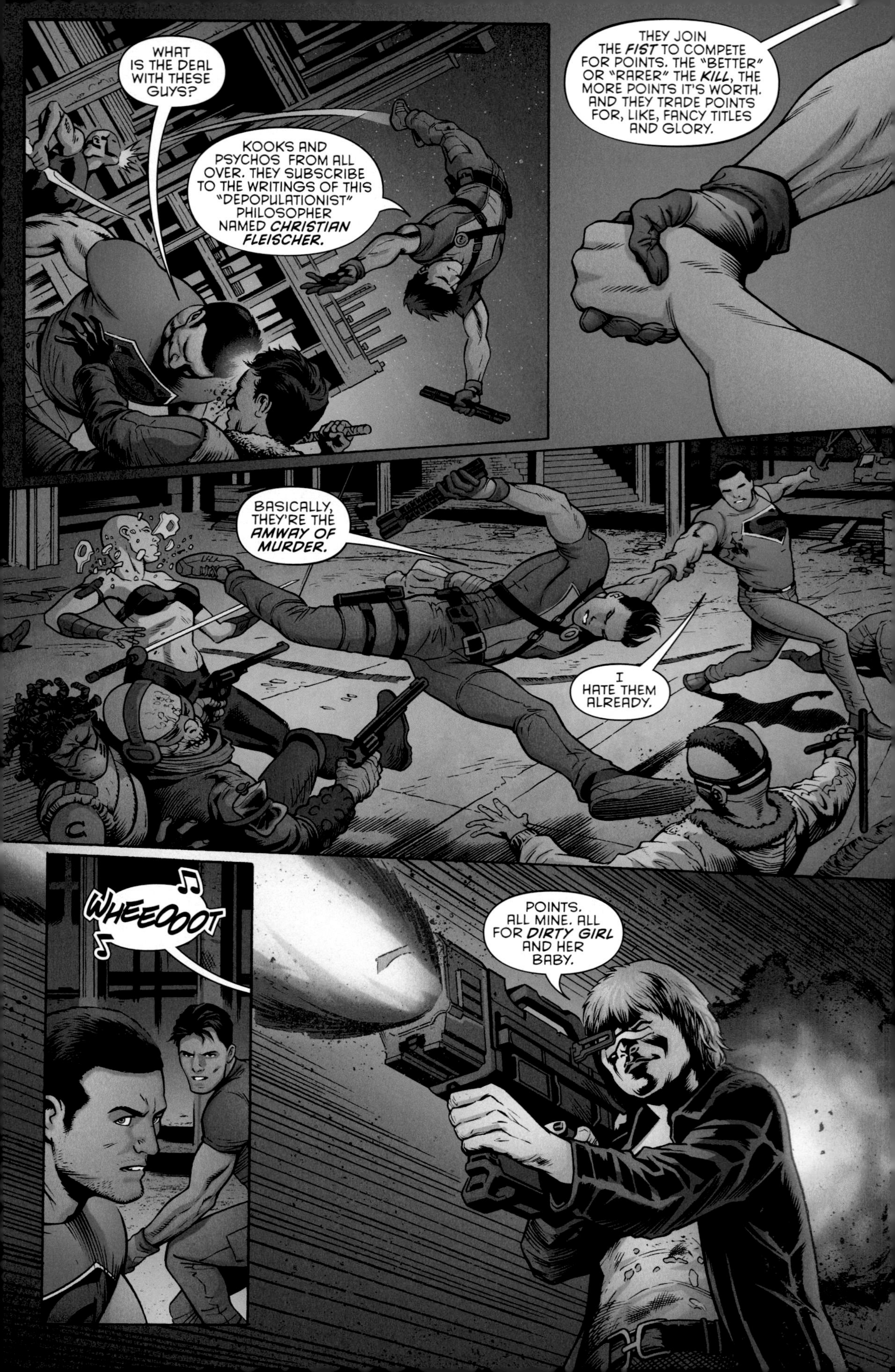
WHAT IS THE DEAL WITH THESE GUYS?
KOOKS AND PSYCHOS FROM ALL OVER. THEY SUBSCRIBE TO THE WRITINGS OF THIS "DEPOPULATIONIST" PHILOSOPHER NAMED CHRISTIAN FLEISCHER.
THEY JOIN THE FIST TO COMPETE FOR POINTS. THE "BETTER" OR "RARER" THE KILL, THE MORE POINTS IT'S WORTH. AND THEY TRADE POINTS FOR, LIKE, FANCY TITLES AND GLORY.
BASICALLY, THEY'RE THE AMWAY OF MURDER.
I HATE THEM ALREADY.
WHEEOOOT
POINTS. ALL MINE. ALL FOR DIRTY GIRL AND HER BABY.

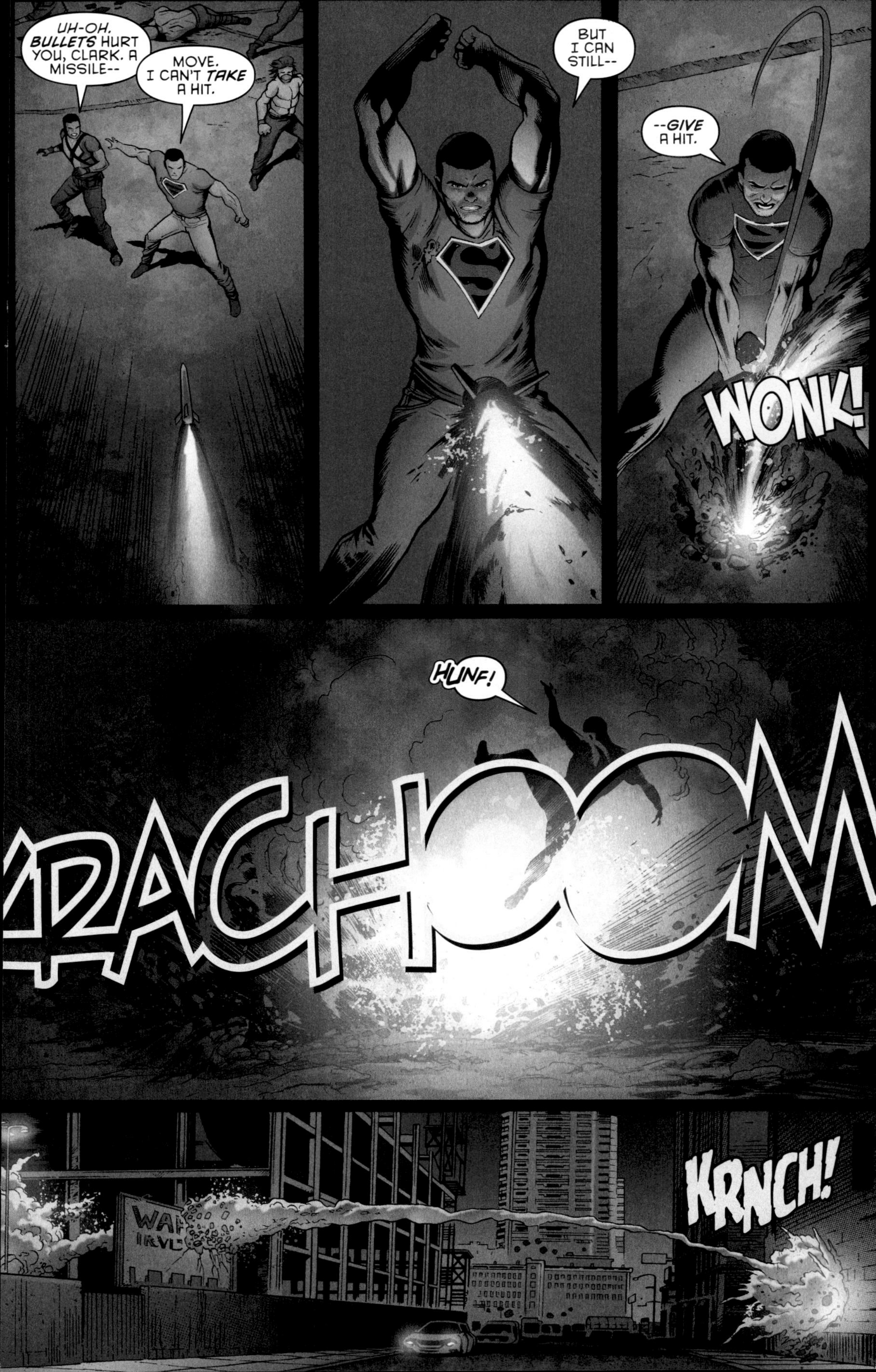
UH-OH. *BULLETS* HURT YOU, CLARK. A MISSILE--
MOVE. I CAN'T *TAKE* A HIT.
BUT I CAN STILL--
--*GIVE* A HIT.
WONK!
HUNF!
RACHOOM!
KRNCH!

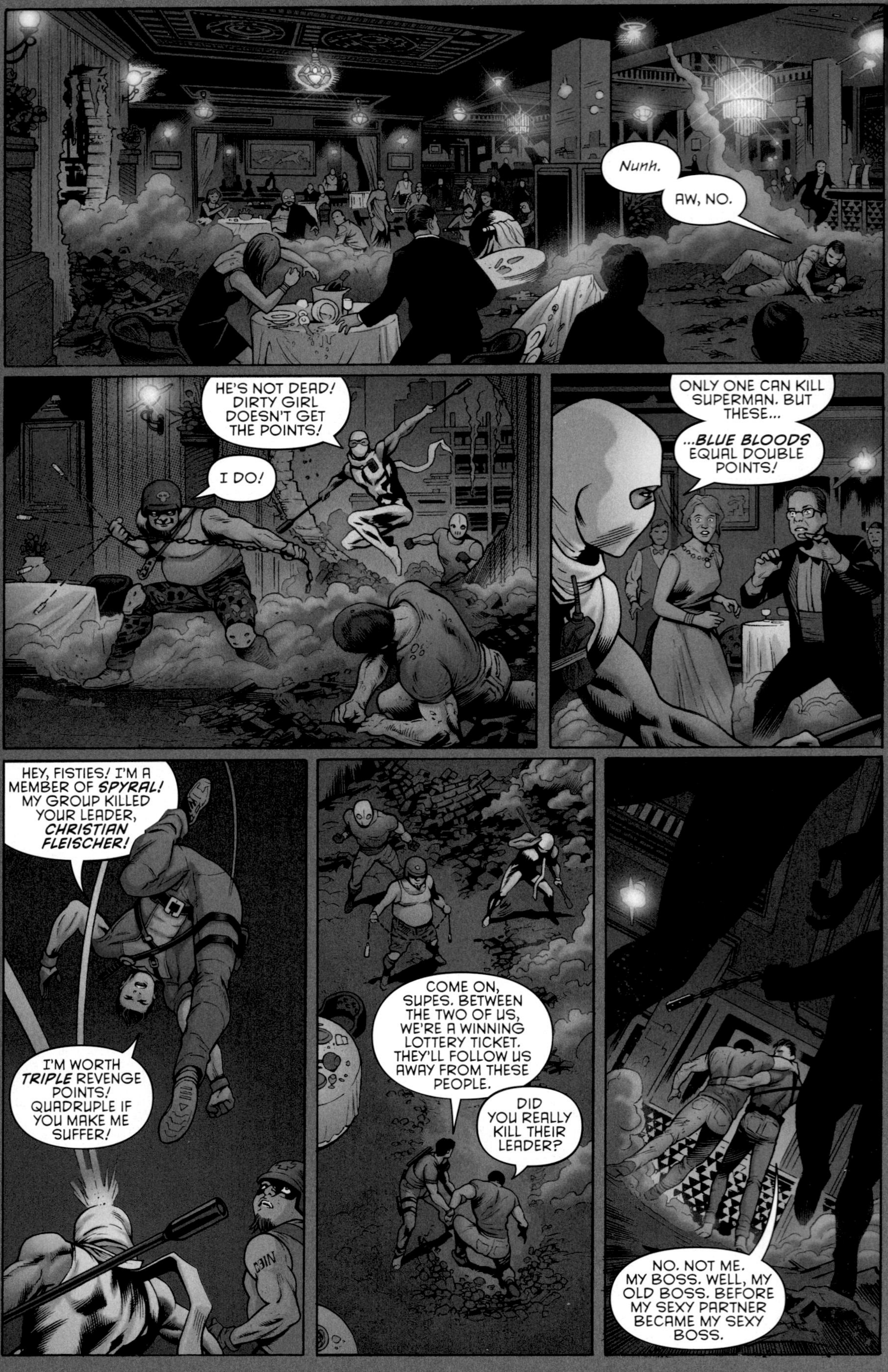
Nunh.
AW, NO.
HE'S NOT DEAD! DIRTY GIRL DOESN'T GET THE POINTS!
I DO!
ONLY ONE CAN KILL SUPERMAN. BUT THESE...
...BLUE BLOODS EQUAL DOUBLE POINTS!
HEY, FISTIES! I'M A MEMBER OF SPYRAL! MY GROUP KILLED YOUR LEADER, CHRISTIAN FLEISCHER!
I'M WORTH TRIPLE REVENGE POINTS! QUADRUPLE IF YOU MAKE ME SUFFER!
COME ON, SUPES. BETWEEN THE TWO OF US, WE'RE A WINNING LOTTERY TICKET. THEY'LL FOLLOW US AWAY FROM THESE PEOPLE.
DID YOU REALLY KILL THEIR LEADER?
NO. NOT ME. MY BOSS. WELL, MY OLD BOSS. BEFORE MY SEXY PARTNER BECAME MY SEXY BOSS.

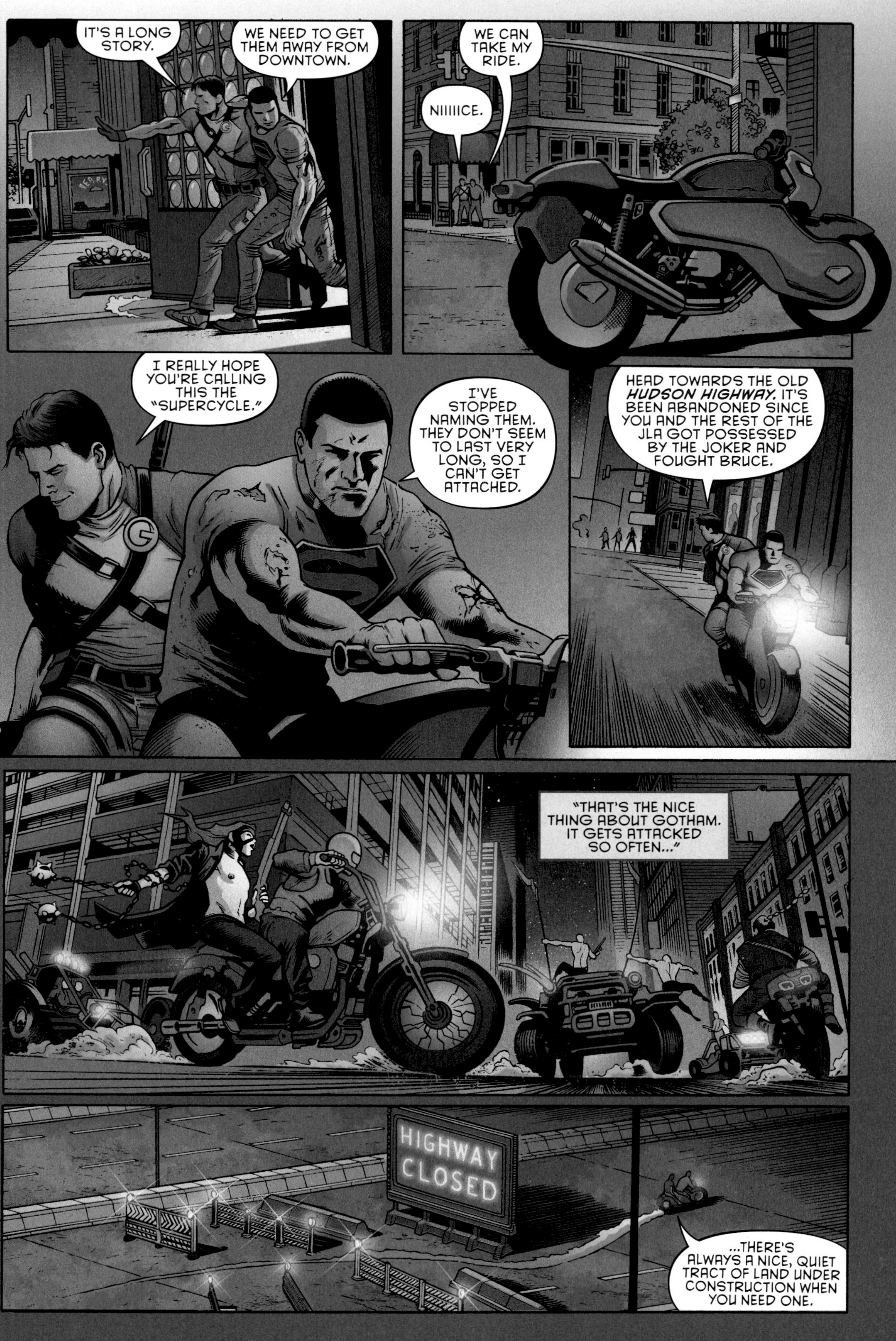
IT'S A LONG STORY.
WE NEED TO GET THEM AWAY FROM DOWNTOWN.
WE CAN TAKE MY RIDE.
NIIIIICE.
I REALLY HOPE YOU'RE CALLING THIS THE "SUPERCYCLE."
I'VE STOPPED NAMING THEM. THEY DON'T SEEM TO LAST VERY LONG, SO I CAN'T GET ATTACHED.
HEAD TOWARDS THE OLD HUDSON HIGHWAY. IT'S BEEN ABANDONED SINCE YOU AND THE REST OF THE JLA GOT POSSESSED BY THE JOKER AND FOUGHT BRUCE.
"THAT'S THE NICE THING ABOUT GOTHAM. IT GETS ATTACKED SO OFTEN..."
HIGHWAY CLOSED
...THERE'S ALWAYS A NICE, QUIET TRACT OF LAND UNDER CONSTRUCTION WHEN YOU NEED ONE.

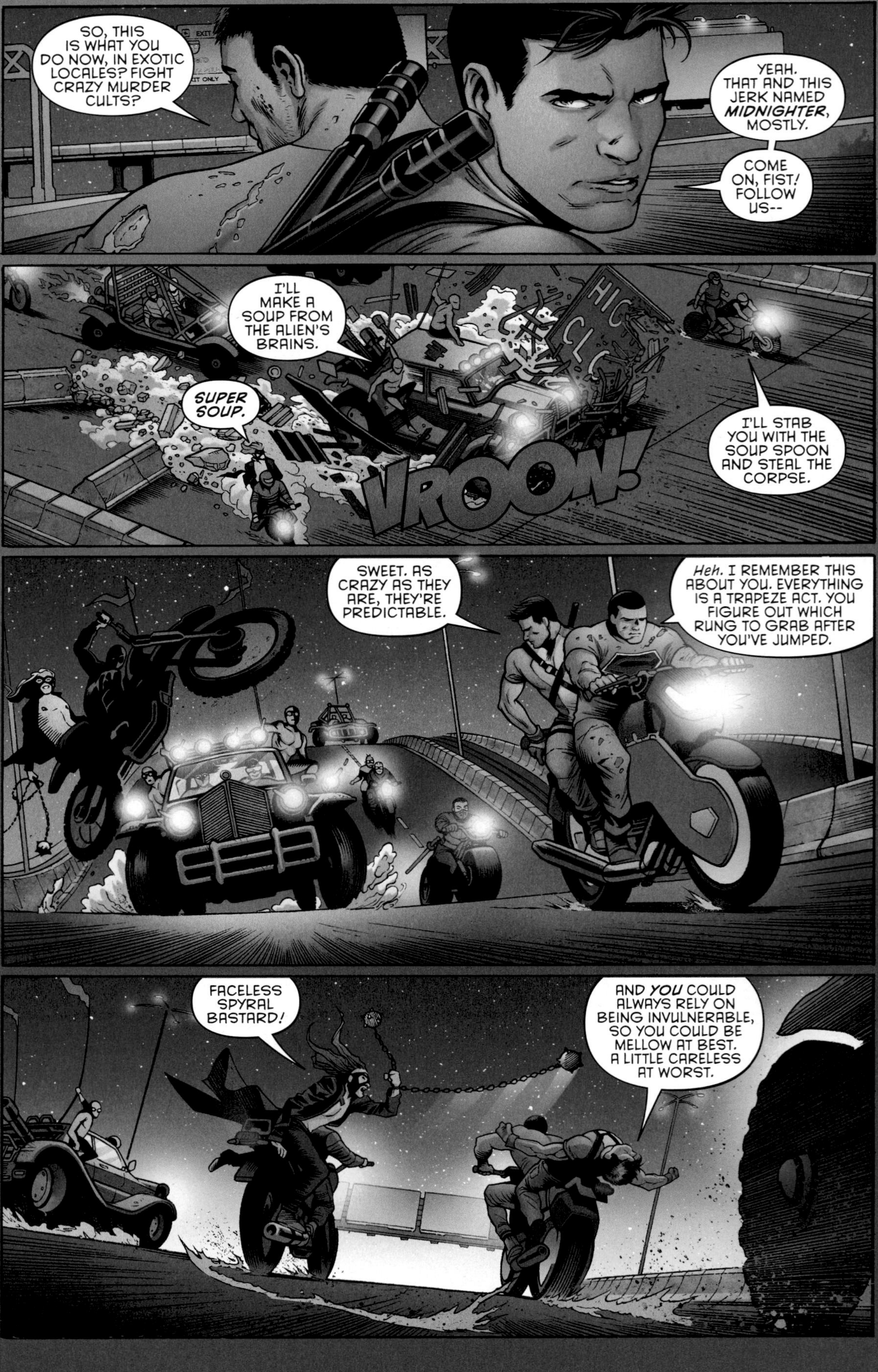

SO, THIS IS WHAT YOU DO NOW, IN EXOTIC LOCALES? FIGHT CRAZY MURDER CULTS?
YEAH. THAT AND THIS JERK NAMED **MIDNIGHTER**, MOSTLY.
COME ON, FIST! FOLLOW US--
I'LL MAKE A SOUP FROM THE ALIEN'S BRAINS.
SUPER SOUP.
I'LL STAB YOU WITH THE SOUP SPOON AND STEAL THE CORPSE.
VROOM!
SWEET. AS CRAZY AS THEY ARE, THEY'RE PREDICTABLE.
Heh. I REMEMBER THIS ABOUT YOU. EVERYTHING IS A TRAPEZE ACT. YOU FIGURE OUT WHICH RUNG TO GRAB AFTER YOU'VE JUMPED.
FACELESS SPYRAL BASTARD!
AND *YOU* COULD ALWAYS RELY ON BEING INVULNERABLE, SO YOU COULD BE MELLOW AT BEST. A LITTLE CARELESS AT WORST.

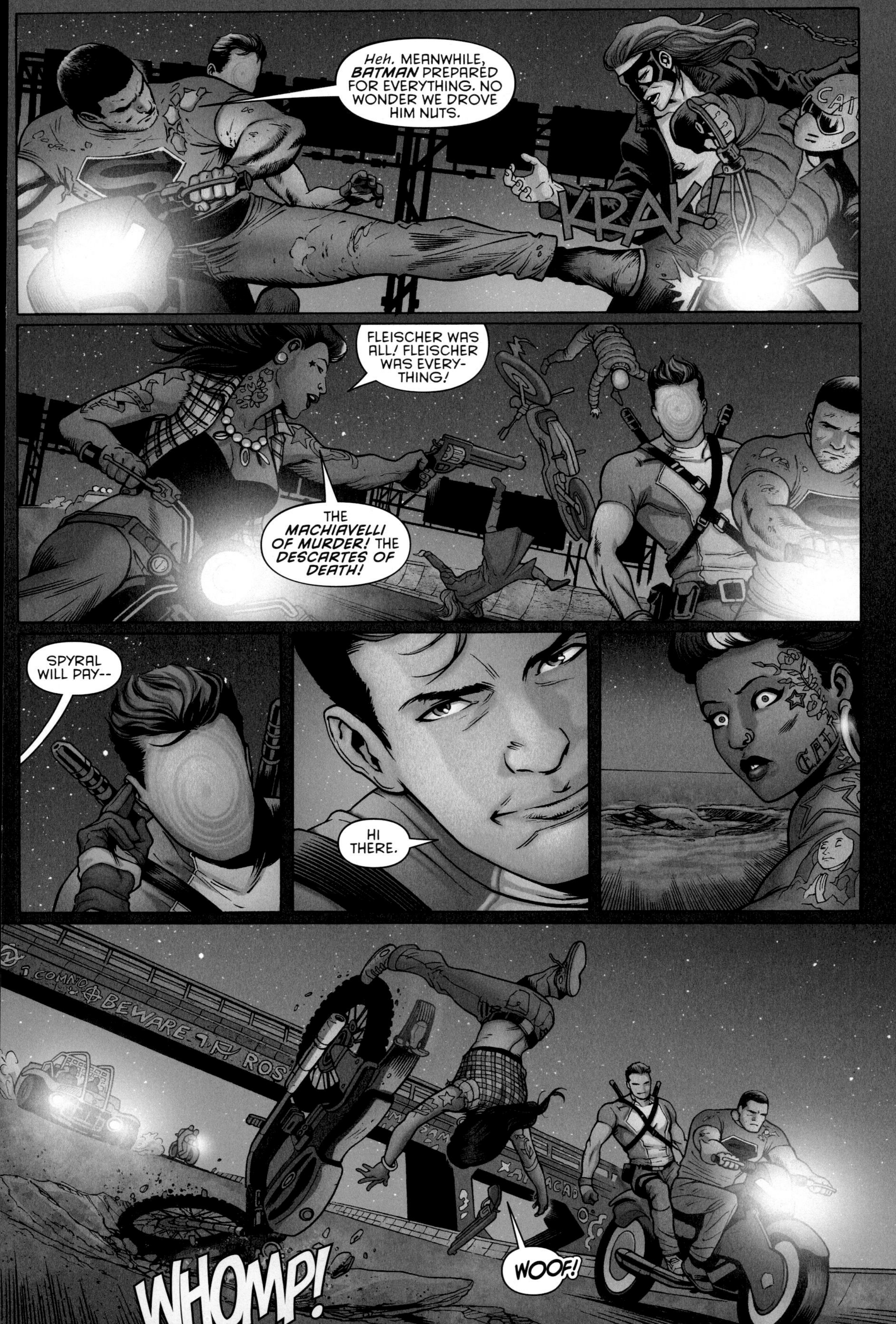
Heh. MEANWHILE, BATMAN PREPARED FOR EVERYTHING. NO WONDER WE DROVE HIM NUTS.
KRAK!
FLEISCHER WAS ALL! FLEISCHER WAS EVERYTHING!
THE MACHIAVELLI OF MURDER! THE DESCARTES OF DEATH!
SPYRAL WILL PAY--
HI THERE.
BEWARE
WHOMP!
WOOF!

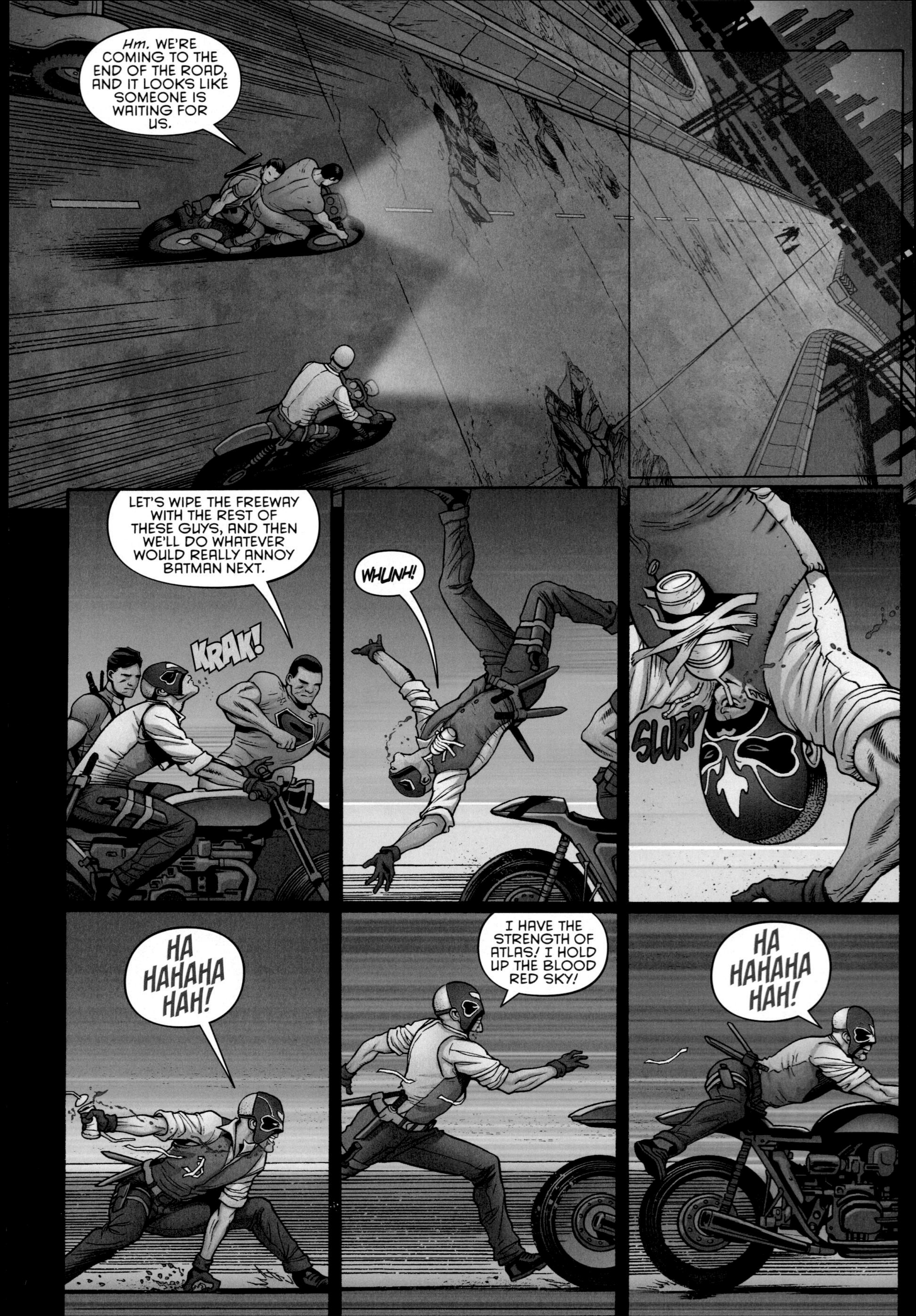

Hm. WE'RE COMING TO THE END OF THE ROAD, AND IT LOOKS LIKE SOMEONE IS WAITING FOR US.
LET'S WIPE THE FREEWAY WITH THE REST OF THESE GUYS, AND THEN WE'LL DO WHATEVER WOULD REALLY ANNOY BATMAN NEXT.
KRAK!
WHUNH!
SLURP
HA HAHAHA HAH!
I HAVE THE STRENGTH OF ATLAS! I HOLD UP THE BLOOD RED SKY!
HA HAHAHA HAH!

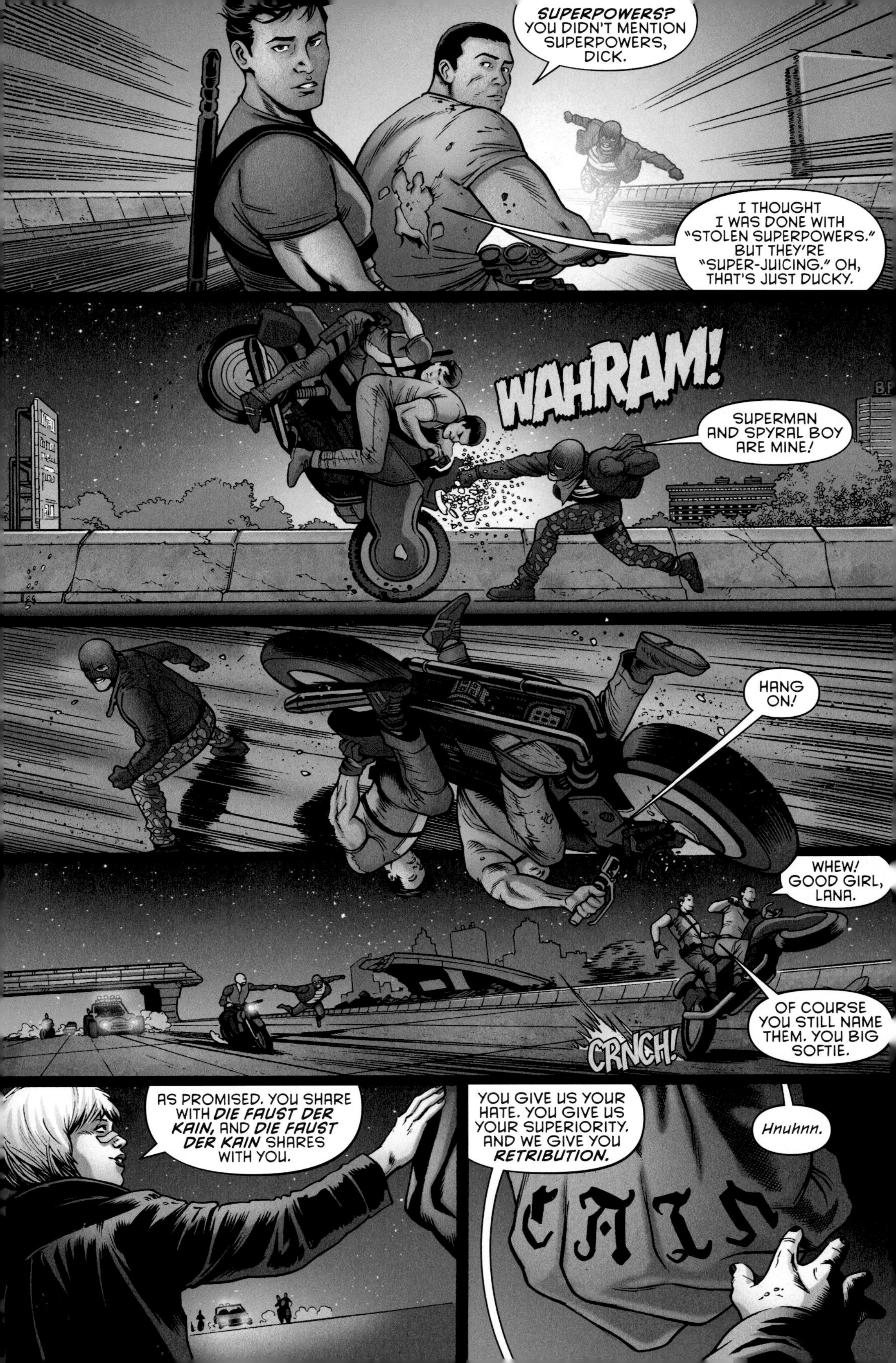
SUPERPOWERS? YOU DIDN'T MENTION SUPERPOWERS, DICK.
I THOUGHT I WAS DONE WITH "STOLEN SUPERPOWERS." BUT THEY'RE "SUPER-JUICING." OH, THAT'S JUST DUCKY.
WAHRAM!
SUPERMAN AND SPYRAL BOY ARE MINE!
HANG ON!
WHEW! GOOD GIRL, LANA.
OF COURSE YOU STILL NAME THEM. YOU BIG SOFTIE.
CRNCH!
AS PROMISED. YOU SHARE WITH DIE FAUST DER KAIN, AND DIE FAUST DER KAIN SHARES WITH YOU.
YOU GIVE US YOUR HATE. YOU GIVE US YOUR SUPERIORITY. AND WE GIVE YOU RETRIBUTION.
Hnuhnn.

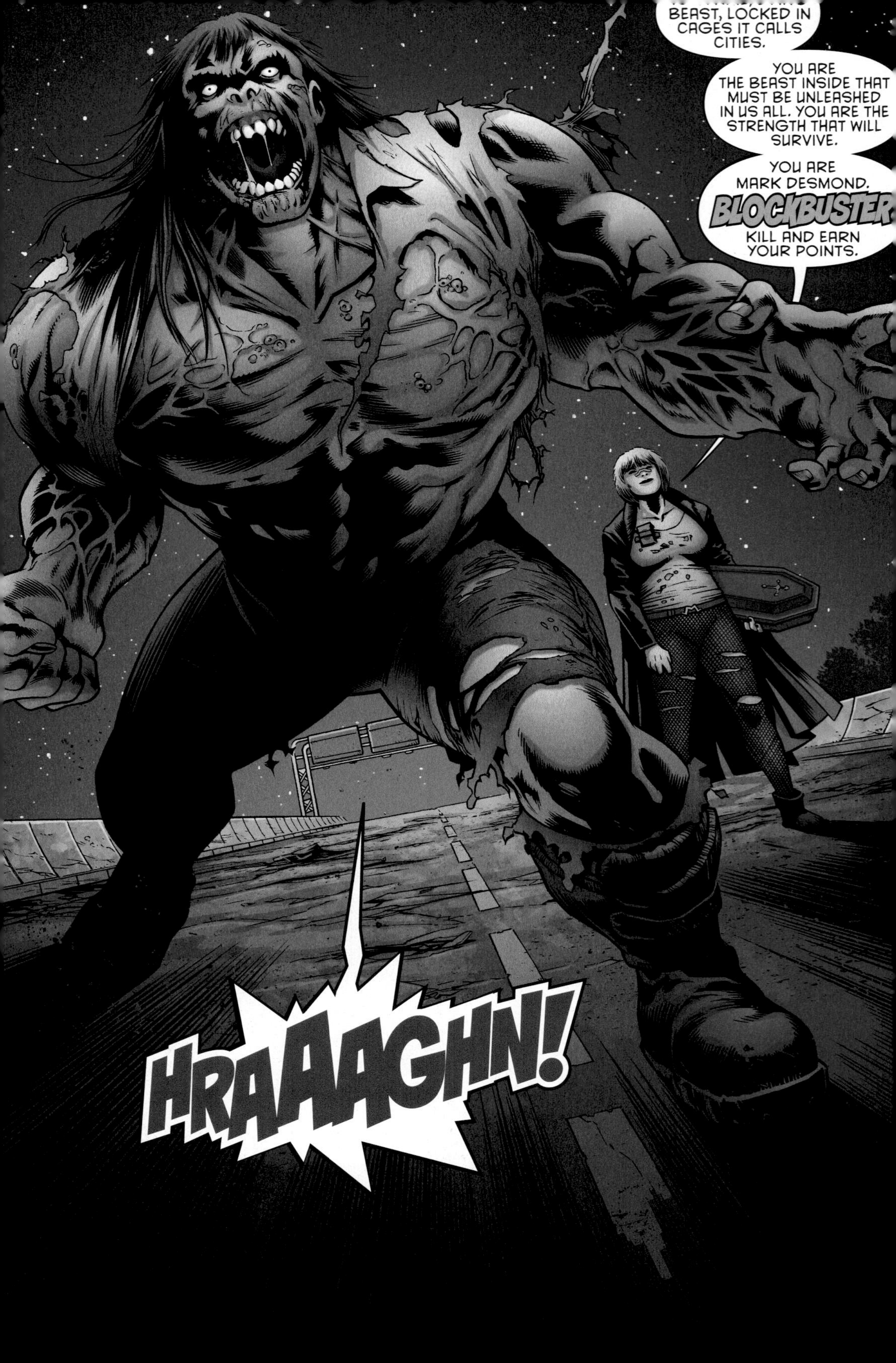
BEAST, LOCKED IN CAGES IT CALLS CITIES.
YOU ARE THE BEAST INSIDE THAT MUST BE UNLEASHED IN US ALL. YOU ARE THE STRENGTH THAT WILL SURVIVE.
YOU ARE MARK DESMOND. BLOCKBUSTER KILL AND EARN YOUR POINTS.
HRAAAGHN!

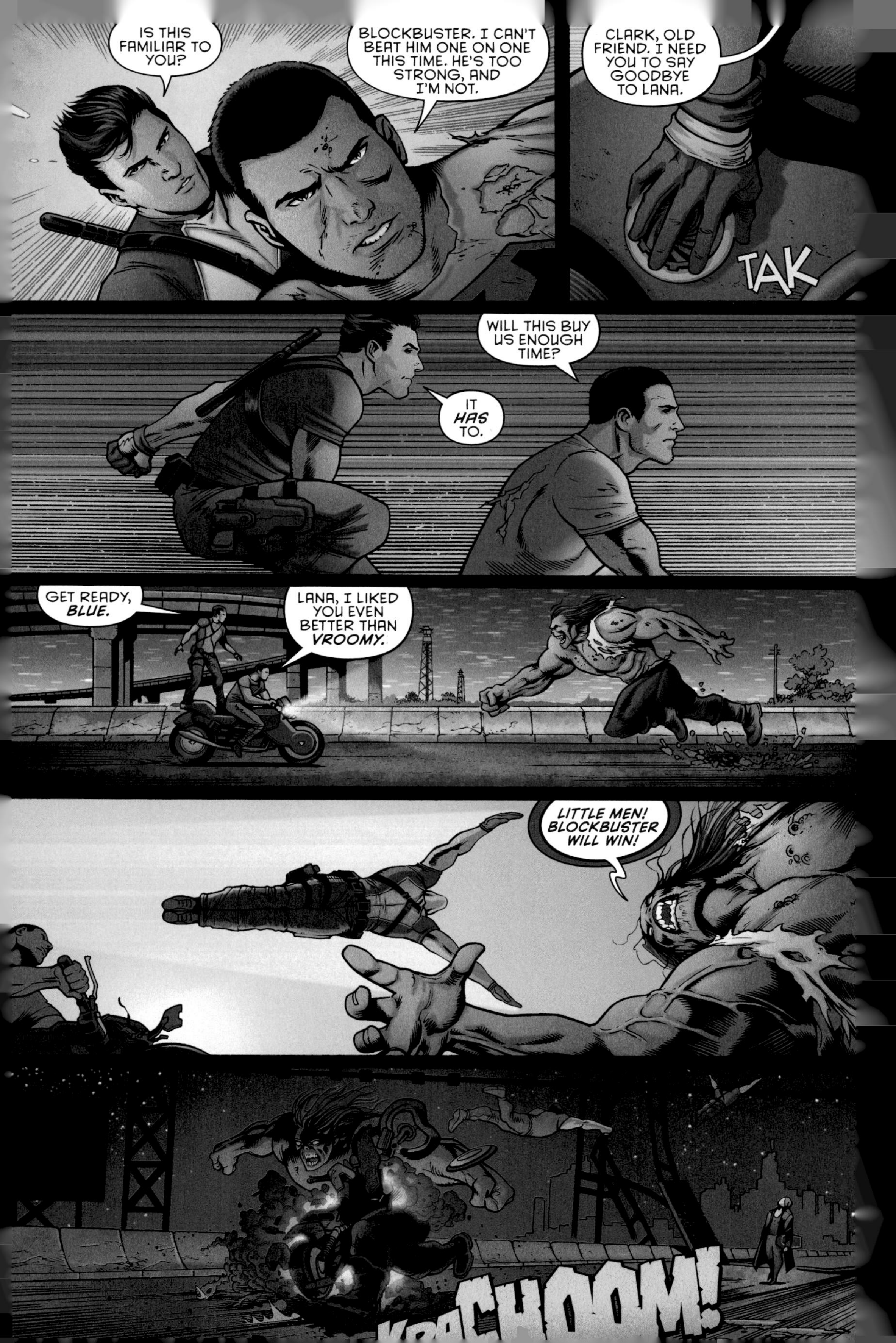
IS THIS FAMILIAR TO YOU?
BLOCKBUSTER. I CAN'T BEAT HIM ONE ON ONE THIS TIME. HE'S TOO STRONG, AND I'M NOT.
CLARK, OLD FRIEND. I NEED YOU TO SAY GOODBYE TO LANA.
TAK
WILL THIS BUY US ENOUGH TIME?
IT *HAS* TO.
GET READY, *BLUE.*
LANA, I LIKED YOU EVEN BETTER THAN *VROOMY.*
LITTLE MEN! BLOCKBUSTER WILL WIN!
KRACHOOM!

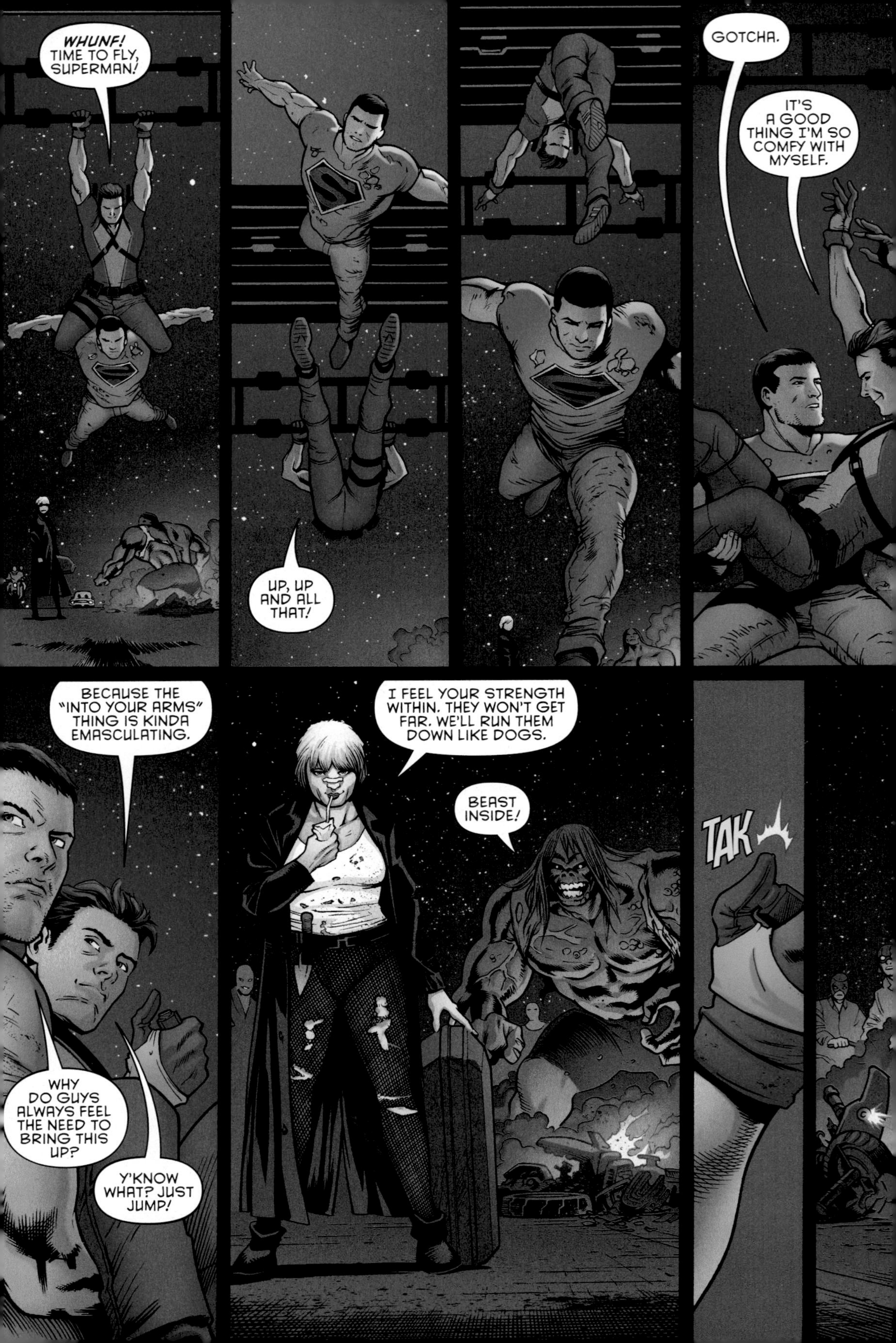
WHUNF! TIME TO FLY, SUPERMAN!
UP, UP AND ALL THAT!
GOTCHA.
IT'S A GOOD THING I'M SO COMFY WITH MYSELF.
BECAUSE THE "INTO YOUR ARMS" THING IS KINDA EMASCULATING.
WHY DO GUYS ALWAYS FEEL THE NEED TO BRING THIS UP?
Y'KNOW WHAT? JUST JUMP!
I FEEL YOUR STRENGTH WITHIN. THEY WON'T GET FAR. WE'LL RUN THEM DOWN LIKE DOGS.
BEAST INSIDE!
TAK

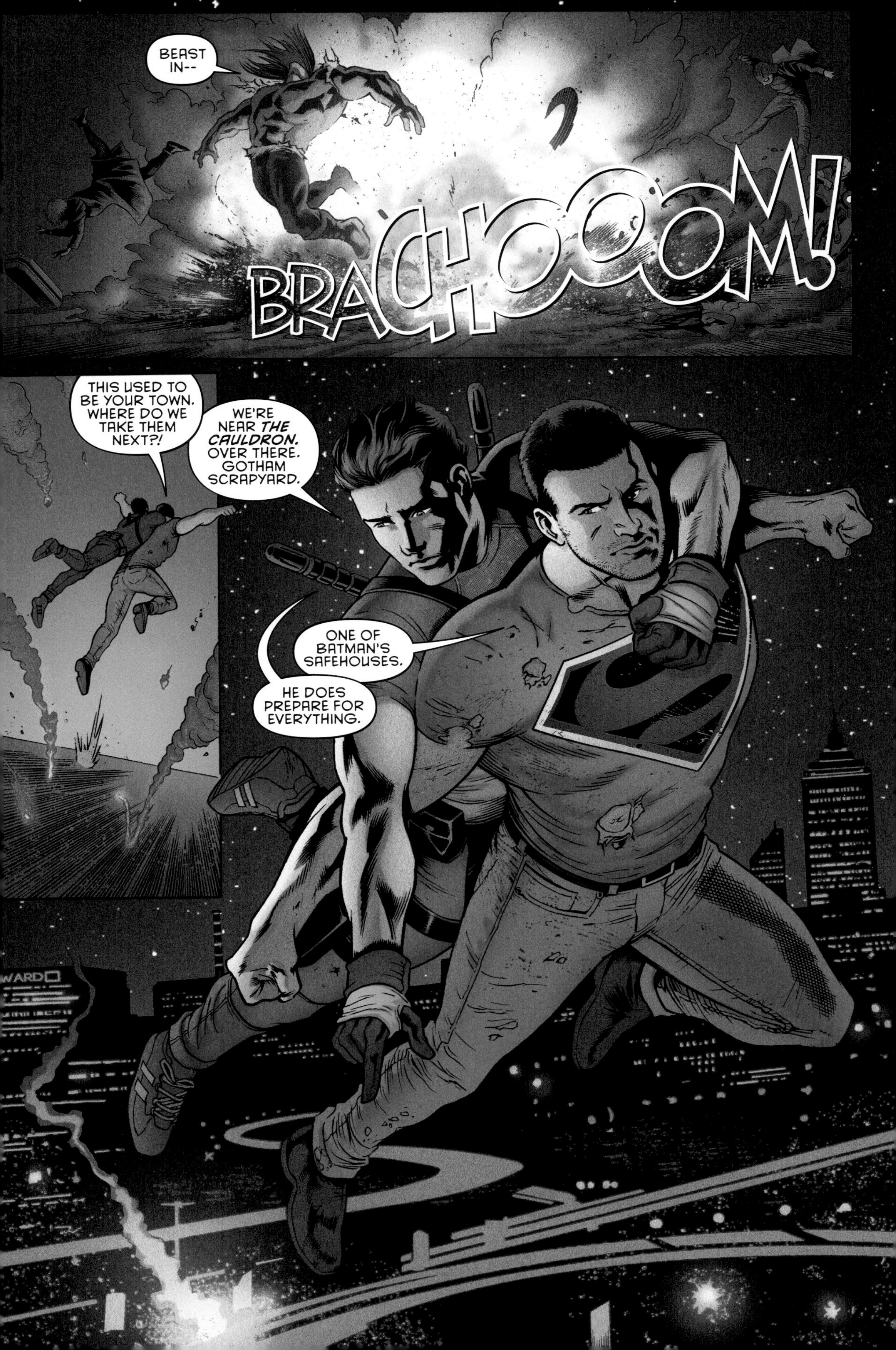
BEAST IN--
BRACHOOOOM!
THIS USED TO BE YOUR TOWN. WHERE DO WE TAKE THEM NEXT?!
WE'RE NEAR *THE CAULDRON.* OVER THERE. GOTHAM SCRAPYARD.
ONE OF BATMAN'S SAFEHOUSES.
HE DOES PREPARE FOR EVERYTHING.

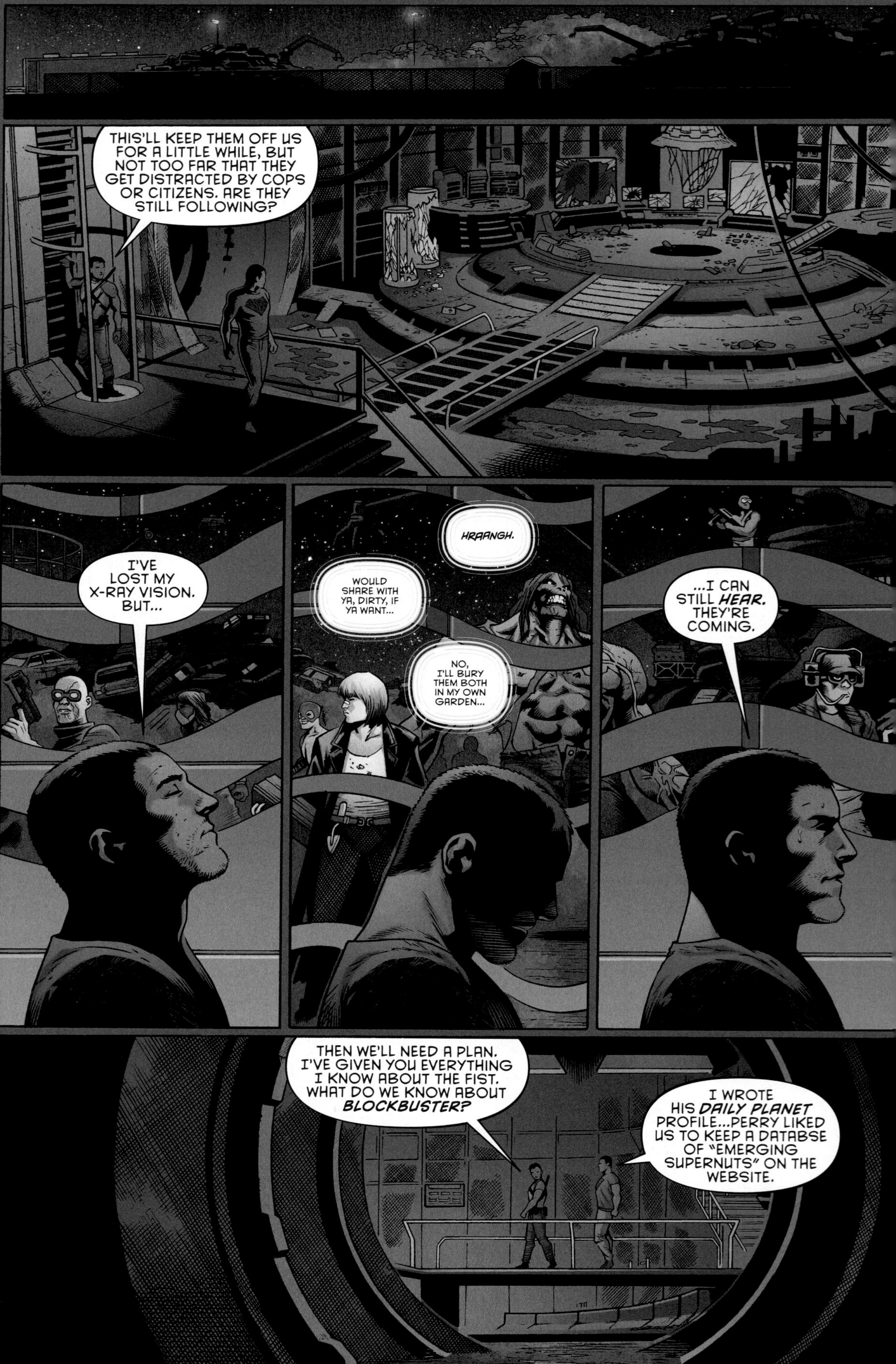

THIS'LL KEEP THEM OFF US FOR A LITTLE WHILE, BUT NOT TOO FAR THAT THEY GET DISTRACTED BY COPS OR CITIZENS. ARE THEY STILL FOLLOWING?
I'VE LOST MY X-RAY VISION. BUT...
HRAANGH.
WOULD SHARE WITH YA, DIRTY, IF YA WANT...
NO, I'LL BURY THEM BOTH IN MY OWN GARDEN...
...I CAN STILL *HEAR.* THEY'RE COMING.
THEN WE'LL NEED A PLAN. I'VE GIVEN YOU EVERYTHING I KNOW ABOUT THE FIST. WHAT DO WE KNOW ABOUT *BLOCKBUSTER?*
I WROTE HIS *DAILY PLANET* PROFILE...PERRY LIKED US TO KEEP A DATABSE OF "EMERGING SUPERNUTS" ON THE WEBSITE.

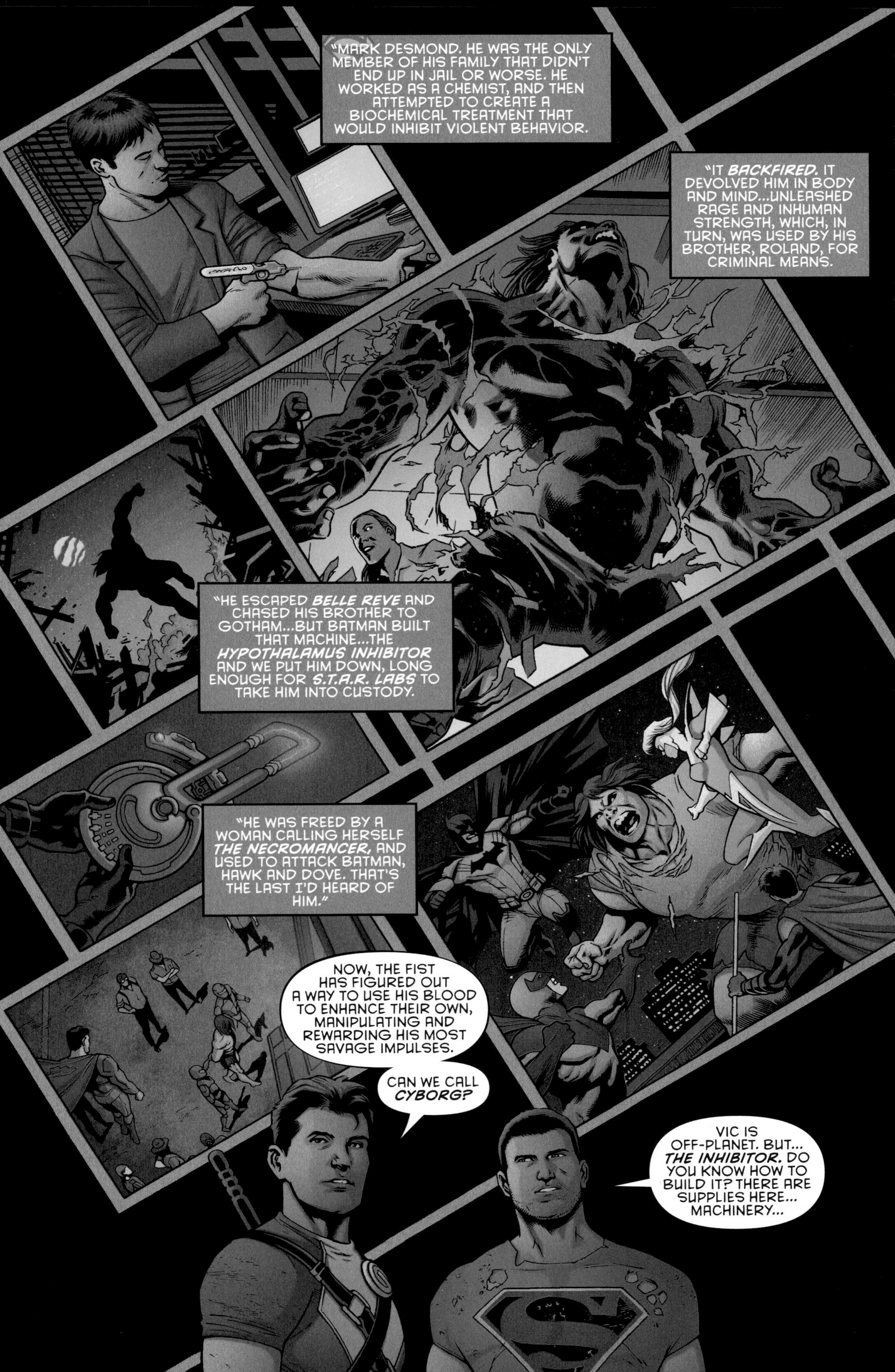
"MARK DESMOND. HE WAS THE ONLY MEMBER OF HIS FAMILY THAT DIDN'T END UP IN JAIL OR WORSE. HE WORKED AS A CHEMIST, AND THEN ATTEMPTED TO CREATE A BIOCHEMICAL TREATMENT THAT WOULD INHIBIT VIOLENT BEHAVIOR.
"IT BACKFIRED. IT DEVOLVED HIM IN BODY AND MIND...UNLEASHED RAGE AND INHUMAN STRENGTH, WHICH, IN TURN, WAS USED BY HIS BROTHER, ROLAND, FOR CRIMINAL MEANS.
"HE ESCAPED BELLE REVE AND CHASED HIS BROTHER TO GOTHAM...BUT BATMAN BUILT THAT MACHINE...THE HYPOTHALAMUS INHIBITOR AND WE PUT HIM DOWN, LONG ENOUGH FOR S.T.A.R. LABS TO TAKE HIM INTO CUSTODY.
"HE WAS FREED BY A WOMAN CALLING HERSELF THE NECROMANCER, AND USED TO ATTACK BATMAN, HAWK AND DOVE. THAT'S THE LAST I'D HEARD OF HIM."
NOW, THE FIST HAS FIGURED OUT A WAY TO USE HIS BLOOD TO ENHANCE THEIR OWN, MANIPULATING AND REWARDING HIS MOST SAVAGE IMPULSES.
CAN WE CALL CYBORG?
VIC IS OFF-PLANET. BUT... THE INHIBITOR. DO YOU KNOW HOW TO BUILD IT? THERE ARE SUPPLIES HERE... MACHINERY...

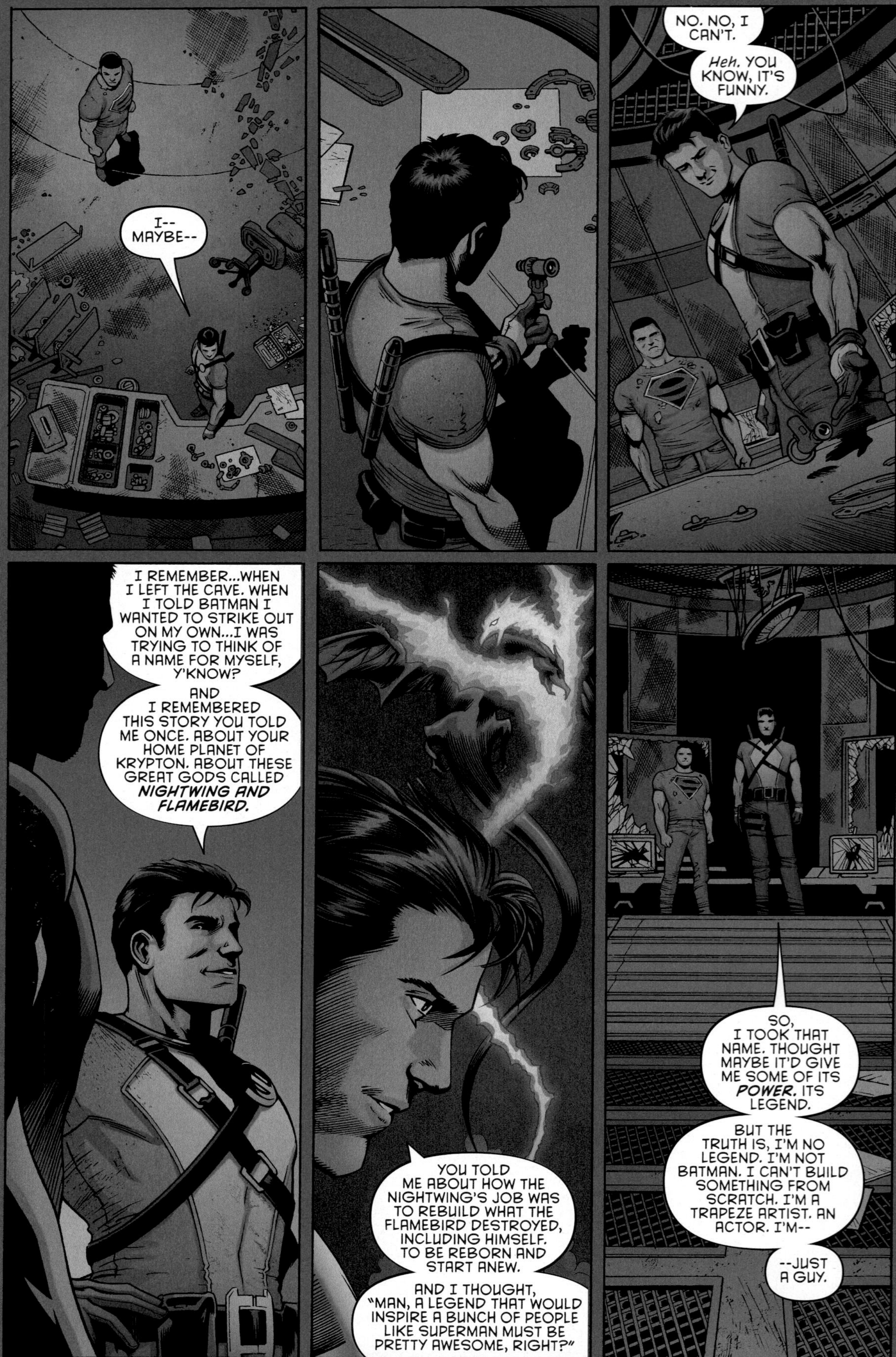
I-- MAYBE--
NO. NO, I CAN'T.
Heh. YOU KNOW, IT'S FUNNY.
I REMEMBER...WHEN I LEFT THE CAVE. WHEN I TOLD BATMAN I WANTED TO STRIKE OUT ON MY OWN...I WAS TRYING TO THINK OF A NAME FOR MYSELF, Y'KNOW?
AND I REMEMBERED THIS STORY YOU TOLD ME ONCE. ABOUT YOUR HOME PLANET OF KRYPTON. ABOUT THESE GREAT GODS CALLED NIGHTWING AND FLAMEBIRD.
YOU TOLD ME ABOUT HOW THE NIGHTWING'S JOB WAS TO REBUILD WHAT THE FLAMEBIRD DESTROYED, INCLUDING HIMSELF. TO BE REBORN AND START ANEW.
AND I THOUGHT, "MAN, A LEGEND THAT WOULD INSPIRE A BUNCH OF PEOPLE LIKE SUPERMAN MUST BE PRETTY AWESOME, RIGHT?"
SO, I TOOK THAT NAME. THOUGHT MAYBE IT'D GIVE ME SOME OF ITS POWER. ITS LEGEND.
BUT THE TRUTH IS, I'M NO LEGEND. I'M NOT BATMAN. I CAN'T BUILD SOMETHING FROM SCRATCH. I'M A TRAPEZE ARTIST. AN ACTOR. I'M--
--JUST A GUY.

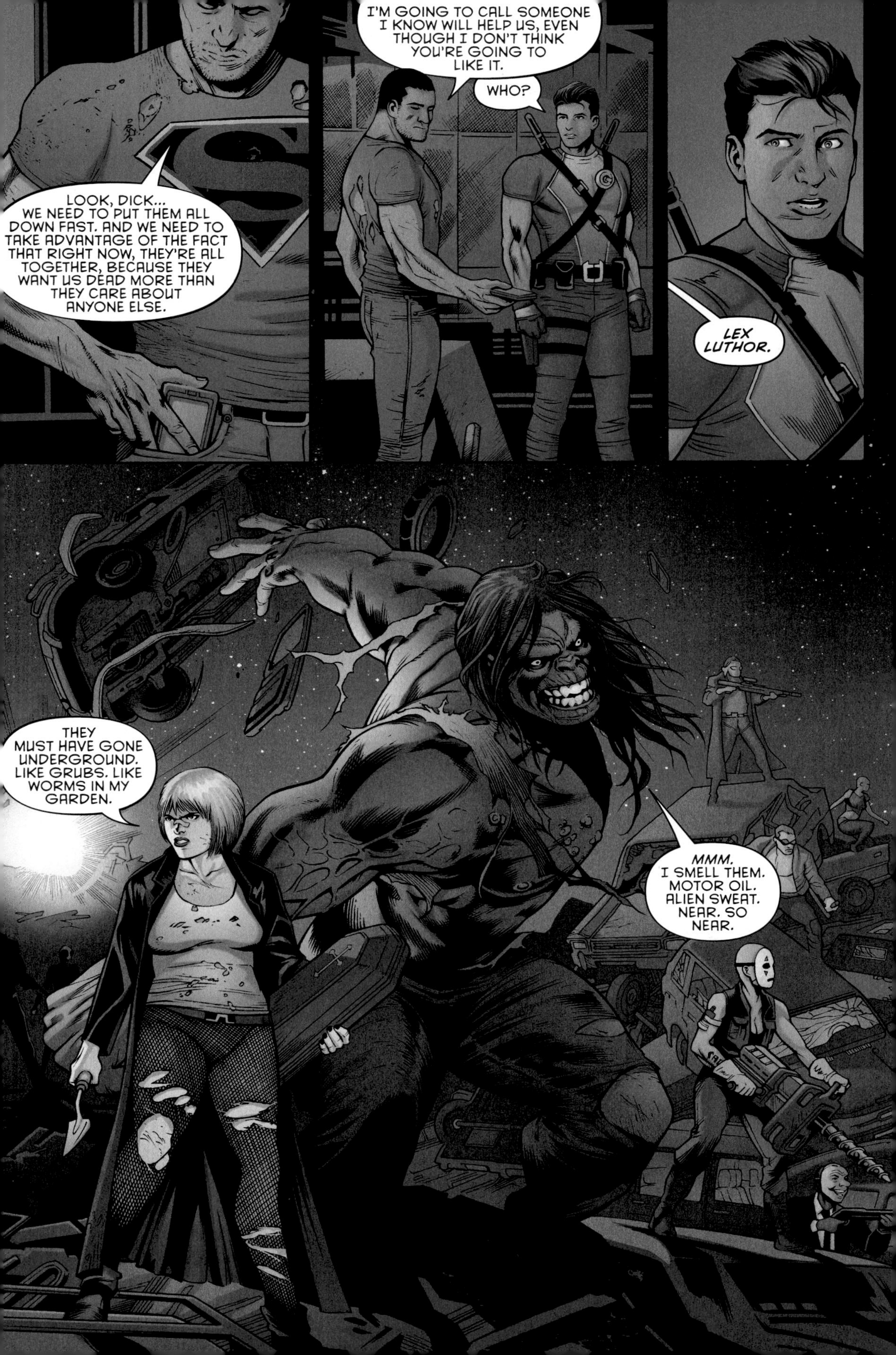
LOOK, DICK... WE NEED TO PUT THEM ALL DOWN FAST. AND WE NEED TO TAKE ADVANTAGE OF THE FACT THAT RIGHT NOW, THEY'RE ALL TOGETHER, BECAUSE THEY WANT US DEAD MORE THAN THEY CARE ABOUT ANYONE ELSE.
I'M GOING TO CALL SOMEONE I KNOW WILL HELP US, EVEN THOUGH I DON'T THINK YOU'RE GOING TO LIKE IT.
WHO?
LEX LUTHOR.
THEY MUST HAVE GONE UNDERGROUND. LIKE GRUBS. LIKE WORMS IN MY GARDEN.
MMM. I SMELL THEM. MOTOR OIL. ALIEN SWEAT. NEAR. SO NEAR.

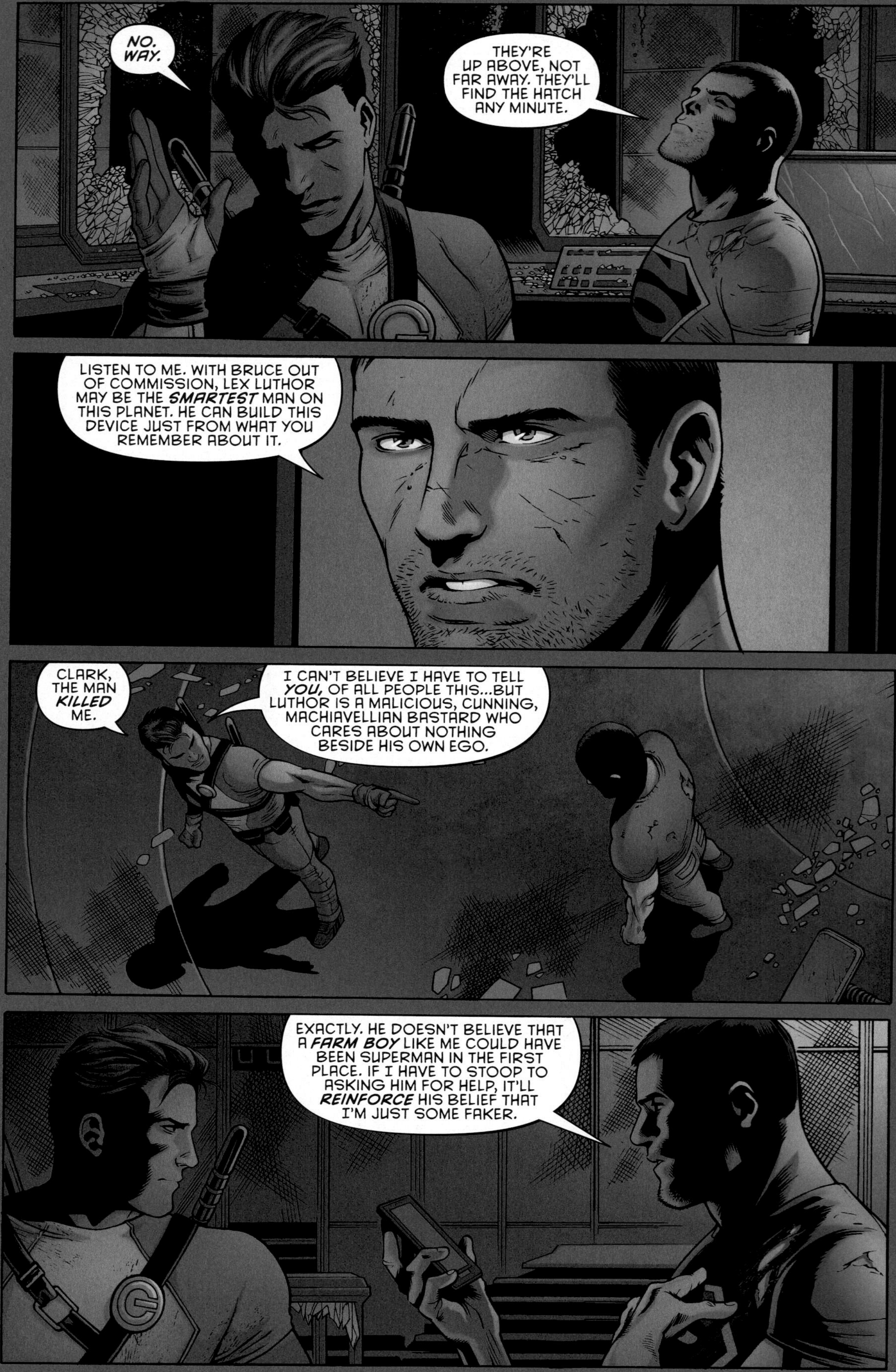
NO. WAY.
THEY'RE UP ABOVE, NOT FAR AWAY. THEY'LL FIND THE HATCH ANY MINUTE.
LISTEN TO ME. WITH BRUCE OUT OF COMMISSION, LEX LUTHOR MAY BE THE SMARTEST MAN ON THIS PLANET. HE CAN BUILD THIS DEVICE JUST FROM WHAT YOU REMEMBER ABOUT IT.
CLARK, THE MAN KILLED ME.
I CAN'T BELIEVE I HAVE TO TELL YOU, OF ALL PEOPLE THIS...BUT LUTHOR IS A MALICIOUS, CUNNING, MACHIAVELLIAN BASTARD WHO CARES ABOUT NOTHING BESIDE HIS OWN EGO.
EXACTLY. HE DOESN'T BELIEVE THAT A FARM BOY LIKE ME COULD HAVE BEEN SUPERMAN IN THE FIRST PLACE. IF I HAVE TO STOOP TO ASKING HIM FOR HELP, IT'LL REINFORCE HIS BELIEF THAT I'M JUST SOME FAKER.

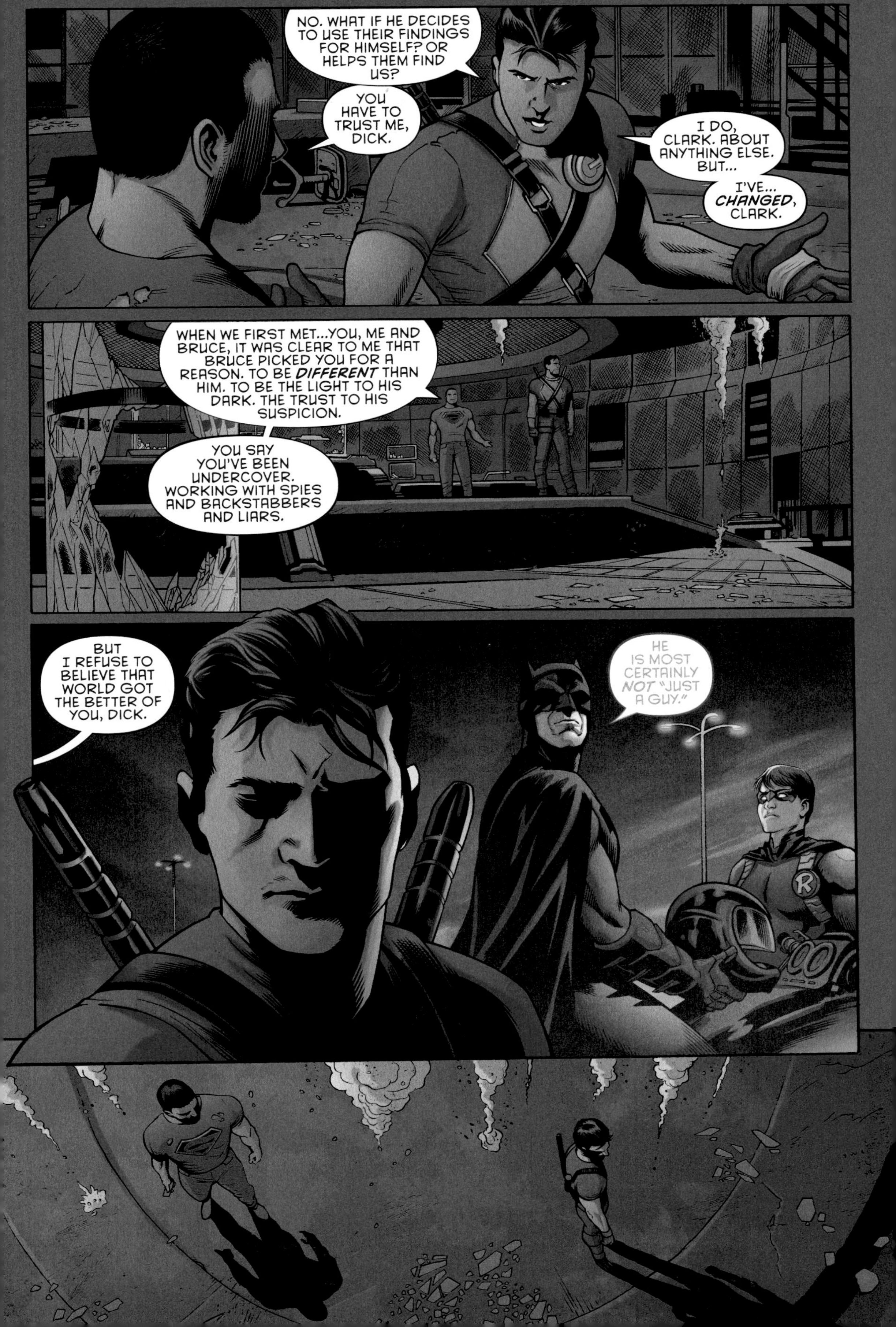
NO. WHAT IF HE DECIDES TO USE THEIR FINDINGS FOR HIMSELF? OR HELPS THEM FIND US?
YOU HAVE TO TRUST ME, DICK.
I DO, CLARK. ABOUT ANYTHING ELSE. BUT...
I'VE... *CHANGED*, CLARK.
WHEN WE FIRST MET...YOU, ME AND BRUCE, IT WAS CLEAR TO ME THAT BRUCE PICKED YOU FOR A REASON. TO BE *DIFFERENT* THAN HIM. TO BE THE LIGHT TO HIS DARK. THE TRUST TO HIS SUSPICION.
YOU SAY YOU'VE BEEN UNDERCOVER. WORKING WITH SPIES AND BACKSTABBERS AND LIARS.
BUT I REFUSE TO BELIEVE THAT WORLD GOT THE BETTER OF YOU, DICK.
HE IS MOST CERTAINLY *NOT* "JUST A GUY."

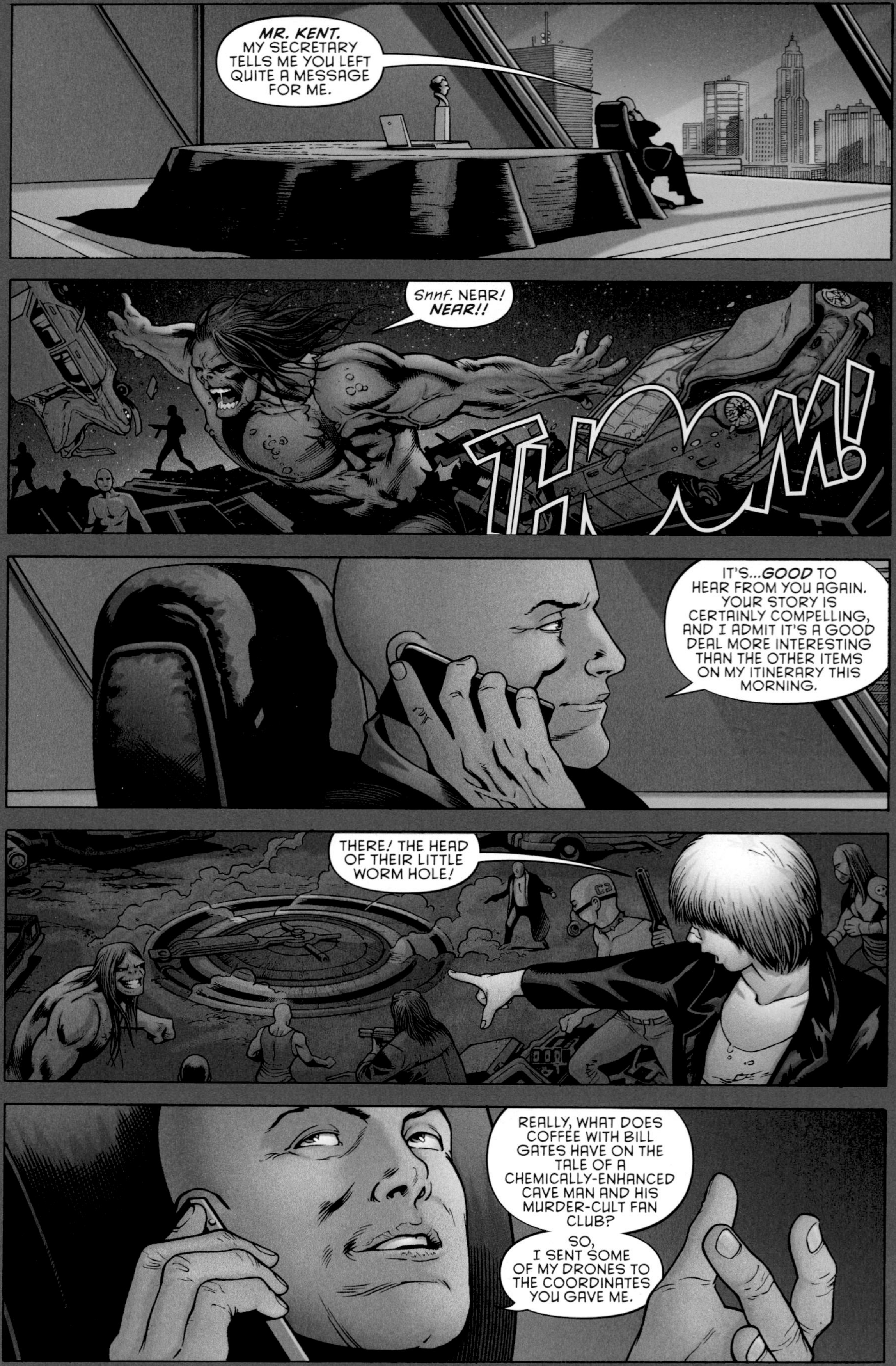
MR. KENT. MY SECRETARY TELLS ME YOU LEFT QUITE A MESSAGE FOR ME.
Snnf. NEAR! NEAR!!
THOOM!
IT'S...GOOD TO HEAR FROM YOU AGAIN. YOUR STORY IS CERTAINLY COMPELLING, AND I ADMIT IT'S A GOOD DEAL MORE INTERESTING THAN THE OTHER ITEMS ON MY ITINERARY THIS MORNING.
THERE! THE HEAD OF THEIR LITTLE WORM HOLE!
REALLY, WHAT DOES COFFEE WITH BILL GATES HAVE ON THE TALE OF A CHEMICALLY-ENHANCED CAVE MAN AND HIS MURDER-CULT FAN CLUB?
SO, I SENT SOME OF MY DRONES TO THE COORDINATES YOU GAVE ME.

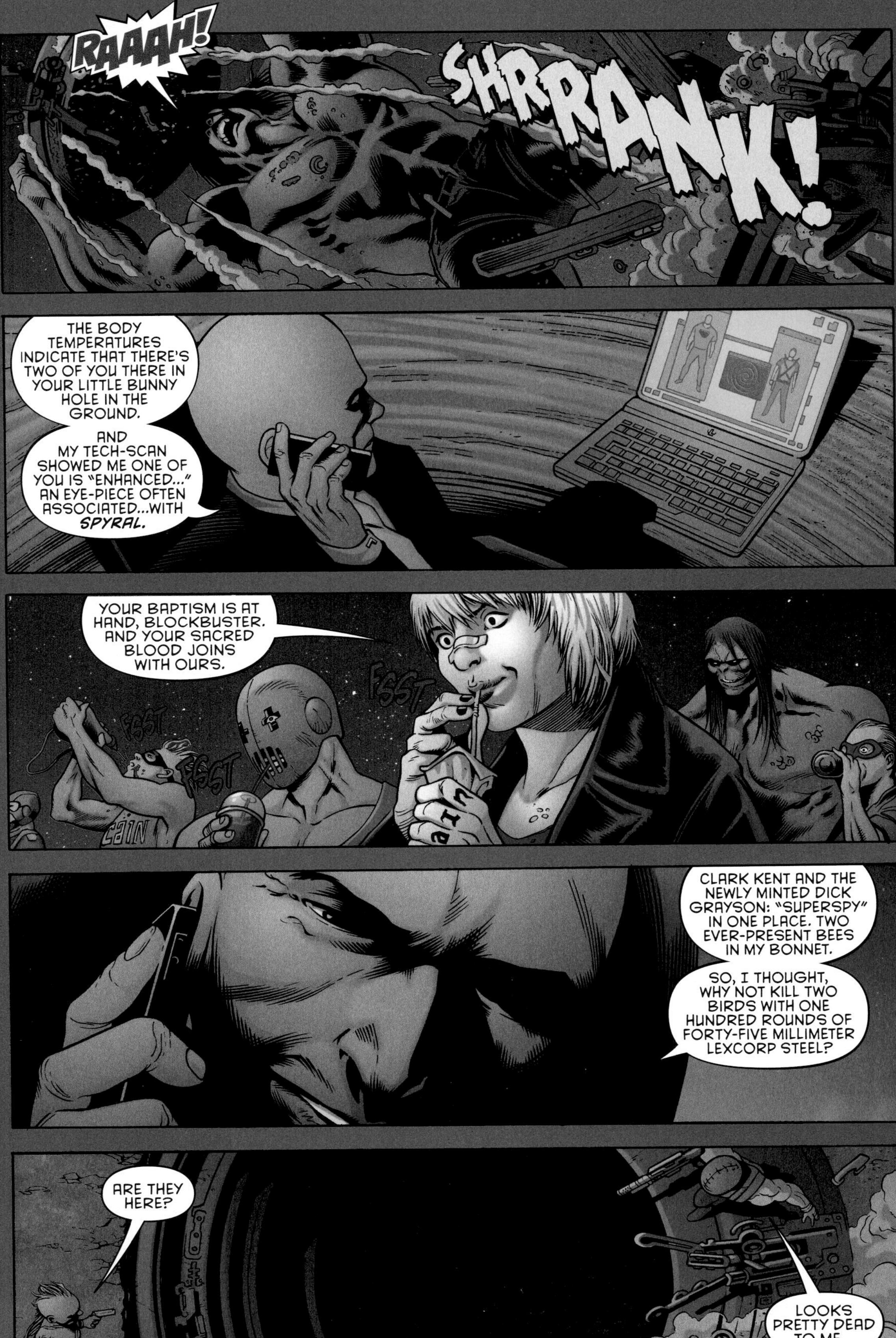

RAAAH!
SHRRANK!
THE BODY TEMPERATURES INDICATE THAT THERE'S TWO OF YOU THERE IN YOUR LITTLE BUNNY HOLE IN THE GROUND.
AND MY TECH-SCAN SHOWED ME ONE OF YOU IS "ENHANCED..." AN EYE-PIECE OFTEN ASSOCIATED...WITH SPYRAL.
YOUR BAPTISM IS AT HAND, BLOCKBUSTER. AND YOUR SACRED BLOOD JOINS WITH OURS.
FSST
FSST
FSST
CAIN
CLARK KENT AND THE NEWLY MINTED DICK GRAYSON: "SUPERSPY" IN ONE PLACE. TWO EVER-PRESENT BEES IN MY BONNET.
SO, I THOUGHT, WHY NOT KILL TWO BIRDS WITH ONE HUNDRED ROUNDS OF FORTY-FIVE MILLIMETER LEXCORP STEEL?
ARE THEY HERE?
LOOKS PRETTY DEAD TO ME...

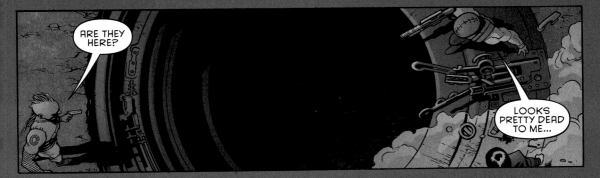

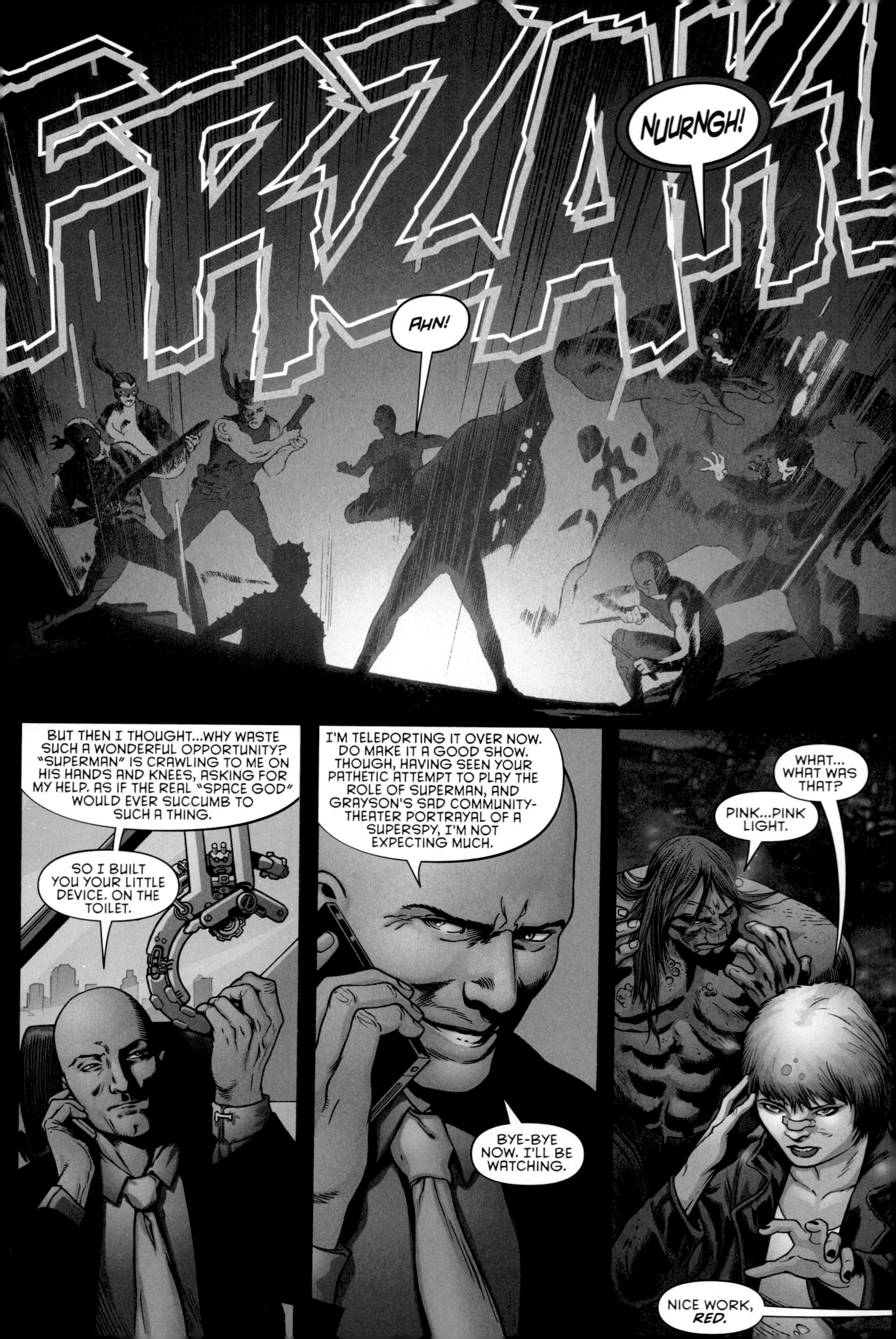
FZZAAK!
NUURNGH!
AHN!
BUT THEN I THOUGHT...WHY WASTE SUCH A WONDERFUL OPPORTUNITY? "SUPERMAN" IS CRAWLING TO ME ON HIS HANDS AND KNEES, ASKING FOR MY HELP. AS IF THE REAL "SPACE GOD" WOULD EVER SUCCUMB TO SUCH A THING.
SO I BUILT YOU YOUR LITTLE DEVICE. ON THE TOILET.
I'M TELEPORTING IT OVER NOW. DO MAKE IT A GOOD SHOW. THOUGH, HAVING SEEN YOUR PATHETIC ATTEMPT TO PLAY THE ROLE OF SUPERMAN, AND GRAYSON'S SAD COMMUNITY-THEATER PORTRAYAL OF A SUPERSPY, I'M NOT EXPECTING MUCH.
BYE-BYE NOW. I'LL BE WATCHING.
WHAT... WHAT WAS THAT?
PINK...PINK LIGHT.
NICE WORK, *RED.*

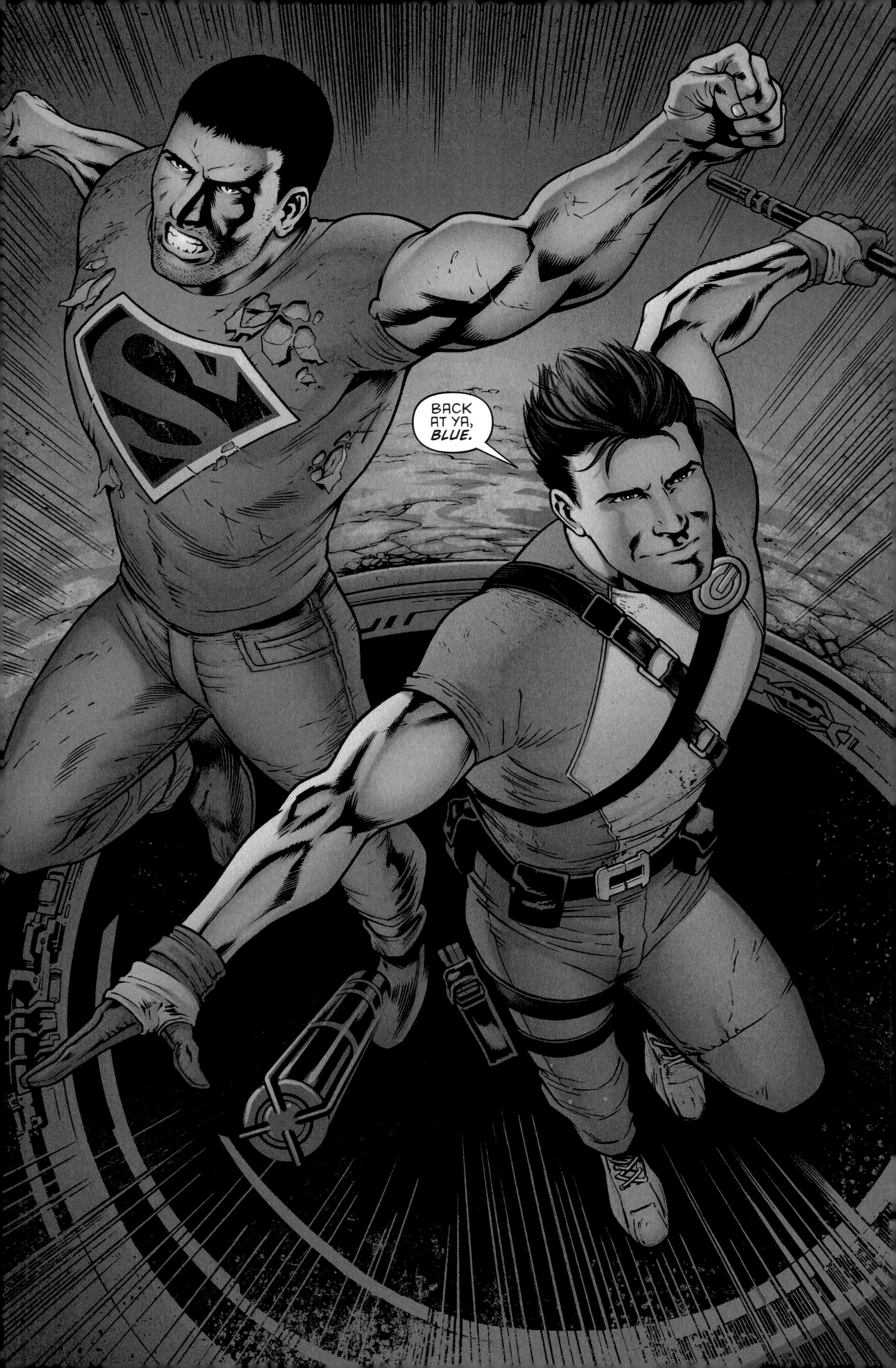
BACK AT YA, *BLUE.*

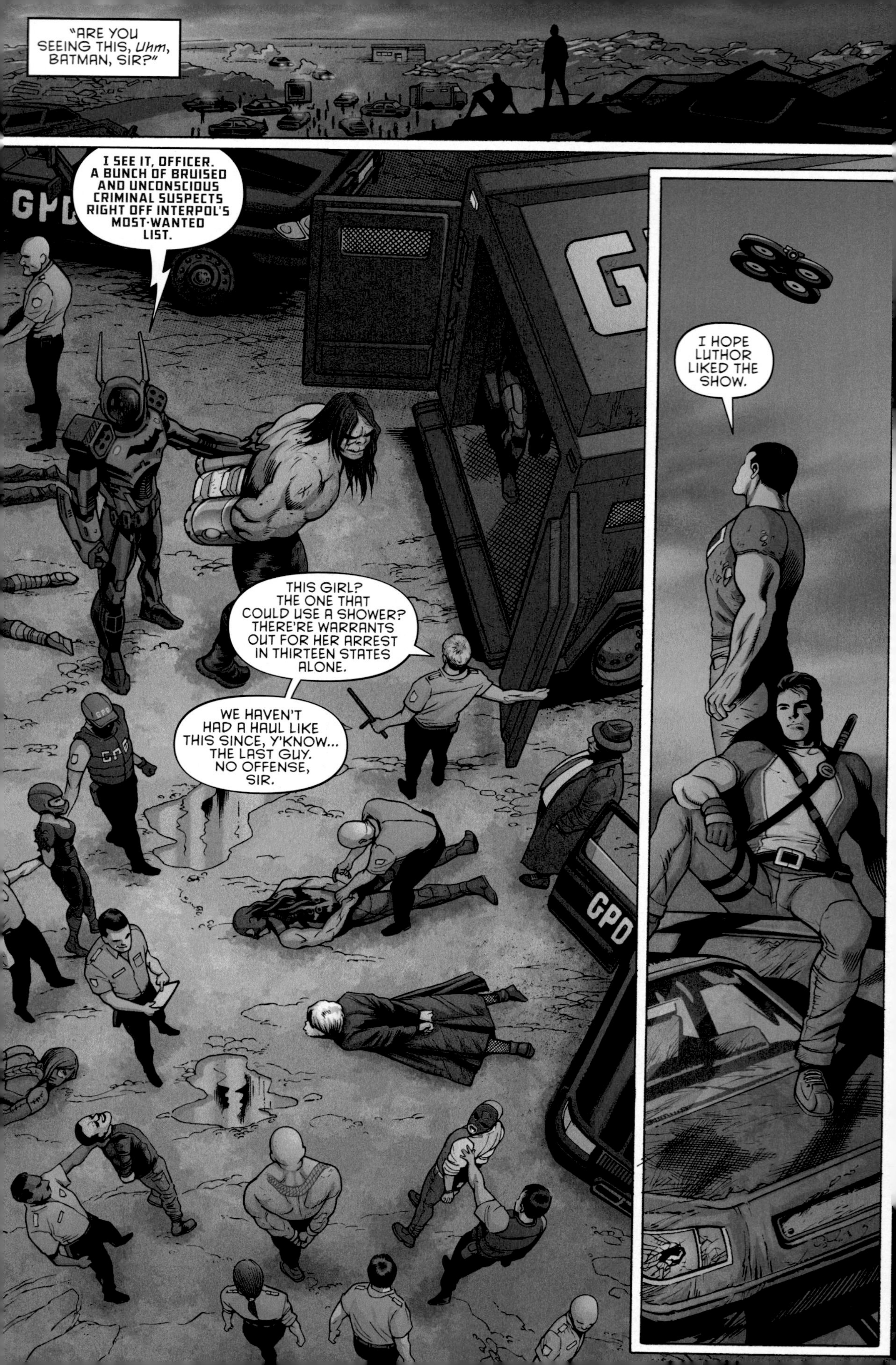
"ARE YOU SEEING THIS, *Uhm,* BATMAN, SIR?"
I SEE IT, OFFICER. A BUNCH OF BRUISED AND UNCONSCIOUS CRIMINAL SUSPECTS RIGHT OFF INTERPOL'S MOST-WANTED LIST.
THIS GIRL? THE ONE THAT COULD USE A SHOWER? THERE'RE WARRANTS OUT FOR HER ARREST IN THIRTEEN STATES ALONE.
WE HAVEN'T HAD A HAUL LIKE THIS SINCE, Y'KNOW... THE LAST GUY. NO OFFENSE, SIR.
I HOPE LUTHOR LIKED THE SHOW.
GPD

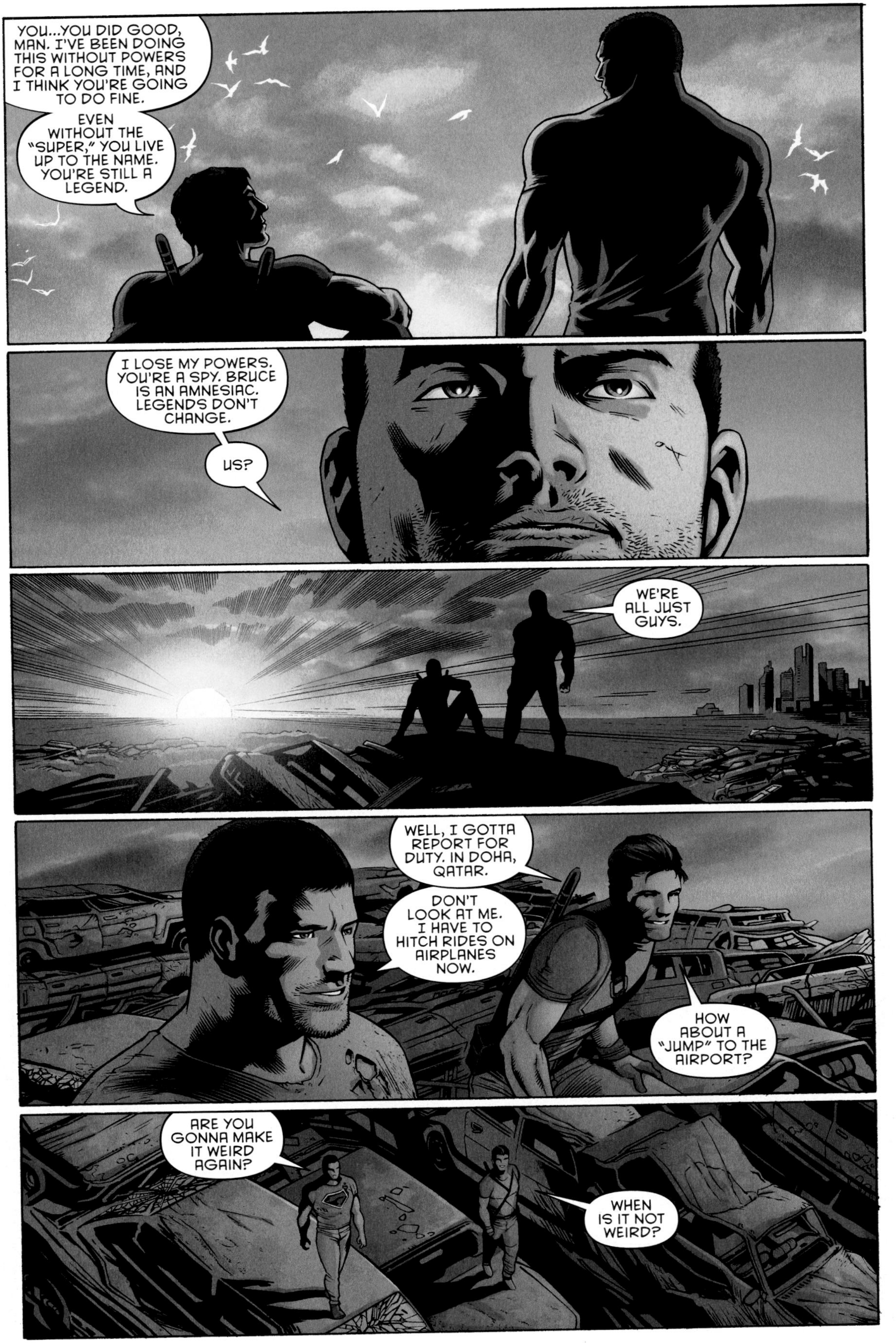
YOU...YOU DID GOOD, MAN. I'VE BEEN DOING THIS WITHOUT POWERS FOR A LONG TIME, AND I THINK YOU'RE GOING TO DO FINE.
EVEN WITHOUT THE "SUPER," YOU LIVE UP TO THE NAME. YOU'RE STILL A LEGEND.
I LOSE MY POWERS. YOU'RE A SPY. BRUCE IS AN AMNESIAC. LEGENDS DON'T CHANGE.
US?
WE'RE ALL JUST GUYS.
WELL, I GOTTA REPORT FOR DUTY. IN DOHA, QATAR.
DON'T LOOK AT ME. I HAVE TO HITCH RIDES ON AIRPLANES NOW.
HOW ABOUT A "JUMP" TO THE AIRPORT?
ARE YOU GONNA MAKE IT WEIRD AGAIN?
WHEN IS IT NOT WEIRD?

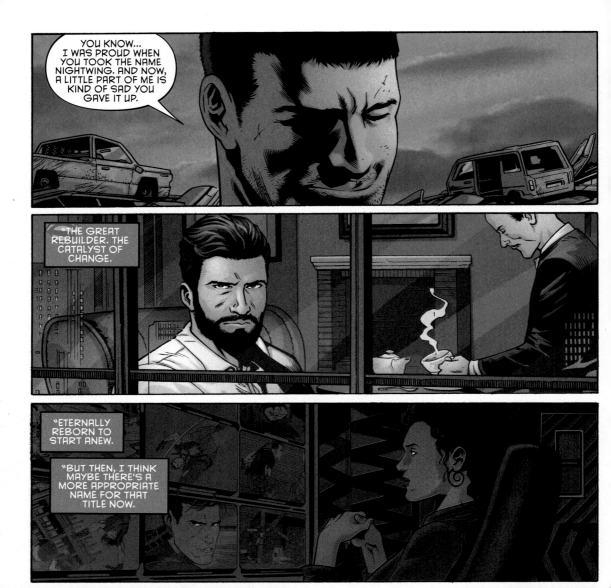

YOU KNOW... I WAS PROUD WHEN YOU TOOK THE NAME NIGHTWING. AND NOW, A LITTLE PART OF ME IS KIND OF SAD YOU GAVE IT UP.

"THE GREAT REBUILDER. THE CATALYST OF CHANGE.

"ETERNALLY REBORN TO START ANEW.

"BUT THEN, I THINK MAYBE THERE'S A MORE APPROPRIATE NAME FOR THAT TITLE NOW.

"GRAYSON."

END

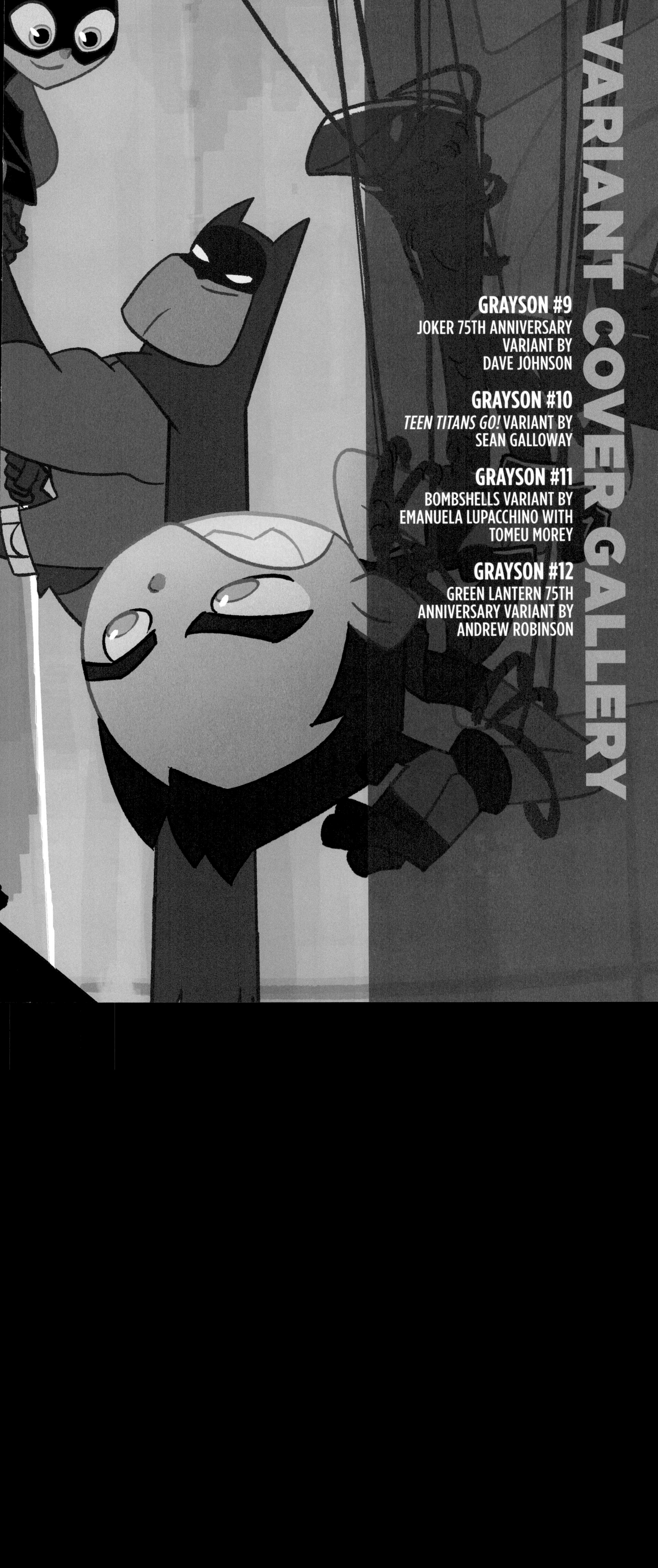

VARIANT COVER GALLERY

GRAYSON #9
JOKER 75TH ANNIVERSARY VARIANT BY DAVE JOHNSON

GRAYSON #10
TEEN TITANS GO! VARIANT BY SEAN GALLOWAY

GRAYSON #11
BOMBSHELLS VARIANT BY EMANUELA LUPACCHINO WITH TOMEU MOREY

GRAYSON #12
GREEN LANTERN 75TH ANNIVERSARY VARIANT BY ANDREW ROBINSON

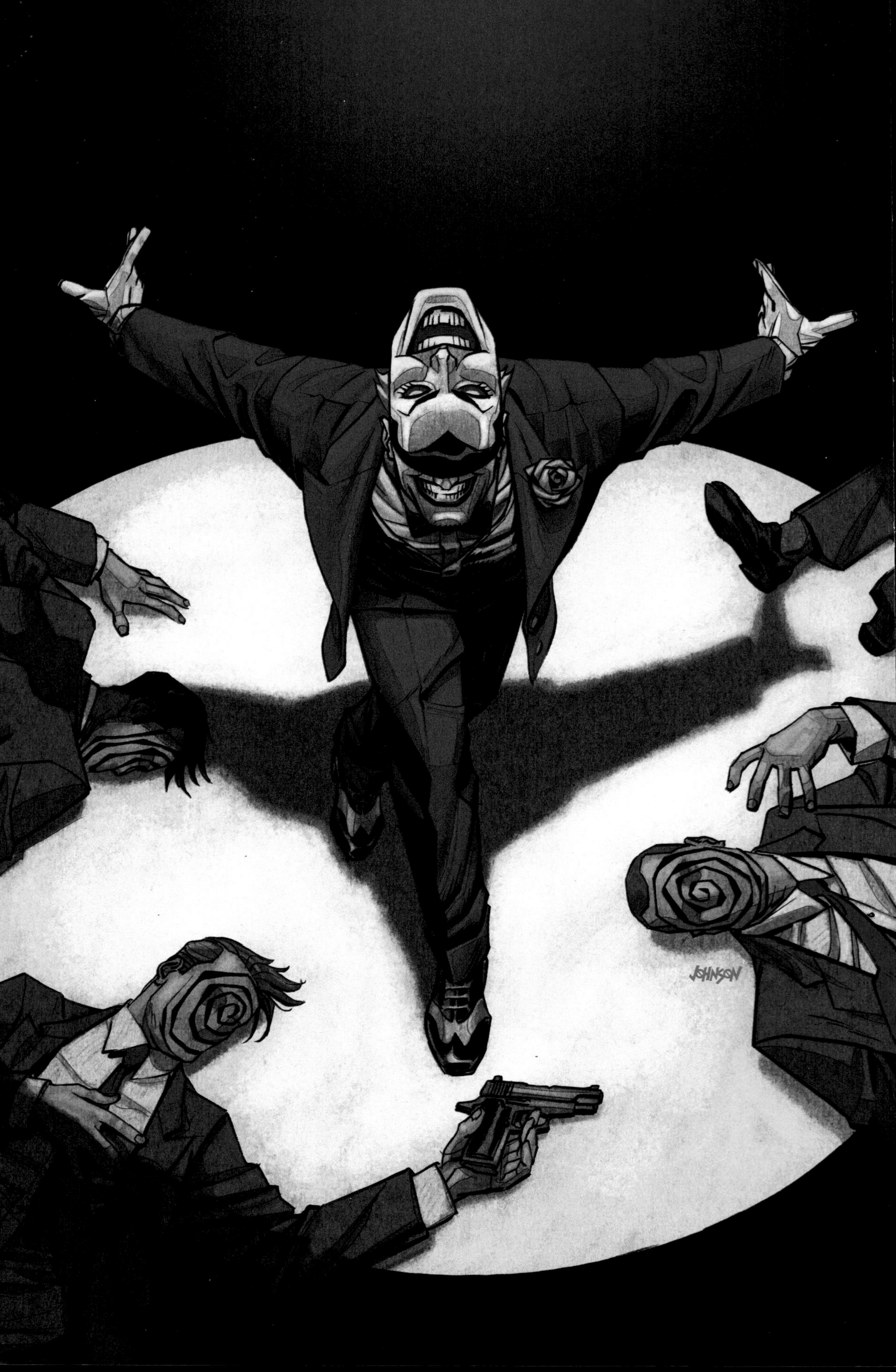
JOHNSON

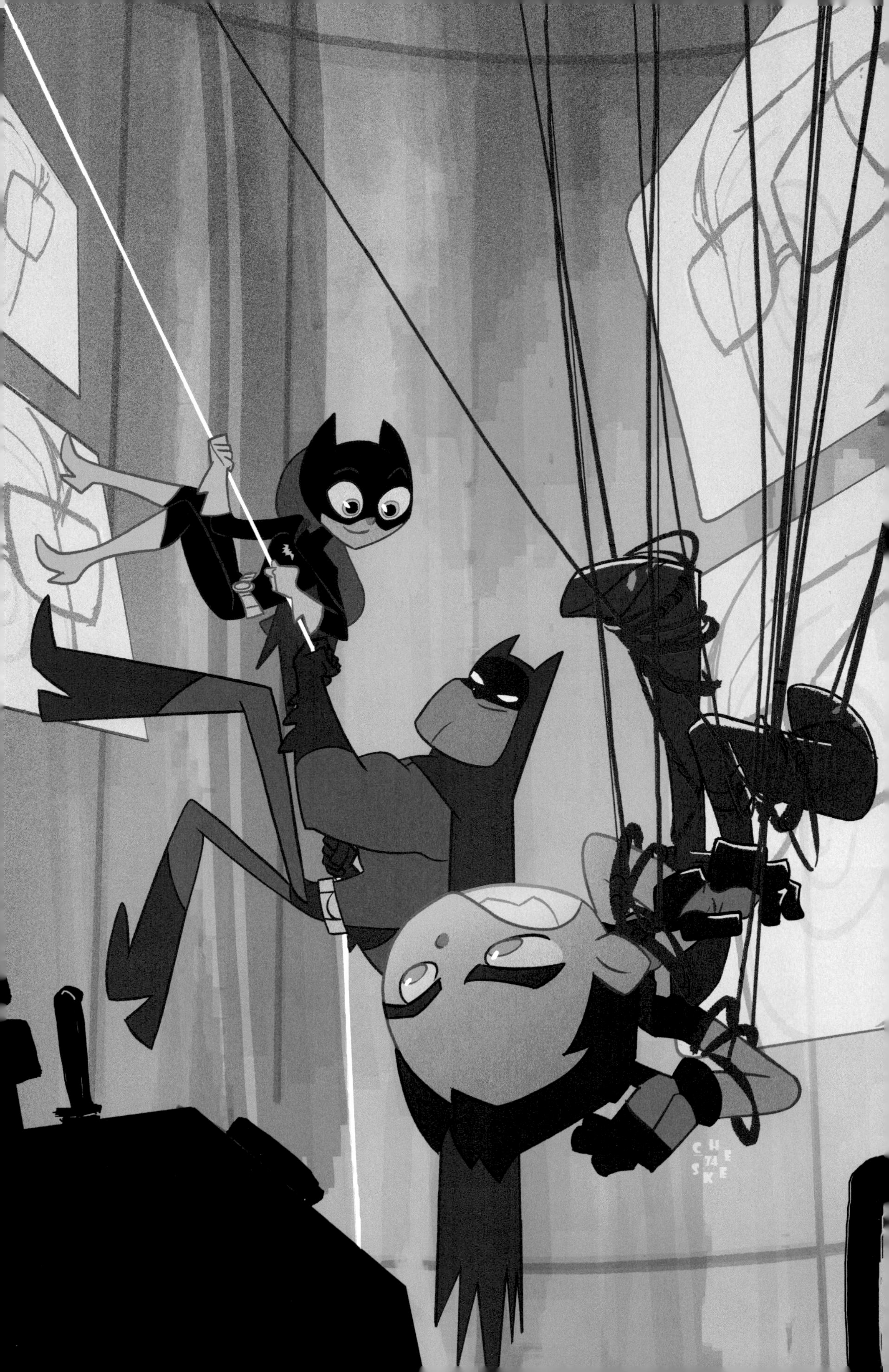

The Incredible
FLYING
GRAYSONS
Dick Grayson
in his
FIRST
SOLO
performance
Exclusively at
HALY'S CIRCUS
GOTHAM
BIG TOP

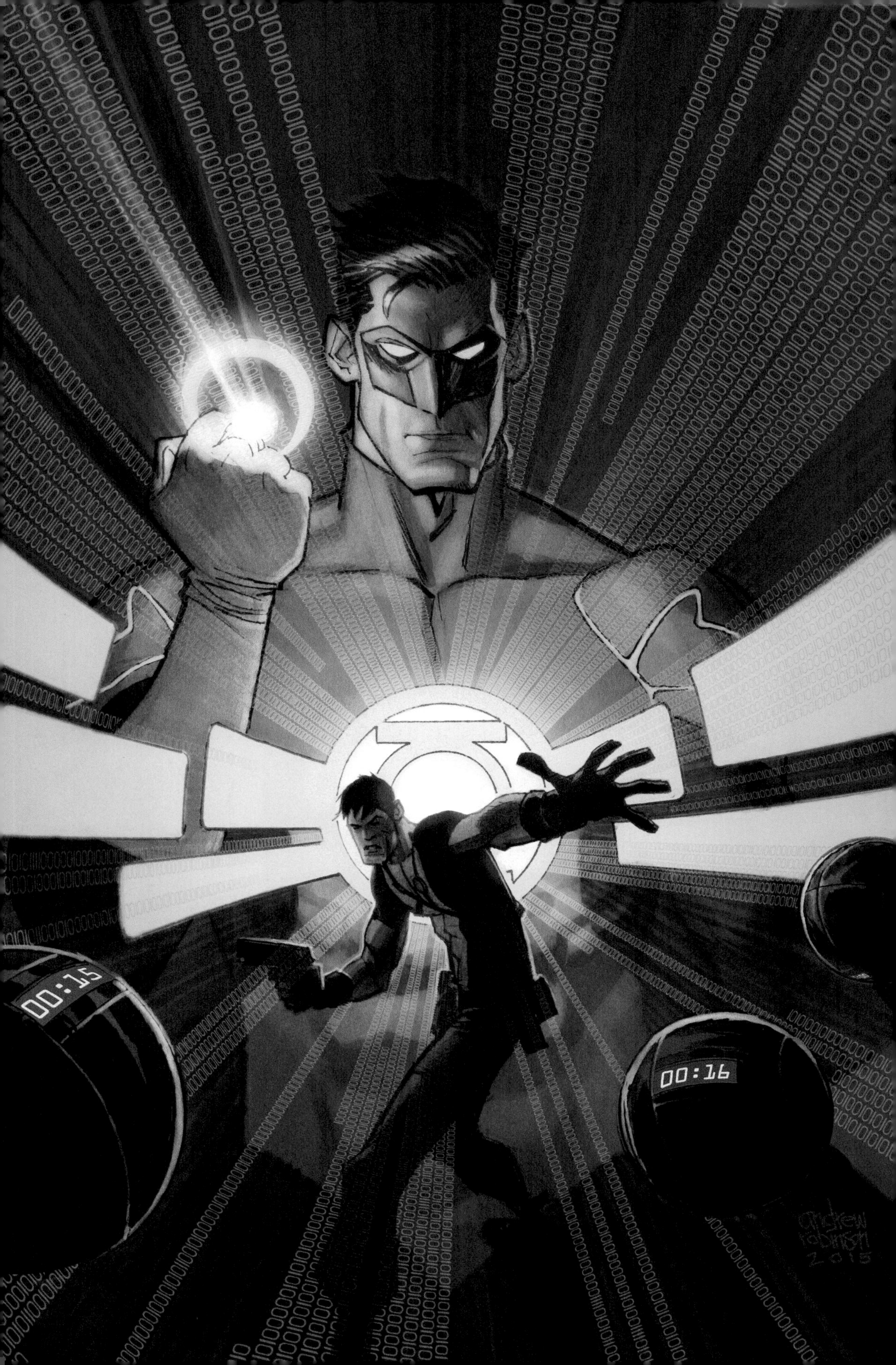
00:15
00:16
ANDREW ROBINSON 2015

ALTERNATE COVER SKETCHES FOR GRAYSON #10 BY MIKEL JANÍN

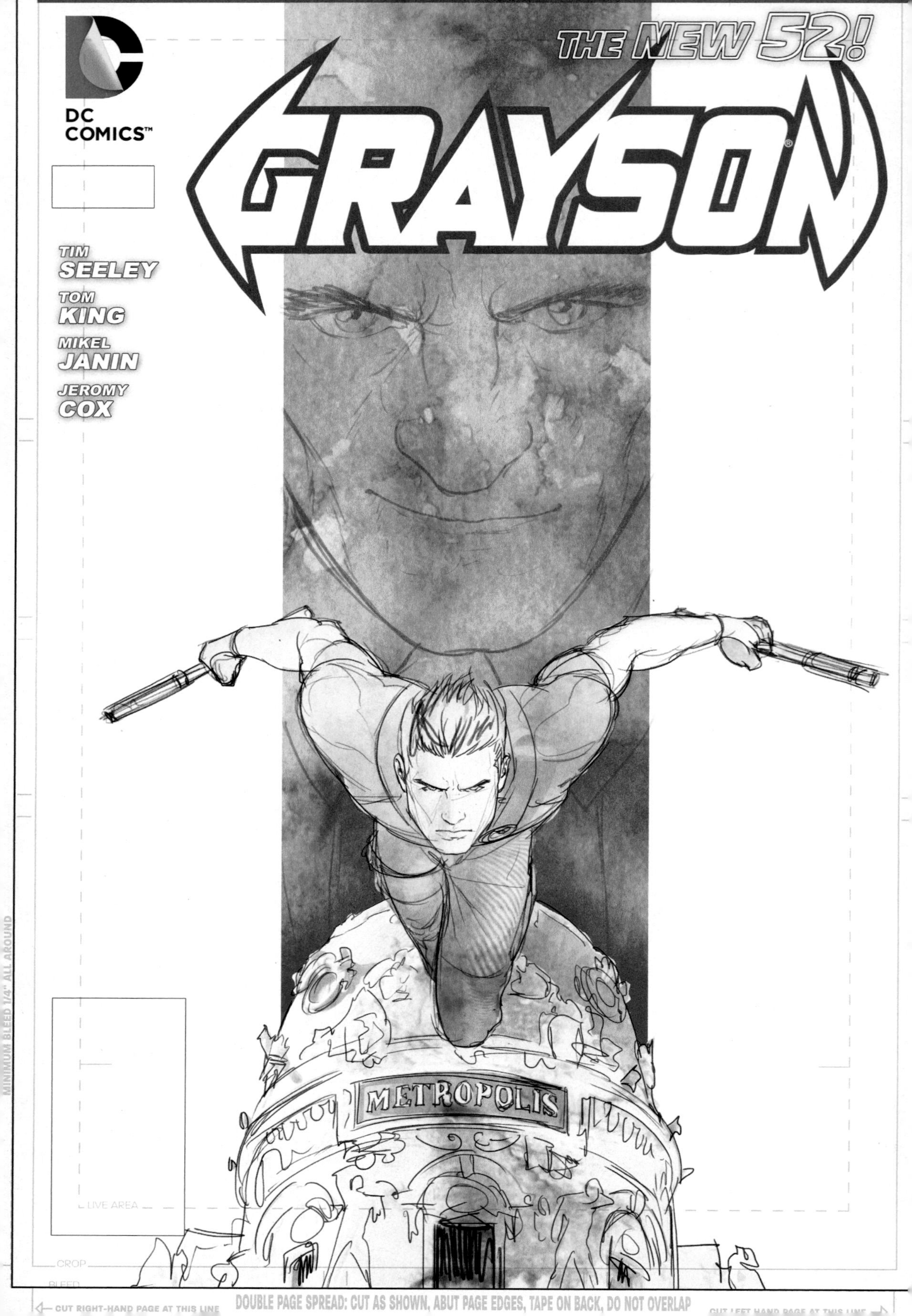
DC COMICS™
THE NEW 52!
GRAYSON
TIM SEELEY
TOM KING
MIKEL JANIN
JEROMY COX
METROPOLIS
LIVE AREA
CROP
BLEED
MINIMUM BLEED 1/4" ALL AROUND
CUT RIGHT-HAND PAGE AT THIS LINE
DOUBLE PAGE SPREAD: CUT AS SHOWN, ABUT PAGE EDGES, TAPE ON BACK, DO NOT OVERLAP
CUT LEFT HAND PAGE AT THIS LINE

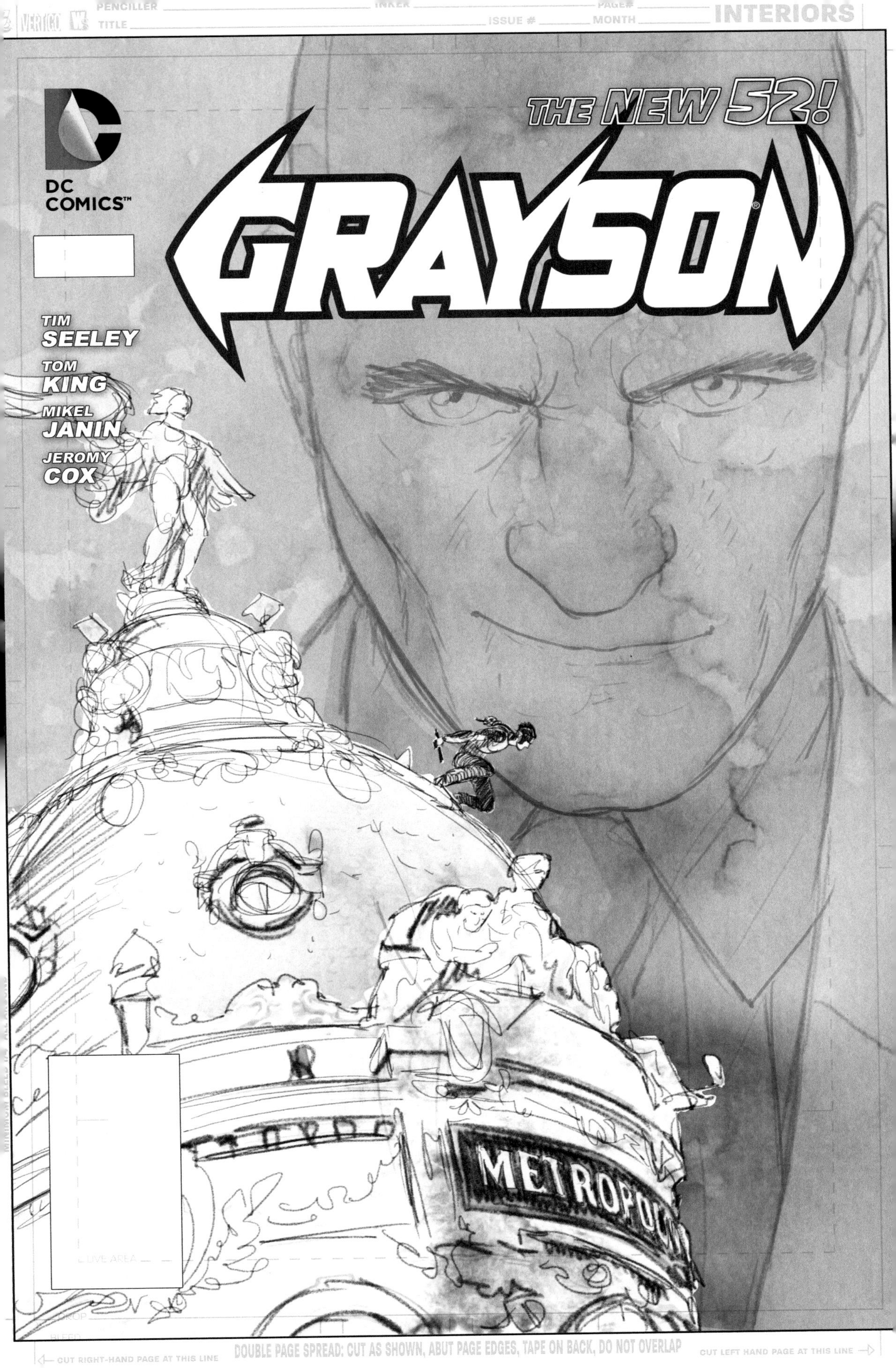
PENCILLER
INKER
PAGE#
TITLE
ISSUE #
MONTH
INTERIORS
DC COMICS™
THE NEW 52!
GRAYSON
TIM SEELEY
TOM KING
MIKEL JANIN
JEROMY COX
LIVE AREA
DOUBLE PAGE SPREAD: CUT AS SHOWN, ABUT PAGE EDGES, TAPE ON BACK, DO NOT OVERLAP
CUT RIGHT-HAND PAGE AT THIS LINE
CUT LEFT HAND PAGE AT THIS LINE

DC COMICS™

THE NEW 52!

GRAYSON

TIM **SEELEY**

TOM **KING**

MIKEL **JANIN**

JEROMY **COX**

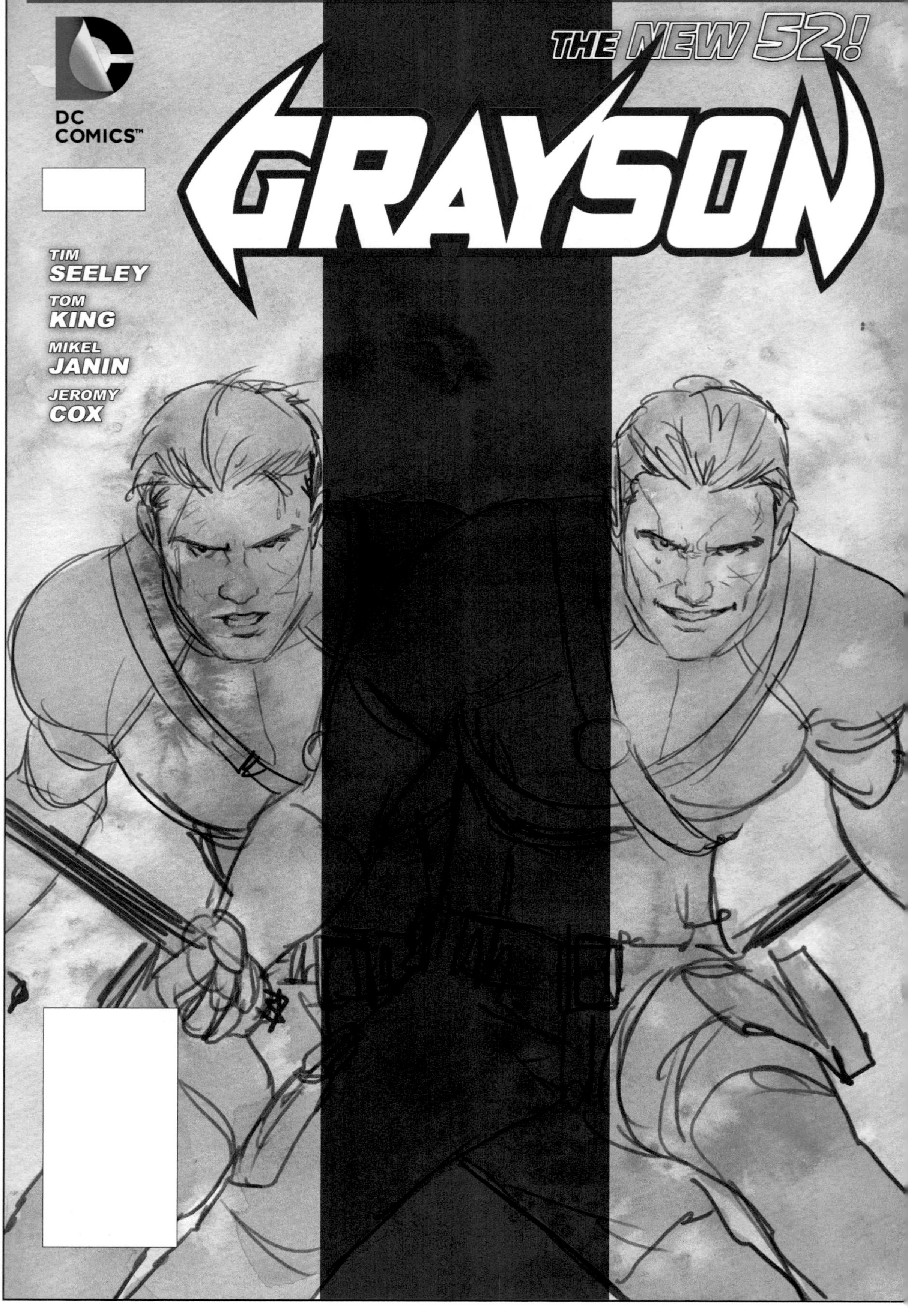

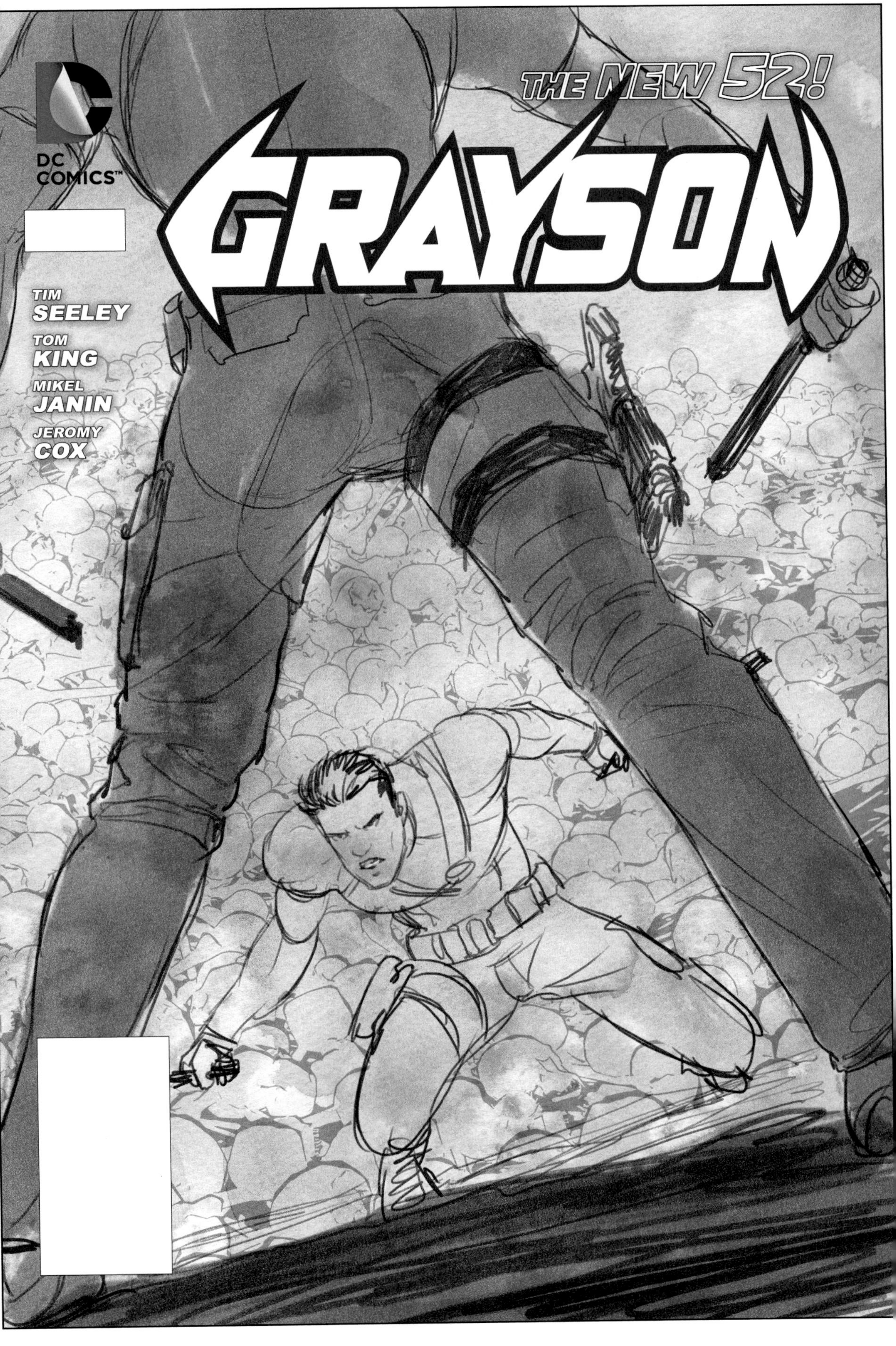
DC COMICS™
THE NEW 52!
GRAYSON
TIM SEELEY
TOM KING
MIKEL JANIN
JEROMY COX

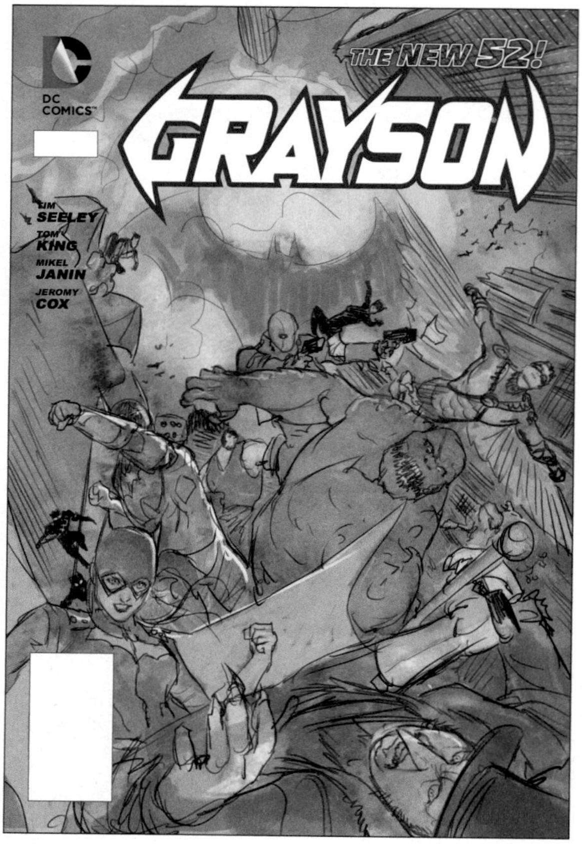
THE NEW 52!
DC COMICS
GRAYSON
TIM SEELEY
TOM KING
MIKEL JANIN
JEROMY COX

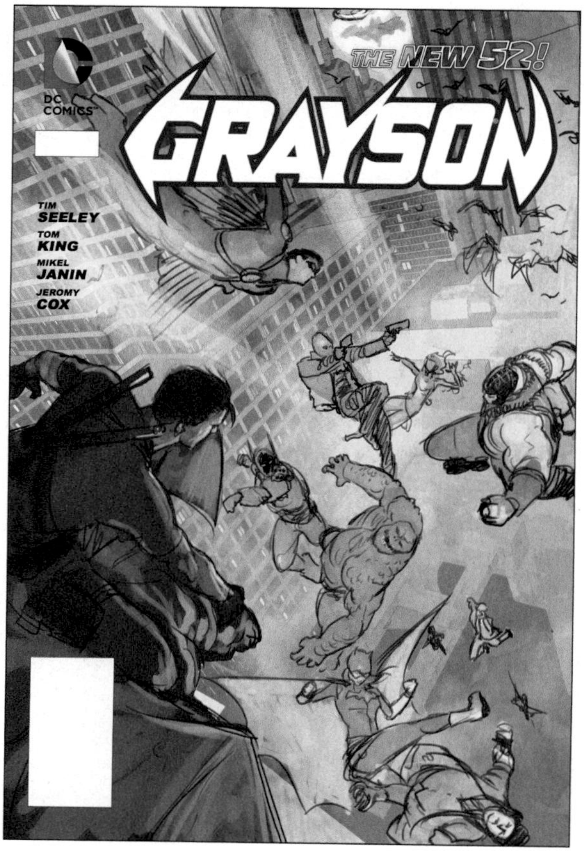
THE NEW 52!
DC COMICS
GRAYSON
TIM SEELEY
TOM KING
MIKEL JANIN
JEROMY COX